Stammering Therapy
from the Inside

Library of Congress Cataloguing in Publication Data
British Library Cataloguing in Publication Data
A catalogue record for this book is available from the British Library
Cover design: Jim Wilkie
Project management, typesetting and design: J&R Publishing Services Ltd, Guildford, Surrey, UK; www.jr-publishingservices.co.uk

Printed and bound by CPI Group (UK) Ltd, Croydon, CR0 4YY

Stammering Therapy from the Inside

New perspectives on working with young people and adults

Carolyn Cheasman, Rachel Everard
and Sam Simpson (Editors)

J&R Press Ltd

Dedication

This book is dedicated to
Renée Byrne
therapist, teacher and mentor
She understood the inside story.

Contents

Acknowledgements

Together Carolyn, Rachel and Sam would like to thank Rachael Wilkie at JR Press for enabling us to finally make this book happen. Particular thanks also go to Jim for carrying out all of the type setting despite getting caught up with the book content. Finally we would jointly like to thank Walt Manning for his enthusiasm and rigorous, thoughtful approach to the foreword.

Carolyn would like to acknowledge: firstly Rachel and Sam – my co-editors - the conception of the idea was relatively easy, but this book has had a long and challenging gestation - thank you both for hanging in there through many hours of discussion and meetings - compromise and good humour have somehow seen us through; my employer, City Lit - I have always been given the opportunity to try out new things and the support to continue my own lifelong learning; to my own speech and language therapists – you helped me begin to allow myself to be someone who stammers; to my colleagues who have given me support and inspiration over the years; a special thanks to Jan for encouragement, wisdom and friendship; to the many clients I have worked with – thank you for sharing your stories and journeys with me; to all of my teachers and friends in the mindfulness world and finally, to my parents – thank you for all of your love and support.

Rachel wants to personally acknowledge: my co-editors, Carolyn and Sam, for their inspiration, vision and determination to create a different type of book about stammering therapy and for inviting me to join them in this worthwhile and exciting project; Neil for his love, support and practical help through the (at times) tortuous process of bringing the book to completion; my parents for their constant love and encouragement; the British Stammering Association which facilitated my own stammering therapy journey and my coming out as a person who stammers; to City Lit, a unique organisation to which I am indebted in so many ways including providing me with first-class therapy when I needed it, for enabling me to fulfil my dream of working with adults who stammer and for helping to make this book a reality; and finally to all the City Lit clients with whom I have worked with over the years and without whom this book would not have been possible.

Sam wants to acknowledge: Carolyn and Rachel, without whom this book would not exist and to whom I feel much closer after the endless discussions, emails and phone calls that the collaborative process of editing has involved;

Jan for her enthusiasm, wisdom and integrity; Carole, for recommending 'Mustn't Grumble' and opening my eyes; Cathy, for her inspiration, creativity and openness to change; Thierry, for his on-going presence, support and patience; Elise, Amy and Anouk for being a continuous source of love, energy and life. Finally, to all my colleagues, clients, friends and family who have made their own unique contribution to my learning process and life over the years. To quote Chris, 'We leave our finger prints on another as we walk through life with them and remain connected in ways which are a mystery'.

About the contributors

Peter Cartwright is a trainer, counsellor and group facilitator who trained at the Gestalt Centre, London. He has always stammered, and had stammering therapy at City Lit in the early 1990s which he found very helpful. He is currently in private practice in London as a Gestalt counsellor, working with clients who face a wide range of difficulties, including some who stammer. Peter also works as a trainer and group facilitator in the counselling and social care fields. He has a specialism in families affected by drug and/or alcohol use, writing and delivering training about this as well as facilitating a weekly group in London for families coping with the impact of substance use.

Carolyn Cheasman has worked with adults who stammer at City Lit, London since 1979. She has experienced interiorized stammering herself and so brings both personal and professional interests to the field. Having done post-qualification training in personal construct psychology and person-centred counselling, she went on to train as a mindfulness teacher and now teaches mindfulness to people who stammer, speech and language therapists and the general public. Carolyn is also involved in student SLT training and is a clinical tutor at City University, London. She has a particular interest in developing counselling skills training at prequalification level as she believes these skills are core to the speech and language therapist role regardless of client group. In 2012, Carolyn was honoured to receive the International Fluency Association Clinician of Distinction award.

Rachel Everard is a specialist speech and language therapist whose decision to train as a therapist stemmed from the fact she stammers herself and from her life-changing experience of receiving therapy at City Lit. Since qualifying in 1996, she has worked in a variety of settings, including community clinics and mainstream primary schools, before joining the City Lit team in 2001. Due to her own personal experience of stammering, she strongly believes in empowering people who stammer and in the benefits of group therapy. She also believes in the value of self-help and has had a long-standing involvement with the British Stammering Association. She is interested in reaching out to different client groups who stammer and has played a key role in developing a programme for people with learning disabilities who stammer. She has recently completed a certificate in person-centred counselling skills.

Jane Fry is a specialist speech and language therapist at the Michael Palin Centre for Stammering, London. She has a post-graduate diploma in Cognitive Therapy from the Oxford Cognitive Therapy Centre, and a Masters in Psychological Counselling. She uses CBT in her practice with children, teenagers, families and adults who stammer and contributes to the national and international teaching programme run by the Michael Palin Centre.

St John Harris has stammered since infancy and undergone various types of stammering therapy through childhood to the present. A life-changing experience for him was the intensive course he attended at City Lit in 1994 which introduced him to both in-block modification techniques and desensitization. Since then, he has attended various courses at City Lit, including the self-advocacy course which is the subject of his chapter. He has previously collaborated with the City Lit team by co-presenting a paper on self-advocacy at the Oxford Dysfluency Conference and giving a client perspective on the course in the BSA *Speaking Out* magazine and the RCSLT *Bulletin*. He has also reviewed books for both these publications. St John is a member of the BSA, and in 2012 took part in the London 10K run to raise money for the charity. St John works in local government, supporting the scrutiny function at Scarborough Borough Council.

Jan Logan is a specialist speech and language therapist and counsellor with over 20 years' experience of working with people who stammer. She enjoys her work at City Lit, a specialist centre for adult stammering therapy, and values the opportunities this presents for group work and collaborative working with clients, who she considers to have been amongst her best teachers. Jan has considerable experience as a counsellor and draws on counselling skills to support her work. She is committed to integrating narrative ideas and practices into her work with groups and individuals who stammer. Jan has an advanced diploma in Humanistic Integrative Counselling and a post-graduate diploma in Narrative Therapy in Counselling from Bristol University. Jan contributes to the development and delivery of the professional training programme offered by City Lit speech therapy, has published numerous articles relating to her work and presented at international conferences.

Debbie Mason qualified as a speech and language therapist in 1994. She has worked with children who stammer throughout her career and began working with adults who stammer in 1999. In 2001, she was introduced to neuro-linguistic programming (NLP) by someone who stammered and used NLP to successfully manage his stammering. She completed her NLP Practitioner training in 2001 and Master Practitioner training in 2003. Further training in neuro-semantics, a field related to NLP, followed in 2004 and 2005. Debbie found herself increasingly using trance (part of the NLP toolkit) to help clients access unconscious resources and in 2007 trained as a hypnotherapist in order to develop her skills in this area. Debbie works both privately and for the NHS in Bristol.

Claire McNeil is a specialist speech and language therapist who graduated in 1982 from Manchester University. She has specialized in working with people who stammer since 1986 and has a particular interest in group therapy and working with teenagers. She is one of the co-founders of the Fluency Trust Charity. She has been running intensive group therapy courses for children and young people who stammer since 1995. From this work she developed the Swindon Fluency Packs which won the Sternberg award for clinical innovation in 2004. She trains speech and language therapists in the use of the packs and has presented at the Oxford Dysfluency Conference. She has become increasingly interested in using a solution-focused approach to therapy and in 2008 completed the Brief Centre Diploma in Solution-Focused Practice.

Deborah M. Plummer has over 25 years' experience of facilitating groups and working individually with children, young people and adults. Formerly a clinical lead speech and language therapist specializing in dysfluency, she contributes to the dysfluency teaching at De Montfort University, Leicester and has extensive experience as a senior lecturer in aspects of health psychology and counselling. Deborah is also an Imagework practitioner and is the author of several titles based on the use of her wellbeing model and imagery in different therapeutic contexts (all published by Jessica Kingsley Publishers). Her books are known internationally and have been translated into more than ten languages.

Sam Simpson is a speech and language therapist, person-centred counsellor, supervisor and facilitator. As a speech and language therapist, she has worked in the fields of stammering and neurorehabilitation since 1995 and was employed as a part-time tutor at City Lit from 1995 until 2001. She co-founded intandem (www.intandem.co.uk) in 2004, an independent speech and language therapy and counselling partnership, which offers a supervision, coaching and training service to healthcare professionals in addition to a range of 1:1 and group therapy services for adults who stammer and adults with experience of brain injury. As a counsellor, she currently works in the contexts of youth counselling and cancer support. She is also a part-time lecturer and visiting clinical tutor at University College London. Sam has a particular interest in the role clinical supervision plays in the development of the creative and ethical practitioner; the integration of person-centred principles into speech and language therapy; empowerment and self-advocacy.

Foreword

This book brings to mind the classic British adventurers who for centuries had the courage to explore the world's oceans and continents. Only a few paragraphs into the introduction by Sam Simpson, the reader can visualize this group of experienced and intrepid clinicians from the UK setting out – along with their clients – to co-author the exploration of contemporary approaches for the treatment for stammering. One feels admiration for these authors who are willing to explore post-modern therapeutic protocols that have only begun to receive support in the literature. Reading through the chapters, the reader shares the authors' sense of enthusiasm and adventure as they consider alternative and creative perspectives of the therapeutic process that we are unaccustomed to seeing in books on stammering. One of the primary goals of the book as described by Simpson in her introduction is 'to broaden the discourse and extend the boundaries of thinking about stammering therapy'. From many perspectives, the authors achieve their goal.

As I read through the near-final drafts of the chapters I found myself making pages of notes that contained a long list of descriptions and quotes I would like to use one day. The notes also included many important themes that resonated throughout the chapters. Though the chapters are authored by different people with different backgrounds and perspectives, the many shared themes helped bind the book together. The following are some examples of these themes.

Perhaps the most distinctive and enjoyable feature of the book is the integration of author and client narratives in the majority of the chapters. As the title of the book suggests, the reader is provided with an insider's view of the stammering experience. Many of the chapters are authored by individuals with a history of stammering. The authors' experiences, combined with the often poignant and elegant narratives of the clients, provide a view through a window that is commonly opaque to the general public and, far too often, to less experienced clinicians. Another primary goal of the book as indicated by Simpson is to develop stammering therapy knowledge by exploring how therapists and clients negotiate and co-construct the therapy process. The blending of narratives by both authors and clients provide the clients with a voice, another theme that echoes throughout the chapters in a variety of forms.

I have had lively discussions with individuals who stammer about whether or not fluent therapists can truly understand the experience of stammering. Without the lived experience, how can the fluent clinician truly appreciate the majority of the stammering experience that lies below the waterline of the iceberg? As a person with a history of stammering, I believe fluent therapists can understand. I know many fluent clinicians and researchers, who by the nature of their approach to therapy and the issues they select for their research, show that they understand. This book provides a road map for understanding.

Perhaps I should indicate that I came to the task of preparing this foreword with my own inclinations concerning the shortcomings of the medical model for informing clinicians about the nature and treatment of stammering. The authors of this book clearly believe as I do that the frequency of stammering tells us little about the severity and scope of the problem for each individual, and that successful therapy is about much more than altering the overt, behavioural characteristics. As a result, I was especially sensitive to the consistency of the authors' perspectives about the respective roles of the clinician and the client during the therapy process. The co-authorship of chapters is a wonderful expression of the view that the therapeutic process is a shared journey where all those who are taking part benefit from the experience. Perhaps this is why the clinicians authoring the chapters reveal obvious enjoyment and enthusiasm for the process. I appreciated the authors understanding that assisting those who stammer is about facilitating more adaptive coping strategies.

I enjoyed the descriptions of therapy activities where the emphasis is not about specific techniques intended to 'fix' the problem but rather the meaning of the techniques and how cognitive and behavioural change leads to the creation of an autonomous and agentic life style. Although paradoxical to many, embracing stammering with mindfulness and acceptance is not an indication of the speaker's resignation or toleration of stammering. As several of the authors stress, acceptance is an active, positive and essential process. Coinciding with the nature of post-modern approaches, each author presents an optimistic view of the speaker's ability to re-conceptualize the nature of their stammering and their relationship with it.

Several authors mention how their clients, predominantly at the outset of therapy, have an overriding desire to achieve fluency. They also often hold firmly to the inflexible and categorical view that stammering is 'undesirable' and fluency is 'desirable'. Each author illustrates how, with a more comprehensive view of stammering, the client begins to expand their understanding and appreciation of goals that are more important and meaningful. Through approaches that foster awareness, externalization of the problem (i.e. the problem is the problem not the person), desensitization, mindfulness and staying in the moment, humour and creativity, the client begins to change his or her relationship with stammering. At its core this journey, as clarified by the authors of this book, is one of moving from a life of fear and avoidance to one of curiosity and exploration.

We began with a metaphor of the early British explorers and we will end with another that illustrates the importance of making such a journey. When paddling a canoe or kayak in turbulent white water it is common to encounter many obstacles in the form of rocks, trees and large waves. As a novice, each obstacle is seen as a threat and your initial (and natural) instinct is to avoid and lean away from the problem. Coping by leaning away (upstream) makes the situation worse and you will quickly find yourself underwater. With proper instruction and experience, you discover that, rather than expending so much effort trying to avoid the obstacles, you will have much better success by moving toward them. For example, as you allow yourself to approach a rock you will notice a cushion of water recoiling off the rock at the waterline that helps you to move around it. Furthermore, by throwing your upper body towards the rock you achieve support and stability. With practice, each obstacle is now seen as an opportunity rather than something to avoid. The journey is no longer one of avoidance but of engagement with the river's flow. The authors of this book provide the reader with such an experience.

Walter H. Manning, PhD
Professor, School of Communication Sciences and Disorders
The University of Memphis
Memphis, USA

Introduction

Sam Simpson

This is a book written by people who stammer and the practitioners who have worked alongside them, with a key aim of co-authoring contemporary stammering therapy knowledge. The idea originated from discussions between Carolyn Cheasman and myself in the early 2000s; however, at that time we struggled to find a publisher who was willing to offer a platform for this shared voice due to the perceived lack of evidence base for such an approach. A decade (and, in my case, three children) later, attitudes towards client accounts as valid evidence had changed. We welcomed Rachel Everard on board, found a publisher, and invited people to contribute who, in our view, reflected the tremendous diversity of stammering therapies currently on offer in the UK, many of which were previously undocumented. Another key aim of this book, therefore, is to bring some of the richness and innovation of contemporary UK stammering therapy into the public domain. Our shared determination has finally paid dividends and I am delighted to be able to introduce you to the end result. I hope you will agree that it was well worth the wait.

It is both a privilege and a pleasure to offer here a personal reflection on the genesis of this book. I am aware that, in so doing, I draw on literature and use terms that remain contentious within the field of stammering. However, throughout my career as a speech and language therapist I have worked with both adults who stammer and adults with experience of traumatic brain injury. As will become evident, this book has as its very basis the cross fertilization of the different theories and ideas from these two fields. My comments contain many biases; none of which I consider to be correct or inaccurate. They simply comprise my perspective and illustrate some of the varied and different threads that have profoundly influenced my personal and professional development; and which together weave the rich, conceptual tapestry from which the book has evolved. I first wrote about some of these ideas with Carolyn in 2000 and it is interesting, over a decade later, to be able to continue this public narrative and take stock of how they have developed over time.

For me, the origins of this publication lie in my first reading of a powerful collection of short stories and poems entitled *Mustn't Grumble* (Keith, 1994), renamed *What Happened to You?* in 1996. This frank, eloquent and controversial collection reflects many varied facets of women's experience of living with a disability. It is a book that is at once both universal and intimately personal. As I read, I felt simultaneously exhilarated and perturbed by the wisdom and humility I encountered on each page. At the time of this book's first publication, I was in my final year of training to become a speech and language therapist and it challenged everything I was learning to the very core.

I was left feeling troubled, inspired and captivated. The principles of respect and value for each individual are deeply important to me and feeling disrespected or seeing others be disrespectful has always made me angry. As I began to read more of the literature I uncovered a deep connection with the radical ideas underpinning the social model of disability. Clearly articulated and angry stories of oppression and exclusion facilitated a painful realization of what it means for me to be 'able bodied' and the automatic social, political and cultural privileges that accompany this identity (Kearney, 1996). I was shocked to discover the pervasive, stereotypical images of disability I had been exposed to in fairytales, films, popular culture, the media, and classical and contemporary literature since my early childhood, which had both subtly and overtly influenced my attitudes, beliefs and openness towards difference as an adult and therapist in training (Barnes, 1994; Shakespeare, 1999).

Writings from the disability movement since the 1990s and the principles of the social model have resulted in a redefinition of disability, clearly locating its primary source within the social environment as opposed to the individual. Thus, according to the social model, people are not disabled because they have an impaired body, mind or means of communication, but because contemporary society neglects their needs and rights, thereby placing barriers in their way. From this perspective, disability is viewed as a human rights issue rather than a medical or therapeutic one (Barton, 1996). This paradigm shift represents a direct challenge to the influential medical model and institutions within which most speech and language therapists have been trained and work. The very principles upon which therapy is based, the roles and relationships therapists establish with clients, the language used, the range of therapies offered and the accessibility and flexibility of service provision have all been called into question (Finkelstein, 1993; Oliver, 1993).

I still vividly recall the fearful sense of confusion that accompanied my deepening appreciation of the powerful influence of the medical model of disability and the implications this has had for speech and language therapy.

With increasing unease, I came to recognize our profession's historical focus on deficit, loss and the need for therapeutic intervention by trained, expert practitioners. Furthermore, as much therapeutic practice has traditionally focused on normalization and the reduction or eradication of difference, I was deeply unsettled by the intrinsic paradox this brings about; the narrow focus of restoration therapy can only serve to reinforce and reaffirm social norms and stigma rather than acting as a vehicle through which these prevailing norms can be challenged and renegotiated (Oliver, 1996). There was something raw, alive and compelling about these disability discourses and their open invitation to engage in a dialogue about difference that extended beyond the focus of loss and adjustment.

My musings on the evolution of speech and language therapy led to an uncomfortable acknowledgement of the historical paucity of involving people with communication disabilities in defining not only their lived experience, but also in determining what therapy, if any, is personally meaningful, timely and effective. It was deeply disconcerting to realize how much of the theory, literature and evidence base that I was being exposed to as a student and qualified speech and language therapist had been written by non-disabled professionals; that is, by people 'outside' of the lived experience of communication disability. More recent trends in social sciences and disability studies have highlighted the paramount importance of exploring insider accounts of chronic conditions when carrying out evidence-based research as 'the definitions people hold of health and illness, as well as the explanatory models they use, affect both their experience and what they do about it' (Conrad, 1990, p.1261). Conclusions were being drawn that it was 'no longer good enough for researchers to look within their own narrow understandings in their attempt to predict the outcome of others. Before we can even begin to predict what people do, we need to gain a better understanding of why people do what they do, based upon *their* understandings of their actions' (Stainton Rogers, 1991, p.233).

An increasing interest in the meaning people attribute to their experience of difference as well as therapy has brought about a welcome break from the traditional therapeutic model in the past two decades, with a number of alternative approaches emerging. Speech and language therapy has been situated as an 'ethical responsibility' with particular importance placed on viewing each individual as part of a personal environment embedded in a larger communal/societal context (Taylor Sarno, 2004). This has resulted in a drive to enrich and enhance professional accounts by including clients as co-authors of therapy knowledge (Gaddis, 2004). As people with communication disabilities have been given a voice and a role in the definition of their lived experience and the evaluation of therapy services, so there has been a call for the focus of therapy to broaden and address the roles that self-identity, society and social stigma play in making the processes of living with a communication disability more challenging (Felson Duchan & Byng, 2004; Downs, 2011). This involves a radical rethinking and reconceptualization of the scope and focus of therapy.

Listening to, bearing witness to and interacting with the stories and expertise of the client is one of the key principles of narrative-based medicine (Greenhalgh & Hurwitz, 1998). The body of literature in the field of speech and language therapy that supports this approach is growing (Kagan, 1995, 1998; Lyon, 1992, 1995, 1996; Parr et al., 1997; Pound, 1999; Pound et al., 2000; Simpson & Pound, 2001; Parr et al., 2003; Felson Duchan & Byng, 2004; Barrow, 2000, 2011), but remains relatively small. Whilst these publications all relate to aphasia therapy, a number of therapists are becoming interested in exploring the relevance of narrative-based practices to stammering therapy (Dilollo et al., 2002; Yaruss & Reeves, 2002; Yaruss, Quesal & Murphy, 2002; Yaruss & Quesal, 2004; Plexico et al., 2005; DiLollo, 2007; Leahy & Warren, 2007; Logan, 2007, Chapter 3 in this book).

Having acknowledged the striking lack of research investigating narrative knowledge with regard to stammering, closer collaboration with people who stammer in evaluating therapy outcomes is being strongly advocated:

> "Still it appears to us that the answer will be forthcoming if we as a field are serious about engaging in a partnership between researchers and the population of people who stutter, for people who stutter can provide the most meaningful metric for determining whether a treatment is viable."

(Yaruss & Quesal, 2004, p.11)

Indeed, due to the variable nature of stammering, client accounts have been positioned by some as the primary and most holistic means of assessing 'a therapy's mettle outside of the confines of the clinic and the clinician's expectation and desired response' (Guntupalli et al., 2006, p.4); and possibly the true 'acid test' of any form of stammering therapy (Kalinowski et al., 2004).

The importance of exploring therapist and client life-narratives and how these intersect is also strongly advocated (Elwyn & Gwyn, 1998; Simmons-

Mackie & Damico, 2011). Every communication exchange is multilayered and coloured by linguistic, personal, contextual, biographical, social and cultural factors. As therapy is co-constructed, the story that is jointly woven defines the therapeutic relationship. This reflects the equal relevance of the narrative frame for clients and practitioners when considering therapeutic effectiveness. Greater appreciation of the narratives employed and preferred by therapists will determine the extent to which they either complement or conflict with those of their clients. Indeed, such collaboration is also being advocated within stammering research:

> "We believe that the challenge is to move beyond controversy and work to find commonality, to learn from one another and work with one another [i.e. clinicians, researchers and people who stammer] in our quest to better define, document, and evaluate the goals and procedures of stuttering treatment."

(Yaruss & Quesal, 2004, p.12)

This publication is a response to the felt need to provide a unique forum for therapists and people who stammer to jointly reflect on and share their perspectives and experiences of stammering and therapy. The motivation is not only to hear from practitioners at the coalface, but to highlight the political significance of listening to people who stammer. The potency of listening to those central to the therapy process, yet often unheard, cannot be underestimated. It is this attempt to provide a shared voice and insight that enables this book to break new ground within the stammering field. This publication hopes to broaden the discourse and extend the boundaries of thinking about stammering therapy. Our intention has been to encourage reflection and subjectivity; to foster difference, collaboration and non-traditional approaches, thereby offering freedom from the rigorous scientific focus of much academic writing. In so doing, we hope this has provided all contributors with a platform to explore aspects of stammering therapy often passed over by prevailing academic discourses.

Commitment, respect, sensitivity, courage, humility, awareness and self-questioning are qualities that all the contributors have in common. The authors write from different contexts: the UK National Health Service (Chapters 6 and 9), adult education (Chapters 3, 4, 5, 7 and 8) and independent practice (Chapters 2, 10, 11 and 12); about their experience of both 1:1 therapy (Chapters

2, 9, 10 and 12) and group work (Chapters 1, 3, 4, 5, 6, 7, 8 and 11). Similarly, chapters take different forms, ranging from in-depth accounts of a particular therapy relationship (Chapters 2 and 9), multiple accounts of a particular approach to therapy (Chapters 3, 4, 5, 6, 7, 8 and 12) through to reflections written solely from the perspective of the client (Chapter 1).

All therapist contributors openly share something about their personal philosophy of stammering and how they embody theory in their therapeutic practice. All client contributors give thought-provoking accounts of their experience of therapy, detailing aspects they found particularly helpful and those they found more challenging, as well as capturing some of the personal growth that the experience of therapy has brought about. What is evident throughout the book is the sense of personal journeys that all the contributors have undertaken. Practitioners and clients unite in their willingness to be open to personal change, to face challenging issues and to consider and learn from their unique experiences.

Many themes emerge throughout the book. Some of these I will signpost here and the rest I will leave you to discover for yourself. One of the most striking relates to the understanding of stammering as being so much more than a speech impairment. This sounds both simplistic and obvious; however, all the chapters attest to the complex, multilayered and unique experience of stammering for each individual. The therapy approaches described are diverse, imaginative and broad-based as a result, focusing on speech and communication, feelings, beliefs, attitudes, thinking processes, identity and lifestyle, and in some cases involving not only the person who stammers but also those with whom they live. None of the chapters takes into account only one of these facets of therapy, but instead illustrates the delicate and challenging negotiation of how these differing components are balanced. It is a testimony to the evolution of stammering therapy and the move far beyond some of the original theories steeped in behavioural language, classical conditioning and the controversial speak-more-fluently and stammer-more-fluently divide.

Another emerging theme relates to therapy being significantly more than the specific topic or focus that it addresses. The role of the therapist and client, the knowledge, skills, personal qualities and respective expertise they bring, how power is balanced and shared, the quality and dynamic of the therapeutic relationship and how the therapy is conducted are also paramount. Many of the chapters explicitly advocate a client-centred approach to therapy rather than a practitioner-dominated one. Much of the therapy described throughout the book is an organic, fluid, lived experience that involves close collaboration and careful negotiation between therapist and client. It is apparent that this dynamic process thrives in the context of a mutually engaging, respectful, authentic and often intimate relationship.

A developing facet of stammering therapy that emerges from several of the chapters is a component that accounts for the role of society. Society's intolerance of difference and the continued stigmatization of stammering are raised by a number of authors. Without proactive, organized initiatives to change society's understanding of and response to stammering, the continued lack of public awareness clearly increases the potential social isolation of people who stammer. There is an urgent need to make stammering more visible and to develop a social environment in which people who stammer are not marginalized, ridiculed or devalued. This starts in the immediate family context, but imperatively needs to broaden out to include educational and other community contexts at large, as well as society as a whole. I celebrate the role played by organizations such as the British Stammering Association and the International Stuttering Association in relation to raising public awareness. Both charities share the mission statement 'a world that understands stammering' and together they provide an invaluable political platform for people to join together as a collective and challenge prevailing negative attitudes.

It is also apparent that the continued stigmatization of stammering poses a direct challenge to therapists. It demands careful consideration and navigation of the intrinsic conflict between supporting clients in their goal of fluency and increased communicative ease whilst not colluding with and reaffirming social stereotypes and norms. There is a tension inherent in all stammering therapy that engages in fluency work and promotes the belief that it is 'OK to stammer'. Given this implicit contradiction, all therapists have a personal, political and ethical responsibility to grapple with the delicate balancing and negotiation of these two dimensions of their work.

This is all the more significant when considering the recurring theme of 'acceptance' or making space for stammering, which is identified by both client and therapist contributors as being central to the change process. The intimate accounts provided show this to be an active process and highlight the complexity and personal challenge involved. The gradual reworking of an individual's personal definition of stammering, their relationship with it and the role it plays in their life is seen to be a highly unique process and the book captures many of the diverse facets that can support this within the therapy context.

Another common thread through the chapters in this book relates to the richness of co-authoring therapy knowledge and integrating therapist and client accounts in both the description and evaluation of stammering therapy. The authors have fulfilled this brief in different ways and I view this diversity positively. It gives credence to the scope and value of including client perspectives when evaluating the efficacy and credibility of stammering therapy. It invites a paradigm shift, where such accounts are included not simply as an adjunct, but as a robust, integral source of information. The voices witnessed in this publication offer a powerful means of evaluation outside the confines of the therapy room, in the many and varied real-life and personally meaningful contexts unique to each individual and over extended periods of time. Given the individualized nature of stammering and its far-reaching consequences, this publication makes a compelling case for the inclusion of client accounts and perspectives as the most holistic, culturally-, socially- and contextually-sensitive measure available. I strongly hope such close collaboration and co-construction of therapy knowledge underpins the future evolution of stammering theory, philosophy and practice.

One of the most recurrent questions asked about stammering therapy, by trainees and therapists alike, is 'How do we do it?'. This collection of chapters offers a rainbow of individual responses to this question, integrating the unique and colourful perspectives of both clients and therapists. It is a highly reflective book capturing the complexity, intricacy and challenge of stammering therapy. It has been deeply satisfying to have taken part in bringing together these chapters exploring the practice and shared client/therapist experience of stammering therapy 'from the inside'. I wholeheartedly believe it to represent UK stammering therapy at its most inspiring and cutting-edge best. I thank everyone who has contributed for their time, self-scrutiny and commitment, and hope that their examples motivate others to consider and debate the various and varied issues that they raise.

References

Barnes, C. (1994) Images of disability. In: S. French (Ed.) *On Equal Terms: Working with disabled people*. London: Butterworth-Heinemann Ltd.

Barrow, R. (2000) Hearing the story: A narrative perspective on aphasia therapy. *Bulletin of the Royal College of Speech and Language Therapists, 576* (April), 8–10.

Barrow, R. (2011) Shaping practice: The benefits of really attending to the person's story. In: R.J. Fourie (Ed.) *Therapeutic Processes for Communication Disorders: A guide for clinicians and students*. Hove: Psychology Press.

Barton, L. (1996) Sociology and disability: Some emerging issues. In: L. Barton (Ed.) *Disability and Society: Emerging issues and insights*. London: Longman.

Conrad, P. (1990) Qualitative research on chronic illness: A commentary on method and conceptual development. *Soc. Sci. Med.*, *30*(11), 1257–1263.

DiLollo, A. (2007) Foxes, scorpions, and stuttering research: How a Constructivist perspective might help us avoid getting stung. In: J. Au-Yeung & M. Leahy (Eds) *Research, Treatment, and Self-Help in Fluency Disorders: New horizons*. Proceedings of the International Fluency Association 5th World Congress on Fluency Disorders, pp.3–9.

DiLollo, A., Neimeyer, R., & Manning, W. (2002) A personal construct view of relapse: Indications for a narrative therapy component to stuttering treatment. *Journal of Fluency Disorders*, *30*(1), 1–22.

Downs, D. (2011) How audiologists and speech-language pathologists can foster and combat stigma in people with communication disorders. In: R.J. Fourie (Ed.) *Therapeutic Processes for Communication Disorders: A guide for clinicians and students*. Hove: Psychology Press.

Elwyn, G. & Gwyn, R. (1998) Stories we hear and stories we tell…analysing talk in clinical practice. In: T. Greenhalgh & B. Hurwitz (Eds) *Narrative Based Medicine: Dialogue and discourse in clinical practice*. London: BMJ Books.

Felson Duchan, J. & Byng, S. (2004) *Challenging Aphasia Therapies: Broadening the discourse and extending the boundaries*. New York: Psychology Press.

Finkelstein, V. (1993) Disability: A social challenge or an administrative responsibility? In: J. Swain, V. Finkelstein, S. French, & M. Oliver (Eds) *Disabling Barriers – Enabling Environments*. London: Sage Publications.

Gaddis, S. (2004) Re-positioning traditional research: Centring clients' accounts in the construction of professional therapy knowledge. *The International Journal of Narrative Therapy & Community Work*, *2*, 37–48.

Greenhalgh, T. & Hurwitz, B. (1988) *Narrative Based Medicine: Dialogue and discourse in clinical practice*. London: BMJ Publishing.

Guntupalli, V., Kalinowski, J., & Saltuklaroglu, T. (2006) The need for self-report data in the assessment of stuttering therapy efficacy: Repetitions and prolongations for speech. The Stuttering Syndrome. *International Journal of Language and Communication Disorders*, *41*(1), 1–18.

Kagan, A. (1995) Revealing the competence of aphasic adults through conversation: A challenge to healthcare professionals. *Topics in Stroke Rehabilitation*, *2*(1), 15–28.

Kagan, A. (1998) Supported conversation for adults with aphasia: Methods and resources for training conversation partners. *Aphasiology*, *12*(9), 816–830.

Kalinowski, J., Guntupalli, V., Stuart, A., and Saltuklaroglu, T. (2004) Self-reported efficacy of an ear-level prosthetic device that delivers altered auditory feedback for the management of stuttering. *International Journal of Rehabilitation and Research*, *27*, 167–170.

Kearney A. (1996) *Counselling, Class and Politics: Undeclared influences in therapy*. Ross-on-Wye: PCCs Books.

Keith, L. (1994) *Mustn't Grumble: Writing by disabled women*. London: The Women's Press.

Leahy, M. & Warren, M. (2007) Making stuttering manageable: The use of narrative therapy. In: J. Au-Yeung & M. Leahy (Eds) *Research, Treatment, and Self-Help in Fluency Disorders: New horizons*. Proceedings of the International Fluency Association 5th World Congress on Fluency Disorders, pp.320–324.

Logan, J. (2007) From client to consultant: Developing 'outsider-witness practices' with adults who stammer. In: J. Au-Yeung & M. Leahy (Eds) *Research, Treatment, and Self-Help in Fluency Disorders: New horizons*. Proceedings of the International Fluency Association 5th World Congress on Fluency Disorders, pp.325–332.

Lyon, J. (1992) Communication use and participation in life for adults with aphasia in natural settings: The scope of the problem. *American Journal of Speech-Language Pathology*, *1*, 7–14.

Lyon, J. (1995) Drawing: Its value as a communication aid for adults with aphasia. *Aphasiology*, *9*, 33–50.

Lyon, J. (1996) Optimising communication and participation in life for aphasic adults and their primary care givers in natural settings: A use model for treatment. In: G. Wallace (Ed.) *Adult Aphasia Rehabilitation*. Boston: Butterworth-Heinemann.

Oliver, M. (1993) Disability and dependency: A creation of industrial societies? In: J. Swain, V. Finkelstein, S. French, & M. Oliver (Eds) *Disabling Barriers – Enabling Environments*. London: Sage Publications.

Oliver, M. (1996) A sociology of disability or a disablist sociology? In: L. Barton (Ed.) *Disability and Society: Emerging issues and insights*. London: Longman.

Parr, S., Byng, S., Gilpin, S., & Ireland, C. (1997) *Talking About Aphasia*. Buckingham: Open University Press.

Parr, S., Duchan, J., & Pound, C. (2003) *Aphasia Inside Out: Reflections on communication disability*. Buckingham: Open University Press.

Plexico, L., Manning, W., & DiLollo, A. (2005) A phenomenological understanding of successful stuttering management. *Journal of Fluency Disorders*, *30*, 1–22.

Pound, C. (1999) *Learning to Listen and Helping to Tell*. Speech & Language Therapy in Practice Conference, Rotterdam, The Netherlands.

Pound, C., Parr, S., Lindsay, J., & Woolf, C. (2000) *Beyond Aphasia: Therapies for living with communication disability*. Oxford: Winslow Press Ltd.

Shakespeare, T. (1999). Arts and lies? Representations of disability on film. In: M. Corker & F. French (Eds) *Disability Discourse*. Buckingham: Open University Press.

Simmons-Mackie, N. & Damico, J. (2011) Narrative, discourse and relationships. In: R.J. Fourie (Ed.) *Therapeutic Processes for Communication Disorders: A guide for clinicians and students*. Hove: Psychology Press.

Simpson, S. & Cheasman, C. (2000) A social model of stammering. *Signal, The Newsletter of Special Interest Group Disorders of Fluency,* Issue 13, 1–3. Available at: http://www.fluencysig.org.uk/new_page_5.htm

Simpson, S. & Pound, C. (2001) *Learning to live with aphasia and disability: Stories of self-identity.* Paper presented at the RCSLT Conference, Birmingham, UK.

Stainton Rogers, W. (1991) *Explaining Health and Illness: An exploration of diversity.* Hemel Hempstead: Harvester Wheatsheaf.

Taylor Sarno, M. (2004) Aphasia therapies: Historical perspectives and moral imperatives. In: J. Felson Duchan & S. Byng (Eds) *Challenging Aphasia Therapies: Broadening the discourse and extending the boundaries.* Hove: Psychology Press.

Yaruss, J.S. & Reeves, L. (2002) *Pioneering Stuttering in the 21st Century: The first joint symposium for scientists and consumers* (Summary Report and Proceedings). Anaheim, CA: National Stuttering Association.

Yaruss, J., Quesal, R., & Murphy, W. (2002) National Stuttering Association members' opinions about stuttering treatment. *Journal of Fluency Disorders, 27,* 227–242.

Yaruss, J.S. & Quesal, R.W. (2004) Partnerships between clinicians, researchers and people who stutter in the evaluation of stuttering treatment outcomes. *Stammering Research, 1*(1), on-line journal.

1 Self-advocacy for people who stammer

St John Harris

Introduction

I have stammered for as long as I can remember and have experienced a wide range of therapeutic approaches in my 44 years. As a child and teenager, I recall a familiar pattern of achieving fluency in a clinical environment, safe in the company of speech and language therapists and sometimes other clients; but then, gradually, back in the outside world, my fluent speech would start to unravel and the old habits would return. In those days, we tended to focus more on the mechanics of speech; however, even then, my therapist would offer me the wise words in conclusion: 'You know, it's OK to stammer.' At the time, it struck me that this was an odd thing to say and I did not believe her. Looking back, I realize that it was because I did not believe her that, paradoxically, I could not achieve a lasting fluency or, as I would prefer to say now, contentment with my way of speaking.

A key goal behind much of the stammering therapy I have had at City Lit has been to be more honest and self-accepting about my stammer. However, it was the self-advocacy course that for the first time really allowed me and, I think, the other participants to explore what it can mean for each and all of us to say, 'It's OK to stammer'. In this chapter, I attempt to explain how and why this was so, as well as the enduring effect the course has had on my life.

Background

Self-advocacy for People Who Stammer was a ground-breaking 10-week course delivered by speech and language therapists Sam Simpson and Carolyn Cheasman at City Lit in London in 2000.

This was stimulating, challenging and in some aspects controversial therapy which gave us the opportunity to examine how we define ourselves, how the social and cultural stigma of stammering has affected our sense of self, what the possibilities are for rehabilitating our self-identity, and how this can be achieved both individually and collectively.

Self-advocacy is a relatively recent term used by the disability rights movement, which in its specific meaning refers to people with disabilities, especially those with learning disabilities, taking control of their own lives and their own care. More broadly, and this is the sense that concerns us, it is about people with disabilities speaking up for themselves, relating their stories, but also being true to themselves.

Of course, the idea of speaking up for oneself has a peculiar resonance for people who stammer, given that it is a condition largely characterized by avoidance of sounds, words, situations, even of role – all in an often vain attempt to preserve a façade of normality. This insight was central to the work of the influential speech pathologist Joseph Sheehan who argued that 'avoidance is the heart and core of stuttering' (quoted in Fraser, 1993, p.74) and advocated openness and acceptance of one's stammer to help counter the fear and shame. An alternative term common to other disabilities and minorities is 'to pass'. Interestingly, a lesbian, gay and transgender self-help group for people who stammer calls itself Passing Twice, in recognition of the common stigmas surrounding both sexuality and stammering. I remember vividly the first time I came across the British Stammering Association (BSA) or, as it was then, the Association for Stammerers: it was through a publicity leaflet with the slogan 'No-one need suffer in silence' and an image of a very embarrassed man on the front cover.

The terms 'disabled' and 'disability' are themselves loaded, and many people who stammer reject them as markers of their identity. This is not unique to stammering. A study published in 2002 revealed that just over 50% of the people with impairments who were surveyed did not identify as disabled. Varied reasons were given, but 'disability was persistently believed to be connected with a physical impairment that typically affected mobility, was visible, led to dependency and incapacity and was a permanent condition' (Reeve, 2004, p.13). The theoretical component of the course was principally about unpacking the multiple meanings of disability, including demonstrating how this most unstable of categories has been appropriated by the disability rights movement as a badge of pride and difference through the articulation of 'the social model'. The most common, lay understanding of disability, known as the medical model, sees the term as a byword for deficit, personal loss, even tragedy – something to be cured or, if not cured, endured. By contrast, the social model makes a fundamental distinction between the impairments people have and the oppression they experience. Disability is, therefore, defined as social oppression, not the form of impairment. The social model was first put forward in the 1970s by disabled activists from the Union of the Physically Impaired Against Segregation (UPIAS). The traditional focus of the social model has, therefore, been on the disabling environment, that is, the physical and social barriers that marginalize disabled people. With the extension of the social model to other impairments, more nuanced and sophisticated interpretations of this model have been developed, which I believe make it more appropriate to stammering.

I refer in particular to the work of Carol Thomas, Donna Reeve and Tom Shakespeare. Thomas has criticized the materialist simplicity of the social model by disputing the attribution of all restrictions of activity experienced by disabled people to external barriers:

> "…our appreciation of the exclusions that constitute disability should include those that work along psychological and emotional pathways. The oppression that disabled people experience operates on the 'inside' as well as on the 'outside': it is about being made to feel of lesser value, worthless, unattractive, or disgusting as well as it is about 'outside' matters such as being turned down for a job because one is 'disabled', not being able to get one's wheelchair into a shop or onto a bus because of steps…"

(Thomas, 2004, pp.9–10)

An impairment, such as short-sightedness, may not be a medium of social oppression; yet facial disfigurement with no impairment effect might well be experienced as a disability. Instead, Thomas advances a 'social relational' model which embraces both the structural and psycho-emotional dimensions of disability, that is, the external and the internal. She argues that the latter have been relegated to the realm of the 'personal' by some social model theorists, and that exclusions that constitute disability should include those that affect one psychologically and emotionally:

> "This form of disability shapes in profound ways what people can *be*, as well as affecting what they *do* as a consequence."

(Thomas, 2004, p.10)

Reeve develops this analysis of the psycho-emotional dimension of disability, noting that it 'can leave disabled people feeling worthless and ashamed, whilst removing others from the social world as surely as structural barriers' (Reeve, 2004). To use Thomas' example of a job, I might not even consider applying, let alone reach the interview stage and be turned down. Both Thomas and Reeve note how the internalized oppression that is a consequence of psycho-emotional disablism has profound effects on one's identity, self-esteem and existential security. The novelist John Updike who writes very eloquently and perceptively about his stammering in his memoir, observes: 'In most people there is a settled place they speak from; in me it remains, unsettled, unfinished, provisional' (Updike, 1989, p.82). Where I speak from is in an important sense how I introduce myself to the world, how I say my name – a task that can be one of the most difficult for people who stammer, myself included. Trying to pass as fluent can deepen this anxiety and self-doubt, as I merely reinforce my ambiguous social position. For many people who stammer, the fear of revealing our dysfluency can become one of the main negative psycho-emotional aspects of the condition.

This is an analysis of the 'problem' of stammering in terms of the social model of disability, which underpinned the self-advocacy course. But what to do about it? Reeve notes that what she calls 'the psycho-emotional pathways of oppression' are 'sustained through imagery, cultural representations and interactions with others' (Reeve, 2004, p.3). By internalizing the oppression, I internalize the prejudices – and the myths and stereotypes behind them – held by the dominant group. Both Thomas and Shakespeare explore the importance of narrative in defining who we are: social narratives in which we locate ourselves, the stories we tell about ourselves and our lives. Both see disability culture as the opportunity to challenge dominant and oppressive social narratives, by sharing experiences, building counter-narratives and providing alternative images of disability. Thomas quotes the cultural critic, Bell Hooks: 'Oppressed people resist by identifying themselves as subjects, by defining their reality, shaping their new identity, naming their history, telling their story' (Thomas, 1999, p.55).

The self-advocacy course provided an exploration of disability culture through the lens of stammering, the centrepiece of which was each participant's personal portfolio.

The course

Week 1: Introductions and orientation to the course

The course was made up of 10 weekly two-hour sessions. The first five weeks focused on giving us the theoretical tools to help us understand our condition and address these questions of identity, and to give us time to prepare our 'personal portfolios'. These were our stories alongside other forms of self and collective expression, to be presented in the second half of the course.

I was also asked to keep a personal learning journal to be completed after each session to enable me to reflect on my personal experiences of the course, and to track my progress in relation to the five aims I had identified:

1. Share my experiences and feelings with others; and in turn listen and learn from their experiences and feelings.

2. Examine both the external and internal factors that influence my identity as a person who stammers.

3. Question stereotypes, challenge received ideas, explore new possibilities.

4. Be more honest and accepting about the person I am.

5. Work to develop a positive collective voice.

What follows is in large part based on my personal learning journal with references to the course materials, and a postscript reflecting on the course and its significance some 10 years later.

My first journal entry expresses my excitement at the start of the course. I had seized particularly on the opportunity to develop a more robust and self-confident identity as someone who stammers, and to embrace our difference as a collective. However, my enthusiasm was tempered by recognition of the difficulty of the project. I had convinced myself of the significance of the social model of disability, but was unsure how the model applied to me in practice:

> "My deeply ingrained impulse is to cover up, minimise the place of impairment in my personal and social life, and so attempt to avoid the stigma of an abnormal, disabled identity. Such are the costs of trying to maintain a normal identity… I am under no illusions that the issue of disability

within the stammering community, but also vis-à-vis the wider disabled community, is fraught with difficulties, but again here is the chance to explore the problems in an open, tolerant way."

But there were also profounder questions at the back of my mind of self-fulfilment and vocation. I had no doubt that stammering had influenced my outlook, temperament and life choices. I wanted in some sense to grasp my fate: to make it a blessing. By doing this I wanted to learn to accept myself and be myself, and thereby achieve some serenity and stability from which 'to speak to the world'.

Week 2: Difference, identity and identity choices

In the second week, we were led through the difficult and potentially awkward area of difference, starting with the multiple aspects in which we can feel different from the majority such as accent, financial situation, ethnic background, political beliefs, religion and class. The group divided into halves to discuss our personal experiences of feeling different in this way, and then brought back our insights to the whole group. The group discussion faltered somewhat. I think we all found it difficult to share, especially hidden differences with others, on only the second occasion we had met. I referred to my speech, but not stammering. My difference, my peculiarity was my lack of a Yorkshire accent, despite having spent most of my childhood in the East Riding of Yorkshire, and having been educated in the local comprehensive school. This anomaly can still provoke adverse reaction in some – that perhaps I am not being 'true' to my upbringing, or that I lack authenticity. Despite the fact that my accent is as natural to me as my breathing, I realize that it has a certain plasticity and can become more neutral or more pronounced as I attempt almost unconsciously to blend in different work and social situations. Another group member who was mixed race spoke of her ambivalence and awkwardness about her ethnic background: east or west? Her appearance and accent do not obviously point to the conclusion that she is mixed race. My accent does not obviously indicate my place of birth and education. This discrepancy between image and reality can be awkward, by our not conforming to powerful social and cultural assumptions of the 'norm'. In terms of stammering, we then discussed what is at stake in either revealing or concealing our difference, attempting either to blend in or to stand apart from the so-called norm. Whilst being open about stammering might well increase people's understanding and reduce pressure and stress, there is a deep-seated fear it could lead to prejudice and diminish people's opinion of me and my competence. By trying to conceal my stammer I might minimize the risk of prejudice, but to maintain the pretence can become an arduous and emotionally costly exercise. In effect, I am like everyone else, but only as long as I hide or minimize my impairment. That the mask slips and the difference becomes apparent on that first introduction can be especially painful. As a group, we lamented that far too often the stammer can dominate the initial impression we give, overwhelming other aspects of our personalities.

Week 3: Stammering and disability – models and issues

Following our discussion the week before, for the third session each one of us was asked to consider 'to what extent the fact that I stammer has led me to construe myself as different' and to study an article by Sally French entitled 'What is disability?' (French, 1994) which explores different understandings of disability and distinguishes in particular between the medical and social models. Here is the extract from my personal learning journal:

> "When I feel different in relation to my stammer, I feel substantially and fundamentally different. When my difference is the most pronounced, the pain and embarrassment I feel at my difference is most acute. In simple terms, the perceived norm is to be able to utter words intelligibly on the phone. On occasions, I find myself at the other pole, reduced to a struggling silence. I wish to break the vicious circle of a damaged sense of self-worth which can prolong and intensify this silence. The more comfortable I feel about my stammer, the more likely the words will escape.
>
> Other times I feel wholly normal. At ease with my partner or a good friend, I hardly stutter. I can forget about other speaking situations, get lulled into a false sense of security and stability, until the not uncommon scenario of, say, meeting a new person jolts me out of my complacency. For example, after a week's holiday when I have spent most of the time with my partner, I can get back to work and

paradoxically find I stammer more; as opposed to the fluency
I might expect from feeling more relaxed and refreshed.
This dichotomy between difference and the norm can be
painful and embarrassing."

Others described similar emotions, some referring to a capricious and fleeting
fluency which would let you down when you most needed it to deliver.

We then proceeded to examine the different models of disability, in
particular medical and social, and describe what each of us felt was meant
by the two models. Some very emotive terms emerged during the discussion:
tragic, diseased, stigma, individual fault and inadequacy.

Our discussion then turned to how stammering could be understood
in terms of the different models. One participant recounted how they had
attained a significant degree of fluency by 'coming out' as a 'disabled person'
and embracing the social model and the rights agenda. This initial liberation
had subsequently succumbed to the old behaviour patterns, as they became
more attached to their identity as a 'fluent' person. This case illustrates how for
many who stammer our identities are claimed from both sides, with the side
of the 'normal' by far the most powerful to which we gravitate. Shakespeare,
Gillespie-Sells and Davies point out that 'people with hidden impairments are
sometimes less likely to "come out" as disabled, and move to a positive acceptance
of difference and a political identity, because it is easier to maintain a "normal"
identity' (quoted in Swain & Cameron, 1999, p.76). Elsewhere, Shakespeare
warns of the dangers of an 'essentialist' approach to disability identity and
disability politics which can lead to an oversimplistic division between 'allies'
and 'oppressors' – between 'them, and 'us' – and therefore to a criticism of
people who pass for somehow betraying their 'real' identity by attempting to
assimilate with the 'normal' majority (Shakespeare, 1996, p.15).

People cope with the stigma of disability in different ways. All of us have
multiple identities and make multiple identity choices in practice – identities
which are neither fixed nor stable. The disability theorist, Carol Thomas, who
was born without a left hand, describes how she inhabits the 'borderlands'
between the disabled and non-disabled worlds (Thomas, 1999, p.55). She
recounts the long history of hiding her impairment in order to appear as normal
as possible which has led to this disjuncture between her disabled sense of
self and how others perceive her. I believe the borderlands are also familiar
territory to people who stammer, although the map of crossings from one realm
to another and the relationship between the disability and the impairment

may be unique to each individual. Thomas notes that the distinction between impairment and disability is not a simple biological/cultural or natural/social dualism, and this I believe is especially pertinent to stammering. The way I stammer is a consequence of the interaction between the disability and the impairment. The degree of oppression and shame I experience, or the pressure I may feel to be fluent, distorts the impairment as I introduce often unhelpful behaviours such as blocks and fillers. At other times, I might be more successful in passing as fluent, but the emotional consequences are just as profound as I attempt to negotiate a comfortable place between my disabled/non-disabled or normal/abnormal selves.

Week 4: Barriers and discrimination

This session focused on the diverse barriers that face those who have disabilities: structural, environmental, linguistic and attitudinal. We considered examples of environmental barriers which people who stammer could have to deal with: an open plan office which removes privacy when making a phone call, or the time pressure of an answering machine with a limited period in which to leave a message. Turns of phrase can also betray unhelpful attitudes, from the downright offensive term 'spastic' to more subtle forms, which can problematize and infantilize impairment. A common term used with stammering, is 'to grow out of it', a possible implication being that if you have retained your stammer as an adult, there is some emotional immaturity or underdevelopment.

In relation to stammering, the most significant barriers are attitudinal: both external (e.g. as displayed by family, friends, employers and society) and the internalization of negative attitudes and self-beliefs. I have already referred to Carol Thomas' work defending the crucial psycho-emotional dimensions of disablism, the manifestations of which should not to be confused with the psychological angst of merely personal problems and therefore relegated to the realm of the private and confessional (Thomas, 2004, pp.9–10 already quoted). In a recent article in *The Independent* newspaper, Martin Stephen recounts his own struggles with stammering, recalling that at the age of 13 he was told he had 'an incurable speech defect'. He goes on to muse: 'How many children accept that they too have an "incurable speech defect", and will perhaps accept compromises in their life that might deny them the chance to be what they could, and should have been?' (Stephen, 2011).

We then divided into two groups to discuss ways of tackling these attitudes. With regard to external attitudes, the emphasis was very much on being more open, honest and communicative about stammering with others, to help rectify mistaken assumptions and unhelpful reactions. One participant referred to how she introduces the fact that she stammers quite early on when meeting new people. This clearly serves to alleviate the tension and burst the bubble of pretence.

Internal attitudes are just as, if not more difficult, to address. Suggested approaches included: questioning why I feel this way about stammering and what I believe about myself; using humour; being positive in my self-expression and remembering positive images of people who stammer.

Week 5: Attitudes and images of difference

The last session in the theoretical half of the course was devoted to representations of stammering in television and other media.

We began by viewing a series of video clips.

'Right to Reply': The first showed Carolyn Cheasman on the television programme 'Right to Reply', protesting at the representation of people who stammer as violent, mentally unhinged victims-turned-aggressors in the crime dramas 'Cracker' and 'Prime Suspect'. I felt Granada TV's reply that the speech impairment was merely incidental to the well-developed portrayal of a character was disingenuous and entirely missed the point. The stammer was a very conspicuous and important part of the impression the character gave the viewer. The association of stammering with derangement was deliberately made for dramatic effect.

'A Fish Called Wanda' – 'The Life of Brian' – 'Open All Hours': All three clips exploited stammering (and other impairments) for comic effect. The severity of stammering in the first two films did not make me laugh, but wince. 'Open All Hours' had a more neutral impact on me. The stammering was very caricatured and unrealistic, and although Arkwright was mimicked, he was not primarily a figure of fun nor a victim.

'Ally McBeal': For me, 'Ally McBeal' was the exception. A key theme of this television series is mild eccentricity or kookiness (in effect being different), not only of the eponymous heroine, but also of her soulmate John Cage, and other less central characters. Ally and her colleagues are rather glamorized in the usual Hollywood fashion, and there is the typical heavy dose of sentimentalism; however, the introspectiveness of the characters and the fact that they do not lose an opportunity to expand on their problems allow for a quite sympathetic and in-depth treatment of a subject like stammering (for example, John Cage's speech on Ally's 30th birthday).

I then gave a précis of Colin Barnes' article 'Images of disability' (Barnes, 1994) which explores the prevalence of negative cultural stereotypes of disability such as the pathetic, tragic victim, the bitter and twisted villain, the brave super-cripple who against the odds has overcome his disability to achieve great things. By contrast, representations which do justice to the complexity of disability experience and show disabled people as responsible and valued members of the community are much more difficult to find.

The group then discussed the moral implications of these images of stammering. What is acceptable and what is not? Should we laugh at 'Open All Hours'? Is not caricature a legitimate comic device? We noted how comic tastes had changed over the years and caricatures of disability had become less acceptable. However, we agreed that all these media representations were powerful forces in determining people's ideas about, and attitudes towards, stammering. Interestingly, outside primetime viewing, the 'Video Diary' programme gave a rounded portrayal of a final-year student with a stammer but was broadcast at midnight on a Sunday evening.

We ended the session by considering the language and images in a range of promotional literature about stammering and how the philanthropic/medical model of disability was used to frame the reader's understanding of the condition for a particular purpose. This could be to impel the reader to donate to an appeal, or to subscribe to a course of stammering therapy.

Weeks 6 and 7: Portfolio presentations

Each member of the group was allotted 20 minutes to present his/her personal portfolio and then take questions. Most of us focused on our own life stories but presented them in a variety of ways: a little booklet divided into years and key events from which we were invited to select a year at random; a life organized according to birthday; Number One hits; or just straightforward story telling. We heard frank and moving accounts of how stammering had impacted on our personal and professional lives – the challenges, the discrimination, the need to prove oneself, the successes, and the missed opportunities.

Mine was a story of a life-changing course at City Lit, but also of my engagement with disability issues by necessity, because of my struggles to develop a career, and to come to terms with 'my shadow':

"The shadow I have fought many years to suppress, which I have not much wished to talk about, and which on many occasions I have pretended is not there. This is the side of me who can't say his name when he introduces himself, who finds himself tongue-tied when trying to begin a telephone conversation, who is prone to seizing up when talking in public. Sometimes it has felt like an achievement just to utter the word, irrespective of the message I wish to convey. The longer the conversation continues, the greater my achievement, simply to do what most people take for granted, like breathing."

I enjoyed the opportunity to tell a little bit about 'my truth' to a receptive and sympathetic audience. I am sure the others felt the same; we all benefited from this exchange of stories about a part of us which is the subject of so much denial and concealment.

We also spent some of the session reviewing the course so far. There was a general feeling that up until the previous week, the course had been heavily weighted towards theory, and the personal portfolios helped restore the balance. Some had problems relating the theory to their life experiences, and so found the course disjointed. I did not have any problems making this connection. My own experiences helped me make sense of the theory and vice-versa.

Week 8: This is me

In this session, we sought to achieve self-expression through our artwork and three images in particular: (i) who I am; (ii) my stammer; and (iii) where I would like to be in relation to my stammer.

Most of us found this a very cathartic and intense experience with vivid and imaginative depictions of self and world. I drew a scene from my walk in the northern Pennines on a lovely summer's evening the previous June. However, in the bottom left-hand corner I was teetering over a black abyss, representing my insecurities and fears even in the midst of such life-affirming beauty. In my second image, it became clearer what the abyss meant. Here I was, a figure trying to straddle a chasm in the earth opening up before him. The widening chasm signified a painful divergence between the world of normality and the world of disability, and my attempt to reconcile both worlds by pretending the latter world did not exist, seduced by the appeal of 'the norm'.

After drawing these two images, the third came quite naturally. This was the happy and relaxed figure enjoying the splendid surroundings of upper Teesdale, and seated on the fault line of the two worlds. The wound in the earth had been healed.

Week 9: Your shout – what do you want to advocate?

This session divided into individual shouts when we were each given a maximum of three minutes in front of the video camera to have 'our say' about stammering, followed by two collective shouts. In mine, I characterized my stammer as a different, but nonetheless valid, way of speaking which encompassed periods of fluency and dysfluency. I referred to its mysterious and unpredictable quality, but that it did not mean that I was afraid, nervous, emotionally unstable or stupid. The desire to suppress it, however, was at the root of much of its pain and sting. I was now trying to live through this paradox instead of trying to fight it. Some other messages were: 'Do not jump to any conclusions about me!', 'Give me a chance to have my say!', 'Give more funding to stammering therapy!'. Each gave a perspective unique to that individual, but complementing and building on the rest to produce a strong collective voice. That voice was further strengthened by the work we did later in the session to produce a group shout.

Week 10 – Where next?

In this final session, we reviewed our individual shouts on the video and decided how we wanted to build on our experiences and lessons from the course. Some of us wanted to publish our experiences and views in a professional journal or in the British Stammering Association magazine. Others wanted to share their own perspectives on stammering through delivering a course. There was a common aspiration to continue this journey of self-expression and self-advocacy and to develop a positive and stronger stammering identity. Both speech and language therapists noted how the course had generated new perspectives on stammering and revealed the significance of narratives in all our lives. For narratives shape who we are and how we see ourselves. In her chapter 'Narrative identity and the disabled self' (Thomas, 1999, p.48) Carol Thomas draws on and quotes Margaret Somers' work:

> "...stories guide action; that people construct identities
> (however multiple and changing) by locating themselves or

being located within the repertoire of emplotted stories; that 'experience' is constituted through narratives; that people make sense of what has happened and is happening to them by attempting to assemble or in some way to integrate these happenings within one or more narratives."

What our foray into disability culture did was to give us a collective context in which to share our ideas, feelings and stories. How far I identify as disabled is ultimately down to individual choice and is not, as we have seen, something simple or straightforward. In 'Disability, identity and difference' Tom Shakespeare concludes that:

"Disability identity is about stories, having the space to tell them, and an audience which will listen. It is also about recognising differences, and isolating the significant attributes and experiences which constitute disability... We may need to develop a nuanced attitude which incorporates ambivalence. But... it all starts with having a voice. As Foucault suggests, our task is to speak the truth about ourselves."

(Shakespeare, 1996, p.18)

Self-Advocacy for People who Stammer was above all a platform to give us a voice.

Postscript

It is now over 10 years since the course, and an opportune time to reflect on how well this platform has served me, how I have progressed in forging a more positive self-identity as a person who stammers, as well as on wider cultural and social developments which have served to counter the taboo of stammering and increase understanding of the stammering experience.

On re-reading my personal learning journal, I realize that I have grown a lot in confidence over the last decade in most speaking situations, and the painful struggles on the phone are a much less common occurrence. Public speaking, which lies in the upper echelons of my hierarchy of speaking situations, still holds its fears, as it does for many people, but also has a certain exhilaration for me, at just being there, centre stage, and managing my stammer. There are all sorts of emotions going on here, largely arising from the powerful interaction of impairment and disability, but part of the rollercoaster experience is some satisfaction that I have brought my stammering into the open, I have made it visible, and still expressed myself.

'The King's Speech'

Donna Reeve maintains that the psycho-emotional dimensions of disability are open to challenge in two ways. She refers first to the experience of disability culture, particularly the provision of positive role models and the exposure of the pervasive nature of prejudices and myths about disability; and secondly, to the increasing presence and visibility of disabled people within mainstream society (Reeve, 2004, p.20).

The enormous box office and critical success of the film 'The King's Speech' has been of incalculable benefit to people who stammer in both these ways. This fact has not been lost on the BSA, which has encouraged its members up and down the country to give media interviews and make the connections between a historical film and their own experiences – another platform to talk about stammering. Personally, I have benefited from the publicity, explaining to work colleagues about the fears and other emotions associated with stammering, about speech and language therapy and coping strategies. I have been congratulated on my public speaking by acquaintances and asked if I was inspired by the film. 'The King's Speech', through its moving, multifaceted portrayal of a man with a stammer who, by accident of birth and circumstance, found himself at the very centre of the mainstream and a living symbol of our country, has provoked an outpouring of 'confessions' and 'coming out' opportunities about stammering, including Martin Stephen's article I quoted earlier.

David Seidler, the screenwriter of the film and a person who stammers, understood this well, when he accepted his Oscar on behalf of all who stammer, proclaiming: 'We have a voice. We have been heard.' Seidler's remarks mirror a particularly poignant scene in the film when the King finds his therapist, Lionel Logue, seated on the coronation throne, St Edward's Chair. The King angrily challenges Logue who asks why he should listen to him. The King replies because he has a voice – a vital recognition which Logue in turn quietly acknowledges. BSA patron and novelist David Mitchell has also used the film to have his say in a brilliantly perceptive article in *Prospect* magazine. Mitchell refers to the taboo of 'the disability which cannot say its name …

the wider cultural "looking away" which translates into political indifference and funding apathy' (Mitchell, 2011). Other commentators have also drawn attention to the underfunding of speech and language therapy on the back of the film at a time of shrinking public sector budgets. On the eve of the Oscars ceremony, Shadow Chancellor of the Exchequer and fellow patron of the BSA, Ed Balls, enthused that the 'film, and Colin Firth's brilliant performance, have done more to advance the understanding of stammering than anything in my lifetime' (Balls, 2011). In the climax of the film, the King with Logue close at hand has to make his first wartime radio address to the nation. With intense drama, the King succeeds in delivering the eponymous speech, but crucially not with complete fluency. 'You still stammered on the "w",' Logue half-jokes after the speech, and the King half-jokes back: 'I had to throw in a few extra ones so they knew it was me.' As people who stammer, both Balls and Mitchell have seized on the significance of this gently ironic remark. There is here more than of a hint of self-acceptance by the King that, provided he can manage his stammer, he is content to see it as part of his identity. This contrasts with earlier scenes in the film, when faced with such torment, all he wishes to do is eradicate his dysfluency. Balls and Mitchell warmly endorse this 'victory'.

That stammering is curable is one of the myths Mitchell wishes to explode in his article – what he calls 'fallacies that make stammerers' lives harder in the long run' (Mitchell, 2011). This fallacy colludes with the medical model of disability that the problem is mine, my failure, and should be removed. Such abnormality should certainly not be made visible: 'the disability which cannot say its name'. The condition has been characterized by this conflict between the desire to destroy it and the desire to come to terms with it – a conflict played out in the BSA's own search for a vision statement some years ago. Two competing visions were proposed: 'A world without stammering' and 'A world that understands stammering'. Happily, the latter statement prevailed. This conflict is another reason why stammering sits so uneasily for many people vis-à-vis the broader disability movement which seeks to subvert the medical model, and why the transition from normal/non-disabled speech to abnormal/disabled speech can be so painful for people who stammer. As Lisette Wesseling shows below (p.30), it can be much harder to accept a condition, and indeed to accept a part of oneself, which is intermittent and variable in nature; and perhaps because we slide so often between fluency and dysfluency in the 'borderlands', to accept a condition so haunted by the fantasy and expectation of a cure. Despite this ambivalence, there was no hand wringing from the BSA about stammering's status as a disability in their reaction to 'The

King's Speech'. The Chief Executive, Norbert Lieckfeldt, was unequivocal: 'It's unseen and unheard. Stammering masks your ability and your intellect. It's a layer between you and the world through which everything gets filtered. It's a serious disability' (quoted in *The Guardian*, 17 January 2011). Such statements accord well with a social relational understanding of disability that the stigma and internalized oppression associated with the impairment tends us towards self-effacement and invisibility. Is stammering legitimate disabled experience? From a social relational point of view, there is no doubt.

Disability art and other vehicles of self-expression

'The King's Speech' was an extraordinary moment in the history of stammering and the production of hitherto silent 'voices', new knowledges, and new subjectivities, which the self-advocacy course set out to facilitate in a much smaller way.

I would now like to examine some other ways in which people who stammer have been allowed to express themselves and so become empowered over the last 10 years.

When the words won't come: Inside the experience of stammering

This was an anthology of children's and adults' poetry published by the BSA in 2003. BSA patron and novelist Margaret Drabble in her foreword describes the collection's power and therapeutic value: 'It is a vivid and moving testimony to the mysterious misery many of us suffer in daily life, and the courage we find to overcome it. It should make us all feel differently when we stammer ourselves, as I do, or meet others who do… There are no easy answers, and none are offered, but there is a sense of sharing here, which offers real encouragement' (British Stammering Association (BSA), 2003, p.I).

By sharing our stories and subjective experiences, we find our common ground and solidarity. Many of the poems are extremely eloquent in facing up to the self-oppression of stammering, and by expressing it, they can counter it. For example, Rosalind Harvey's cleverly titled poem 'The Sentence' (BSA, 2003, p.21):

> 'How can I begin to tell you this tale
> of a life-serving prisoner in this puzzling jail?
> A jail with no shackles, no whips and no chains –
> But a jailer most wicked who never refrains

> From a continual strapping of words to the soul –
> A legacy of suffering is his only goal.
> His testing and teasing, his taunts and his lies,
> and unkind regard for the need of replies,
> I question him curtly, "When will I be free?"
> The jailer turns slowly – the jailer is me.'

Time2talk

Time2talk (Doncaster Stammering Association, 2007) is a collection of six songs performed by youth and adult members of the Doncaster Stammering Association with the support of professional musicians and specialist speech and language therapist, Hilary Liddle. Like *When the Words Won't Come*, the songs are based on real-life experiences of the participants, and seek not only to convey the tribulations of stammering, but also to build a positive collective identity out of these experiences. Children are singing about a condition often characterized by avoidance and embarrassment, in a dynamic act of self-advocacy. Here is 'Don't Finish My Sentence':

> 'Don't finish my sentence
> I don't want you to
> Don't finish my sentence
> 'Cause I don't finish for you
> We keep on trying
> We don't give up
> We're never alone
> You may pick on us
> We keep on going
> We will fight'

Speaking Out magazine

The BSA's *Speaking Out* magazine is an important organ in which people who stammer can publish their stories and experiences. In the Winter 2008 edition, Lisette Wesseling compares her stammering with her blindness, maintaining that the former is much more difficult to live with. Blind from birth, she has a strong blind self-identity shored up by positive blind role models and a sense of pride in using Braille. By contrast, her dysfluency 'is something I have struggled to make a part of myself due to a world which really does not understand stammering at all' (Wesseling, 2008, p.6). Blindness is consistent and permanent, whereas her stammer is variable and unpredictable, causing shock and surprise in her listener. Friendships with other people who stammer have helped her overcome the stigma of stammering and manage it better. The combination of two disabilities is illuminating by further pointing up the difficulties in accepting a complex condition, which is intermittent and so possible to conceal. Her BSA article is of course the opposite of an act of concealment – a sharing of her experience to help promote understanding.

Stammering's status as a disability

The disability debate around stammering has certainly moved on since 2000, particularly in the arena of employment where I first came across discrimination and the disability movement.

Allan Tyrer's website, stammeringlaw.org.uk, has done much to trace the development of disability discrimination legislation over the last 12 years and its implications for people who stammer, including examples of legal cases.

Tyrer explains that it is 'fairly easy' for stammering to fall within the Equality Act which replaced the Disability Discrimination Act in 2010:

> "Broadly, a stammer is covered if it has a substantial adverse effect on one's ability to carry out normal day-to-day activities, such as having a conversation or using the phone."

(Tyrer, 1999–2012)

But crucially, there are still likely to be substantial effects if the stammering is intermittent. This could be because of the usual attempts to hide or avoid stammering through word substitutions, inserting additional words, or avoiding speaking situations such as telephone calls. In other words, the guidance, which informs the legislation, explicitly recognizes how the stigma and self-oppression of stammering affects its manifestation, or in social model terms, how the disability distorts the impairment.

What I find most interesting about stammeringlaw.org.uk is the page which addresses and challenges the widespread reluctance by people who stammer to consider their stammer as a disability, or to identify as 'disabled'.

Tyrer's initial concern is that people who stammer may not wish to make use of the Equality Act which is there to protect them because of the negative connotations associated with the terms 'disability' and 'disabled'. He points out that these terms have a specific legal definition within the Act, which in most cases embraces stammering, and that by using the Act, you do not have to accept that you have a disability in the broader sense. But then he goes on to explore what this broader sense means, the problems with the term because of its inherent connotations of deficit and loss, but how through the social model, the disability community has reinvented the term as a marker of social oppression. He then discusses various reasons people cite for not regarding their stammer as a disability: 'I'm normal', 'If I say I'm disabled, then I'm saying there is something wrong with me', 'I'm perfectly able', 'Only people with quite a severe stammer are genuinely disabled by it', 'It limits me to see myself as disabled'. On closer analysis, these statements are all likely to reflect a deeply engrained wish to distance oneself not just from the stigma of disability but also from the stigma of stammering, understood in terms of the medical model. Such a wish is common, especially among those with interiorized stammers who are adept enough to pass as fluent (despite the emotional cost), and so self-identify strongly with the 'normal' non-disabled constituency. By instead using the social model to shed light on stammering, Tyrer places the condition in the context of other disabilities, which are the subject of negative imagery, misconceptions and stereotypes.

In his article 'The debilitating 'd' word' posted as part of the International Stuttering Association Online Conference in 2010, Grant Meredith similarly describes this cultural estrangement between stammering and other disabilities. His PhD study showed him that, as a consequence of this estrangement, Australian university students who stammer miss out on the help available to other students with disabilities, even though their speech had impacted upon their grades and general academic performance. By people who stammer occupying what I have previously referred to as the borderlands between the disabled and non-disabled worlds, it can seem at times that our experiences belong to neither world. What to do about 'the disability which cannot say its name'? Meredith's advice is emphatic:

> "By taking pride and being open that you have at times a disability you will help to redefine the negative social stigmas that are commonly attached to that word. There is absolutely no shame at all with admitting that your stuttering at times may cause restrictions and limitations upon your

day to day life and as a result could be termed as having a disabling effect on your life from time to time.

When the **need** arises say it loud and say it proud. **I AM DISABLED.**"

(Meredith, 2010)

In 2005, the International Stuttering Association, the umbrella organization for national stammering self-help and support groups throughout the world, debated the issue of whether stammering is a disability and concluded in favour. Among their reasons, they wished to align the condition with the disability movement so that people who stammer could find strength and support in the movement if they wish. Mark Irwin, Chair of the Board of the International Stuttering Association, counters the argument that many people who stutter (as with many other disabilities) do not regard themselves as disabled. This he attributes to the shame, embarrassment and denial which people who stammer too readily feel and which is the major role of self-help groups and speech and language therapists to address. With an assertiveness characteristic of the disability movement, the ISA has also agreed a Bill of Rights and Responsibilities for People Who Stutter:

> "The general concept is one of individual rights for the person who stutters. In other words, some may choose to live with their stuttering while others may work at overcoming it—the path is for each individual to decide. But with either path the word disability remains. Stuttering can be seen as a disability to be lived with, or as a disability to be overcome."

(Irwin, 2005)

Conclusions

The work of Tyrer and Meredith and organizations such as the British Stammering Association and the International Stuttering Association suggests that attitudes towards stammering have shifted over the last 10 years and the ideas explored in the self-advocacy course have become more widely accepted.

The phenomenon of 'The King's Speech' film has also been enormously encouraging.

I have already stated that how much one invests in a disabled identity will ultimately remain a matter of individual choice. My own journey began with the despair of discrimination, but from this negative starting point many positives have resulted. I count among these the joy and solidarity of shared experiences and creative responses I have found in group courses at City Lit, not only the self-advocacy course. I identify strongly with people with disabilities, and thinking about disability issues has become an important part of my intellectual life. On the other hand, I can pass quite well as 'fluent' in certain company. It is those transitional moments from fluent to non-fluent, those progressions up and down the speaking hierarchy which I need to keep a weather eye on. A thorough grounding in the social relational model of disability helps me understand the forces with which I must contend, the courage it takes to speak and the thrill it gives me. This will never be the stable and settled place I had hoped to speak from by the end of the self-advocacy course. To borrow a visual metaphor from the images I sketched on the course, there will always be a fissure in the earth. But as Tom Shakespeare said: 'It all starts with having a voice... our task is to speak the truth about ourselves' (Shakespeare, 1996, p.18).

References

Balls, E. (2011) 'The King's Speech must win for proving a stammer is nothing to be ashamed of', *Daily Mail*, 28 February 2011.

Barnes, C. (1994) Images of disability In S. French (Ed.) *On Equal Terms: Working with disabled people*. London: Butterworth-Heinemann, pp.35–45.

British Stammering Association (2003) *When the Words won't Come: Inside the experience of stammering*. London: British Stammering Association.

Doncaster Stammering Association (2007) *Time2talk: Stammering awareness project* music CD.

Fraser, M. (1993) *Self-therapy for the Stutterer*. Memphis, TN: Stuttering Foundation of America.

French, S. (1994) What is disability? In S. French (Ed.) *On Equal Terms: Working with disabled people*. London: Butterworth-Heinemann, pp.3–16.

Irwin, M. (2005) 'Stuttering as a Disability—the Controversy'. International Stuttering Association, linked at *stammeringlaw.org.uk* website.

'The King's Speech means stammerers understood', *The Guardian*, 17 January 2011.

Meredith, G. (2010) 'The debilitating "d" word', *International Stuttering Awareness Day Online Conference 2010*.

Mitchell, D. (2011) 'Lost for words', *Prospect Magazine*, Issue 180, 23 February 2011.

Reeve, D. (2004) Psycho-emotional dimensions of disability and the social model. In: C. Barnes and G. Mercer (Eds) *Implementing the Social Model of Disability: Theory and research.* The Disability Archive UK website www.leeds.ac.uk/disability-studies/archiveuk/

Shakespeare, T. (1996) Disability, identity and difference. In C. Barnes and G. Mercer (Eds) *Exploring the Divide.* The Disability Archive UK website www.leeds.ac.uk/disability-studies/archiveuk/

Stephen, M. (2011) 'Every child deserves the right to speak', *The Independent*, 27 January 2011.

Swain, J. & Cameron, C. (1999) Unless otherwise stated: Discourses of labelling and identity in coming out. In: M. Corker and S. French (Eds) *Disability Discourse*. Buckingham: Open University Press, pp.68–78.

Thomas, C. (1999) Narrative and the disabled self. In: M. Corker and S. French (Eds) *Disability Discourse.* Buckingham: Open University Press, pp.47–55.

Thomas, C. (2004) Developing the social relational in the social model of disability: A theoretical agenda. In C. Barnes and G. Mercer (Eds) *Implementing the Social Model of Disability: Theory and research.* The Disability Archive UK website www.leeds.ac.uk/disability-studies/archiveuk/

Tyrer, A (1999–2012) *stammeringlaw.org.uk* website.

Updike, J. (1989) *Self-Consciousness – Memoirs.* London: Random House.

Wesseling, L. (2008) 'Stammering or blindness – which is harder?', *Speaking Out*, Winter 2008.

2 1:1 therapy revisited

Jan Logan, Sam Simpson, Dan Durling and Ed Balls

Introduction

We write from diverse perspectives – Jan as a speech and language therapist and counsellor working within adult education, and Sam as a speech and language therapist and counsellor working in the independent, educational and voluntary sectors – and also from what we share together: a fundamental belief in the principles of person-centred therapy, the centrality of the therapeutic relationship and the potential for stammering therapy to facilitate the development of alternative narratives and future identities. Whilst this chapter focuses on individual therapy with adults who stammer, we bring a shared commitment to stammering therapy in a group context. We consider this to be a positive choice for people who stammer (PWS), facilitating the development of a collective identity. In addition to working with groups, Sam has transitioned into offering regular 1:1 stammering therapy over the past 10 years whilst Jan has recently returned to 1:1 work on an occasional basis.

This chapter aims to capture the voices of two clients, Ed Balls and Dan Durling, in order to explore the 1:1 therapy experience from their different perspectives. Their personal accounts have provided us with a unique platform to explore our common and different experiences of working with block modification in the 1:1 context. The process of writing this chapter has been exciting, challenging and personally enriching for all involved, as initial reflections have taken clearer form and shape during the many discussions that we have had in different combinations. We welcome this opportunity to share Dan and Ed's moments of insight, alongside our own, with a broader audience interested in the co-authorship of therapy knowledge.

The experience of 1:1 therapy: The client perspective

Dan and Ed have chosen to share their individual accounts in different formats. Dan starts with a personal written account of his experiences. This is then followed by Ed's reflections in the form of a transcribed conversation with Jan. Whilst both Dan and Ed have covert (interiorized) stammering patterns, we believe that the issues raised are equally relevant to people with more overt (exteriorized) stammering.

Dan's story

My stammering history

I have stammered all my life, I don't remember a time when I didn't have a stammer. As a boy, I don't remember being bothered by it until I reached school, when I became frustrated at not being able to say what I wanted. As I grew up, I began to experience other negative feelings related to my speech, such as anxiety, embarrassment and doubt. These feelings deepened as I became more self-conscious. Many of my memories are more about my fear of stammering than actual memories of blocking. I can still vividly remember my extreme upset and worry as I spoke to my mother every night before bed about something I might have to do in class. With hindsight, I don't remember getting upset because I had any traumatic blocks, it was more the prospect. This is a theme that has stayed with me most of my life. The thought of stammering has at times been terrifying. As my negative feelings grew, so did the 'techniques' I used to avoid situations where I might stammer and to modify my speech. I avoided the phone, classes at school, tutorials at university and presentations at work and developed a huge web of strategies to stammer less.

Over time my speech varied. I have had times when I have been more fluent and times when my blocks became more frequent. I have had periods when my confidence has grown and my fluency improved, but have also had times when I relapsed and feelings of embarrassment, fear and doubt reappeared. When my confidence is at its highest, my speech is something I only think about a couple of times a day. At its worst, it is the first thing I think about in the morning and the last thing I think about before bed.

What led me to therapy?

In my role as a salesperson, I am often required to make presentations. On one occasion I was asked to present in front of colleagues. I found myself blocking on certain words and substituting others that did not make sense. I was mortified. I went home that night and explained the ordeal to my wife;

I was very emotional. It was that night I decided I needed to find someone who could help me.

My hopes and expectations of therapy

Throughout my time in therapy my hopes and expectations have changed. When I first thought about therapy it scared me. Thinking I needed therapy meant I was owning up to having a problem. Even though the thought of stammering in public had filled me with dread over the years, I did not believe I had 'a problem'. As I got better at hiding my stammer I thought of therapy as something for 'real stammerers', that is, people who block all the time. I had always seen stammering in very black-and-white terms. You either stammer or you do not. It is only now I see it as more of a continuum with fluent people speaking dysfluently at times. I had a view on the 'sort of person who should see a speech and language therapist' and I did not fit that type. I realize now my knowledge of stammering was limited. I had created a set of beliefs around PWS and my speech, which was based on my own limited experience. I had never spoken to anyone about this or read anything, so looking back these beliefs were pretty inaccurate and unfounded.

I found the experience of seeking therapy very difficult. I had previously thought hiding my stammer and not talking about it might mean it would go away. I was worried that owning up to having a problem might make me stammer more. Also, once I had decided to do some investigation, it took me some time to find a local speech and language therapist. This was disheartening.

The first time I met Sam I was extremely anxious because I had talked about my stammer with so few people. We talked for an hour and some of the content moved me to the point of tears. I was surprised at how emotional I became – I had locked so many feelings away and meeting Sam felt like a release. This confirmed to me that I definitely needed to speak to someone about how I was feeling.

I remember thinking that this first session was the first step to being cured. With hindsight, I thought of my speech as a sport or technique where someone could show me a new way of doing it which would help me stammer less. To me, this was very black and white. Sam made me feel comfortable by assuring me there were techniques we could investigate, but also seeded the idea that therapy involved more than just working on how I spoke. It also included working on my feelings about my speech. She never overtly told me there wasn't a magic cure, but was careful to set my expectations. Sam explained there was more than one approach to stammering therapy and that she focused on the 'stammer-more-fluently' rather than 'speak-more-fluently' approach. Looking back, I don't remember considering the differences between these approaches, but do remember feeling comfortable and impressed enough by her explanation to want to continue. Sam's approach was very invitational. My overriding feeling from her was one of trust and that I wanted to continue our work.

Experience of therapy

In the early sessions, Sam set out the framework for the work. She explained we would be moving through the three stages of block modification – identification, desensitization and modification. Knowing there was some order to the work was reassuring. I don't think I would have responded as well if I hadn't known what was coming. At first, hearing that modification would be the final stage in the process was disappointing as I was eager to work on my speech. However, as Sam explained both identification and desensitization, it became clear these would be the most important for me.

My thoughts on therapy

I had never thought of speech and language therapy to be true 'therapy'. In my mind, I considered it to be a 'speech class' where you learn techniques to make you stammer less. Even though Sam had explained the mix of work we would be doing (both around how I felt about my speech and my speech itself) I think I only focused on the latter.

I considered 'therapy' to be serious work to help with deeper issues such as anxiety or depression. I initially did not recognize this as relevant to me. In my eyes, I was seeing Sam to improve the way I spoke and had not entertained the idea of exploring my feelings. It became obvious from the first few sessions that we would be exploring some deeper psychological issues I had around my speech, which was a new and at times quite uncomfortable experience. It took me time to get used to this as I was impatient to target my speech and find a cure. Sam introduced the idea that my efforts to hide my stammer might actually be contributing to my blocks. This seemed counterintuitive at first, but with time made sense to me. I have seen a dramatic change in my attitude towards my stammer; I avoid difficult words far less now, which means I stammer more openly.

Aspects I found most helpful

I have always been someone who enjoys both theory and practice. In other areas of my life I have enjoyed learning through study and this was the case throughout my work with Sam. Our sessions would follow a similar format whereby Sam would introduce a new concept, for example an aspect of the work of Sheehan or Van Riper, which we would explore and then investigate the practical implications. The use of models and theory interested me and appealed to my academic side. By making stammering a theoretical problem, I felt I could learn my way to an improvement.

Sam would usually cover a new subject with me in the one-hour session and then set me some work to think about before our next meeting. At first she would suggest this, but over time it became a two-way discussion. With two to three weeks between sessions, it allowed time to practise. I was able to do some reading and put together my thoughts on the subject covered. Examples include the stammering iceberg, thinking about all the ways I avoided or my speaking hierarchies. Later, my time between sessions was used to practise the techniques we covered, for example, experimenting with voluntary stammering to help with desensitization. With two or three weeks between sessions I was able to experiment in my own time and did not feel under pressure to rush into it. However, that length of break also meant that if I had any problems I knew I did not have to wait too long to see Sam. Seeing her weekly would have been too often and not given me the chance to experiment, do the reading and put my thoughts together. As someone who works and was at the time studying for a Masters degree I was always under time pressure. In one week I may not have had time to do the work. With three weeks I could fit everything in.

The aspects of my work with Sam that resonated with me the most were the onion and iceberg analogies, hierarchies, the identification of my web of avoidance and the phonetics work that we undertook. The onion analogy helped me understand that I had surrounded my stammer with layers of avoidance techniques and negative feelings which, when I stripped them back, left my core stammer. This is simply a speech block, yet in the process of blocking, my head would fill with many complex negative thoughts and feelings. By identifying these and challenging them I have been able to understand the difference between the thoughts and feelings I have around my speech and my actual speech. This concept resonated with me as I found the work we did allowed me to peel back all the thoughts and feelings that made me feel rubbish about my speech.

The stammering iceberg helped me identify feelings and behaviours around my speech. I began to understand all the negativity I had around my stammer: feelings such as fear, shame, humiliation, panic, stress, frustration, exhaustion and anger. These were feelings I had felt for years, but never associated with stammering.

The work we did on hierarchies helped me start to open up about my speech. By identifying friends and colleagues who I had never spoken to about my stammer, I could slowly 'out' myself in a more controlled manner. Over the first few months I made real progress in this area. Speaking to my friends about my therapy and speech gave me the confidence to speak to colleagues at work. I always received a positive reaction, which was hugely helpful as it made me realize my speech was not as big an issue as I had made it out to be in my mind.

Before working with Sam I never realized I avoided on so many levels. Sheehan's levels of avoidance helped me realize all the techniques I had developed over the years to get me through situations. These included looking away, touching my nose, tapping, coughing, swallowing, and licking my lips, as well as others. I also came to understand that I was avoiding at the role level. All my life I had tried to be someone I wasn't; I had a stammer, but was trying to be someone without one. Becoming aware of this made me realize I was making my situation worse through my efforts to mask who I really was and how I spoke. By identifying this I was able to start doing something about them. I set myself goals, for example to look people in the eye when I stammered, which helped. Every day I would have small wins, which created a positive momentum.

Incredibly, even though I had stammered for so many years I never realized what my mouth was doing, especially when I blocked. By showing me the different features of speech sounds (i.e. where they were made and how they were made) I started to understand my blocks. I realized most of my blocks were plosives, in particular 'Ds' and 'Ps'. This awareness allowed me to work on the transitions between sounds. Realizing what my mouth needed to do allowed me to be better prepared for words I might block on and helped me with the modification stage.

I enjoyed the pace of our sessions for the majority of time. I knew we were working to a framework, but always felt we had the right amount of flexibility within our schedule of sessions. Sam was very consultative about our work, especially as we got to know each other. I never felt she had every session mapped out or was ever rushing me through the stages. If I thought I wasn't getting a technique or some aspect of the theory then we would take more time on that area.

Aspects I have found challenging

Making the decision to see a therapist, finding a therapist, making the call and organizing to see Sam were all big and difficult decisions. Once I had made that step I was keen to get on with it as quickly as possible. The pace of early sessions, therefore, sometimes felt slow. In my head, we would be making me speak more fluently in every session. After the first two to three sessions it became obvious this was not the case. It took me a few weeks to understand the process even though Sam made it clear from the outset. I remember driving home feeling a little disappointed and impatient on occasions; however, the fact that I knew I was now taking action kept me motivated.

Some sessions were hard work. They were challenging in terms of the subject matter, but also the nature of the work. Even though sessions were only an hour long, they were quite intense at times. I had to get used to sitting in a room one-on-one with someone that I didn't know well, answering questions which required me to think deeply. Sessions were often characterized by silence and pauses where I had to search for answers to questions like 'How did I feel about…?' and 'What was I thinking when…?' There were never any simple 'yes' or 'no' questions. I had worked all day, driven over to Sam's house and then spent an hour deep in concentration, discussing thoughts and feelings which I didn't know were meaningful or important. I sometimes just wanted to say 'I don't know' and move on. Looking back on this, I know these sessions were important because it helped me unpick some of the deep beliefs I had around my speech, but at the time it was exhausting.

Talking to friends and colleagues about my stammer was challenging. However, opening up about stammering was a key stage in my therapy. Today, I find this easier which shows progress, but the first few times I did it I hated it. I had built my stammer up as a big issue I was particularly sensitive about and thought it would be 'weird' to talk to people about. It took me a few months to discuss my stammer with colleagues. I was shaking when I spoke to them, but the results were great. I consistently met with the view that it was 'no big deal' and that I thought more of it than they did.

I remember finding it hard to hear there wasn't a quick fix. All I wanted when I started therapy was to be shown how to speak fluently. It became obvious from our conversations this was unrealistic. I initially found this difficult; in my mind I was expecting to learn how to be more fluent after each session. When I realized I would be shown how to stammer more for a time rather than less, I was disappointed. However, the trust I had built with Sam meant I was always going to carry on. I also knew that the third stage would be modification. This was the area that most interested me and it kept me motivated.

Finally, in one session we used art materials to represent my relationship with stammering. The idea was to use the more creative part of my brain to help unlock feelings or insights. Strangely, I am interested in hypnosis, meditation and art, but I remember not finding the session that helpful. I always left Sam's session feeling like I had learned something; however, on this occasion it was different. It felt a little forced and I questioned whether I was expressing myself honestly in the painting. I wasn't sure if I was showing Sam what I thought she wanted to see or what was true to me. Looking back, it would have been helpful to have explained this to her at the time. I think she could see I was not as engaged and we moved on. Maybe it would have been helpful to have pursued it for longer or possibly Sam could have challenged me more.

Key turning points

In an early session, Sam showed me the DVD 'Transcending Stuttering' by Phil Schneider, an American speech and language therapist, showing his work with a group of stammerers of different ages over a number of years.

We watched some of the DVD together and then she lent it to me. It was a significant moment as I had never come into contact with anyone who stammered. I had spent my life trying to shut my stammer away and avoid any mention of stammering. I would turn over if I saw stammering on TV and avoid anyone if I knew they blocked. For the first time, I was listening to complete strangers tell stories I could relate to. The feelings they grew up with and the challenges they faced were the same as my experiences. At first I found it difficult to watch; however, their stories and successes were also fascinating. The more I watched, the more interested I became; it was the realization that other people lived and coped with the same feelings as me. I think seeing the DVD early in my sessions with Sam helped me prepare for the work we were going to do and allowed me to open up more than I would have otherwise. Much of our work focused around desensitization and the DVD was a helpful first step on this journey to opening up about my stammer.

1:1 vs. group therapy

Sam encouraged me from an early stage to look into group therapy sessions, which at first I was reluctant to do. I did not think I was ready to share my experiences with a group. However, it was a general feeling of ease with Sam, a sense I was progressing and seeing other people with stammers through DVDs and second-hand accounts that led me to contact City Lit. I had been in 1:1 therapy for 18 months when I joined a group there and my change in attitude to group therapy was a sign of progress. I had changed from being someone who couldn't think of anything worse than sharing my inner secrets about my speech in a group to someone who was comfortable with this. When I first called Sam I was nervous and worried about the thought of therapy. When I first put myself on the group course and subsequently turned up for group work I was pretty relaxed.

My experience with the group was rewarding. I quickly felt comfortable in the sessions following my 1:1 experience and the material was familiar. I was ready to share my feelings, experiences and thoughts with the group and they welcomed this. I also learned a huge amount from others in terms of how they dealt with situations and how they felt about stammering. The group felt safe and gave me a chance to experiment with techniques and share sensitive information. When I was reintroduced to the idea of hierarchies it made more sense. I definitely had my order of people in my life that I would either 'out' myself to, for example family and close friends, and those that I would not, like some of my colleagues and senior management. I found it difficult to talk openly about my stammer and feelings around my speech with anyone outside my 'inner circle'. The group offered an opportunity to extend that inner circle, which was helpful. It allowed us to play with ideas and concepts before we took them to the 'outside world'.

Whilst on the City Lit course my group agreed it would be useful to hear from someone who had been through the course. In the year after I finished I went back twice to share my thoughts with new groups. I found this hugely beneficial as it made me re-read my notes and reminded me how far I had come. I was now comfortable talking to complete strangers about my biggest insecurities, which was a huge step forward from the time when I locked my stammer away so deeply that I never discussed it with anyone.

Changes

Since starting therapy I have seen many aspects of my life change; my goals, my speech and my attitude to therapy have also changed. The word 'cure' no longer seems appropriate. I still want to block less, but now understand that the biggest issue I face is my fear of stammering rather than my stammer itself. Success came to mean reducing my feelings around my speech and being more open about stammering. My stammer is something I have more control over as I am able to modify it using modification strategies. I can relax my mouth at times when I know I will block and I am less worried about my blocks when they do happen.

Future

My work with Sam helped me hugely; however, I feel my stammering therapy is an on-going journey. I have continued to see Sam, but less frequently, and have agreed to go back to City Lit to do further short talks to groups. It is very easy to fall back into old habits if the work is not at the front of my mind. I am now more accepting when this happens, able to recognize it and to remind myself to do something differently next time. I still have weeks where I find myself more fluent and some when my blocks are more frequent. When this happens, I try to use this as a prompt to re-read my notes and think about my work with Sam. Without someone to continuously remind me about it, I know I will have to work hard to do it myself.

Writing this chapter with Sam has been a great exercise as it has allowed me to celebrate how far I have come. I am looking forward to getting involved in more talks and projects that will allow me to explore my learning further.

Ed's story

Jan: What led you to have stammering therapy at the particular time in your life that you did?

Ed: After being selected as a Member of Parliament (MP) in July 2004, I did my first 'Newsnight'[1] interview – then 'Any Questions'[1] – a few weeks later, and both times I struggled to be fluent. I had big pauses in the middle of sentences when I couldn't get the words out. I knew at that point there was an issue. After 'Any Questions', my Dad rang me up and said, 'You have the same thing I've had all my life' – although he did not call it a 'stammer'. It was a big shock – I hadn't realized the difficulties I had with public speaking at different times in my life, particularly as a teenager, were all the same issue. I thought I had got over my teenage problems with public speaking, and suddenly there it was back again. The next couple of years as an MP and Cabinet Minister[2], I sometimes found speaking in the House of Commons[3] and on television difficult. But when I got into the Cabinet, I was suddenly much more exposed. After my first speech, which I hadn't written myself, colleagues came to me and said, 'Why weren't you more confident?' I thought, well I was confident – but the few moments when I had blocked were misconstrued as lack of confidence. So I decided I needed somebody who understood these things – and that's how I came to you.

Jan: And what was it like acknowledging you needed some help?

Ed: At the time, really risky. If you're a senior politician, there's always a bit of a stigma about getting help, especially if it is seen as 'therapy'. It's ridiculous, there's no stigma about politicians having a personal trainer to get fit but there is a question for me if I want to get professional help to deal with a problem. Politicians often have media training; for me media training was always unhelpful because it never got to the heart of the problem. From 2004, I had been making progress, but was frustrated to be tripped up from time to time with my speech, especially in the House of Commons. My worry was I'd go backwards, that I would get locked into a process that would mean I lost control, that would suddenly destabilize me. It's always a worry that people will want to take you to pieces and put you back together again. I didn't really have the time to be taken to pieces.

Jan: So time was a factor…

Ed: It's one thing if you are somebody who needs to go through a process of learning to come out the other end in a better place, and can write off three months to go through that process. However, I was in the Cabinet, standing up to speak regularly in the House of Commons and on television three or four times a week. I couldn't write off three months and couldn't go backwards.

Jan: When you were seeking therapy, did you have a sense of what therapy might involve?

Ed: Not really. At the start, I didn't even realize it was a stammer. Over that summer of 2007, I read a bunch of stuff about stammering on websites, but don't think I really had any idea. Which is why I said to Francine (Special Advisor[4]), 'You have to find out how to do this… what do you do?' and she came back and said, 'I think I've found the person, you should just go and see what happens.' It was reading which made me understand there was something called an interiorized stammer – that was a revelation. I had always thought stammering was overt. I don't think I would have used the word 'stammer' until I started reading about it. So the diagnosis was really helpful, I thought, 'Well, we must be able to do something about this.' Previously, I don't think it occurred to me there were things I could do. There were things I did to try to be fluent – steel, concentration, resolve and getting through it – which of course was part of the problem.

Jan: What were you expecting when you started?

Ed: If I am honest, I had low expectations and a lot of worries. I thought it would be a good thing to try, but had equally strong feelings that it might be counterproductive and make things worse. In a way, understanding was the starting point.

Jan: That came across to me, that sense of not wanting to be taken apart.

Ed: I couldn't really afford to.

Jan: That became a real consideration for me in our work.

Ed: I saw very quickly in our discussions, there were things I was doing which were absolutely the right things for me to do. But there were other things which were counterproductive.

Jan: Can you remember the things you were doing that were helpful?

Ed: For me, dealing with my stammer was about a state of mind – how I dealt with the situation and the confidence I had in that situation – more than it being about a physical need to learn a technique. That was partly because I was worried if I attempted any techniques it would be destabilizing. There were some House of Commons exchanges, speeches or television interviews where my speech was fine and there were others which were very hard; it was a different feeling, the mental state was different. I felt that was important, I knew what made the difference was whether I had done it before, whether I knew the audience, whether I felt I was connecting with them, whether I was talking from 'me', whether I was genuine, whether I was relaxed, or I would use the phrase 'in the zone'. There were also things like concentrating hard on fluency, trying to avoid a block, trying to get to the end of what I was saying, that really did not help. I remember once in our discussions using the analogy of being on a tightrope. Sometimes you lose your balance – my instinct was to speed up because if you can get to the other side you won't fall off, whereas what happens is you actually lose your balance more. What you need to do on a tightrope is stop and regain your composure before moving on… But the deeper point was, I thought these were ways I could deal with it, control it, suppress it, cure it, avoid it.

The most important things I learned in the early period were that, firstly, I did have this issue. I think I spent quite a lot of time thinking, 'Maybe I'm just making this up? Are you sure…?' Secondly, it was never going to go away. Thirdly, it was made much worse by trying to make it go away. The most important thing for me was the positive mental state, which I always wanted to get into. This was a mental state where I could relax and be accepting of how things were. The difficult mental state was what I call the 'avoidance' mental state. This was where I didn't know the audience; I felt I had to present a particular view of myself and conceal the stammer. The most important thing I learned was to be open, but it took a long time to realize what that really meant. To be honest, just talking to you about it in the first six months was quite a step forward. That was quite open… on reflection it wasn't very open, but it felt like it was.

Jan: Early on I felt there were limits to how far you wanted to go with talking about your feelings about stammering…?

Ed: I hadn't talked to anyone about it for pretty much 40 years. It takes time. I remember early on discussing what I had read on one of the websites about the iceberg with the stammer on the surface and this huge thing underneath. But if you've had years where it's all been underneath, it takes time to think being more open may be a good thing. You assume you should keep it underneath.

Jan: Any aspects you found most helpful?

Ed: I learned the more I moved towards authenticity, the easier it became. That was the big revelation – because I had totally underestimated, in fact, I didn't believe at all really that it would relieve the pressure to be open. I remember you saying that and I thought, well that's very easy for you to say, but it was true. Secondly, I learned that openness about my stammer would help and it did. Thirdly, that it was possible to get out of some of the things I was doing wrong. That took a long time because I started off being sceptical that there was a better way of doing it. I was worried about going backwards. It's quite risky – my experimenting with my speech was always in the House of Commons chamber or live on national television. It always felt risky trying things in a different way.

Jan: That was something I found difficult. We encourage people working on their speech to start with the least challenging situations, then gradually increase the challenge. You didn't have those 'in between' steps.

Ed: If I was in a group or chairing meetings I wouldn't have a problem. It was only difficult when I had to give a bigger performance; therefore, given that was where the problem was, that was where I had to solve it. In the early period when you would make me read out a text into the camera I'd think, 'Well, OK, I will, but I'm not sure why I'm doing this because reading out the text to a camera at home is not difficult for me.' It's much harder to speak when you're standing up at the despatch box[5] in the House of Commons or on live television, or prerecorded onto camera. However, I learned things from doing that which led to a better understanding, but I don't think I knew it at the time.

Jan: You talked about being more open about stammering. Can you remember the first time you were more open?

Ed: There was one strategy, which merged into another over three or four years. When we started in 2007 only three or four people knew. Now and then something would go wrong, there'd be a block or pause and Jon Sopel or Jon Snow[6] would look at me oddly or somebody would write, 'Why does EB pause?' or 'Why did he have his eyes open wide'? Therefore, strategy one was about preparing the ground, telling people about the issue so if I had a bad moment people would understand what was going on. I started talking to people. I spoke to Michael Palin and the Michael Palin Centre[7] staff and John Bercow[8] who was doing a report on speech and language therapy. I think in part I was thinking if something goes wrong I need people who understand stammering who will come out and defend me. What happened was, slowly I was persuaded by you that it wasn't simply about defensive strategy; that a strategy of being open was important and would itself make a difference. Following the interim report of the Bercow review[8] I was interviewed for the 10 O'Clock News and talked about myself for the first time. It felt a deeply destabilizing thing to do. But then at the 2009 Labour Party Conference[9] I did my speech without notes – I had found that much easier to deal with over the past couple of years than trying to read from a script. It went well, but I had a couple of points where I blocked. The audience liked it, I got a standing ovation, but the jokes from journalists were destabilizing. A couple of times they said, 'He was awkward', or 'Did he forget what he was going to say?' One journalist bizarrely wrote that he assumed I had an earpiece telling me the words and that there was a disruption on the line so I had to pause while I waited for the next sentence. I thought, 'This is madness.' This is making me more under pressure because these guys don't understand this. I thought I've got to start talking about this. I am going to go out there and be open about it. I decided to speak privately to the BBC[10] Political Editor, Nick Robinson, about it. I found it quite liberating, it took the pressure away. I thought if they understand, that will be alright. But I still had not gone fully public. There's no doubt that being berated by a parent for not talking about myself in front of some children who stammer – 'cowardly' was his word – did also have a big impact on me. As a result, I spoke about myself at a Downing Street[11] reception for the British Stammering Association[12] and then in an interview on the day of the Northern Stammering Centre appeal launch at Clarence House[13] in March 2010. That was a big moment. In the morning, Michael Palin and I went on television about it, then we had the Clarence House event, then I did an interview on Sky – and that was sort of my 'coming out' day. I felt so much better it was actually relieving the pressure. So it wasn't about getting my defences in by that point, it was about being open, being myself.

Jan: It sounds like openness was one of the biggest challenges?

Ed: The biggest learning was that things I was doing to avoid the problem weren't helping, therefore I just had to be myself and roll with it. I had to stop trying to be perfect 'Radio 4' and just become 'Radio 5 Live'[14]. I had to talk publicly on television and in speeches as a normal person would – with maybe a block or pause in it – and the attempt to be fluent was my biggest problem. The biggest intellectual strategic challenge was the acceptance of dysfluency, the biggest reliever of pressure was realizing that people knowing about it made it better. When I think back now to the huge stress and pressure of avoidance, it's massive, it's like a huge weight being lifted. Even now people say, 'I read your piece on "The King's Speech"[15] and I never knew you used to have a stammer', and I will immediately say, 'I still do, it'll never go away and it's totally part of me.' I've got beyond all that pressure and avoidance so it doesn't trip me up. If I'm standing up in the House of Commons or on the Andrew Marr[16] programme now, a block wouldn't worry me. I could acknowledge it and move on and it wouldn't matter. Whereas four years ago the block itself, and any acknowledgement of it, would have felt like a massive failure, a blow to my self-esteem, a question mark over my capability, a defeat. I'd battled all this time thinking it was possible to be a senior politician and have a stammer and in the end it would have been, 'OK, you couldn't do it'. Now it wouldn't make a big difference to me at all, because it doesn't matter, so what?

Jan: I had a number of concerns initially because I was thinking about a particular format for people with interiorized stammering.

Ed: You'd normally do it in groups?

Jan: That's right…

Ed: I've never met other people with an interiorized stammer and would love to meet them. I'm sure for lots of people group sessions are very good, but it wasn't an option for me on a practical level. Also, because I was concerned at the beginning about any acknowledgement.

Jan: As we weren't able to meet on a regular basis I was initially reluctant to focus on emotional aspects in case it opened things up, leaving you with 'live' issues which might be destabilizing. I wanted to keep it very structured, very safe.

Ed: By the time we started working together, I was much more 'mental state' orientated, partly because of the reading. Initially, you were inclined to think I needed technique and I was totally against technique. That was partly about not wanting to try a new way of doing things in case it made things worse, it was also because I believed it was somehow about mental states, not simply about physical things.

Jan: I gradually decided to follow your lead. I realized your own coping strategies had supported you when faced with challenging situations. I was aware you were in a new job and believed if you could be supported whilst you built up some new positive experiences of dealing with the new situations, it would allow you time to find your feet. But I didn't think you were going to be willing to be open about stammering. I thought being open was going to be a 'no go'. I thought, 'He's a public figure. He's not going to want to be open.' Quite an assumption!

Ed: At the beginning I definitely thought it was going to be a 'no go' as well, and then I thought about doing a little subtle preparing of the ground in case anything goes wrong, but it took a long time to realize the openness was part of it.

Jan: What struck me was we would talk about something that I considered might be quite challenging for you, then you'd come back and say you'd done it!

Ed: The best example was I didn't like doing television clips standing up; partly because sitting down was more relaxed, but also I had had some difficult experiences standing up. You said, 'What happens when you stand up?' I said I get shortness of breath and blocking. I clasp my hands together to help me concentrate on getting it right. You said, 'Holding your hands like that is part of the problem because what you are doing is tensing up in the chest and making it harder to breathe. Avoiding standing up doesn't help in the long run, why don't you just try doing a television clip standing up?' The next day I was doing an interview which I would normally do sitting down. I said, 'I'll stand up.' I used my hands and stopped clasping them together. It was a revelation, and I did it two or three times. Nowadays, if I do a standing up clip I wouldn't be worried because I know I can speak standing up. Before, it was like 'maybe I can't, I've got to avoid it'. It was a good example of how we diagnosed the problem and I acted on it. I would go and try it out – it's just that I had to try it in the House of Commons or on national television and that's just the way it was.

Jan: I was aware of wanting the work to be safe and yet it was hard because there was no middle ground.

Ed: Trying that out in a group wouldn't have made any difference because it was the insight I needed rather than the practice. I was practising all the time between sessions. There was always some reluctance on my part to accept any of it. Was it real? Could there be techniques? Should you talk about it? Could you overcome these things? But also I was happy to try it out.

Jan: So you had lots of outside practice with the occasional 1:1 session?

Ed: To me it felt regular. It came round quickly because there was a lot going on in the meantime. Initially it was more frequent and then became less so. It would partly be the diary would go wrong, and my secretary would say, 'I have to cancel Jan' and I would think, to be honest I'm making progress, it's fine. Now and then I would need a top-up. If I was getting close to the Party Conference or if I had a setback, I'd think I'd better see Jan. I remember, after making a lot of progress, I had two or three baddish experiences; nobody would have noticed, but I knew. I thought three different things – What's happened? Have I lost it? Have I gone backwards? I decided to talk to you about it, so that you could probably say, 'Well, of course that happens every now and then, don't worry.' That was during the period when I was still not quite willing to be too open… when I was still in a bit of denial.

Jan: I remember saying, 'You've done really well and you've only had eleven sessions', and you said, 'I've been doing this for two and a half years actually!' I realized I'd weighted the session times as more important. It reminded me it's what goes on between sessions; that's when the work is done.

Ed: In that early period I was working on my speech every day because I had no choice. I thought about the things we talked about and worked on them continually. In my mind, the hour and a half that we would talk about it was not the session – it was what I did in real time.

Jan: It took commitment.

Ed: It was partly commitment, partly just how it was. Another thing was you wrote me a detailed summary note after each session and I read them. I'd go back to them, look at them again and think about it. I was overtly practising and consciously thinking about things. I read the notes quite a few times, it helped me track progress and remember how it had been. The feeling of making progress is important to carrying on. I could see that progress over the year.

Jan: I hoped the notes might fill the gap between sessions…?

Ed: I felt you were challenging me to do certain things. I realized after our conversations that if there were some things I had to do, I would go and do them and report back. If I'd done them and they'd gone badly I might have come back quicker, but the truth was I wanted to come back and say, "I have done this; I've done that; this works." It was like reporting back, it was a conscious thing to do that.

Jan: I wanted to mention involving Francine in our work. Initially I was reluctant to say too much to her as I was mindful our work was confidential. However, once I'd talked about it with both of you I spoke with her regularly. Looking back, involving Francine contributed significantly to the work.

Ed: My conversations with Francine changed over time. In the early period, she was more involved, I had taken a big risk doing this. She had found you, but you and I, for different reasons were worried whether we could make this work. Francine was the person holding it together, mediating and saying, 'It'll be OK'. She would say to me, 'It's totally private and we can fit around it, I think you should carry on, I think it will work', and I suspect she was saying to you, 'I will make sure he comes, I'll make sure he gets the letters', therefore she was dealing with both our anxieties.

Jan: Francine was brilliant, having her in the loop was invaluable. We had great conversations about stammering, the nature of stammering, issues for someone in the public eye doing stammering therapy... .

Ed: There were lots of things in my work we did better because Francine was involved; we tried autocues, speech writing and doing it without notes. She spent a lot of time explaining to others what was going on and things we needed without me having to have all those conversations because the truth was, at the beginning, I didn't find it that easy to have those conversations. Francine was a big deal in my becoming more open because she kept saying to me, 'You've got to do it, you've got to do it'.

Jan: And you did!

The experience of 1:1 therapy: The therapist perspective

What informs us as therapists: Theoretical underpinnings

We have come to appreciate the importance of having a strong and broad theoretical knowledge base from which to work as therapists. We recognize that, whilst our learning about stammering is rooted in the stammering therapy literature, it has been shaped by the many and varied experiences of stammering shared with us by our clients. They have been some of our best teachers.

We see stammering as complex and multifaceted; its overt and covert dimensions incorporating cognitive and behavioural components alongside the more emotional and psychological aspects of stammering. Our approach to therapy is based largely on the work of Sheehan (1958, 1970) and Van Riper (1973) as we consider avoidance to be the central maintaining dynamic of stammering and value the therapeutic components of desensitization, avoidance reduction and self-acceptance as a person who stammers (Montgomery, 2006; Plexico, Manning & Levitt, 2009). We support Manning's view of therapy as involving 'so much more than simply fixing the stuttering...' and similarly strive to support people to 'live life in a broader and deeper manner... [to] become "unstuck", not only from their speech, but from a life of restricted decision making' (Manning, 2001, p.218). We share the belief that for many PWS this work is most readily carried out in a group context as peer support is available, alternative narratives can be witnessed, stereotypes challenged and a collective identity negotiated. However, we recognize that for some people a group context can feel too exposing and public an arena within which to explore stammering openly. Consequently, the confidential space afforded by 1:1 therapy offers a more comfortable starting point.

For the client, the process of developing openness, self-acceptance and renegotiating their identity as a person who stammers is a challenging one. A person-centred approach (Rogers, 1959) assists us in holding a therapeutic space within which the client can explore experiences and develop a revised relationship with stammering at their own pace. Counselling research indicates that therapeutic change is most likely to occur where the therapist is able to communicate attitudes of empathy, unconditional positive regard and congruence or genuineness. (Rogers, 1951, 1961; Berenson & Carkhuff, 1967). These attitudes are the key components of a person-centred approach to therapy. Additionally, clear boundaries provide a 'container for the process of therapy' (Gray, 1994, p.58), creating a safe space where feelings can be held and self-understanding deepened. Valuing the client and trusting their process supports the non-medical model of therapy, which we strongly adhere to, and offers us a way to share power and work in partnership with clients (Rogers, 1951, 1978).

Narrative ideas and practices also play a part in our therapy approach (Logan, Chapter 3 in this book). The notion of the client as a social being, in a system which includes family, friends, community and society at large, is central. As a result, we are keen for therapy to address the client in context and take account of the client's social situation. Furthermore, we are interested in creating a therapeutic space, which allows for the role of society in the development of a stammering identity to be discussed and challenged (Peters, 1996; Simpson & Cheasman, 2000).

Having a rich theory base to draw on is particularly valuable in 1:1 work, where we need to be flexible and creative in terms of addressing the individual wants of each client. PWS come to therapy with unique experiences of stammering. Each person will have developed individual stammering behaviours and coping strategies in the context of the needs and demands of their personal, social and work life. The timing of therapy will also influence their readiness for and pace of therapy (Prochaska & DiClemente, 1992). PWS will, consequently, respond differently to the content and format of therapy. In negotiating therapy with our clients, it is important not only to attend to the individual accounts of stammering (Corcoran & Stewart, 1998), but also to ensure that these accounts influence each therapy pathway (Hayhow & Stewart, 2006).

In line with Manning (2001), we embrace creativity in therapy. To this end, we look outwards, beyond the stammering literature, to explore other ways of approaching therapy or adapting our therapeutic approach. Developments in the field of counselling, narrative medicine and therapy, sociology, disability studies and aphasia therapy have been key influences. Within these fields, defining and exploring the client experience and personal meanings is paramount – both in terms of developing our understanding of living with difference and the experience of therapy. Increasingly, stammering therapy research has identified the need to listen more closely to the client's experience of stammering and therapy (Yaruss & Quesal, 2004). However, much stammering therapy literature remains heavily based on professional knowledge. We advocate increasing partnerships between clients and therapists in order to co-author the therapy experience, thereby broadening and deepening professional knowledge. We are encouraged to see that there is an increasing interest and recognition of the value for such partnerships amongst other clinicians and researchers (Yaruss, 2012; Reitzes & Reitzes, 2012).

Both Ed and Dan's accounts highlight that a rich theory base is equally valued by clients. In the true spirit of collaboration and transparency, we believe therapy involves sharing our theoretical foundations and understanding of stammering with clients, as well as the dilemmas and challenges of stammering therapy.

Therapy as education: 'Knowledge is all'

It is evident from Ed and Dan's commentaries that they both entered therapy with extensive *experience* of stammering, but a limited *understanding* of it. This fuelled a keen interest in stammering theory. As their knowledge of stammering grew, a parallel process of increased self-understanding was set in motion, which offered them alternative ways of relating to their stammering.

Ed initially sought relevant reading on the internet where he learned about interiorized stammering: a revelatory experience for him. His work and commitment to supporting children and young people experiencing difficulties in their lives took him to the Michael Palin Centre for Stammering Children. Thus, independent reading and conversations with Jan, together with his interest in the experiences of children who stammer gave him a sound understanding of the nature of stammering, which in turn played a significant role in his own change process.

Dan's account illustrates that approaching therapy from a theoretical standpoint initially appealed to him as it tapped into his knowledge of himself as 'academically able', giving him a sense of his own competency and personal resources in tackling his stammering, something he had previously experienced as being out of his control. Having ready access to different models or ways of framing stammering gave him a language through which he could explore and make sense of his own experience. Furthermore, it gave him a shared language through which he could make connections and comparisons with other people's experiences of stammering, as evident when watching the Transcending Stuttering DVD[17].

Both Dan and Ed refer to the value of being introduced to the iceberg model (Sheehan, 1958) early on in therapy as this offered them a valuable insight into their experience of stammering. It proved clarifying, validating and offered a framework within which they could place their personal experience. Dan also found metaphors (e.g. avoidance construed as layers on an onion concealing his core stammering pattern), visual frameworks (e.g. levels of avoidance (Sheehan, 1958)); and people/speaking hierarchies helpful. For Ed, the challenges in relation to his speech were related to specific speaking situations, such as giving speeches, presentations or doing televised interviews, therefore the notion of hierarchies was less personally relevant.

Both Dan and Ed had developed a range of coping/avoidance strategies in an attempt to manage moments of stammering and present as fluent. Interestingly, they both refer to the moment of realization that these strategies were at times counterproductive. This insight signifies a turning point in therapy, leading to an active reduction in coping strategies determined as less helpful and an increase in more valued forms of coping responses.

Perhaps what is important is that Ed and Dan have developed an overarching understanding of the complexity of stammering. They demonstrate an awareness of its different dimensions (e.g. overt/covert; physical, psychological, cognitive, behavioural), an appreciation of the interplay of these components – with all of its inconsistencies and contradictions; as well as the fundamental realization that avoidance can be both helpful and unhelpful. We believe it is important that avoidance-reduction work does not become a tyranny in itself. Instead, we are interested in finding ways to offer a therapy that opens up possibilities; where conversations can create space to consider the choices around avoidance and the possible consequences or gains.

Therapy can be seen as an unfolding dialogue that enables a shift from a more polarized, fixed conceptualization of fluency and stammering (wanted/unwanted) to a less simplistic, more integrated understanding; a process that enables clients to re-evaluate and creatively re-work their personal definitions of stammering and their relationship with it.

Negotiating the format of therapy: A move towards greater flexibility

Whilst group therapy for people with interiorized stammering is positively indicated (Levy, 1987; Cheasman & Everard, Chapter 4 in this book), our beliefs around the scope of 1:1 therapy for this client group have evolved over time. Our experience of 1:1 work has affirmed its potential to offer a flexible, individually-tailored therapy which takes into account important aspects of our clients' lives such as their readiness for a group, availability and geographical access, as well as time constraints resulting from the competing demands of work and family life.

The structure and demands of Ed's work, in addition to his public status and family commitments, resulted in him not considering group work an option when first entering into therapy. He later acknowledged reluctance on his part to talk openly about his speech in a group context at that time. For Dan, the competing demands of a management role, MBA studies and a growing young family meant 1:1 therapy that was geographically closer to home, and which could frame time more flexibly, was more viable. Additionally, whilst

Dan's MBA experiences led him to be open to the benefits of group work, he acknowledged not feeling ready for this on entering therapy, although identifying it early on as something that could be worked towards.

Work with Ed was a valuable learning experience for Jan, leading to a change in perspective in relation to the format and scope of 1:1 therapy:

> "I realize I took into our early sessions a limited vision of what was possible given the demands of Ed's work and time available. I felt a group would be best, but this was not possible. I wanted to offer block modification and had in mind an 'ideal' format for our work. I initially proposed frequent and regular sessions as I considered it would not be possible to address the covert/emotional aspects of stammering if sessions were less frequent. It felt important for me to keep the work as safe as possible so I was reluctant to step outside the familiar parameters of what I believed worked best. As the therapy developed I responded to Ed's issues, concerns and beliefs about what was driving his stammering, which took us to productive work that did allow a focus on the emotional/attitudinal aspects of stammering."

This in turn has led Sam to reflect on changes in her practice since transitioning from exclusively group stammering therapy to working primarily 1:1:

> "Early encounters with the work of Prochaska and DiClemente (1986) fuelled an interest in the timing of therapy. I have come to realise the importance of inviting an open exploration of the client's readiness for change at the beginning of the therapy relationship, both in the context of their stammering and within the broader context of their lives. Having an opportunity to openly explore their commitment to the change process and to negotiate the timing and frequency of sessions in relation to their other life commitments enables the client to take self-responsibility within the relationship from the outset. This makes sense to me philosophically in that it feels fundamental to establishing a more equal power dynamic and collaborative approach to therapy. Discussions with Jan

have highlighted my increasing willingness to honour the individual over any pre-ordained structure, based on the belief that rigid contracts can block a person's growth and restrict the potential for mutuality within the relationship" (Worrall, 2006).

We are aware that, in the current economic climate, time-limited contracts of 6–12 consecutive speech and language therapy sessions have become the norm within the UK National Health Service. We believe this is largely historical, originating from financial, budget-driven and practical considerations. However, to our knowledge there is little clinical research in support of this format and number of sessions within the field. Our work with Ed and Dan has led us to question the way time is currently framed within the NHS as well as having fixed time limits. Are regular, consecutive sessions the most useful and, indeed, the only way of structuring time if a prescribed amount is available? Are there alternative ways of working that might increase client choice and maximize the efficacy of sessions which are time-limited in number?

An influential framework within the field of counselling is the contractual model of 'time-conscious therapy' developed by Elton Wilson (1996). Offering a no-obligation 'introductory or exploratory session' to start provides both the therapist and the client with an experimental precurser prior to committing to a more regular therapeutic engagement. The option of then negotiating a 'mini commitment' (e.g. two to three sessions) with a review gives the client an opportunity to gain some experience of therapy and what it can offer, prior to agreeing on a further 'mini commitment' (e.g. two to three sessions) or a new 'time-extended contract' (e.g. three to six sessions). Flexibility in frequency, timing, breaks and periods of consolidation are viewed favourably in order to encourage self-autonomy and the generalization of skills.

We acknowledge that both Ed and Dan are highly self-directed, and some clients may require greater support to take increased self-responsibility. However, our work with them has illustrated that breaking free of the weekly-session format offers us a different perspective to therapy. It has given us an opportunity to move from a narrow focus on what happens *in* sessions to a broader focus on what happens *in and between* sessions, thereby enhancing the value of the time *outside* of therapy. For both of us, working with Ed and Dan once every two, three or four plus weeks has involved moving from a fixed, self-limiting position, focusing on what work cannot be done, to an opening up to the possibility of just how much can be achieved. Engaging with the opportunity this shift in perspective creates, coupled with a commitment to integrate work in therapy with our clients' daily lives, works in favour of the client. We believe that this creates a healthier therapy/work/home/life balance, promoting client autonomy and self-efficacy. This revised conceptualization of therapy has also changed the language we use to describe it. For example, presenting therapy as primarily 'self-directed with the occasional 1:1 session': this has required a paradigm shift away from the medical model and the seductive 'role power' granted to the 'expert' therapist (Proctor, 2006) towards a position of greater personal humility, a willingness to challenge our own sense of importance and a greater awareness of the limitations of our own role (Taft, 1932). Our shared philosophical allegiance with the principles of person-centred therapy (Rogers, 1959) further affirms our belief in clients being instrumental in their own change process.

Re-defining therapy and what is therapeutic: The potential of each session

Therapy with PWS inevitably touches on an individual's feelings about stammering and their identity as a PWS. As a result, ensuring psychological safety in our client work is of paramount importance and we have both chosen to undergo additional counselling training in order to support this. Our work with Dan and Ed has invited us to explore the extent to which a session can be 'holding' if it is fortnightly or monthly. This has led us to reflect on and challenge our beliefs about the depth of psychological work that is possible when sessions are less frequent and less predictable. Balancing our clients' wants and preferences with the personal challenges of adapting block modification and avoidance reduction therapy to a less regular format highlighted for us the value of the counselling literature that we draw upon to support our work.

The concept of time is implicit in the very word 'therapy' as the Greek noun from which the term is derived means 'a servant' and the verb means 'to wait' (Taft, 1932, p.1). The term 'servant' is indicative of the power dynamic that we aim to establish in therapy; furthermore, the concept of waiting implies patience and respect for the client's own pace/process. Thorne (1999, p.8) also identifies the concept of companionship to be central to person-centred counselling: 'To be a faithful companion to the client and to accompany where the client leads.' To walk alongside, by definition, means to walk 'in time'.

Ed and Dan's reflections on their experience of therapy have affirmed our belief in the person-centred principle of trusting the client's innate capacity to determine what is self-healing. Ed and Dan clearly appreciated being involved in determining the frequency, timing and focus of sessions. Equally important was our willingness, as therapists, to walk in time with them, to enter positively into a therapy relationship and explore how we might work creatively in order to adapt therapy to fit their wants and desired pace. It is interesting to note from their commentaries that both Ed and Dan *experienced* their sessions as regular, thereby highlighting our possible over-concern as therapists with *chronos* (i.e. chronological) time and underestimation of the therapeutic importance of *kairos* time (i.e. a client's own appropriate time).

Our discussions have highlighted a shared move away from the more traditional conceptualization of therapy within our profession as having a natural progression involving a discrete beginning, middle and end phase to an increased valuing of each individual session in its own right. Construing each therapy hour in this way has enhanced the attention we give to each and every session beginning and ending, independent of those that have come before or may come afterwards. Interestingly, our experience has consistently revealed this to have a liberating effect for therapist and client alike rather than limiting the possibilities of each therapy session. Indeed, Taft (1932, p.3) writes that time is '…valuable in and for itself when it is actually used in the passing moment without dependence on the next time', thereby describing the healing properties of the present moment and highlighting the value of what might be achieved even in a short time frame.

Working in this way places great emphasis on the quality of the therapeutic relationship:

> "I am the remedy at this moment if there is any and I can no longer escape my responsibility, not for the client but for myself and my role in the situation. Here is just one hour to be lived through as it goes, one hour of present immediate relationship, however limited, with another human being who has brought himself to the point of asking for help."
>
> (Taft, 1932, p.4)

Thus, the collaborative therapeutic relationship intrinsic to person-centred work is an important supporting factor in our 1:1 stammering work.

Trust: The importance of the therapeutic relationship

Corcoran and Stewart (1995) highlight the importance of the client/therapist relationship in gaining a deeper understanding of the client's personal experience of stammering. We also consider the development of a close working relationship to be essential for truly collaborative work to take place. However, it is a process that cannot be hurried (Mearns & Thorne, 1988).

Clients inevitably bring initial expectations and concerns to therapy. Ed described himself as coming to therapy with 'low expectations'. The immediate demands of his career meant it was crucial that therapy did not 'take him apart' and that he did not 'go backwards'. These concerns were based largely on his beliefs about what therapy might involve and fears that it could be counterproductive. Dan also came to therapy with negative preconceived ideas as to the 'sort of person who needed stammering therapy', strongly wanting to dissociate himself from this stereotype and the perceived stigma attached to attending therapy. He also brought an overriding fear that choosing to explore his stammering within the therapy context rather than avoid and keep it hidden (from himself as well as others) would serve to exacerbate it.

Developing a collaborative therapeutic relationship, which included trust, proved to be central to our work with both Ed and Dan. Giving clients an opportunity to share their hopes and fears about therapy and to have these taken seriously is key. Similarly, honesty on the part of the clinician is paramount; for example, sharing her understanding of stammering, what might be therapeutically possible and following the client's lead in terms of what is important contributes to the development of trust, allowing space for the therapeutic relationship to develop over time.

It is evident from Dan's account that he entered therapy with a fixed view of what it would comprise (i.e. 'work on my speech'), which was consistent with his initial understanding of his stammering as primarily a physical problem. Whilst Sam was transparent about her understanding of stammering from the outset and the dual focus on the physical and psychological aspects of stammering that therapy would embrace, it is evident that Dan needed a combination of knowledge about stammering, experience of therapy and time to fully understand the relevance and importance of this combined approach – a process that was clearly challenging, frustrating and disappointing at times. Being able to talk honestly and openly about these feelings was an important part of the therapy process and only possible in the context of a mutually trusting and respectful therapeutic relationship. Regular review opportunities to explore both the client's and the therapist's experience of therapy facilitate such metaconversations as they enable both client and therapist to momentarily hover above the therapy process and share their discrete vantage points. We are well aware that therapy can be a rocky road and does not always flow seamlessly for both the client and the therapist. A willingness and openness to explore the challenges together provide invaluable opportunities to further develop trust and deepen the therapeutic relationship. Dan's reflections on his experience of image work are an illustration of his increased self-responsibility and with hindsight identify an opportunity missed.

Trust: The client as the agent of change

Empowering clients to become their own therapist is central to our approach. To this end, we strive to create a therapeutic space where clients can develop increased insight into stammering, self-knowledge and self-efficacy. The concept of personal agency defines an individual's ability to 'live out their lives according to intentions that they embrace in the pursuit of what they give value to in life' (White, 2007, p.103). Van Inwagen (1983) describes it as a process whereby a person develops new ways of thinking and acting and in doing so becomes their own agent of change.

Achieving agency leads an individual to:

> "…acknowledge possibilities that did not appear available before, discover intentions that have informed or underlined their decision-making process and take the therapist's input and modify it to achieve their own personal needs and goals."

(Plexico, Manning & Levitt, 2009, p.120)

Manning (2001) refers to Zinker, a gestalt therapist and writer who reflects on the self-directed/agentic client as follows:

> "At a certain point in the self-generated event, the client experiences an Aha! He says, "Now I understand how I am" or "Yes, that's how I feel", or "Now I know what I need to do, how I need to act to get what I want in this situation." He is his own teacher."

(Zinker, 1977, p.125)

Both Ed and Dan's accounts illustrate such moments. For example, both of them experienced a turning point when they became aware that many of their avoidance strategies were unhelpful. This moment of insight marked an important transition from an avoidance-based reaction to stammering to an approach-oriented response. This involved actively reappraising the effects of the coping strategies they had been using and shifting focus to what was needed in order to 'accomplish change in their speech and quality of life' (Plexico et al., 2009, p.120).

Person-centred principles assist us in resisting the seductive lure of wanting to 'fix' a client's problem, which places us in a position of control or authority. Instead, our commitment is to valuing the innate knowledge of the client, based on our belief that clients have within themselves the capacity and resources for their own self-development (Rogers, 1959, 1961). Our challenge is not to take over, but to get out of our clients' way. We believe having shared open conversations with our clients that reflect our uncertainties, speculations or questions opens up new understandings and possibilities for action.

Therapeutic documents: Supporting less regular therapy

Following the influence of narrative practices, using therapeutic documents is a key aspect of our way of working. The documents we use range from handwritten mind-maps or sketches/visual representations of an established or emerging pattern that captures a conversation within a session, through to grids or notes summarizing the content of a discussion (such as a video review) and therapeutic letters/notes (see Logan, Chapter 3 in this book). Such documents are not only a useful way of capturing individual sessions (Fox, 2003; White & Epston, 1990; Speedy, 2000), but also provide us with opportunities to focus and reflect on the work.

Our motivation in using such documents is to supplement face-to-face sessions. When shared or created in collaboration with clients, such documents can act as ramps between sessions that are less regular. Our intention is to capture our clients' moments of insight and make tangible links between sessions.

Documents may serve to maintain the therapeutic relationship/connection (for us as well as for the client) between sessions. A written record not only captures the client's achievements, emerging patterns and personal reflections, but more firmly records tentative or fleeting change. As a result, it is more likely to support further self-reflection on the part of the client and generalization of learning outside of sessions. Indeed, Ed's comment that such documents helped him to track progress, recall sessions and to keep going suggests that therapeutic documents can provide motivational support and assist with generalization and maintenance. Of course, documents could, if the client wishes, be shared with others and so can provide a platform for clients to educate others about stammering and therapy as well as to gain support for themselves.

We are aware that using documents in this way challenges some of the 'taken for granted' assumptions within speech and language therapy. Consequently, a number of considerations need to be taken into account. The first relates to the issue of therapeutic boundaries as contact with clients between sessions can challenge these. There may also be concerns that contact with clients between sessions might open up communication, unsettle the equity we aim to achieve across all our clients or raise difficult issues for the client between sessions.

We have discovered that the process of writing, when carried out transparently and collaboratively, can be done both therapeutically and safely, in a way that assists clients in making sense of their therapy journey. It is important that any writing is fully negotiated. Opportunities for the client and therapist to review this communication, discuss how the documents are being used and the value of them need to be built in, thereby underlining the collaborative nature of the practice.

Whilst writing therapeutic documents can be time-consuming, Freeman, Epston and Lobovits (1997) make the case for it saving therapist time. Informal clinical research asking clients how many sessions of therapy each letter represented for them indicated that one letter was as useful as four and a half sessions of therapy (White & Epston, 1990). White (White & Epston, 1990) suggests that letter-writing can also be brief, with short, 'one-off' letters being equally valuable. In these terms, spending time writing therapeutic documents is highly cost-effective.

Involving others in the process of therapy

We both endeavour to adopt a systemic approach to therapy in that we consider it important for a client's personal experience of stammering and therapy to be viewed within the context of their broader social network. Whilst we openly encourage our clients to involve other key people in their therapy, we appreciate that this might not fit with their wants and expectations. It is our experience that many people with an interiorized stammer enter therapy 'in secret', choosing not to let anyone else know. This is likely to influence their readiness and willingness to include others, directly or indirectly, in their therapy.

We consequently believe in always remaining *invitational* with regards to encouraging clients to involve family, friends or work colleagues in their therapy, as well as being *fully respectful* of their views on the relevance, timing and format this might take. We appreciate each individual's need to establish their own degrees of privacy as they negotiate their individual path between absolute secrecy ('I don't want anyone to know!') and absolute openness ('I don't care who knows!'). Therapy affords clients the opportunity to explore what it is like to be neither fully secretive nor absolutely open about their stammering. Additionally, visual frameworks in the form of confidentiality trees[18], people hierarchies (Van Riper, 1973) or Johari's window (Luft & Ingham, 1955) serve as useful 'loosening' processes (if used as a 'one off') or as a means of tracking change over time (if used sequentially).

Giving clients an opportunity to begin to articulate what they would like people to know about their stammering provides rehearsal and practice opportunities which, irrespective of whether they remain hypothetical or are subsequently reenacted outside of the therapy room, enable an unfolding personal dialogue, exploring the gradations of avoidance and openness. Creativity is also required at times in co-constructing 'ramps' with clients to facilitate initial discussions with key people. This can take the form of: meeting other PWS and learning from their experience; paired or family sessions; creative writing or video recordings of the client talking about their experiences of stammering to then share with people of his/her choice; through to developing a lending library of DVDs and books for clients to take away and discuss with others.

Involving key people from a client's social circle in therapy is not without its challenges. In particular, ethical considerations relating to confidentiality and professional boundaries come to the fore, as illustrated by Jan's account below:

> "My initial contact with Ed was through his Special Advisor (Francine). As the work commenced I spoke with her following each session. I was unsure how to deal with this and felt a conflict: Should I be speaking to her? How much was it appropriate to share with her? What about client confidentiality? After discussing this with Ed and Francine I was given the 'go ahead' to share whatever felt relevant

> with her. Whilst initially slightly uncomfortable with this, I developed confidence in this way of communicating and began to use this opportunity to share my understanding of stammering and therapy goals with her. I now recognize that Francine played a crucial role in the therapy. She educated people around Ed about the nature of stammering, me about the communication demands of a senior politician and acted as a valuable 'sounding board' for Ed. Her contribution was the 'glue' that held the therapy together."

We acknowledge that this way of working is highly unique and somewhat unusual. Furthermore, whilst such close collaboration facilitated the therapy process for Ed, we recognize that it could be unhelpful for clients in other contexts. Whilst we both uphold the ethical importance of boundaries within the therapeutic relationship, we appreciate the merit of compromise and a willingness at times to break traditional norms in the service of the client.

'Coming out': "The most important thing I learned was to be open"

The fact that PWS are also fluent some of the time creates a complex dynamic in relation to avoidance in an 'attempt to preserve the façade of normality' (Harris, p.14, this book). The dilemma of whether to reveal or conceal stammering, particularly for those with an interiorized stammering pattern, can be a challenging one as both options have the potential for positive and negative outcomes (French, 1994).

Pinderhughes (1989) explores how the experience of 'difference' is primarily associated with feelings of being 'less than' and 'not as good as' on a comparative level. It is often the stigmatizing values and assumptions in society (Blood, Blood, Tellis, & Gabel, 2003) that lead PWS to adopt avoidance as their main coping strategy in spite of the limitations this generally imposes. White (2007, p.165) claims that 'rituals of contemporary culture' lead individuals to judge themselves against socially-constructed norms; often judging themselves to be 'not up to the mark'. In these terms, it is understandable that embracing an identity that includes stammering is complex and challenging.

White (2002) identifies 'acts of refusal and resistance' as ways in which people may respond to the experience of 'difference' which do not reproduce socially-constructed norms. Thus, in choosing to become more open about stammering and resisting the attempt to always present as fluent (and in Ed's case taking the decision not to use stammering management techniques), both Dan and Ed undertake such acts of resistance. In doing so they re-vision stammering, contributing to the opening up of alternative ways of 'thinking and being in the world' (White, 1999, p.6) and honouring their right to be fully themselves.

Both Dan and Ed's reflections on therapy highlight the significant role that talking about stammering and becoming more open with friends, family, work colleagues and the general public has played in their respective change processes. What was clearly important for both of them is that they determined the timing, format and progression that this took; with initial small gains leading to greater experimentation, openness and self-disclosure. Therapy sessions served as both a springboard and sounding-board in support of this process, involving the regular renegotiation of boundaries and roles.

It is evident from Dan's account that his increasing openness about stammering was positively received both in his personal and professional relationships. For Ed, becoming more open about stammering ultimately supported his own process of change. Interestingly, it was his interest in supporting children and young people who stammer which provided the spark and began the process of him speaking more openly about his experiences of stammering.

A paradox in stammering therapy is that increased fluency can occur as a byproduct of being more open. This can in turn shift the focus of therapy and a client's personal goals to fluency; a further barrier to working on openness and acceptance of stammering as an end in itself. However, we believe therapy that focuses solely on fluency runs the risk of endorsing mainstream thinking and reinforcing negative perceptions of stammering. We consider it crucial to be alert to cultural stereotypes, prejudice and stigma in relation to stammering and to provide clients with opportunities to question mainstream thinking and develop a more political voice (e.g. self-advocacy, see Harris, Chapter 1 in this book). One of the challenges for therapists working 1:1 is to explore ways of providing clients with opportunities for communal interaction in order to develop a collective voice, which can further contribute to the process of identity reconstruction.

Group experiences

We share a commitment to group work for PWS and, similar to Manning (2001), believe that the group experience plays a significant role in facilitating change. Not only does it offer a supportive environment with positive role models, but it also provides ready access to a sense of community and a space where alternative narratives of stammering can be developed and witnessed (Logan, Chapter 3 in this book; Logan, 2007; Leahy, O'Dwyer & Ryan, (2012)). This sense of community and communal interaction is a key component underlying identity revision (Peters, 1996; White, 1999; Simpson, 2000). In 1:1 work we aim to be flexible and creative in order to make these aspects of the group experience available to our individual clients.

This can be done in a variety of ways. Bringing a 'third person' into the room *through their words and experiences* can be affirming or normalizing for a client who feels isolated or different, and can pave the way for them to speak more directly about their own experiences. To this end, we have collected written stories or video 'shouts' by clients reflecting on their experiences of stammering and therapy with a view to this being shared with other PWS (Logan, 2007).

Other ways we have experimented with providing 'virtual' group experiences include developing a lending library of DVDs, articles and books. This supports the collaborative nature of therapy and gives clients access to other people's experience of stammering and therapy. Communities of acknowledgement may be created by arranging meetings with a peer, either individually or in a small group, which offers a one-off opportunity for a 'group experience'. We also regularly arrange opportunities for interested clients to talk to groups of other PWS about their experiences, to be involved in speech and language therapy student training or to co-present at professional study days. This places them in a consultancy role, thereby recognizing their knowledge and expertise as well as supporting their change process. Additionally, we have found that signposting opportunities for connections with other PWS through websites or Facebook and sharing information about group opportunities (such as group stammering courses, self-help groups or Toastmasters for PWS) offer other ways for our clients to gain access to the broader stammering community.

Dan's personal commentary highlights the value for him of having experienced therapy in both 1:1 and group contexts and of having been able to determine the timing of both. He shows a clear appreciation of the potential advantages and disadvantages of therapy in each setting, concluding on the complementarity of a combined approach. We are well aware that stammering therapy provision in the current UK National Health Service climate varies hugely and, sadly, remains a geographical lottery. To this end, we embrace a collaborative approach to stammering therapy that brings together specialist, generalist, public health, educational, independent and voluntary services offering both 1:1 and group opportunities. Involving PWS more actively in determining what service provision they would like to access across these different sectors, as well as identifying what they have found particularly helpful and unhelpful in therapy, will further serve to forge stronger partnerships and joint working practices.

Conclusion

The privilege of being allowed into someone's inner experience of stammering and their therapy process, their moments of insight and their struggles, their hope and despair, is a gift that touches us as therapists in ways that are difficult to put into words. In this chapter, we have attempted to capture what we have learned through our work and collaboration with Ed and Dan, as well as with each other. By sharing these reflections on our own and our clients' process we hope to inform, enrich and inspire other therapists to reflect on the 1:1 therapy they offer in conjunction with their clients. We have been moved by the potency of this shared exploration and its potential to expand our therapy knowledge and practice in surprising and creative ways.

We would like to thank Elaine Childs and Liz Taylor for their assistance with transcribing the interview with Ed Balls.

References

Berenson, B.G. & Carkhuff, R.R. (1967) *Sources of Gain in Counselling and Psychotherapy.* New York: Holt, Rinehart & Winston.

Blood, G., Blood, I., Tellis G., & Gabel, R. (2003). A preliminary study of self-esteem, stigma and disclosure in adolescents who stutter. *Journal of Fluency Disorders, 28,* 143–159.

Corcoran, J. & Stewart, M. (1995) Therapeutic experiences of people who stutter. *Journal of Speech-Language Pathology and Audiology, 19*, 89–96.

Corcoran, J. and Stewart, M., (1998) Stories of stuttering: A qualitative analysis of interview narratives. *Journal of Fluency Disorders, 23*, 247–264.

Fox. H. (2003) Using therapeutic documents: A review. *The International Journal of Narrative Therapy and Community Work, 4*, 26–36.

Freeman, J., Epston, D., & Lobovits, D. (1997) *Playful Approaches to Serious Problems: Narrative therapy with children and their families.* New York: Norton.

French. S. (1994) Dimensions of disability and impairment. In French S. (Ed.) *On Equal Terms: Working with disabled people.* Oxford: Butterworth-Heinemann.

Gray, A. (1994) *An Introduction to the Therapeutic Frame.* London: Routledge.

Hayhow, R. & Stewart, T. (2006) Introduction to qualitative research and its application to stuttering. *International Journal of Language and Communication Disorders, 41*(5), 475–493.

Leahy, O'Dwyer & Ryan (2012). Witnessing stories: Definitional ceremonies in narrative therapy with adults who stutter. *Journal of Fluency Disorders, 37*(4), 234–241. Special Issue: 9th Oxford Dysfluency Conference.

Levy, C. (Ed.) (1987) *Stuttering Therapies: Practical approaches.* London: Croom Helm.

Logan, J. (2007) From client to consultant: Developing 'outsider-witness practices' with adults who stammer. In: J. Au-Yeung & M.M. Leahy (Eds), *Research, Treatment and Self-Help in Fluency Disorders: New horizons.* Proceedings of the 5th World Congress on Fluency Disorders, pp.325–332.

Manning, W. (2001) *Clinical Decision Making in Fluency Disorders.* New York: Singular.

Mearns, D. & Thorne, B. (1988) *Person-centred Counselling in Action.* London: Sage Publications.

Montgomerey, C. (2006) The treatment of stuttering: From the hub to the spoke. In: Nan Bernstein Ratner & John Tetnowski (Eds) *Current Issues in Stuttering Research and Practice.* New Jersey, London: Lawrence Earlbaum Associates.

Peters, S. (1996) The politics of disability identity. In: L. Barton (Ed.) *Disability and Society: Emerging issues and insights.* London: Longman.

Pinderhughes, E.B. (1989) *Understanding Race, Ethnicity and Power.* New York: Free Press.

Plexico, L.W., Manning, W.H., & Levitt, H. (2009) Coping responses by adults who stutter: Part I. Protecting the self and others. *Journal of Fluency Disorders, 34*, 87–107.

Prochaska, J.O. & DiClemente, C.C. (1992) Stages of change in the modification of problem behaviours. In: M. Herson, R. Eisler, & P. Miller (Eds), *Progress in Behaviour Modification.* Sycamore, IL: Sycamore Publishing Company, p.184–218.

Proctor G. (2006) *The Dynamics of Power in Counselling and Psychotherapy: Ethics, politics and practice*. Ross-on Wye: PCCS Books.

Reitzel P. & Reitzel D. (Eds) (2012) *Stuttering: Inspiring stories and personal wisdom*. StutterTalk, Inc.

Rogers, C. (1951) *Client-centred Therapy*. Boston: Houghton Mifflin.

Rogers, Carl (1959) A theory of therapy, personality and interpersonal relationships as developed in the client-centered framework. In: S. Koch (Ed.) *Psychology: A study of a science. Vol. 3: Formulations of the Person and the Social Context*. New York: McGraw Hill.

Rogers, C. (1961) *On Becoming a Person*. Boston: Houghton Mifflin.

Rogers, C. (1978) *Carl Rogers on Personal Power: Inner strength and its revolutionary impact*. London: Constable & Robinson.

Sheehan, J. (1958) Conflict theory and avoidance-reduction therapy. In: J. Eisenson (Ed.) *Stuttering – A Second Symposium*. London: Harper & Row.

Sheehan, J. (1970) *Stuttering Research and Therapy*. London: Harper & Row.

Simpson, S. (2000) Making sense of aphasia and disability: The impact of aphasia on sense of self and factors influencing identity reconstruction. Unpublished MSc Project, City University.

Simpson, S. & Cheasman, C. (2000) A social model of stammering. Available at: http://www.fluencysig.org.uk/new_page_5.htm

Speedy, J. (2000) The 'storied' helper: An introduction to narrative ideas and practices in counselling and psychotherapy. *The European Journal of Psychotherapy, Counselling and Health, 3*(3), 361–375.

Taft, J. (1932) The Time Element in Therapy. Paper at the National Conference of Social Work in Philadelphia.

Thorne B. (1999) The move towards Brief Therapy: Its dangers and its challenges. *Counselling 10*(1), 7–12.

Van Ingwagen, P. (1983) *An Essay on Free Will*. Oxford, UK: Clarendon.

Van Riper, C. (1973) *The Treatment of Stuttering*. Englewood Cliffs, NJ: Prentice-Hall.

White, M. (1999) Reflecting-team work as definitional ceremony revisited. *Gecko: A Journal of Deconstruction and Narrative Ideas in Therapeutic Practice*. Adelaide: Dulwich Centre Publications.

White, M. & Epston, D. (1990) *Narrative Means to Therapeutic Ends*. Philadelphia: W.W. Norton & Company Ltd.

White, M. (2000) *Reflection on Narrative Practice: Essays and interviews*. Adelaide: Dulwich Centre Publications.

White, M. (2002) Addressing Personal Failure. Part 1: Modern power and the production of failure. Part 2: Refusal. *The International Journal of Narrative Therapy and Community Work, 3*,

White, M. (2007) *Maps of Narrative Practice*. Philadelphia: W.W. Norton & Company Ltd.

Worrall M. (2006) Contracting within person-centred counselling and psychotherapy. In Sills C. (Ed.) *Contracts in Counselling and Psychotherapy* (2nd ed.) London: Sage Publications.

Yaruss, S. & Quesal, R. (2004) Partnership between clinicians, researchers and people who stutter in the evaluation of stuttering treatment outcomes. *Stammering Research*, 1, 1–15.

Yaruss, J.S. (2012) Understanding the speaker's experience of stuttering: Implications for treatment outcomes research. International Fluency Association, 7th World Congress on Fluency Disorders, 2–5th July 2012, Tours, France.

Zinker, J. (1977) *Creative Process in Gestalt Therapy*. New York: Random House.

Endnotes

1. Newsnight and Any Questions: political debate programmes on television in the UK.

2. Cabinet Minister: government minister.

3. House of Commons: Centre of Parliament in the UK.

4. A Special Adviser works in a supporting role to the British government. Their duty is to assist and advise government ministers.

5. Despatch box: a lectern from which Members of Parliament deliver speeches in the parliamentary chamber.

6. Jon Sopel and Jon Snow: political journalists and presenters.

7. Michael Palin: an English comedian, actor, write and television presenter. He gave his name to the Michael Palin Centre for Stammering Children in memory of his father who stammered severely. MPC is a centre of excellence in the UK for the treatment of children who stammer: www.stammeringcentre.org

8. John Bercow: British politician and Speaker of the House of Commons. He was responsible for the Bercow Report, which examined the provision of support and speech and language therapy for children with speech, language and communication needs.

9. Labour Party: political party in the UK.

10. BBC: British Broadcasting Corporation.

11. 10 Downing Street: official residence of the Prime Minister in the UK. Receptions may be held there.

12. British Stammering Association: the UK's national charity for stammering, supporting adults and children who stammer: www.stammering.org

13. Clarence House: official residence of some members of the Royal family.

14. Radio 4 is a fairly formal UK radio station. Radio 5 Live is the less formal UK home of live news and sport on the radio.

15. 'The King's Speech': a recent film about King George VI, who stammered.

16. Andrew Marr Show: a weekly political programme on television.

17. Transcending Stuttering (http://video.google.com/videoplay?docid=3654482395702 325018)

18. Confidentiality tree: the client draws a tree with five branches, allocating each branch to a different area of their life: friends, family, work colleagues, partner, other. These can be broken down into further 'branches' to differentiate between close friends/ acquaintances, close/distant family members, etc. The client then fills in the 'leaves' by writing the initials (or a letter) for each person represented. Following this they cross off all the people with whom they have talked about their stammering. This provides them with a clear visual image to begin to explore levels of openness about stammering, any emerging patterns and possible changes they would like to make.

3 New stories of stammering

A narrative approach

Jan Logan

> Narrative therapy seeks to be a respectful, non-blaming approach to counselling and community work, which centres people as the experts in their own lives. It views problems as separate from people and assumes people have many skills, competencies, beliefs, values, commitments and abilities that will assist them to change their relationship with problems in their lives.
>
> (Morgan, 2000, p.2)

My story

I am particularly drawn to a narrative approach to therapy as it is client-centred, appreciates each person's lived experience and acknowledges the complexity of people's lives by placing the client's experience within a social context. In this chapter, I do not intend to give a full account of narrative therapy as this can be found elsewhere (Morgan, 2000; Payne, 2000; White, 2007). Instead, I hope to share enough of my own understanding to illustrate the relevance and application of these ways of working to stammering therapy.

A key theme in narrative therapy is the understanding that our lives are shaped by the stories we tell about ourselves and the stories told by others about us, so it seems apt to begin with my story of engaging with narrative ideas and practices. My commitment to developing a narrative-based practice began some years ago in conversations with a colleague, Sam Simpson, whose work with adults with aphasia was influenced by developments in disability theory and narrative medicine.

Interest in these developments took me to the social model of disability, which challenges the traditional medical or philanthropic models of disability (Oliver, 1990). The social model invites a consideration of the barriers preventing people with impairments from participating fully in society and locates the problem within the environment rather than placing responsibility solely with the individual. I was also introduced to the concept of narrative medicine (Greenhalgh & Hurwitz, 1998), which takes into account an individual's narrative or personal experience of illness, thus fostering a more holistic approach to healthcare. An example of this approach is the work of Frank (1995), who explores 'insider accounts' of chronic illness and disability.

As therapists working with adults who stammer (AWS), Sam and I considered these ideas highly relevant for our client group. We were curious as to why they were influencing aphasia therapy (Parr, Byng, Gilpin, & Ireland, 1997; Pound, Parr, Lindsay, & Woolf, 2000; Parr, Duchan, & Pound, 2003; Felson Duchan & Byng, 2004) yet had no similar impact on stammering therapy. These conversations sparked my interest.

As a result, I looked for ways to bring my therapy more in line with social model thinking and responded to an invitation to co-run a self-advocacy group for AWS based on these ideas (Logan, Cheasman & Harris, 2003; Harris, Chapter 1 this volume). Rather than being impairment-focused, the course was designed to offer clients an opportunity to share personal stories of stammering, identify and challenge barriers to communication and develop a more robust identity as a person who stammers. However, whilst the response was positive, over time, my experience was that introducing the notion of disability in relation to stammering often proved to be contentious. The social model, disability theory and narrative medicine continued to influence my thinking about stammering and therapy. It seemed to me a narrative approach might be a way forward. When I came across a diploma course in counselling, offering a 'narrative pathway', I joined the programme.

My literature degree had introduced me to post-structuralist thinking through literary criticism (Belsey, 1980). This offered an insight into new ways of looking, not only at literary texts, but at the world, catching my interest and imagination. Discovering narrative therapy, influenced as it is by post-structuralism (Thomas, 2002), rekindled much of this original excitement. I was interested to discover my experience was similar to those of other people when beginning to engage with narrative ideas and practices. It felt like a 'homecoming' (Freedman & Combs, 1996; Speedy, 2000). A narrative approach encompassed aspects of narrative medicine and disability theory and fitted well with my model of stammering and what might help. I could see the relevance of narrative practices for adult stammering therapy. My journey as student, therapist and counsellor had come full circle.

After completing the diploma in narrative therapy, I began to draw on narrative ideas and practices in my work. The response of clients has strengthened my commitment to further developing a narrative-based practice. Working eclectically, I devised an adult stammering therapy course integrating narrative ideas and practices within a block modification approach (Van Riper, 1973). In this chapter, I share my own and my clients' experiences and reflections about this course.

It has been interesting and encouraging to note that more recent stammering therapy research has shown increased interest in the client's experience of stammering and therapy (Yaruss & Quesal, 2004; Plexico, Manning, & DiLollo, 2005; Plexico, Manning, & Levitt, 2009; Yaruss, 2012). Narrative approaches, which offer opportunities for therapists to hear the clients' personal stories of stammering, have in turn begun to influence adult stammering therapy (DiLollo, Neimeyer, & Manning, 2002; DiLollo, 2007; Logan, 2007; Leahy & Warren, 2007; Leahy, O'Dwyer & Ryan, 2012; Reitzes & Reitzes, 2012). I look forward to sharing my ideas, experiences and learning in relation to narrative ways of working with both therapists and AWS.

Narrative therapy: Orientations and intentions

Narrative therapy is a collaborative and creative approach to counselling developed by Michael White and David Epston (White & Epston, 1990). It is informed by post-structuralist thinkers, such as Michel Foucault (1980), in that it holds an understanding that a person's sense of self is shaped in social and relational contexts. A narrative approach offers a way to acknowledge and respond to the effects of power and normalizing discourses on people's lives, and assists people in discovering the knowledge and abilities they have which may help them address problems. Rather than focusing solely on the individual, narrative practitioners see individuals as social beings in relational contexts; as a result, they may involve the client's family, friends or other therapists in the therapy process. Narrative approaches have been successfully applied to a range of problems affecting the lives of adults and children, including attention deficit-hyperactivity disorder, anorexia, sexual or alcohol abuse and trauma (White & Denborough,1998; White, 2000; Denborough, 2005; White, 2007).

Influences: Post-structuralism

Post-structuralism is a theory, or a group of theories, offering an alternative way of viewing the world and questions 'taken for granted' assumptions we have about what it means to be a human being (Belsey, 1980). Its origins can be found in the work of French philosophers such as Derrida (1978) and Foucault (1980), and it looks at the relationship between power, knowledge, language and meaning by taking apart or 'deconstructing' accepted models and frameworks (Epston & White, 1992; Speedy, 2000).

From this perspective, some of our assumptions about what assists people to deal with problems in their lives may be challenged. A more traditional *structuralist* approach to counselling and therapy is based on the notion that going 'deeper' and exploring inner feelings helps to address problems. A narrative (*post-structuralist*) approach steps back from the idea that identity is 'a given'. Instead, it is based on the notion that life is multi-storied and individuals may be helped by discovering alternative or preferred narratives about themselves and their lives. This is achieved through the telling of stories (Speedy, 2000). Rather than exploring issues more 'deeply', a narrative approach uses metaphors and differentiates between 'thick' versus 'thin' descriptions to talk about an individual's life and experience. A 'thin' narrative is where there are just small traces of a new story. A 'thick' or 'rich' description means the new story is captured and substantiated through making links with other similar events and experiences.

Identity formation: Hearing the dominant story

> Amongst my people, questions are often answered with stories. The first story almost always evokes another which summons another, until the answer to the question has become several stories long. A sequence of tales is thought to offer broader and deeper insight than a single story alone.
>
> (Pinkola Estes, 1993, p.1)

In developing narrative therapy, White and Epston (1990) drew on the work of Bruner (1986), who proposed that people achieve meaning by taking their experiences into a storyline composed of events linked in sequence, through time, according to a plot. White (2007) describes identity as a public and social achievement, suggesting people form and re-form their identities through their experience of the world and interactions with others, resulting in multi-storied lives (Thomas, 2002). However, it is likely that some stories will dominate, overshadowing others. This can sometimes be unhelpful. For example, an individual may have a dominant story about being 'a loser', 'weak-willed' or 'not up to the mark'. This perception of self often comes to be seen as 'the truth', obscuring other stories of competency and knowledge. Therapists influenced by narrative ways of working are interested in neglected storylines that contradict the dominant 'problem' story.

Deconstruction

The stories people tell about themselves not only reflect experience, but shape it too (White & Denborough, 1998; White, 1999; Morgan, 2000). For example, culture, class, sexuality, disability and discourses of 'how you should be' influence an individual's understanding of themselves and others. Many people experiencing problems discount the impact of the environment on themselves and their circumstances. Narrative therapists, along with their clients, are interested in exploring ideas and beliefs in society that may be contributing to the problem. Deconstruction conversations (White, 1990, 2001) are designed to examine, 'unpack' or 'take apart' elements within the broader context that could contribute to or sustain problem stories. Through conversation, 'taken for granted' ideas and assumptions are made visible. As a result, the person is able to reconsider where the problem is located:

> These conversations often enable people to break further
> from a sense of guilt or blame as they come to see their
> problem no longer speaks of their identity.

(Morgan, 2000, p.50)

Finding alternative narratives: 'Sparkling moments'

Whilst hearing the dominant story is crucial, one of the intentions of narrative therapy is to assist people to find alternative narratives. Ways into these stories might be understood as 'sparkling moments' (Winslade & Monk, 1999) or 'unique outcomes' (White & Epson, 1990, 1992) and are opportunities for identity re-formation. Sparkling moments are events or expressions of life which stand outside the dominant storyline and act as points of entry for 'rich' story development. An example of this is when someone who stammers has kept the stammering hidden, and then begins to speak openly about it. Once a 'sparkling moment' has been identified and acknowledged by the client, it is important they have opportunities to 'thicken' or 'richly describe' this new storyline. Through this process, alternative narratives and preferred identities may be co-authored.

The client as expert

> The best source of information about the client is the client (Reimen, 1986, p.290). As clinicians taking this position, we are able to relinquish our role as the 'experts'. We are no longer in the role of the 'unquestioned authority'…
>
> (Manning, 2006, p.152)

A key aspect of narrative practice is that the therapist takes a 'decentred' yet 'influential' position (White, 2007). This acknowledges the collaborative nature of the work whilst recognizing the position of relative power held by the therapist. Therapeutic conversations are collaborative and clients take a leading role in determining the direction of therapy. Rather than having a hypothesis, narrative therapists listen both curiously and respectfully, asking questions from a place of 'not-knowing' (Speedy, 2000). Reflecting on the range of questions therapists might ask their clients, Jill Freedman (2011, p.7) shares a question which she asks herself when working with clients: 'What else do I want to know to be able to really see, hear and feel what the person is describing?' This illustrates how, whilst asking questions, the therapist can remain 'decentred', following the client's lead

Narrative practices

Externalizing: The problem is the problem

> One of the first things that a narrative therapist is interested in is to separate the person's identity from the problem for which they seek assistance.
>
> (Morgan, 2000, p.17)

The practice of 'externalizing', that is, separating the person from the problem, is central to a narrative approach (Carey & Russell, 2002). Many people experiencing problems in their lives locate the problem within themselves, believing it is to do with their personality or identity. White (2001, 2007) identifies 'disabling identity conclusions' such as 'hopeless', 'inadequate' or 'a failure'. These conclusions may leave people feeling 'stuck' with no hope of a way forward. Externalizing conversations separate the problem from the person and their identity, often making relevant links between the problem and the context of their lives. This practice can help people achieve some distance from limiting identity conclusions, opening up other options and leading to increased clarity.

One way of externalizing problems is through using language in a particular way. For example, a client might speak about problems in terms of their identity:

'I've always been an anxious person...'

'I just get so angry, I can't help it...'

'I'm quite a depressive sort of person really...'

A narrative therapist may instead talk about '**the** anxiety', '**the** depression' or '**the** anger' asking questions such as, 'How long has **the anxiety** been influencing you?' or 'Are there times when **the anxiety** is not around, or is less so?'

Shifting the focus of the conversation to the *relationship* between the client and the problem opens up possibilities that may not be recognized when it is seen and experienced as an integral part of their 'personality'.

Whilst all narrative therapy conversations are externalizing, White (2007) offers a framework[1] or 'Statement of Position Map' which supports externalizing conversations. There are four categories of enquiry which invite people to state their position in relation to the effects of the problem:

1. Negotiate an experience-near definition of the problem, i.e. the client names the problem and explores the history of the problem.

2. Explore the effects of these issues/concerns in the client's life.

3. Evaluate the extent of these issues/concerns.

4. Justify this evaluation/judgement about the extent of the issues/ concerns.

This map can be adapted for work with AWS. It is client-centred; allows the story to be fully heard; the problem to be identified and named; the effects of the problem to be described in terms of relationships and life circumstances and, finally, invites the client to voice what is important to them in their life (i.e. values and hopes). For a fuller account see Epston and White (1990) and White (2007).

Re-authoring: Using questions to invite new possibilities

Once the history and the effects of the problem have been fully heard using the Statement of Position Map, narrative therapists are interested in finding out about events that stand outside the problem story and indicate preferred ways of living. Based on the work of Bruner (1986), White's 'Re-Authoring Conversations Map' (2007) acts as a guide to therapeutic conversations and assists the development of alternative storylines. Single alternative events may be dotted through a person's history, offering possibilities for alternative stories to be discovered; however, if not connected, new stories remain vulnerable. Our intention is to find ways to bring these isolated events into a plotline which exists over time, thus contributing to subordinate storyline development. From a narrative perspective, rather than the client re-telling the familiar problem story, the therapist's intention is to use questions that provide a scaffold inviting clients to move from the 'known and familiar' to new territory, that is, what it 'might be possible to know'.

Bruner proposed that stories are composed of two 'landscapes': a 'landscape of action' (experiences and events) and 'landscape of identity' (thoughts and feelings to do with identity). Once a 'sparkling moment' has been identified, therapists might ask a question based on the 'landscape of action' to help 'thicken' this new story. For example, 'Can you say something about what happened then?' 'Who else was there?' or 'Have you ever done something like this before?' These questions invite clients to link actions and events, thus developing alternative storylines.

Questions based on the 'landscape of identity' assist people to explore their identity, inviting them to reflect differently on it. The following questions are examples taken from conversations with AWS:

> 'When you spoke openly about stammering what were you hoping for? What does this say about how you want to live your life?'

> 'You said you were more candid and honest about stammering with your family. Why is this important to you? What difference does this make to your life?'

'When you retrieved the glove for the woman, in spite of the fear of stammering, what led you to do this? What does this action say about how you want to live your life? Why are you proud of that?'

These questions offer opportunities for individuals to speak about their values and what is important to them. Re-authoring conversations move between 'landscape of identity' and 'landscape of action' questions, inviting people to reflect on actions, events, commitments, values, beliefs, hopes and dreams. In narrative conversations it is 'radical interest' or curiosity and 'not knowing' that underpins the kinds of questions a therapist might ask.

Communities of acknowledgement: Supporting new storylines

The process of identity re-vision can be challenging and new narratives may remain vulnerable. White (2000) emphasizes the importance of creating ways for people's revised identities to be witnessed by others. It is through joining with others that alternative stories can be 'thickened' and further developed (Behan, 1999; Morgan, 2000). Narrative therapy offers us a number of ways of doing this. Here I outline three.

'Definitional ceremonies'

Definitional ceremonies (DCs) offer opportunities for people to engage with their preferred identities and have these acknowledged by an appropriate audience called 'outsider-witnesses'. DCs, as developed by White (1999), originate in the work of cultural anthropologist Barbara Myerhoff, who described how a community of elderly Jewish people participated in group activities, actively redefining their preferred identities:

> Definitional ceremonies deal with the problems of invisibility and marginality; they are strategies that provide opportunities for being seen in one's own terms, garnering witness to one's worth, vitality and being...

> (Myerhoff, 1986, p.267)

DCs engage people in re-authoring conversations with 'outsider-witnesses' present. The responses of witnesses 'thicken' new stories and acknowledge revised identities as valid. People with 'insider-knowledge', that is, experience of dealing with similar problems, can be a valuable resource when recruited as witnesses. DCs consist of three parts:

> *The telling*: a conversation where the therapist facilitates a re-authoring conversation in front of an audience acting as witnesses.
>
> *The re-telling*: witnesses respond according to specific guidelines, known as practices of acknowledgement (White, 1999, 2004). Audience responses are not about pointing out positives or congratulating people. Instead, re-tellings link the stories of the person at the centre of the telling to those of the witnesses through shared experiences, themes and values.
>
> *The re-telling of the re-telling*: the client shares which of these images or expressions resonated for them and how they were moved by the comments of the witnesses.

For a fuller account of DCs see White (1999, 2004), Carey and Russell (2003), Logan (2007) and Leahy et al. (2012). The latter two references relate specifically to the application of DCs to stammering therapy.

Consulting our clients

In addition to DCs, narrative therapy offers other ways to support developing storylines. Consulting clients about the changes they have made, and sharing these stories, not only supports others but leads them to feel more able to deal with their own lives and problems (Epston & White, 1992). The consultation focuses on the history of the person's struggle with the problem and the knowledges they have gained. Questions asked invite responses that:

- Bring the knowledge gained to the fore
- Uncover details of steps taken leading to change
- Identify skills, qualities and resources
- Identify ways others might deal with similar problems.

An important aspect of this process is documenting this conversation. 'Therapeutic documents' are useful here, as by capturing the conversation they emphasize the value of the learning, substantiate it, and (with the client's permission) make it available to others dealing with similar difficulties.

Therapeutic documents

For narrative practitioners, 'document making' is a collaborative project and part of the therapeutic process. Therapeutic documents capture new knowledges and preferred changes that have become part of the person's revised identity (Payne, 2000). They can be used to provide links between sessions, capture key moments, thicken emerging stories and remind people about how their stories change over time (Speedy, 2004). For a fuller account of therapeutic documents see White and Epston (1990) and Fox (2003).

Narrative practice and stammering therapy: The possibilities

> Stories set the inner-life into motion, and this is particularly important where the inner-life is frightened, wedged or cornered. Story greases the hoists and pulleys, it causes the adrenaline to surge, shows us the way out…cuts for us fine wide doors in previously blank walls…
>
> (Pinkola Estes, 1992, p.20)

In this section, I develop my exploration of narrative ideas and practices and explore their relevance for therapy with AWS. It is by no means an exhaustive summary; there are many aspects of narrative practice that could be creatively integrated into stammering therapy. I hope other interested therapists will develop and share their own ways of incorporating narrative practices in their work and that AWS will contribute to professional knowledge by sharing their experiences of stammering and therapy.

The role of the therapist: Working collaboratively

Much stammering therapy research identifies the value of hearing the client's personal experience of stammering and therapy (Corcoran & Stewart, 1995, 1998; Crichton-Smith, 2002; Yaruss & Quesal, 2004; Yaruss, 2012). Hayhow and Stewart (2006) recommend therapists offer opportunities for AWS to tell their stories. Narrative therapy provides this opportunity (see the section on 'The client as expert' above). As a therapist without personal experience of stammering, I consider it important to find ways of assisting clients to access their 'insider-knowledge' about stammering, so working from a decentred position is highly relevant. Placing the client and their experience at the centre of the work also fits well with my approach to stammering, which is collaborative and based on a partnership where the AWS brings a wealth of experience to therapy.

Yaruss (2012) talks about the central importance of the clinician coming to understand the experience of the person who stutters. Adopting a decentred and non-expert stance as therapist provides an opportunity to develop this understanding, gaining an insight into the meaning stammering holds for the client. This fosters an attitude of trust, deepening the therapeutic relationship and creating an invitational space for the client to step into, maybe taking the lead in the therapy process as experts on their own lives (Stewart & Leahy, 2010). The resulting therapeutic alliance ensures clinical decision making is influenced by the client's needs and experiences.

Deconstruction: Addressing the stigma

> People who stutter live in an environment in which the general public stereotypes or stigmatizes them or their disorder.
>
> (St Louis, Reichel, Yaruss, & Lubker, 2009, p.12)

Stammering therapy research studies that examine the attitudes and perceptions of those who interact with AWS have shown stammering to be stigmatized (Blood, Blood, Tellis, & Gabel, 2003; Craig, Tan, & Craig, 2003). Stereotypes of stammering have been held by a number of groups, including the general public (Craig et al., 2003), teachers (Dorsey & Guenther, 2000), speech and language therapists (Cooper & Cooper, 1996) and school-age children (Frank, Jackson, Pimentel, & Greenwood, 2003).

In my experience, many AWS come to therapy with a dominant stuttering-saturated narrative. If, as a narrative approach suggests, people form identities out of the materials of the wider society (McAdams, 1993), then stereotypes and negative perceptions of stammering are likely to influence the stories AWS tell about themselves (McKenzie & Monk, 1997). This may lead to the internalization of negative perceptions of stammering and self-limiting beliefs, as illustrated by Tiffany Summerlin who shares her experiences of stammering:

> To me stuttering is a very shameful thing. I know I shouldn't
> feel that way, but I don't want anybody to know…Stuttering
> has a stigma about it that people who stutter must have
> something wrong with them…

(St Louis, 2001, p.31)

In Logan et al. (2003, p.15), Harris explains: "Stammering is an expression of social oppression. I feel shame. I block. I feel further shame… ."

Personal narratives such as these may come to dominate an individual's view of themselves, leading them to interpret experience in ways that maintain the dominant story. Separation from guilt or blame seems crucial if AWS are to come to alternative identity conclusions and self-acceptance as a person who stammers. (See the section on 'Deconstruction' p.83 above and 'Deconstruction conversations and stammering' p.93, below.)

I found White's writings on 'Modern power and the production of failure' (2002) illuminating in relation to internalized oppression and stammering. He identifies practices of power in society which I consider are likely to impact on individuals who stammer, in turn contributing to internalized negative perceptions of self and stammering. He suggests that power relations in society encourage people to actively participate in measuring themselves and each other against socially-constructed norms, often judging themselves to be 'inadequate, incompetent, disordered and a failure in terms of their identities' (White, 2007, p.165). White calls these judgements 'normalizing judgements' (White, 2002, p.43). In my experience, many AWS measure themselves against the 'norm' of fluency, leading to a negative self-identity as a person who stammers. White suggests that, in order to 'fit in' and feel acceptable within our communities, individuals undertake acts of 'management of the self' in an attempt to gain 'a small grant of normative worth' (White, 1999, p.3).

It is well documented that avoidance or coping strategies are often used by AWS to present as fluent, even though these may significantly restrict their life (Plexico et al., 2009). These actions could be seen as examples of the normalizing judgement White (1999) refers to. In these terms, some people might hold back from speaking, change words, avoid relationships, and forgo career choices in return for this 'small grant of normative worth', in other words, to be accepted as fluent – part of the norm.

Interestingly, I have found that even in the face of powerful influences such as these, many AWS do challenge mainstream thinking and the status quo by undertaking 'acts of refusal' (White, 2002, 2003). These acts are evident in the actions of those individuals who accept aspects of their lives and identities that may not fit with norms and standards associated with contemporary culture and, as a result, refuse to live their lives in the pursuit of a fluent identity. I see these acts of refusal in many of my clients: those AWS who begin to accept stammering as part of themselves, those who begin to challenge their avoidance strategies, mention they stammer or join with others to advocate for AWS. It is often through collective involvement such as this that identity shifts take place (Peters, 1996; White, 1999), challenging negative images of stammering and offering AWS new and preferred places to stand in the world. These acts of refusal come to form the basis for their new stories.

Identity re-vision

My approach to therapy is influenced by the work of Sheehan (1958) and Van Riper (1973), with desensitization and increased self-acceptance as an AWS central to the process (Plexico et al., 2009). Sheehan's 'role conflict theory' (1958, 1970) suggests the dynamic underlying stammering is linked to self-concept and social roles, in other words, is a problem of identity. I believe re-negotiating identity to include stammering and the development of a robust sense of self is a crucial aspect of change for successful therapy. For this to happen, I see therapy as needing to be systemic, addressing clients in the broader social context. However, much stammering therapy focuses on the individual, with only limited attention given to increasing clients' awareness of external 'barriers', rights, entitlements or the impact of the context on their sense of self. In my experience, inviting clients to carry out a public survey about stammering is often part of the therapy programme. One of the therapeutic aims is for AWS to recognize that the general public's response to stammering may be positive or neutral. Whilst this can indeed be beneficial, I believe it is equally important that therapy creates space for stigma and cultural stereotypes in relation to stammering to be named and discussed, opening possibilities for clients to challenge mainstream thinking about stammering. For the client in a system where negative attitudes to stammering still exist, working on the process of desensitization and self-acceptance is likely to be particularly challenging if the wider social context is not addressed.

Whilst I recognize there has been a gradual increase in awareness of communication disabilities (Everard, 2008; Ayre, 2011) and welcome some of the more balanced information about stammering as a result of the film 'The King's Speech'[2], it seems that stammering therapy still does not fully address the values in society that stigmatize people who speak differently and, as a result, can often make stammering so difficult for AWS to accept. Narrative therapy addresses the person in the wider social context (see the section on 'Narrative therapy: Orientations and intentions' pp.81–83, above) and, as a result, does create space for therapy to challenge stigma and negative mainstream thinking.

Deconstruction conversations and stammering

Deconstruction conversations assist the client to 'take apart' dominant 'problem-saturated' narratives of stammering and reconstruct alternative, less restrictive, more fulfilling stories (DiLollo et al., 2002). DiLollo et al. (2002, p.32) adapt White and Epston's framework for deconstruction conversations (1990) for use with AWS. The steps are as follows:

1. *Externalizing the problem*: e.g. 'When did *Stuttering* first enter your life?'

2. *Mapping the influences of the problem on the person's life and relationships*: e.g. 'How does *Stuttering* affect your life, your relationships?'

3. *Mapping the influence of the person in the life of the problem*: e.g. 'It seems that you accepted the invitation to speak to your church group even though you had some concerns about how *Stuttering* might steal the show. What strategies did you use to keep yourself on centre stage?'

A series of suggested questions takes the client through this process. The third step highlights the person's experiences that may stand outside of the 'problem-saturated' dominant story and provides an opening to alternative narratives or sparkling moments. It is here that we can assist our clients in re-authoring their story of stammering. For a fuller account see DiLollo et al. (2002).

Externalizing stammering

Externalizing conversations can be a useful first step in identity re-vision:

> ...the term 'stutterer' is a pathologizing label, which locates
> the problem within the client, implying that 'this is who I

> am' and which may present a barrier to successful, long-term outcomes of therapy.
>
> (DiLollo et al., 2002, p.32)

Manning (2006) suggests that externalizing broadens perspectives, leading to more flexibility and increased problem-solving. The notion of externalizing stammering initially challenged my beliefs about the importance of clients taking responsibility for the stammering. However, this apparent incompatibility need not be the case:

> ...acceptance of and desensitization to stuttering does not require one to accept him or herself as 'a stutterer' as much as accepting that stuttering is a problem and "I am a person who stutters.
>
> (DiLollo et al., 2002, p.38)

I now talk with clients about how they might *revise their relationship* with stammering or *reduce the influence* of avoidance. Externalizing feelings about stammering can be useful; for example, "How long has **the** fear kept you from telling people that you stammer?" or "How has **the** embarrassment stopped you asking for what you want in a restaurant?" Externalizing personal qualities that have sustained people coping with stammering leads to these being more richly described, for example, talking about the 'history of courage', which helped an individual to apply for work involving lots of talking.

Communities of acknowledgement: Supporting new storylines

> The new story... will remain vulnerable to subversion by the treachery of the old story, because of the powerful outside influences that authored this account initially... it becomes very important that revisions be given every opportunity to become strong, especially while in their infancy.
>
> (Parry & Doan,1994, p.157)

Prochaska and Di Clemente (1992) have identified minor slips and relapse as an integral part of the change process and research identifies relapse as a risk for AWS following therapy (Craig, 1998; Manning, 2001; DiLollo et al.,

2002). I too have found that many people develop a revised relationship with stammering during therapy, and come to a preferred identity which includes stammering and supports easier speech. However, once back in the outside world, many lose touch with this new story, leading to a return to familiar coping strategies of avoidance, restricted lifestyle and increased stammering. Narrative practices offer creative ways to assist clients in the maintenance of change.

Definitional ceremonies

For new stories to survive, it is important they are witnessed and interwoven with stories of others (see 'Communities of acknowledgement' p.87, above). Engaging AWS in re-authoring conversations with outsider-witnesses present links lives through shared themes and values and supports new identities in becoming established. Interestingly, this is borne out by Leahy et al. (2012) who point out the links between a reconstruing of self, the development of personal agency and the maintenance of change. In the absence of a group, 'virtual' meetings can be provided through the use of DVDs, such as Transcending Stuttering[3] or clips of other AWS who agree to share their stories of stammering and therapy. Audiences with whom people share their story may be arranged, comprising of colleagues, AWS or speech and language therapy (SLT) students.

Consulting clients

> I never tire of speaking about stuttering. It has been the most intimate experience of my life, and in the lives of almost everyone I have come to know and love in the stuttering community. And what do we love most of all? Telling our stories...

> (Ahlbach, 2001, p.25)

Inviting clients to speak about their experience of stammering and therapy 'thickens' new stories, providing a guide for other AWS dealing with similar difficulties. Parry and Doan (1994) offer suggestions for ways of supporting story re-visions:

- Making videotapes of clients to share with other AWS

- Arranging for clients to speak to groups

- Involving clients in therapy sessions with others.

Therapeutic writing

> Persons who have virtually lost their lives to problems find it difficult to escape despair, even when evidence suggests that they have had some success in reclaiming themselves. This despair can make them oblivious to their progress...

> (White & Epston, 1990, p.115)

White (2000) argues that it is imperative that people dealing with difficulties in their lives have devices which enable them to chart their progress as this offers hope (see 'Therapeutic documents' p.89, above). In my experience, 'therapeutic writing' fulfils this function for AWS and supports the client's ability to accomplish and maintain change. There are numerous categories of document, such as letters recording sessions, documents of knowledge and documents contributing to rites of passage (Fox, 2003). Here I refer to two.

Documents of knowledge

> Documents of knowledge can be extremely useful...in situations where under stress people forget the knowledges and skills that they most need at exactly those times of stress.

> (Fox, 2003, p.30)

Co-constructing documents recording the skills and knowledges that AWS have gained during therapy may support them in maintaining revised attitudes as well as the stammering management strategies they have learned. Clients are invited to keep this document so it is available to them when facing challenging situations. Here is an example of one such document:

> On my course I have gained knowledge and developed skills which help me to manage stammering more effectively. This document records what I have gained so far.
>
> **Self-advertising** – If I let people know I stammer sometimes, they won't be surprised if I do.
>
> **Speak more slowly and pause** – rather than putting pressure on myself to speak as quickly as I think other people are speaking or want me to speak
>
> **Give myself permission to stammer** – rather than trying to hide it.
>
> **Keep eye contact** – this feels more natural and gives the message I am OK with my stammer
>
> **Recognise Negative Automatic Thoughts** – this helps me question unhelpful thoughts and find more supportive ones e.g., 'I don't have to be 100% fluent.'

A 'book of knowledge'

Collecting stories by AWS about their personal experiences of stammering and therapy acts as a valuable resource for other AWS starting therapy. The following questions, adapted from Parry and Doan (1994), could be offered as a guide to clients willing to share their experiences of stammering and therapy:

- Could you give a brief description of your old story and how it influenced your life?
- How are things different for you now?
- What was the first thing you managed to do that you recognized was the beginning of a new story for yourself?
- What would be the most important thing for other people wanting to have a new relationship with stammering to know?

Narrative stammering therapy: An integrative model

Drawing on narrative ideas and practices, I devised a therapy programme using elements of narrative therapy within a block modification therapy approach (Van Riper, 1973). The course included key elements of block modification and selected narrative practices. With a colleague, Matthew Mills, I co-ran a weekly stammering therapy group based on this model. There were 10 adults and the course ran for two hours a week over 25 weeks.

Our narrative intentions were for clients to: tell the dominant stories of stammering; discover alternative stories of stammering; manage stammering in a more effective way; become aware of their resources, strengths and values; develop a robust self-identity which included stammering; 'thicken' their revised identities; and use their experiences to support other AWS. Here I illustrate the narrative elements of the course through the experiences of two clients: Aide, a young woman with an interiorized stammer, and Alex, a man with an overt stammer. Both had experienced significant negative feelings about stammering.

Identifying the problem story

In order to tell their story of stammering and as part of the *identification* process, individuals were invited to respond in writing to questions (see Appendix A) adapted by DiLollo (2002) and based on White and Epston's (1990) framework for identity re-vision. The work was carried out between sessions and individual responses discussed the following week in small groups. Each person chose what they were comfortable sharing, thus offering a way to safely explore their dominant story and for this to be fully heard.

Excerpts from Aide's response

- When did the stammering first enter your life?

  I stammered since I was a child but I only remember from the age of 11 when I started secondary school. It's remained with me since.

- Have you found the stammering to be a problem in your life? If so, when did it first become a problem and what kind of problem is it?

Yes, a big problem. I've never not minded the fact that I stammer, but hated it more the older I got. It restricts my life in terms of activities I might have taken part in, in school and in work.

- How does the stammering affect your life now?

It's constantly on my mind... am I going to be able to get through this alright? I'm not a shy person so it doesn't stop me from socializing. It makes me apprehensive to carry on conversations sometimes.

- What has it led you to think or say about yourself?

I imagine people to think/say negative things which makes me feel embarrassed, frustrated/angry and sometimes worthless.

- Of the significant people in your life who else should know that you are working on developing a different relationship with stammering? What difference would it make to their attitude towards you if they knew this?

My boyfriend knows. This helps me because he is encouraging. I don't feel telling anyone else will add value. If I told my family it might slow my progress because they will expect great changes and miracle cures. They are supportive, but can also put pressure on me without meaning to.

Aide's responses illustrate how these questions offer clients and clinicians an opportunity to understand more fully the role stammering has played in their lives/the lives of their clients. For Aide, the experience of looking at stammering this way helped her gain some distance from the stammering: 'It helped me learn about my stammer, and my relationship with it. I could look at my stammer objectively.'

Externalizing the problem

Once clients had identified the problem or dominant story, we provided further opportunities for individuals to externalize stammering. I adapted questions by Roth and Epston (1996) designed to be responded to from the perspective of 'the problem'; in this case stammering. The group were invited to work in pairs, taking turns to ask/respond to these questions.

Aide's responses

Q: To what extent do you think you've been a problem in Aide's life?

Aide: *I have been a problem... not in terms of holding her back from what she wants to do, but how she sees me, and to what extent she thinks I impact on her life.*

Q: How did your involvement get started?

Aide: *I crept up on her when she was about 11, at secondary school, although her parents say they remember her stammering when she was about 4.*

Q: Have you had any effect on her social life, family, friendship or other social relationships?

Aide: *I don't think I've held her back making friends or from doing anything... Maybe at work I hold her back from saying what she wants and make her feel a bit tense in some speaking situations.*

Q: Are you able to have an impact on how Aide thinks or feels?

Aide: *Yeah... I have a huge impact on her. She's a bit too sensitive about me or too aware that I'm there and when I trip her up, I definitely make her aware that she's not by herself.*

Q: In the past have you influenced her performance at school?

Aide: *Not academically, but she would have wanted to speak at the school assembly...*

Q: Are you able to affect her ability to dream of the future?

Aide: *It's mostly to do with immediate speaking situations... so I don't think I will hold her back from attempting to achieve anything in the future.*

Q: Currently, what control over Aide's life do you have?

Aide: *A huge amount because she has to speak a lot of the time...*

Q: Even with all that has happened what is her goal right now?

Aide: *It's being able to control her speech as best she can... not to let anything hold her back in life, whether it's speech or anything else.*

I asked Aide what it had been like responding to these questions: 'Initially it was odd…it was hard to separate the stammer from me. It helped in reinforcing the fact that my stammer is not who I am, it's just part of me.' This separation is important as it opened up possibilities Aide may not have recognized when she saw the problem as 'who I am'. I was struck by Aide's determination not to let stammering restrict her life. Whilst stammering clearly had a great deal of control over her life, I was also interested in finding out more about:

- How it was that she had not allowed stammering to prevent her from doing/achieving what she wanted to in life?

- What name would she give to the part of her that does not allow stammering to restrict her life?

Responding to my questions Aide identified qualities of 'determination' ('maybe stubbornness') and values, such as the importance of 'trying to fulfil your potential', as factors that prevented stammering from stopping her doing what she wanted in life.

Metaphors

The language we use in therapy can often represent experience as static, leading people to become trapped in positions dictated by the language of binary oppositions, for example: fluent/dysfluent, approach/avoid, open/not open, normal/abnormal. Bird (2004) suggests we can also use language in a way that indicates movement, thus opening space beyond these polarities. She believes metaphors create such a space, offering places for people to inhabit that are less restricting. I noticed that Manning (2006) used metaphors when applying the narrative practice of externalizing to stammering. In the light of these influences, we invited clients to think of two metaphors (see Appendix B) – one describing their relationship with stammering and another illustrating how they would like it to be. This enabled them to explore their dominant story of stammering, visualize a different story and, when returned to later in the course, identify change.

Aide's metaphor

Start of therapy: 'It's like I'm walking along the path and every now and then a deep gully suddenly appears and I fall in and I have to do everything I can to climb out.'

(Aide did not include a metaphor to describe how she would like her relationship with stammering to be.)

Aide updated her metaphor later in the course: 'I walk along the path without gullies appearing... but if they do, they're more like a little dip in the road and I can pass over with ease. I'm more open with people at work... I feel more able to try new things and I don't really care as much if I do stammer.'

Interested in finding out more about this emerging story or 'sparkling moment', I asked the following questions:

- What difference has caring less about stammering made to your relationships at work?

- What were the first small steps you took in becoming more open about stammering?

Aide noticed the more she tried to conceal stammering the more it took over her life. Whilst being more open at work was challenging, it led to her feeling less stressed and more 'herself'. This conversation allowed Aide to 'thicken' her new responses to stammering and substantiate the beginnings of change.

Desensitization and identifying 'sparkling moments'

As part of the process of desensitization, our intention was to capture stories that stood outside of each person's dominant story of stammering. We listened out for 'sparkling moments'; that is, times when stammering had less influence, for events that did not fit with the dominant 'problem' story or for any reduction in avoidance strategies. We took notes using the clients' own words in order to capture these changes, asked questions to explore these events further and make links between events, thus supporting the development of alternative storylines.

Alex's 'sparkling moments'

- Saying what he wanted to say and feeling more 'candid and honest'

- Speaking to his dad and girlfriend about 'going for the word'

- Telling his family about the ways he 'concealed stammering'

- Being more 'honest' with himself and others about stammering – finding the 'honest/straightforward approach' paid dividends.

We were interested in Alex's new response to stammering. To find out more and assist the development of emerging storylines we asked questions such as:

- We wondered what difference having the conversation with your dad and girlfriend made to your relationship with them? Have you had this kind of conversation with anyone else?

- We were interested in what being candid and honest about stammering might mean for how you want to live your life?

- This change in attitude you mention, can you think of other examples of this? How did you know your attitude to stammering was beginning to change?

Sparkling moments present as thin traces of a new storyline which, unless substantiated, remain vulnerable. Inviting Alex to reflect on his experience assisted 'rich story development', offering him an opportunity to make links between actions/events, identify values, explore his understanding of his identity and maybe reflect differently on it.

Deconstruction: Unpacking the dominant story

I was keen to provide an opportunity for participants to make links between their experience of stammering and the role played by society in the construction of their identity as an AWS (see 'Deconstruction: Addressing the stigma' p.90 above). I looked for a way to introduce 'deconstruction' conversations to the group. Morse and Morgan (2003) devised questions for a group of women who had experienced violence. Their questions highlighted the context of the womens' lives and built connections between them. I felt there were common issues for AWS to do with locating responsibility for the difficulties they were dealing with in their lives as a result of stammering, and adapted the questions as follows:

- What ideas about stammering get promoted by society?

- How do you think these ideas impact on the lives of AWS?

- Do you think these ideas are OK ideas or not so OK ideas?

- Are there names for these kinds of attitudes?

- What in our society might lead some AWS to conceal stammering?

- What do you think would be good ideas to put out there about stammering?

The group discussed stereotypes of stammering and their conversation made the social construction of stammering more transparent. A group member took notes and afterwards distributed them to group members. Points from the discussion included: the nature and complexity of stammering is misunderstood in society; the 'norm' is the expectation of fluency; people who laugh at AWS should be seen as behaving in an unacceptable way; change should come from AWS themselves. Their conversation acknowledged the social construction of stammering, how this had impacted on their view of stammering and highlighted the beginnings of self-advocacy with individuals beginning to become their own agent for change.

Therapeutic documents: Capturing change

When working on avoidance reduction, the changes people make are often difficult to sustain or sometimes are not acknowledged as important. I wanted to respond to White's suggestion (see section on 'Therapeutic writing', p.96, above) that, in order to support change, clients need devices that enable them to chart their progress. I used therapeutic documents, art therapy and definitional ceremonies. To capture change, verbatim notes of clients' reflections were taken during weekly 'check-in' sessions and, with the clients' agreement, half-way through the course a letter was sent to each client. I wrote the letters following guidelines referred to by Fox (2003) and included questions that had occurred to me after sessions.

Extract from the letter to Alex

Dear Alex,

We wanted to share our recollections of what you have been working on this term. We hope they resonate for you, but if not, feel free to disregard.

At the start of the course you described the problem as 'a bubbling under the surface annoyance'. Your goal was to speak more easily, gain confidence and reduce the influence of stammering in your life. Can you think of what steps you have taken this term towards these goals?

When working towards reducing avoidance strategies, you said it was challenging to say what you wanted to say, you felt you were doing the 'classic stammer', however, you recognized you were being more 'candid and honest'. We wonder if you could think of times when you said what you wanted to say in spite of the challenges? You spoke to your dad and girlfriend about 'going for the word' and got positive feedback. We are interested in what difference having this conversation made to you? You said you were beginning to realize it's better to go for what you wanted to say rather than 'umming and aahing'. You noticed an attitudinal change. You spoke to your family about your aims and said: 'I was telling them about all the things I do to conceal stammering – they didn't have a clue... I've been more honest with myself and others... the honest/straightforward approach is paying dividends, speaking to people at work and not feeling bothered.' Could you say more about how this straightforward approach is paying dividends?

We hope this fits with your experience, feel free to respond to any of the questions that may interest you. We would be interested to hear, but if not that's fine.

Best wishes,

We were keen to know how clients received the letters and discussed them in the group, asking how it felt to receive them and what they would do with them. Alex commented:

> "The letter is good because we've covered a lot of ground on the course and I'd forgotten lots of things I said... I started off quite negative, the first bit is all my doubts and the metaphors I used to describe what it's like trying to speak and have things that I want to say. But the letter reads like someone coming to terms with their issues and starting to look more analytically at what they do and learn from

different experiences. It would be good to use as a reference
to go back to. Yes, I think I'll keep it and use it."

This illustrated the value of the letter for Alex and the way such documents
could be used to capture and 'thicken' clients' revised stories.

Art therapy

Towards the end of the course, a speech and language therapist who is also
an art psychotherapist, Matthew and I co-facilitated a session on the theme
'Looking back – looking forward'. Our intentions were for clients to have
opportunities to reflect on their stammering therapy journey, 'thicken' new
stories of change and identify future hopes. The image-work provided a medium
for these conversations. Clients created their image, discussed them in pairs
and finally, those who wished to, talked about them in the group. Some people
took photographs of their image to keep on their mobile phones. This seemed
a helpful and creative way of literally 'capturing' change.

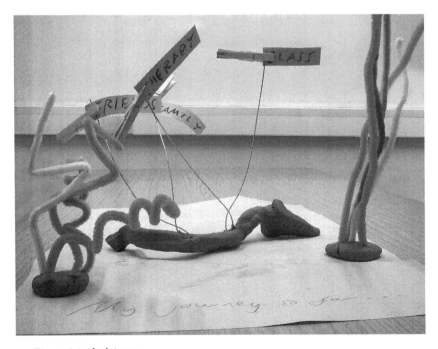

Figure 3.1 Alex's image.

Alex used his image (Figure 3.1) to illustrate changes in his feelings about stammering, the challenges he had faced and overcome and what and who had sustained him on this journey. He said:

> "The emotions I attempted to convey with the image... the arrow (my journey) originates from a place marked by the jagged, sharp angles of frustration, but it points to a destination where lines are more at ease signifying less tension and frustration. Though the journey is never straight and smooth, supportive signposts (friends, family, classmates) light the way and steady my hand (or mouth!!)."

Definitional ceremonies

Clients were invited to prepare a presentation using Doan's questions (see section, A 'book of knowledge' p.97,) as guidelines. Mindful that identity revision needs to take place in a communal setting, with the group's permission, I invited prospective SLT students to be 'witnesses' to the presentations. They were briefed in 'practices of acknowledgement' (see 'Definitional ceremonies' above, p. 88) and responded to each person's story following specific guidelines. With the client's permission, presentations were videoed to be shared with SLTs or AWS. Any written stories were collected for inclusion in a 'Book of Knowledge'.

Aide and Alex's stories

Aide and Alex volunteered to write about their experiences of therapy for inclusion in this chapter. I wondered how to go about collecting their stories. To give chapters a common framework, the editors had provided contributors with a list of suggested questions to share with clients. I used these as a starting point, but asked additional questions, either to assist Aide and Alex in responding to the questions given, or where I felt narrative-based interventions might be useful.

Clearly not all the outcomes for Alex and Aide can be attributed solely to the narrative-based elements of the course; rather, they are a response to a course where different practices were woven together. Other elements inevitably came into play: the timing of therapy; what therapy clients had done before;

the fact that therapy was in a group and had two therapists. With hindsight, it might have been interesting to explore Aide and Alex's responses to the narrative elements of the course more fully. To do this, the questions would have needed to be more specific.

I hope their stories offer a glimpse of how two individuals responded to a course integrating elements of narrative practice and block modification therapy. The course I have described is not intended as a 'blueprint' for including narrative practices in stammering therapy. There is no single, 'right' way and no textbook questions to ask. My questions during therapy and afterwards were led by interest and 'not knowing' and, as a result, may be different to those of someone else. The outcomes were the result of the experiences of two clients wanting to find a way forward with stammering, a small group of AWS and two therapists whose imagination had been captured by narrative ideas and practices, keen to explore new ways of working.

I collected Alex and Aide's stories in different ways. Alex preferred to be interviewed. I asked him the suggested questions (along with some spontaneous questions arising from his responses), captured this on video, transcribed the conversation and sent it to Alex who edited his story and returned it to me. I then responded with any additional questions I had. Aide began writing in response to the questions given, then sent me what she had written, asking for assistance as she felt 'stuck'. I responded by asking interested questions where I felt it appropriate and adding optional questions to assist story development. These 'conversations' were carried out via email. Both stories involved the process of emails going back and forth over distance and time between myself and each client.

Aide's story

The initial question Aide responded to was, 'What has brought you to stammering therapy and what aspects of the course stand out for you?' Aide's response was:

> "Imprisoned by my emotions towards my stammer and searching for a way out – is the best way to describe why I sought therapy. Feelings, like frustration, anger and embarrassment, led me to want to gain some control over my speech, which I felt I had no control over. I am my own worst critic, always striving to maintain my standards of how I should portray myself. My speech was getting in the

way of that. Each time I heard myself stammer it made
me shudder. Even hearing others stammer was difficult to
listen to. Stammering can be extremely isolating, I never
spoke to anyone about my stammer, with the exception
of my boyfriend. Even when I did speak to him about my
feelings, he wasn't allowed to have any opinions. I thought
he doesn't stammer so can't possibly understand how I feel.
In opening up to him, I was still very guarded.

I found myself thinking, speaking is primarily how we
communicate. How can I live the rest of my life scared of
my own voice? I felt I was playing the victim. Everyone
has their bag of bricks to lug around life and stammering
is mine."

Reflecting on Aide's story now, I realize I might have asked an externalizing
question here, inviting Aide to think about where the 'standards' she strived
so hard to maintain may have originated. As I was interested in hearing more
about Aide's experience of stammering, I asked the following question to assist
story development: 'I wonder whether it was these thoughts that led you to
start speech therapy or perhaps there were others?'

"I wanted more from life; not to have my whole existence
dominated with something as mundane as speaking. I wanted
to be 'normal'. My stammer made me feel abnormal; I felt it
made me look odd. I sought therapy to stop feeling this way.
I wanted to be able to open my mouth and have the words
flow and stop the feeling of drowning in my own words,
the disappointment I felt in myself after each stammered
word. The disappointment I imagined my loved ones felt
after I stammered. I wanted to be free… therapy helped
me take a step away from my stammer. Prior to therapy,
stammering was eating me up. I was extremely sensitive
about it. I couldn't separate myself from it and would not
accept myself as someone who stammered. I was raw with
emotion every time I had a bad stammering experience. I
felt helpless… Therapy helped me see the more I run away
from my stammer and pretend it's not there, the more it
imprisons me. It helped me realize my stammer does not

> define me and should not take over every aspect of my life. Therapy has been liberating. I feel like I am knocking years off my life-sentence. It is OK to stammer."

Here Aide describes the experience of gaining some distance from stammering (externalizing). Her use of language (normal/abnormal, free/imprisoned, liberated/victim) illustrates her movement from the position of 'victim', where stammering imprisoned her, to one where she is able to separate herself from stammering, feels liberated and where it is 'OK to stammer'.

I was interested in finding out about what components of the course had been helpful. Using externalization to support distance and perspective, I asked: 'This feels like important learning. I wonder what aspects of the course might have led you to take this step away from the stammer?'

> "Meeting other people who share the same experiences as me. Hearing their stories and feelings about their stammer, yet being able to separate the people from their stammer made me realize that my stammer didn't define who I was. It put things into perspective. Hearing other people try something different, taking that step to conquer their stammer inspired me. Your words, Jan, that the 'old way hasn't worked' reinforced the fact I had to do something different, something new. I had to try to change my mindset – begin to believe I am more than my stammer."

Aide's experience here bears out the narrative notion that externalizing the problem and interacting with others dealing with similar difficulties supports identity change. Her reflections bear this out: 'My stammer doesn't define who I am.' My next question was: 'Initially you found voluntary stammering challenging, but had a change of heart about using it. Can you explain how this came about and what difference it made?' My intention in asking this question was for Aide to connect her action (beginning to use voluntary stammering) with meaning (what difference did it make?) and to elaborate this new story.

> "I realized my old ways weren't working, I had to try something different... face my demons head on. This meant accepting myself as someone who stammers. A big part of this acceptance was allowing myself to be vulnerable enough to put myself in feared situations (i.e. stammering).

Voluntary stammering empowers me, and makes me more
confident with my speech."

I was curious to find out more about Aide's experiences of responding differently
to stammering and chose to ask a broader question rather than enquire further
about her shifting personal narrative, so I asked: 'What difference have the
changes you have made so far made to your life?'

"When I do have moments of stammering I let them go, I
don't carry them with me for hours, days, months like I used
to. I see past the stammering and realize I will come out the
other end, as opposed to being so wrapped up in it I drown.
I now know stammering is just **part** of me and not **who** I
am, so even in difficult periods where my stammering gets
bad I remain optimistic and hold my head up as opposed
to recoiling in shame and embarrassment."

My 'conversation' with Aide via email might have gone in a number of directions.
I could have made an enquiry connecting action to meaning, such as, 'What
does that mean for you when you hold your head up?' Alternatively, I might
have asked questions linking other similar events to form a new story. For
example, 'Can you think of any other occasions when you "held your head up"
rather than "recoiling in shame"?' Aide's response to my question illustrates
how her story of gaining distance from stammering allowed optimism to step
in along with a new response to stammering. She now is able to 'hold her head
up'; a 'sparkling moment' worth capturing.

Alex's story

Jan: Why did you choose stammering therapy at this stage of your
life?

Alex: I was becoming less confident and grinding to a halt in terms of
my communication. There was an incident at work where a manager
took me aside and made an issue about my speech in an unprofessional
way. It was upsetting and I thought rather than cower away from it, try
and seek help because I'm always going to have to speak…

Jan: Was this having an impact in other areas of your life?

Alex: No, because I have good friends and a supportive family it's never been an issue, but in a new job I felt people were making judgements.

Jan: What sort of judgements?

Alex: Judging me on how I say things rather than what I say. Only noticing the struggle with my words and not what I'm trying to express.

Jan: What effects might these judgements have on people who experience speech difficulties?

Alex: Judgements make people more introverted, doubting of themselves, it perpetuates the problem... negativity feeds negativity.

Rather than asking Alex a more personal question to do with the impact of these judgements on him, my question was an invitation to 'unpack' or 'deconstruct' the impact negative perceptions of stammering may have on AWS. It also had the potential for him to make connections between his experiences, those of other AWS and the effects of social 'norms'.

Jan: How did this fit with your hopes for the course?

Alex: It led me to deal with the prospect of therapy by being guarded about what it would be like and the people that would be there. It was more than healthy scepticism; I found myself getting quite arrogant about what people would be like... I'm going to use a horrible word... thinking they would be slightly 'retarded'...

Jan: I wonder if you have any idea where these ideas about AWS being 'retarded' might have come from?

Alex: I don't mean the word in the actual sense, as horrible and derogatory as it is. I suppose I was projecting onto others my fears about myself, almost bullying, like the kid in the playground who is the bully is always the one with the most insecurities. In a weird way it was like that; a way to separate myself, they had the 'disability', and I was OK. Perhaps projecting onto others the fears I had about myself was a way to hide away from uncomfortable realities about my own speech. It shows how unwilling I was (before the class) to look deep into myself, I found it easier to be judgemental about others. Stepping inside the room on the first day was excruciating. But the more I got into the course I found my classmates were all articulate, interesting, engaging people with careers and social circles. What's more, we were coping with the situation we all had to deal with – stammering.

My question had provided Alex with an opportunity to identify the impact of social norms and attitudes to stammering on his beliefs and perceptions of stammering. His response illustrates the extent to which he had internalized negative stereotypes of stammering and was himself bringing judgements. The question allowed him to take a step back and develop valuable insights about where these negative beliefs might have originated. His response also illustrates his transition from standing outside the stammering community to forming strong connections with his classmates which contributed to a changed personal identity which included stammering.

> **Jan:** Which stage of the course was most challenging?

> **Alex:** Identification: I felt an impatient feeling in the room. I thought we know what we do; we just need some strategies to stop stammering… I wanted somebody to sort it out.

> **Jan:** Were there any points when the course started to fall into place?

Asking about turning points allows people an opportunity to identify and explore a change of direction from a less preferred to a preferred direction, and invites a consideration of the initiatives they took to make this change (Freedman, 2011).

> **Alex:** The more I talked to people in the group about stammering and related to situations they had been through, the easier the process became. My self-confidence went up. Before the course, I hadn't met anyone who stammered. Meeting other AWS put things into perspective. It was the shared experience and sense of all working towards a single goal that made the difference. Now, even if a conversation on the phone didn't go well and the listener noticed I stammer, I think, 'who cares, let's just get on with it'… I have a happier, sunnier attitude.

I was interested in Alex's use of the words 'sunnier attitude' and wondered what meaning he attributed to these words.

> **Jan:** What has this sunnier attitude and increased confidence made more possible in your life?

Alex: Communicating at work is a lot easier. I'm not so bothered if someone notices I stammer. In the past, I was reluctant to open my mouth in certain situations, I speak more now. I feel more confident speaking about stammering and have spoken with people at work about it. Things I used to do when stammering, I don't do as much now. I'm sticking to the word I want to say rather than using similar words... there are other changes too; I'm trying to say the audible sound I want, rather than holding back.

Jan: Have these changes affected relationships at work?

Alex: I feel I can I get on. Some of the same things are still there. I went to a meeting the other day and some new people had come into the work-place. I still had the fear we were going to go round the table and say our names... I can't say that at times I wouldn't do some of the things I used to do; excuse myself, put the phone down on someone to avoid stammering. But I'm more confident now.

Jan: At the start of the course you described stammering as a 'bubbling under the surface annoyance'. How would you describe stammering now?

Alex: 'Simmering' rather than bubbling. It's still there, but doesn't get me down in the same way. I've accepted it's always going to be there. I think the period it takes me to get over a difficult moment with my speech is less than it was.

Here, Alex's response illustrates the value of metaphors; rather than the limited 'either/or' binary positions determined by language (fluent/dysfluent, change/no change, success/failure), metaphors open up other possibilities, allowing therapist and client to notice gradations of change, such as 'simmering' rather than 'bubbling'.

Jan: Knowing what you know now, what advice would you give others thinking about speech therapy?

Alex: I would say leave your cynicism at the door and take the plunge – it's good to talk about it!

Reflections

Both Alex and Aide achieved the narrative therapy intentions identified at the start of the course (see 'Narrative stammering therapy' p.98 above). Aide discovered a new relationship with stammering, one where stammering no longer defined her. She moved from a problem-dominated story of stammering, where she felt 'abnormal' and 'helpless', to one where she experienced stammering as a part of her – it was 'OK to stammer'; this was a liberating experience. Her identity re-vision developed or 'thickened' as the course progressed and contributed to her finding new and easier ways to manage her speech. Aide also became more aware of the personal skills, knowledges and values that sustain her in facing the challenges of working on her speech. She identified determination, stubbornness and a strong belief in the importance of fulfilling your potential.

Alex came to the course with deeply-held negative views of stammering. He too was able to develop a more accepting relationship with stammering, which assisted him in managing stammering in an easier way. The movement he made was from an initial position of internalized oppression – not wanting to be identified as someone who stammered – to one where his perception of AWS and ultimately of himself changed. This stands out for me in Alex's story. His new story of stammering included a 'happier, sunnier attitude'. He moved from a starting point where his expectations were about practical solutions to the problem of stammering; he was looking for someone else to take responsibility and 'sort it out'. He gradually became his own agent for change and, ultimately, it was his interaction with other AWS that contributed to the changes he made. He reports: 'It was the shared experience and sense of all working towards a single goal that made the difference.'

Alex identified values important to him, such as being 'candid and honest', which assisted him when facing challenging situations working on his speech. His message to others, 'leave your cynicism at the door – it's good to talk' highlights his new story and the knowledge gained. Cynicism was initially part of his dominant story of stammering, underpinning his initial response to the course and classmates. The above message illustrates important learning for Alex and could be interpreted as advice he might give himself were he to start the course again.

Aide and Alex arrived at new conclusions about their lives and identities, moving from positions where they held negative feelings about stammering to one where they hoped, by sharing their experiences, that other AWS may benefit. Whilst sharing personal experiences was sometimes challenging, Alex spoke to a group of SaLTs and Aide allowed her story to be shared with SaLTs on professional training courses. Both have contributed to therapy knowledge by documenting their respective stories for inclusion in this book.

In narrative terms, the process for Aide and Alex of responding to my questions and writing about their experiences formed yet another 're-telling' of their respective stories, thus contributing to a 'rich description' supporting their new stories. This chapter forms yet another 're-telling'.

Final thoughts

Writing this chapter has been exciting and challenging. The overriding experience was one of pleasure as I have had the opportunity to share my experiences, dilemmas and enthusiasm about this way of working. It has been rewarding to work with Aide and Alex and hear their stories. I hope the chapter offers a realistic description of the therapy process and conveys a sense of the ways in which narrative ideas and practices can contribute to new story development and identity re-vision in the lives of AWS.

This chapter describes a 'work in progress' and is intended to invite therapists and clients alike who are interested in narrative practice and stammering to enter into the discussion, sharing ideas and experiences. I welcome this dialogue. Whilst this work is in its infancy, I am encouraged by the response of my clients. Witnessing their stories gave me the opportunity to learn from them, and hearing their feedback helped me envisage how I might develop this work. Their stories give me encouragement and sustain my belief in the importance of drawing on clients' insider-knowledge, in the ability of clients to determine what they need from therapy and the value of collaborative working. Drawing on narrative practices has offered clients a different place to stand in relation to stammering and me a broader landscape within which to work and learn. This learning continues to inform and enrich my work.

I thank Aide and Alex for their contributions and commitment, other group members for the parts they played in the story and the following people who were involved in different ways in the generation of this chapter: Sarah Walter, Matthew Mills and Catherine O'Neill.

References

Ahlbach, J. & Benson, V. In K.O. St Louis (Ed.) (2001) *Living with Stuttering – Stories, Basics Resources and Hope*. Morgantown, West Virginia: Populore Publishing Company.

Ayre, A. (2011) Talkcoach. *Signal: The Newsletter of SIG Disorders of Fluency*, Issue 34, Winter 2010/11. http://www.talkcoach.co.uk/who-we-are.php

Behan, C. (1999) Linking lives around shared themes: Narrative group therapy with gay men. *Gecko – A Journal of Deconstruction and Narrative Ideas in Therapeutic Practice, 2*, 18–34.

Belsey, C. (1980) *Critical Practice*. London: Routledge.

Bird, J. (2004) *Talk That Sings – Therapy in a new linguistic key*. New Zealand: Edge Press.

Blood, G.W., Blood, I.M., Tellis, G.M., & Gabel, R.M. (2003) A preliminary study of self-esteem, stigma and disclosure in adolescents who stutter. *Journal of Fluency Disorders, 28*, 143–159.

Bruner, J. (1986) *Actual Minds, Possible Worlds*. Cambridge, MA: Harvard University Press.

Carey, M. & Russell, S. (2002) Externalising – commonly asked questions. *The International Journal of Narrative Therapy and Community Work, 2*, 76–84.

Carey, M. & Russell, S. (2003) Outsider-witness practices: Some answers to commonly asked questions. *The International Journal of Narrative Therapy and Community Work, 1*, 3–16.

Cooper, E.B. & Cooper, C.S. (1996) Clinician attitudes towards stuttering: Two decades of change. *Journal of Fluency Disorders, 21*, 119–135.

Corcoran, J. & Stewart, M. (1995) Therapeutic experiences of people who stutter. *Journal of Speech-Language Pathology and Audiology, 19*, 89–96.

Corcoran, J. & Stewart, M. (1998) Stories of stuttering: A qualitative analysis of interview narratives. *Journal of Fluency Disorders, 23*, 247–264.

Craig, A. (1998) Relapse following treatment for stuttering: A critical review and correlative data. *Journal of Fluency Disorders, 23*, 1–30.

Craig, A., Tan, C., & Craig, M. (2003) Stereotypes towards stuttering for those who have never had direct contact with people who stutter: A randomized and stratified study. *Perceptual and Motor Skills, 97*, 235–245.

Crichton-Smith, I. (2002) Communicating in the real world: Accounts from people who stammer. *Journal of Fluency Disorders, 27*(4), 333–352.

Denborough, D. (2005) A framework for receiving and documenting testimonies of trauma. *The International Journal of Narrative Therapy and Community Work, 3&4*, 34–42.

Derrida, J. (1978) *Writing and Difference*. Chicago: University of Chicago Press.

Di Lollo, A. (2007) Foxes, scorpions, and stuttering research: How a constructivist perspective might help us avoid getting stung. In: J. Au-Yeung & M.M. Leahy (Eds) *Research, Treatment, and Self-Help in Fluency Disorders: New horizons.* Proceedings of the International Fluency Association 5th World Congress on Fluency Disorders, pp.3–9.

DiLollo, A., Neimeyer, R., & Manning, W. (2002) A personal construct psychology view of relapse: Indications for a narrative therapy component to stuttering treatment. *Journal of Fluency Disorders, 27,* 19–42.

Dorsey, M., & Guenther, R.K. (2000) Attitudes of professors and students towards college students who stutter. *Journal of Fluency Disorders, 25,* 77–83.

Epston, D. & White, M. (1992) *Experience, Contradiction, Narrative & Imagination: Selected papers of David Epston and Michael White 1989-1991.* South Australia: Dulwich Centre Publications.

Everard, R. (2008) Help City Lit spread awareness. *Speaking Out,* Spring 2008.

Fox. H. (2003) Using therapeutic documents: A review. *The International Journal of Narrative Therapy and Community Work, 4,* 26–36.

Felson Duchan, J. & Byng, S. (2004) *Challenging Aphasia Therapy: Broadening the discourse and extending the boundaries.* Hove: Psychology Press.

Foucault, M. (1980) *Power/Knowledge: Selected interviews and other writings.* New York: Pantheon Books.

Frank, A. (1995) *The Wounded Storyteller: Body illness and ethics.* Chicago: University of Chicago Press.

Frank, A.L., Jackson. R.A., Pimentel, J.T., & Greenwood, G.S. (2003) School-age children's perception of a person who stutters. *Journal of Fluency Disorders, 28,* 1–15.

Freedman, J. (2011) My favourite questions. *The International Journal of Narrative Therapy and Community Work, 4,* 3–8, www.dulwichcentre.com.au

Freedman, J. & Combs, G. (1996), *Narrative Therapy: The social construction of preferred Realities.* Norton, New York.

Greenhalgh, T. & Hurwitz, B. (1998) *Narrative Based Medicine: Dialogue and discourse in clinical practice.* London: BMJ Books.

Hayhow, R. & Stewart, T. (2006) Introduction to qualitative research and its application to stuttering. *International Journal of Language and Communication Disorders, 41*(5), 475–493.

Leahy, M., O'Dwyer, M., & Ryan, F. (2012). Witnessing stories: Definitional ceremonies in narrative therapy with adults who stutter. *Journal of Fluency Disorders, 37*(4), 234–241 (Special Issue: 9th Oxford Dysfluency Conference).

Leahy, M. & Warren, A. (2007) Making stuttering manageable: The use of narrative therapy. In: J. Au-Yeung & M.M. Leahy (Eds) *Research, Treatment and Self-Help in Fluency*

Disorders: New horizons. Proceedings of the 5th World Congress on Fluency Disorders, pp.320–324.

Logan, J. (2007) From client to consultant: Developing 'outsider-witness practices' with adults who stammer. In: J. Au-Yeung & M.M. Leahy (Eds) *Research, Treatment and Self-Help in Fluency Disorders: New horizons.* Proceedings of the 5th World Congress on Fluency Disorders, pp.325–332.

Logan, J., Cheasman, C., & Harris, St J. (2003) Self-advocacy for people who stutter. In: K.L. Baker (Ed.) *Proceedings of the 6th Oxford Dysfluency Conference.* Leicester, UK: K.L.B. Publications.

Manning, W. (2001) *Clinical Decision Making in Fluency Disorders.* New York: Singular.

Manning, W. (2006) Therapeutic change and the nature of our evidence: Improving our ability to help. In: N. Bernstein Ratner, & J. Tetnowski, (Eds) *Current Issues in Stuttering Research and Practice.* Mahwah, NJ: Lawrence Earlbaum Associates.

McAdams, D. (1993) *The Stories We Live By: Personal myths and the making of the self.* New York and London: The Guildford Press.

McKenzie, W. & Monk, G. (1997) Learning and teaching narrative ideas. In: G. Monk, J. Winslade, K. Crocket, & D. Epston (Eds) *Narrative Therapy in Practice: The archaeology of hope.* San Francisco: Jossey-Bass, pp.82–117.

Morgan, A. (2000) *What is Narrative Therapy? An easy to read introduction.* Adelaide: Dulwich Centre Publications.

Morse, J. & Morgan, A. (2003) Groupwork with women who have experienced violence. *The International Journal of Narrative Therapy and Community Work, 4,* 37–47.

Myerhoff, B. (1986) Life not death in Venice: Its second life. In: V. Turner & E. Bruner (Eds) *The Anthropology of Experience.* Chicago: University of Illinois Press.

Oliver, M. (1990) *The Politics of Disablement.* London: Macmillan.

Parr, S., Byng, S., Gilpin, S., & Ireland, C. (1997) *Talking about Aphasia: Living with loss of language after stroke.* Buckingham, UK: Open University Press.

Parr, S., Duchan, J., & Pound, C. (Eds) (2003) *Aphasia Inside Out: Reflections on communication disability.* Maidenhead: Open University Press/McGraw Hill Education.

Parry, A. & Doan, R. (1994) *Story Revisions – Narrative Therapy in the Postmodern World.* New York/London: The Guilford Press.

Payne, M. (2000) *Narrative Therapy – An introduction for counsellors.* London: Sage.

Peters, S. (1996) The politics of disability identity. In: L. Barton (Ed.) *Disability and Society: Emerging issues and insights.* London: Longman.

Pinkola Estes, C. (1993). *The Gift of Story: A wise tale about what is enough.* New York: Rider.

Pinkola Estes, C. (1992) *Women Who Run With the Wolves: Contacting the power of the wild woman.* New York: Rider.

Plexico, L.W., Manning, W.H., & Levitt, H. (2009) Coping responses by adults who stutter: Part I. Protecting the self and others. *Journal of Fluency Disorders, 34*, 87–107. Part II. Approaching the problem and achieving agency. *Journal of Fluency Disorders, 34*, 108–126.

Plexico, L., Manning, W.H., & DiLollo, A. (2005) A phenomenological understanding of successful stuttering management. *Journal of Fluency Disorders, 30*, 1–22.

Pound, C., Parr, S., Lindsay, J., & Woolf, C. (2000) *Beyond Aphasia – Therapies for living with communication disability.* Bicester: Winslow Press.

Prochaska, J.O. & Di Clemente, C.C. (1992) Stages of change in the modification of problem behaviours. In: M. Herson, R. Eisler, & P. Miller (Eds) *Progress in Behaviour Modification.* Sycamore, IL: Sycamore Publishing Company, pp.184–218.

Reimen, D.J. (1986) The essential structure of a caring interaction: Doing phenomonology. In: P.M. Munhall & C.J. Oiler (Eds) *Nursing Research: A qualitative perspective.* Norwalk, CT: Appleton-Century-Crofts, pp.85–105.

Roth, S. & Epston, D. (1996) Developing externalising conversations: An exercise. *Journal of Systemic Therapies, 15*(1), 5–12.

Reitzes, P. & Reitzes, D. (2012) *Stuttering: Inspiring stories and personal wisdom.* StutterTalk, INC.

Sheehan, J. (1958) Conflict theory and avoidance – reduction therapy. In: J. Eisenson (Ed.) *Stuttering – A Second Symposium.* New York: Harper Row.

Sheehan, J. (1970) *Stuttering: Research and therapy.* New York: Harper Row.

Speedy, J. (2000) The 'storied' helper: An introduction to narrative ideas and practices in counselling and psychotherapy. *European Journal of Counselling, Psychotherapy and Health, 3*(3), 361–375.

Speedy, J. (2004) Using therapeutic documents in narrative therapy practices. In: G. Bolton, S. Howlett, C. Lago & J. Wright (Eds) *The Writing Cure: An introductory handbook of writing, counselling and therapy.* London: Routledge, pp.25–34.

Stewart, T. & Leahy, M.M. (2010) Uniqueness and individuality in stuttering therapy. In: A. Weiss (Ed.) *Perspectives on Individual Differences Affecting Therapeutic Change in Communication Disorders.* New York: Psychology Press.

St Louis, K. (2001) *Living with Stuttering: Stories, basics, resources and hope.* Morgantown, West Virginia: Populore.

St. Louis, K.O., Reichel, I.K., Yaruss, J.S., & Lubker, B.B. (2009) Construct and concurrent validity of a prototype questionnaire to survey public attitudes toward stuttering. *Journal of Fluency Disorders, 34*, 11–28.

Thomas, L. (2002) Post-structuralism and therapy–what's it all about? *The International Journal of Narrative Therapy and Community Work, 2.*

Van Riper, C. (1973) *The Treatment of Stuttering*. Englewood Cliffs, NJ: Prentice-Hall.

White, C. & Denborough, D. (1998) *Introducing Narrative Therapy: A collection of practice-based writings*. Adelaide: Dulwich Centre Publications.

White, M. (1992) Deconstruction and therapy. In: D. Epston & M. White, *Experience, Contradiction, Narrative & Imagination: Selected papers of David Epston and Michael White 1989–1991*. Adelaide: Dulwich Centre Publications, pp.109–151.

White, M. (1999) *Different Faces of Power*. Adelaide: Dulwich Centre Publications, Teaching Notes.

White, M. (1999) Reflecting-team work as definitional ceremony revisited. *Gecko – A Journal of Deconstruction and Narrative Ideas in Therapeutic Practice*, 2, 55–82.

White, M. (2000) *Reflections on Narrative Practice – Essays and interviews*. Adelaide: Dulwich Centre Publications.

White, M. (2002) Addressing personal failure. Part 1: Modern power and the production of failure. Part 2: Refusal. *The International Journal of Narrative Therapy and Community Work*, 3, 33–52.

White, M. (2004) Working with people who are suffering the consequences of multiple trauma: A narrative perspective. *The International Journal of Narrative Therapy and Community Work*, 1, 45–59.

White, M. (2007) *Maps of Narrative Practice*. New York: W.W. Norton & Company.

White, M. & Epston, D. (1990) *Narrative Means to Therapeutic Ends*. New York: W.W. Norton & Company.

Winslade, J. & Monk, G. (1999) *Narrative Counselling in Schools: Powerful and brief*. Thousand Oaks, CA: Corwin Press.

Yaruss, J.S. (2012) Understanding the speaker's experience of stuttering: Implications for treatment outcomes research. International Fluency Association, 7th World Congress on Fluency Disorders, 2–5 July 2012, Tours.

Yaruss, S. & Quesal, R. (2004) Partnership between clinicians, researchers and people who stutter in the evaluation of stuttering treatment outcomes. *Stammering Research*, 1, 1–15.

Websites

Roth, S. & Epston, D. (2003) Framework for a White/Epston type interview. Accessed at: http://narrativeapproaches.com/narrative%20papers%20folder/white_interview.htm

White, M. (2001) Narrative practice and the unpacking of identity conclusions. Accessed at: http://www.dulwichcentre.com.au/narrativepractice.html

White, M. (2003) Distinctions between traditional and modern power. Accessed at: http//www.dulwichcentre.com.au/workshopnotes.htm

Endnotes

1. See also Roth & Epston (2003) Framework for a White/Epston type interview

2. 'The King's Speech'. Recent film about King George VI who stammered.

3. Transcending Stuttering: http://video.google.com/videoplay?docid=36544823957023 25018

Appendix A

Relationship with stammering – Some questions

- When did the stammering first come into your life? Did it start gradually, or has it always been around?
- Have you found the stammering to be a problem in your life? If so, when did it first become a problem and what kind of problem is it?
- What name would you give to this problem?
- How does the stammering affect your life now? How does it lead you to relate to other people?
- What has it led other people to think/say about you?
- What has it led you to think or say about yourself?
- Does the stammering ever influence your decisions for you? If so, can you think of any decisions it has affected?
- Have there been times when you have been able to overcome the influence the stammering can sometimes have in your life?
- How did you accomplish that?
- How did you feel when this happened?
- What does this achievement say about:
  - the sort of person you are
  - the kind of relationship you want to develop with the stammering
  - what you want for yourself in your life.
- Of the significant people in your life, who else should know that you are working on developing a different relationship with the stammering? What difference would it make to their attitude towards you if they knew this?

Adapted from: DiLollo, A., Neimeyer, R., & Manning, W. (2002) A personal construct psychology view of relapse: Indications for a narrative therapy component to stuttering treatment. *Journal of Fluency Disorders, 27*(1).

Appendix B: Metaphors

Handout: finding your own metaphor to describe your experience of stammering.

How would you describe your experience of stammering?

Walt Manning, a Speech and Language Pathologist in the USA who specializes in stammering therapy (and stammers himself), wrote about the experiences of some of his clients:

> One young man who had recently begun a course of speech therapy came up with this metaphor to explain what it was like for him to stammer. After thinking about it for a moment he said: 'It is like I am a butterfly trying to fly, but I am constantly buffeted by strong winds. I cannot move forward like I want and it's frustrating...'

> Another person who stammers talked about stammering and the experience of using avoidance strategies said: 'It's like walking on thin ice, treading carefully but always aware that at some point I might fall through!'

> Another person, a 24-year-old university student said, 'When I stammer I feel like a deer in the headlights...' When asked how he might rewrite that metaphor into what he would like to become, he said, 'A performer in the spotlight.'

Walt commented: 'Based on his current success, I believe he is well on his way.'

- What metaphor would you use to describe your experience of stammering?
- How might you rewrite that metaphor to illustrate how you would like things to be?

Adapted from Manning, W. (2006) *Therapeutic Change and the Nature of Our Evidence: Improving our ability to help.* The University of Memphis.

4 Interiorized (covert) stammering

The therapy journey

Carolyn Cheasman and Rachel Everard

Introduction

For some people who stammer (PWS), their stammering remains largely hidden from view and is often perceived as a dark, shameful secret that might well cause immense embarrassment and anguish should it be discovered. This particular group is described as having interiorized stammering, the main characteristics of which include high levels of fluency, extensive use of avoidance strategies to conceal stammering and deep-seated negative feelings about their stammering. At City Lit, a UK specialist centre in adult stammering therapy, evening courses are run specifically for people with interiorized stammering, a unique provision for this group of clients.

In this chapter, we include a brief overview of the past and present literature on interiorized stammering, a description of interiorized stammering and a detailed commentary on the therapy process specifically tailored to meet the needs of this particular group, illustrated by comments from clients attending the course. Central to the chapter are longer contributions from clients giving an overview of their experience of therapy. The chapter concludes with results from a recent study looking at the outcomes of our therapy programme.

We use the term 'interiorized stammering' for this chapter; however, it is sometimes referred to as 'covert stammering'. Some therapists describe this type of stammering as mild. We feel this is misleading and inaccurate as, whilst for some people the overt behaviours may be mild, the covert aspects are significant.

Authors' personal experience

We see this chapter as a unique opportunity to bring together our personal and professional experience of interiorized stammering. In 2003, we presented a paper at the International Fluency Association conference in Montreal on our approach to this area of work and were encouraged by many present to share this through writing about it. Some years later, we are pleased to have this opportunity to share our thoughts with a wider audience.

Carolyn's story

I first became aware of stammering aged nine years. All the evidence I have indicates that I did not stammer prior to this. I know that I did not stammer frequently and almost immediately resorted to avoidance strategies to cope. I changed words and stayed quiet in certain situations. The low frequency of the stammering, coupled with my increasingly wide vocabulary and my fear of revealing what I perceived to be a deeply embarrassing difficulty, meant that it quickly became a secret problem, an almost totally submerged iceberg. The fear of being 'found out' rapidly became the dominant issue and ruled my teenage years. The GP referred me to a psychologist who did an IQ test and little else. I was excused all oral reading at school and went through university never attending a tutorial. It was only when I left university that I felt I needed to address the hidden demon. By some miracle, I ended up at City Lit. I attended an intensive course where I was the only 'interiorized' person in the group. Some of my fellow group members openly wondered why I was there: 'If I spoke like you I would be so happy', is one comment I remember. I was taught a fluency technique, syllable-timed speech (Andrews & Harris, 1964), which I now recognize as being inappropriate but, despite all of this, it was a key breakthrough. For the first time I met speech and language therapists who understood why this apparently insignificant problem was ruling my life. I was introduced to the concept of avoidance and challenged to start to reduce some of my coping strategies. I started to tell friends that I stammered and would even read books on stammering in public without covering them in brown paper. Whilst I went on to have more therapy and the journey was long and bumpy at times, this first course truly was a life-changing event. I started to be able to say 'I stammer' and, more to the point, started to allow myself to stammer openly.

Rachel's story

My story fits neatly into the multifactorial model of stammering (Kelman & Nicholas, 2008), where a number of predisposing factors led me to start stammering. There is a family history of stammering; I was born into a busy family with two noisy older brothers; my speech and language skills were somewhat delayed; and I was highly sensitive to the differences in my speech compared to my family and peers. I started stammering as soon as I started speaking and received some help around the age of 11. By this stage, I had become adept at using a range of avoidance strategies and, therefore, therapy was fairly brief and my stammering was considered 'sorted' by the therapist. I colluded with this decision, but continued to dread certain situations, such as reading out in class, taking part in oral examinations and giving presentations. It was only in my 20s that I decided enough was enough and sought therapy. With an immense sense of relief I finally attended a City Lit interiorized stammering group and for the first time found myself among other people with similar experiences, thoughts and feelings. That first experience of therapy and subsequent courses affected my life beyond measure: I became actively involved in the British Stammering Association and retrained to become a speech and language therapist. The key for me was becoming more open and accepting of my stammering and seeing it as a positive part of my identity, not something to be ashamed of and kept hidden.

Past and present knowledge of interiorized stammering

'Internal' stammering was mentioned in the literature as early as the 1800s (Ssikorsky, 1891) and since then the terms 'covert', 'masked' and 'interiorized' have been used interchangeably to describe this particular type of dysfluency. In 1952, Douglas and Quarrington published their important study 'The Differentiation of Interiorized and Exteriorized Secondary Stuttering', a two-year study of 20 people with interiorized stammering seeking treatment for their difficulties. They make the very valid observation that stammering is not a static characteristic but develops over time, and suggest that a process of interiorization takes place which involves adopting an increasingly sophisticated repertoire of avoidance strategies to conceal stammering. They propose a number of ways in which interiorized stammering can be distinguished from exteriorized stammering, which include:

- The main communicative goal for those with interiorized stammering is to avoid stammering at all costs.

- Since avoidance is the main coping strategy, this leads to greater difficulty in predicting the involuntary pattern of stammering for people with interiorized stammering than is the case for people with more overt stammering.

- People with interiorized stammering demonstrate heightened sensitivity to the social world and anxiety to conform, which leads to the desire for fluency at all possible costs.

- Those with interiorized stammering are likely to come from a family with high parental expectations and early concern about speech behaviours.

- Those with interiorized stammering place value on gaining recognition in the community and professionally.

Douglas and Quarrington propose that people with exteriorized stammering supposedly do not share these characteristics. From our clinical experience this is clearly not the case. In our opinion, the distinction between interiorized and exteriorized stammering is not so clear-cut.

The research carried out by Kroll (1978) also raises more questions than it answers. The study involved 53 PWS, divided into two groups of interiorized and exteriorized stammering. He collected data on eight variables which included stuttering severity, stuttering adaptation, socio-economic status, level of concern about stuttering, communicative goals, level of awareness of stuttering problem, group affiliation characteristics and Rotter's test of locus of control (Rotter, 1966). Rather surprisingly, he found that only three of these variables distinguished significantly between the two subgroups:

- **Communicative goals**: people with an interiorized stammer avoided communication in order to avoid stammering.

- **Level of awareness**: people with an interiorized stammer were less aware of their speech problems.

- **Group affiliation**: people with an interiorized stammer sought to please people with superior status more than friends of their own age.

Whilst we would question these findings which do not tally with our clinical experience, we find it useful that Kroll suggests the need to generate new forms of therapy for interiorized stuttering with the initial phase focusing on modifying attitudes rather than speech. This is very much in line with our own way of thinking.

Levy (1987) suggests that instead of viewing interiorized stammering as a diagnostic category, as proposed by Douglas and Quarrington (1952), it could be viewed as one pole on an axis along which a person who stutters may move. One end of the pole is interiorized stuttering, the other end exteriorized stuttering. She goes on to explain that this way of viewing stuttering will help us to understand fluctuations in behaviour and make predictions about changes that could result from therapy. She also describes other diagnostic constructs or axes, which include:

- High avoidance/low avoidance
- Silent blocks/stuttering more openly
- Infrequent stuttering/frequent stuttering
- Mild overt behaviours/severe overt behaviours
- Stuttering catastrophic/stuttering a relief.

Therefore, someone with an interiorized stammer might demonstrate high levels of avoidance, may block silently and, when they do stammer overtly, it may be mild. We would question this latter point as some of our clients with an interiorized pattern of stammering can stammer severely on occasions. Levy talks about the strongly negative feelings someone with an interiorized stammer may experience and the fact that, when they do stammer, it is perceived as a catastrophic event. This way of viewing interiorized stammering fits more closely with our clinical experiences. No two PWS are the same and this remains true for people with interiorized stammering. Whilst it may be clinically helpful to have clearly defined criteria for diagnosing interiorized stammering, it is of course important to allow for individual variation and to have the freedom to decide on a person-by-person basis the type of therapy most beneficial for a particular client. Some clients we see appear to have what we would describe as more borderline interiorized stammering; for example, someone may be extremely sensitive about stammering and uses a range of avoidance strategies but demonstrates a higher percentage of overt stammering behaviours than we would normally expect in this group.

The above studies give us an idea of the characteristics of interiorized stammering. What is interesting is that there appears to be little or no data on its incidence, the male:female ratio, different treatments available and treatment outcomes. These would be interesting areas to research further. We have observed that a greater percentage of women attend our interiorized stammering groups than our other types of courses (for example, in a group of 10 clients on an interiorized stammering course four or five might be women, whereas this number reduces to zero, one or two on our other courses).

In conclusion, we would identify someone as having an interiorized stammer if they demonstrate high levels of fluency, very strong negative feelings and resort to using avoidance strategies when at all possible to maintain the outward appearance of being a fluent speaker, motivated by the fear that they will be negatively judged if observed to stammer.

Description of interiorized stammering

Levy (1987), writing as a speech and language therapist, provides us with a very powerful description of what it is like to have an interiorized stammer:

> "For those who cannot tolerate the sound of themselves stuttering, there is but one tortuous course of action open to them: they must at all costs prevent themselves from stuttering. But there is a price to pay: the freedom of speech. From now on speaking will be viewed as an obstacle course of difficult sounds and words. In order to hide stuttering, perfect predictions of future difficulties will need to be made. Words about to be uttered will be scrolled through the window of our speaker's mind to be checked for their stuttering potential. Uttered speech will be severely censored. Somehow, fluency will be achieved and no outsider will guess how much has not been said."
>
> (Levy, 1987, p.104)

One of our clients, giving an insider account, described her experiences as follows:

> "Having an interiorized stammer is incredibly frustrating for me because I am a very vocal and social person and I consider myself to be fairly highly functioning. It's something I always carry around with me and it's always something that is a worry. It's something I particularly worry about in the workplace, in situations where things feel more

stressful. It's something I plan for; I think a lot about how I can get around this in my job and I figure out ways in which I can either avoid stressful situations or how I can manage the situation a bit better. I have my list of things that I know I can turn to help me get through some of those situations. I've only recently really thought about how invasive that is to my life and I didn't realise how the anxiety that I have about it and the negativity I feel about it has fed into it a lot."

The internet has enabled the self-help movement for PWS to flourish and grow beyond recognition and many useful personal accounts of covert stammering are available. For example, StutterTalk (www.StutterTalk.com), a weekly free podcast, has devoted many episodes specifically to the topic of interiorized stammering. The Stuttering Homepage (www.mnsu.edu/comdis/kuster/stutter.html) also has numerous articles on interiorized stuttering, mainly written by people who themselves stammer. In addition, there is the Yahoo group, Covert-S, which encourages discussion between people who experience interiorized stammering.

Our interiorized stammering programme

As a specialist centre in adult stammering therapy, City Lit has been offering evening courses specifically for people with interiorized stuttering since the early 1980s. As far as we are aware, this type of programme remains unique. Our rationale for offering the programme is based on the recognition of key differences experienced by people with interiorized stammering, identified above. These differences indicate the need for an adapted therapy programme, with more emphasis on the covert aspects of stammering and the desensitization process, as we will go on to describe. We also believe it is important for clients to share their experiences and to work through the therapy process with others with interiorized stammering. If someone is placed in a group with others who stammer more overtly, they can quickly feel different and be perceived as different. This is neatly summarized by Hood and Roach, 2001:

"Ironically we're viewed suspiciously in the stuttering community for being fluent just as we're ostracized in the fluent community for stuttering."

This sense of belonging to neither the stammering nor the fluent world but instead somewhere in-between reflects the idea of 'inhabiting the borderlands' described by Harris (Chapter 1, this volume). Through avoidance people with interiorized stammering can move relatively easily between both worlds and may not feel fully accepted by either.

At City Lit, we are fortunate to be based in central London and with such a high density population it is easier for us to recruit people with interiorized stammering than it is for many other therapists. We also work within a college of adult education, which means we are easily able to offer evening courses, another advantage for ensuring our numbers for these types of groups remain high. The majority of participants are in full-paid employment and would find it difficult to access therapy during the day.

We believe strongly that the group aspect of the programme is a vital part of the therapy for a number of reasons. For anyone who stammers, group therapy has the advantage of helping to reduce feelings of isolation (Van Riper, 1973). A person with an interiorized stammer is likely to feel even more isolated, as their overriding concern might well be to keep it secret from everyone else around them. In our experience, the group quickly becomes a safe environment where people feel confident to share their thoughts and feelings, and for many it is an enormous relief to be able to talk openly about something they have hidden away from others for so long.

Group therapy also helps people with an interiorized stammer to address crucial issues of identity, and at this point it is useful to make comparisons with the literature on negotiating identity in aphasia therapy (Pound, Parr, Lindsay & Woolf, 2000; Simmons-Mackie & Elman, 2011). These authors make the point that identity and communication are intricately linked since we use language to shape our own experiences and create an image for others. People who stammer may believe that their identity has been compromised by their difficulties with expressing themselves and that other people as a result do not see them as they truly are. Moreover, for people with interiorized stammering (and this may well be true of those who stammer more openly), they might oscillate between two different identities: that of a fluent person and that of someone who stammers. The temptation to present themselves as a fluent speaker can be very great and leads to different forms of avoidance, described later.

Pound et al. (2000) suggest that the goal of identity work is to 'incorporate' disability into a healthy robust sense of self rather than deny disability or make disability equal to the self (that is 'I am my disability'). Whilst we are cautious about labelling stammering as a disability, this way of working with identity links closely with our focus on supporting clients to become more accepting of their stammering and to start to view their stammering as just one of the many different aspects of themselves, not as something that defines them. With the latter point in mind, we use the term a 'person who stammers' rather than 'stammerer' and encourage clients to reflect on how they describe themselves.

The group plays a key role in helping individual members to achieve some degree of acceptance as it promotes the development of a shared identity. With the added strength and support this collective identity brings, individuals are more willing and able to address the reveal/conceal dilemma (French, 1994) experienced by all people who stammer: 'Shall I take the risk of saying something about my stammering? And what will other people think of me once they know? Or shall I continue hiding my stammering? And what is this going to cost me?' This dilemma is particularly significant for someone with an interiorized stammer as they can more often than not 'pass' as a fluent person.

A further complicating factor in relation to being open about stammering is that when someone with an interiorized stammer does reveal they stammer, they are faced with well-meaning, but sometimes unhelpful responses, such as, 'Oh. I never noticed' or 'It doesn't seem to be a problem'. It is much easier for an individual to confront these issues with the support of the group than on their own and this will be explored further when describing 'coming out' as a person who stammers (p.138).

The group aspect of the programme also provides the opportunity for people to get to know each other and to set up a support network, which often continues beyond the end of the course. Right from the start, we encourage participants to communicate with each other between sessions by facilitating the formation of an email group. Each week one person takes responsibility for taking minutes of the session which they then circulate to the other group members. If anyone misses a particular session, the minutes serve as a useful record and at the end of the 25-week course each member has a complete record of every session, a useful reminder of the work covered and the progress made.

Overview of the structure and content of the programme

The course comprises 25 two-hour evening sessions and takes place over two terms with a three-week break. The maximum group size is 10 and the courses are invariably full, indicating the demand. Broadly speaking, the therapy programme is based on block modification (Van Riper, 1973) and avoidance reduction therapy (Sheehan, 1970). Over time, the course has evolved to include aspects of mindfulness meditation (Kabat-Zinn, 1996), acceptance and commitment therapy (Hayes, Strosahl & Wilson,1999) and cognitive behaviour therapy (Beck, 1995); also see Chapters 7, 8 and 9 in this book. The sequence of therapy follows Van Riper's programme of identification, desensitization and modification but changes have been made to the ordering of some stages.

Identification

Traditionally, identification of the overt aspects of stammering precedes identification of covert aspects (Van Riper, 1973). However, in interiorized groups we begin by exploring the covert aspects. Sheehan's iceberg metaphor views stammering as comprising overt, observable behaviours (above the water line) and covert aspects, including thoughts, feelings and avoidance strategies (below the water line). The iceberg metaphor indicates that for most people the majority of the stammering is below the water line, i.e. it is the internal aspects that represent the more significant part of the difficulty. In interiorized stammering, this ratio is magnified and we can see the overt stammering as being literally just the 'tip of the iceberg' or the iceberg may be completely submerged.

We start with exploring the covert dimension as this is usually the aspect clients with interiorized stammering most closely identify with. Some clients come to therapy with feelings of guilt: 'It's not as bad as other people's', 'I know I shouldn't make a fuss'. Some may even have been told by SLTs that they cannot be helped as they are 'not stammering'. Starting therapy with covert identification validates clients' experiences. It acknowledges that this is a real issue for people. It is not just 'mild stammering' or 'less of a problem than overt stammering' but a **different** kind of problem. Participants feel they are being heard and understood and, importantly for group forming (Tuckman, 1965), they can quickly appreciate that they are finally in a group of others with similar issues. This identification with others is potent and an important first stage of the healing process. There are other reasons for starting off in this way. Usually there is very little overt stammering to be identified in these groups, partly because the frequency is much lower, but also because of high levels of avoidance. In addition, clients are often threatened by the experience of seeing themselves stammer. Spending time exploring other aspects and allowing for some group bonding and trust to form means that people are more ready to look at overt stammering behaviours when invited to.

A collective group iceberg is drawn and feelings are shared as with any other group. Clients then draw their own personal icebergs (see Figure 4.1).

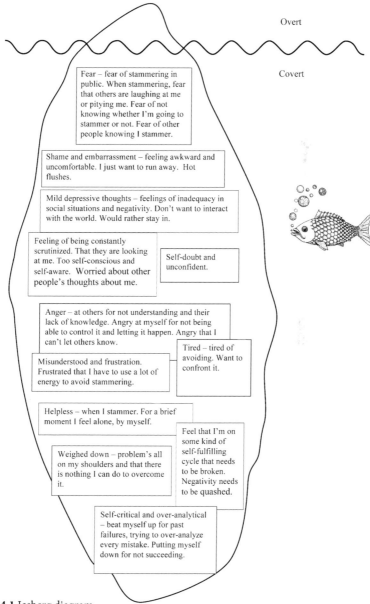

Figure 4.1 Iceberg diagram.

The group is asked about the consequences of feeling like this about their stammering, what it is likely to lead to in behavioural terms and this naturally flows into the major issue of avoidance. It helps to frame avoidances as understandable coping strategies – if someone feels this bad about something then why would they want to do it. A modified version of Sheehan's (1970) levels of avoidance is used to structure this part of identification.

We describe the levels of avoidance as follows:

- **Sound level**: Things you do to try to not stammer, but you still go ahead and say the word you want to. Strategies include starters, fillers, pausing, backtracking, coughing, etc.

- **Word level**: Changing the word to a synonym or omitting the feared word.

- **Speech level**: Opting out of speaking – this may mean saying less or staying silent, e.g. in a meeting.

- **Situation level**: Not going into a situation, e.g. not attending a meeting.

- **Feelings level**: There are two aspects to this: (i) not letting others know how you feel about stammering; (ii) cutting off from your feelings yourself – a form of denial.

- **Relationship level**: Avoiding certain types of relationship, e.g. authority figures or intimate relationships.

- **Role level**: Due to its more abstract nature, this is described in 'Coming out as a person who stammers' below (p.138).

We are also interested in helping clients identify aspects of their thinking as thoughts and beliefs play such a key role in driving the stammering cycles of fear and avoidance. Clients are introduced to the cognitive cycle (Greenberger & Padesky, 1995) and to the concept of negative automatic thoughts (NATs) (Beck, 1995). They spend time between sessions identifying or 'catching' some NATs and discussion in the group helps to identify some of the deeper underlying beliefs, e.g. 'I shouldn't stammer', 'stammering is bad, wrong and unacceptable', 'people will see my weakness and feel they have power over me'. The person with interiorized stammering often has negative thoughts around what others will think if they find out about their stammering. The fear of 'being found out' is often profound and is driven by negative, catastrophizing thoughts such as 'If they know I stammer they will think I can't do my job.'

Time is then devoted to exploring the overt behaviours. Basic information on speech and voice production is given and clients use a vocabulary of stammering-related words to start to identify some of their own behaviours. They are also given the opportunity to see themselves on video. It is often surprising how valuable clients find this given how little stammering there is. However, it may be that one of the reasons for this is that some participants start to recognize that they do have strong communication skills. They have often been so focused on stammering or avoiding it that other aspects of their communication have gone unnoticed. Equally, they may start to identify aspects which they would like to modify, such as rate or volume or loss of eye contact. This is also useful information. Some do have stammering and avoidance behaviours to identify and some have become a little more willing to let themselves stammer than would have been likely earlier on in the course.

Desensitization

Desensitization becomes the explicit focus of the course from Session 8. The long-term goals of desensitization are for people to become more open and accepting of stammering and for negative emotions about stammering to reduce. Many of the strategies described by Van Riper (1973) and Sheehan (1970) are as relevant to people with interiorized stammering as to any other people who stammer. These include avoidance reduction, voluntary stammering and self-advertising. This phase of the programme also includes more work based on CBT to help clients start to challenge, and 'loosen', some of their negative thinking about the consequences of stammering.

For people with interiorized stammering, desensitization is the central pillar of the therapy programme and the key to change. It is often vital that people tackle avoidance reduction in a very gradual and highly structured manner, setting goals for themselves to work on as they gradually extend the area in which they can allow themselves to stammer. Introducing goal-setting strategies such as SMART goals (specific, measurable, achievable, relevant/ realistic, time limited; Doran, 1981), hierarchies (Van Riper, 1973) and the concept of increasing comfort zones are valuable here. Ideas and practices from mindfulness work (Kabat-Zinn, 1996; Cheasman, Chapter 7 in this book) and acceptance and commitment therapy (Hayes et al., 1999; Cheasman &

Everard, Chapter 8 in this book) are also included to support what can be a hugely challenging process for people. Mindfulness-based approaches help to cultivate openness and acceptance of difficult experience. ACT focuses explicitly on encouraging a willingness to experience uncomfortable emotions in the service of moving in valued directions. For example, one student on a recent interiorized stammering course commented on how he had avoided attending his children's parents' evening as he was anxious about school staff becoming aware of his stammering. However, he identified that one of his key values was to be a good parent and therefore recognized that avoiding such meetings was not in the best interests of his children. He realized that it was important for him to be willing to experience this anxiety and to go ahead with attending such events.

'Coming out' as a person who stammers

For many in these groups stammering is a secret, often a secret coloured with shame. In his levels of avoidance model, Sheehan describes role avoidance. The vast majority of PWS can speak fluently some of the time, so as well as having a stammering 'role' they also have a fluent 'role'. Avoidance at the role level takes place when someone is, for whatever reason, going to stammer and they do not want to let this happen; they do not want to be this person who stammers so they choose to avoid it in some way. It is the most fundamental and deep-seated of all of the levels of avoidance and it drives many of the other avoidance-based coping strategies. Role level avoidance taps into profound issues of identity, and whilst it is a conflict for many PWS, it is particularly central to the dilemma facing those with interiorized stammering. People with more overt stammering may not want to be someone who stammers, but from the outside it is more readily apparent that they do. Those with interiorized stammering can 'play' the 'avoidance at the role level' game and apparently get away with it. They may avoid a word, say a bit less, not make a phone call and because they have such high levels of fluency the fact that they stammer is not seen or heard. This is a seductive game with a big pay-off but one which comes at a personal cost.

One activity on the course is called 'avoidance: the pay-offs and the prices'. Avoidance is described as a choice and clients are asked to list as many pay-offs and prices as they can think of that link to making this choice. They are then given a diagram depicting the central part of a set of scales and are asked to draw in how the scales would sit. Are the pay-offs or prices higher (see Figure 4.2)?

Pay-offs
- Stammering is kept hidden
- Appear fluent
- Easier (less effort)
- In some way, makes you feel in control of your stammer
- Avoid embarrassment
- Peace of mind (short-term)
- Short-term solution
- People don't know that I stammer
- Avoid being judged as a stammerer
- Keep problem hidden so don't have to deal with it
- It's a quick fix
- Feel normal

Prices
- You can't say the words you want to say
- Not get your meaning/point across
- Hard to explain a simple thing
- Miss out on interactions
- Inability to contribute effectively
- Didn't date
- Impact negatively at work
- Failed interviews
- I don't make myself understood
- You stop making sense
- You aren't being honest with yourself
- You'll never fully accept your stammer
- Become shy/reclusive
- You can't be yourself
- Not at ease with yourself
- Miss out on communication
- Miss out on situations – social
- Don't take part in conversations
- Harder to get things done
- Sense of failure
- Missing opportunities
- Not empowering
- Not starting to solve problem – doing something about it
- Perception of me (shy/nervous/lacking confidence)
- Adds to the frustration
- Increases fear for next time
- Might appear like you don't know what you're talking about

Figure 4.2 Avoidance as a way of coping – the pay-offs and prices.

This is not just a numbers game – there may be more pay-offs than prices listed, but the cost of the prices might be seen as higher...or not. It is often when the prices of avoidance are experienced as outweighing the pay-offs that people come along to therapy in the first place. After this activity clients regularly conclude that the pay-offs, whilst powerful and frequently numerous, are generally short-term, whereas the costs have long-term impacts.

For many with interiorized stammering the world at large and sometimes even their closest friends and family do not know that they stammer. It is for this reason that 'coming out' as someone who stammers is a defining part of the change process in a way that is different to those who stammer more openly. The extent to which someone can do this is likely to have a major impact on how liberating therapy will be for them. Desensitization strategies, whether behavioural, cognitive or mindfulness-based, will support this process. For many, starting to tell people in their lives that they stammer is key. Often the fact that someone is going to a stammering therapy group is kept secret and so for some letting others know where they go to on a particular evening is part of 'coming out'. A challenge for clients with interiorized stammering is that when they do find the courage to start telling others about it they are often met with responses like 'Oh, I do that too', or 'You don't really stammer'. This is a useful illustration of what would be described as an attitudinal barrier according to the social model (Thomas, 2004). One client comments:

> "At various times through my life I have tried to discuss my stammer with friends and family. This has almost always been a frustrating experience on both sides: it has been extremely difficult for my friends and family to understand that there is a problem or to understand even superficially the nature of the problem. This is not for want of trying on their part. Perhaps I have not been able to describe the problem in terms that make sense to someone who does not stammer."

Whilst it might be helpful for the person who stammers to hear that others do not consider it to be a problem, it is often invalidating for them to feel that their very real difficulty is not being understood or appreciated. It is clear that the group aspect of the therapy is of immense importance in counterbalancing such responses. As previously described, people with interiorized stammering can find it hard to identify with those who stammer more overtly. They equally do not feel they fit with the majority group, fluent speakers. When people join an interiorized group they can recognize, often for the first time, that there are other people like them and this ability to identify with others can provide the foundation on which increased openness and 'coming out' will be based.

A few weeks into the desensitization phase, we invite a client from a previous course to come and talk to the group about their experiences. Participants are often inspired and encouraged to hear someone who has been through the whole process talk about what it has been like for them. Our experience has shown this to be a good time for clients to hear about the lived experience of someone who has already engaged with the challenges of the therapy. By now, participants have generally started to open up to the philosophy of the therapy and are more receptive to hearing that, whilst the programme can be enormously liberating, it is not about 'cure' or not stammering. Below is an extract from a client's email to the visitor:

> "Just wanted to let you know how much your visit helped
> me and that I really appreciate you coming to see us all.
> Almost everything you said had so many familiarities to the
> experiences I've had, and although much of your talk was
> the type of thing I hear each week from the group, I found
> it inspirational. Perhaps it was hearing how you have coped
> after the course finished that helped so much? Maybe it was
> hearing how your sensitivity to your stammer has changed
> and how your life has changed as a whole? I thought it was
> an excellent talk – very open and honest."

Voluntary stammering

It might seem that voluntary stammering (Sheehan, 1970) would be an ideal tool for those for whom 'coming out' as someone who stammers is a therapy objective. In many ways it is, but our experience tells us that, whilst people might use it easily in the therapy room, it is far more challenging in the outside world where they are often still trying not to be someone who stammers. Many do not actually ever use it in outside situations but it can be powerful for those who do. Here is a comment from someone writing immediately after the voluntary stammering session:

> "The day after the first session on voluntary stammering
> I woke up at five in the morning as the prospect of doing

> something I had literally spent my whole life avoiding was
> a little bit overbearing for me. Nevertheless, I plucked up
> the courage to tell one of the people at work about the task
> I planned to carry out. They were supportive and helped
> me set a goal of voluntarily stammering three times with
> her that day. I laughed uncomfortably the first time as it
> felt weird. Once the novelty wore off I stammered more
> frequently in front of her and it wasn't bad at all! The
> experience gave me the courage to stammer voluntarily
> over the phone with some clients I didn't know. These
> are the first steps for me and I still can't fully let go with
> clients I do know."

This affirms the value of developing skills in using SMART goals and hierarchies to help start to tackle something which is very fearful.

End-of-term review

At the end of Term 1, usually after 12 or 13 sessions, participants are asked to identify their key learning and key challenges. People are just starting to scratch the surface of working with the covert issues and it is instructive to read some of their comments.

> "Key learning is that stammering is part of me and I can live
> with that – I am not trying to be perfect all the time and I
> am not thinking that everything has a solution or needs to
> be eliminated. I still dread moments like, e.g. the round of
> introductions at meetings, but not hours/days in advance
> like I used to and when it comes I am less worried about
> the consequences of not being able to introduce myself.
> The challenge is being open about it."

This illustrates what many people experience at this stage of therapy: a growing acceptance of stammering accompanied by less anxiety about speaking situations on the one hand, and on the other hand, a reluctance to be more open about stammering.

> "Key learning is that assumptions can be challenged quite
> successfully. The challenge is the process of internalizing

the new mindset and keeping in mind that I am going to face ups and downs."

Here someone acknowledges the importance of challenging assumptions and beliefs but also recognizes that to do this in practice takes time and will not always be easy.

"It is not as bad as I thought in my mind – seeing the video helped and telling people I am coming to speech therapy has challenged some of my perceptions. Voluntary stammering is a key challenge because I have tried to hide it for so long."

These comments confirm both the value of overt identification and the challenge of using voluntary stammering for this client group.

"Fear faced head on almost always reduces. Avoidance almost always makes things worse. The therapy so far has freed up my thoughts so I can think about other things. The challenges for me are letting go of the goal of trying to be perfect – the mindset of 'if something isn't right I need to fix it'. Voluntary stammering is one of my biggest challenges."

This person has realized the detrimental effects of using avoidance in the long term and the importance of facing their fears, whilst recognizing their perfectionist tendencies. Once again voluntary stammering is cited as a major challenge.

"The key learning is that stammering is a part of me and I need to not dislike that part of me so actively. When I was 14 a friend said, 'It's just a part of you' and I was very upset. I now see I need to embrace that part more. This for me is also the biggest challenge."

Here is someone saying they understand the theory, they know what will help, but it is very difficult to put it into practice.

"The key learning is that the covert part is the magnitude of the problem – the iceberg was very powerful and helpful – I had never thought that was the main issue till now. Working with negative thoughts rather than being overwhelmed by them has helped. The challenge for me is working on things between sessions."

This last point highlights what is often a challenge for people – taking the learning from the therapy room into their lives outside.

Course break

The three-week break between the two terms often throws up challenges for participants in relation to keeping the work going. We help participants to set up a 'buddy system' so they have someone to contact during the break. Despite this, and despite spending time during the first term setting goals, many find they do little active work on their speech during the break. However, this is all useful learning for when the course comes to an end. We spend time helping people to reflect on what it was like without the weekly support of the group and our hope is that this discussion helps them start to anticipate what some of the issues might be when the course ends.

Desensitization review

A review of desensitization is carried out in Week 16. Participants are asked to reflect on what has changed so far, what has helped this change, what has been harder to change and how they plan to continue the work. Here are some of their comments:

> "The main change so far has been in my attitude – I am getting curious about it – as a result I am more willing to put myself in situations where I might stammer and see what happens. I also don't let circumstances dictate the pace of my speech. I feel I need to talk about it more and carry on experimenting."

These comments pick up on an the attitudinal stance of curiosity and experimentation that we encourage throughout the therapy process.

> "Progress has been steady, but not so rapid that I can say it's because of this or that. I would have been more nervous about things at the start of the course. The fear has lessened.

> There are important differences in the way I approach speaking in general – with less anxiety and anticipatory fear. Having a better understanding of the challenges, talking to others and challenging assumptions has helped reduce the fear. I need to put myself out there more and make more time for it."

The work on desensitization has clearly been useful and has led to a reduction in fear. Cognitive therapy aspects are identified as contributing to this process.

> "Change is more to do with how I feel – I used to hate stammering so much. Now I feel I do not want to carry on torturing myself – I just accept it. Sharing has helped and working with NATs. I still feel it's so hard to talk about it at work."

The depth of negative feeling that someone with interiorized stammering can experience is vividly described here. Again cognitive therapy has been helpful alongside being in a group.

> "I have greater self-awareness and am more confident – my thinking now is that I might stammer and if I do I'll get back on the horse. My negative thinking has reduced. I need to push the boundaries out a bit more. I am edging up to it more and more now and am thinking I might just do some of these scary things now."

This is a clear illustration of working with extending comfort zones.

> "I am still not telling people that I stammer but I am not feeling so bad if I do stammer. I feel I need to work on it more –I'm not trying to hide it in the same way."

For some people the opposite is true at this stage in that they have started to let some others know that they stammer but they still find it very hard to actually do it.

> "Since self-advertising I feel I am stammering more. I think in my own mind if I tell someone I stammer then I won't do it."

This is interesting and illustrates how when people start using desensitization strategies to support a 'trying not to stammer' agenda things can backfire. The paradox of stammering is that people may do it less when they truly open to the possibility of letting it be.

> "An area I am stuck with is not being self-aware when I block – I tend to go into a state where everything blurs. A key change though is that overall I don't care so much. I feel I need to work more on my negative thinking."

The opening comment here indicates that this person is probably still very emotionally reactive to stammering and is likely to need to become more desensitized if they are to make productive use of modification techniques when the time comes. Another possibility is that having some success with modification later on might reduce the reactivity.

> "Self-advertising has been the key for me – especially during phone calls and doing the survey [the group go outside one evening and conduct a survey with the general public on attitudes to stammering]. This really got to my assumptions that people would be critical and has helped me to accept myself more. I never thought I could make a phone call and say, 'Can you bear with me as I have a stammer'. I thought the worst and it wasn't like that at all – people were friendly. I don't mind so much that I stammer now."

This last phrase encapsulates what we would see as a helpful outcome of therapy. It is not that he is no longer bothered at all by stammering, but that he does not mind as much.

Modification

The programme moves on to the modification stage at Week 17. This is not because the desensitization process is complete, as this is likely to be on-going work for most participants, but strategies to help modify moments of stammering need to be introduced, with enough time to offer practice opportunities prior to the end of the course. Cancellation (post-block modification), pull-outs (in-block modification) and pre-sets (pre-block modification) are taught as described by Van Riper (1973), but another adaptation for this group of clients is that the sequencing of therapy is changed.

Traditionally, cancellation is taught first followed by pull-outs and pre-sets. However, because participants are still likely to be sensitive to the experience of overt stammering we consider they are unlikely to use cancellation in everyday life. Our experience leads us to believe that only the clients who are most willing to stammer openly with low reaction are likely to implement cancellation out of the therapy room. It carries penalties and can in itself be seen as a desensitization tool as it involves open acknowledgement of having stammered. On the interiorized programme we teach pull-outs first and then follow this up with cancellation and finally pre-sets.

As with all of our modification programmes we encourage people not to view pull-outs as a 'control' strategy. We believe that stammering is most successfully modified when the client can 'let themself stammer' and work with this in an 'allowing' as opposed to 'trying to control' manner. The control agenda can be most unhelpful in stammering therapy and many of the core and secondary behaviours have come about as unsuccessful attempts to try to control. We also approach the introduction of pre-sets with caution. If pre-sets are implemented successfully there may be very little apparent stammering. This has clear benefits, but the danger is that people can quickly get hooked back into trying not to allow stammering to show on the outside. This may be particularly unhelpful for those with interiorized stammering, where the pattern of keeping dysfluency as covert as possible has been strong. Too much focus on using pre-sets can lead to greater avoidance again.

Although at the start of therapy clients can be impatient to be taught modification strategies, it is interesting to note that by the time we come to introduce them many are recognizing that they are not going to be the most important aspect to focus on once the course has ended.

Ending

In the closing sessions of the course we devote considerable time to looking to the future. We know that the weekly group support has been an important part of the change process, and we encourage groups to think about how they can keep support going. We also know that people are often just starting the 'coming out' process and, despite having had 50 hours of therapy on the programme, we highly recommend that they continue with some form of formal follow-up therapy. Interiorized groups often form particularly strong bonds and they frequently continue to meet up in some less formal way after the course has ended. Some people join dedicated internet groups. This probably reflects some of the previously mentioned identity issues. High levels of fluency and the ability to 'pass' as a fluent speaker mean that participants can be seduced back into the avoidance game. Having ongoing ways of connecting with others who are dealing with the same dilemmas is often key to maintaining and developing change. Making use of technology through email, social networking sites and internet forums can greatly facilitate this process.

End-of-course reflections

At the end of the course, participants are asked to reflect on their learning and here are some of their comments which we think illustrate some of the key outcomes. A unifying theme is how expectations, assumptions and predictions are often challenged and changed through the therapy process.

> "I realize I can be open and stammering is not something that can be cured. I accept it is part of me for the rest of my life. Acceptance is key. I wouldn't have imagined that I would let people know I stammer, but I have told some. I feel I am still in the phase of desensitization."

> "I realize it's not as bad as I thought – this is through desensitization and through telling people who hadn't noticed."

> "Non-avoidance is the key – it has helped a lot. When I arrived I was expecting to learn a technique to make me fluent. When I found it wasn't going to be like that I thought, 'Oh crap'!"

> "Recognizing how I react and perceive things has been key for me – all the work on thoughts and NATs. People's perceptions are not what I thought they were. Telling people and not getting much reaction has been helpful. I now think that what I say is more important than how I say it."

Client contributions

These three reflections on the experience of therapy illustrate the individual nature of each person's journey.

Amanda Almeida – her story

Life before therapy

I believe my stammer started when I was about eight years old. Around this time I had a best friend called Adele and I suddenly found it hard to say her name. My mother wasn't pleased about my stammering and I was put to the test by my next-door neighbour and my mother one day when playing in the garden. My neighbour called me over and asked me the name of my best friend. I stood there in silence. I didn't try to say the name 'Adele'. My neighbour laughed and said, "Fancy forgetting your friend's name." I felt really stupid, but carried on avoiding words I felt I couldn't say.

Of course, over time this avoidance builds and builds until there is a great sense of fear with saying certain words, my name being one of them. I spoke to no-one about my stammer and felt that I must be the only person with this problem.

I went through school, college, marriage, babies not telling anyone about my stammer. Through the British Stammering Association I found out about stammering therapy in my area which helped me tremendously. The therapist told me about City Lit.

The City Lit course

When I read about the interiorized stammering course I was immediately attracted to it for the following reasons:

- I was fed up living with my stammer for the last 40 years and believed there must be a better way of communicating. I wanted 'free' communication – to say what I wanted to say and when I wanted to say it.

- I didn't want to live another 40 years (hopefully) being ashamed of my stammer and hiding it, avoiding words/situations/planning ahead, etc. ...It becomes exhausting.

- I read a past student's comments about the course and identified myself with everything – I couldn't wait to get started.

- I hoped the interiorized stammering course would give me a freedom of speech I hadn't had before. My hope was I would become completely desensitized to stammering and be able to tell everyone and openly stammer. I was afraid of starting the course – the name thing – the introductions – the journey to London – asking for a ticket – maybe asking strangers the way if I got lost. It was outside my safety zone.

The main part of the course was the desensitization. I was lucky in the fact that 'The King's Speech' was released whilst doing this part of the course. I went to see the film with my husband and younger daughter (who was 18) and it enabled me to talk to them in some depth (for the first time) about my stammer and speech. My elder daughter gave me a lot of support and encouragement and was always interested in how I was doing on the course. I spoke to her in great depth about my stammering. I was able to tell my two sisters about my stammer – the elder one remembering I had a stammer when I was little and my younger sister who seemed surprised about my stammer. I kept it that well hidden!! I also spoke to my father about my stammer (again for the first time) and to my disappointment, he didn't seem to know about my struggle with my speech. Again, I suppose that shows how well I hid it. I'm sad that I never had the opportunity to discuss my speech with my mother. I think this is another reason for doing the course – I didn't want to continue with my life the way it was. I began to think that I could pass on and nobody would ever have known about my battle with my speech.

The other part of the course dealt with the techniques to get us through a stammering moment. The techniques are useful – pre-block, in-block and post-block, but for me the best way forward is to be open and tell people about my stammer – then the fear is gone. This seems so easy now, but before the course it was so hard to do.

Facing up to my stammer and becoming desensitized was the hardest part of the course and the most challenging. Having my daughter come to one of the sessions with me speaking about my stammer was very difficult. I hadn't imagined it would ever be that hard. It was years and years of hiding and avoidance coming out.

Where I am now

The course has made me a stronger person and I want to go and reach out for new opportunities. I have become a volunteer for Thrive (a charity that uses gardening to help change the lives of disabled people) and I am about to start on a training programme to gain an award in Social and Therapeutic Horticulture. My goal is to become a horticultural therapist. This is all something I would never have done before attending the course – it would have been too challenging and not safe enough.

The course lived up to my expectations because it has enabled me to make so many changes. I've stopped planning and worrying days/weeks ahead of an event/appointment. Thinking about it now, I don't notice the negative thoughts I used to pay so much attention to. The course teaches you about negative thoughts and feelings in the desensitization programme. I have stopped planning in my head – I live life as it comes. I can do this because I'm not afraid of my speech.

Amanda's story describes the sense of isolation that someone with interiorized stammering can feel. For her, stammering had been a secret shared with no-one. The exhaustion of trying to keep it hidden comes across and her account is an example of how people often seek out therapy when the costs of avoidance finally become too high. She identifies desensitization as the key part of the programme for her and concludes by illustrating how therapy had freed her up to take on new challenges in life.

John Whitamore – his story

Introduction

I started stuttering when I was about eight or nine years old. I didn't consider having speech therapy, even when it was offered to me at school. My stammer was my problem, for me to deal with. Something that I wasn't proud of and that I didn't want to discuss. Anyway, I had it completely under control. Nobody could tell that I stammered.

I had tricks to conceal my stammer. For example, I would force words out by speaking more loudly or slide them out by speaking more softly. But the tricks weren't entirely successful. The effort of trying to say something would make my face tense, making me look inexplicably angry. Or I would talk so fast that I just gabbled. Sometimes I wouldn't speak even when I should have. Or I would talk too much, to keep the words coming so that they wouldn't get stuck.

The effort of controlling my speech consciously, meticulously, continuously took enormous amounts of energy. I would feel myself becoming exhausted, making me even more 'stammery'.

Stammering therapy

I was 44 when I started having therapy. For some years the balance between my tricks and my speech had been wavering. I could feel myself becoming more jittery and less confident. In conversations I would find myself exhausted, shaking, struggling to speak. But, nonetheless, still speaking, despite the cost. Still speaking so that no-one would know about my stammer.

I tried to explain it occasionally, to friends and family. But I didn't explain it very well. Even those closest to me found it frustrating and difficult to understand. I could speak perfectly well. Better than most people, even. What was the problem?

In my 40s, as I became more bothered by my stammering, I slowly began to realize that I should do something about it. I signed up for the interiorized stammering course, but my hopes were low. I didn't feel that I needed therapy: isn't that for people with psychological problems? And if I was going to have therapy, I didn't want to have it with a group of strangers.

On the first evening of the course, I sat in a room and listened to that group of strangers talk about their experiences of interiorized stammering. Every word that was spoken described something that I had felt, something that I had struggled with. I could see other people having the same reaction: heads were nodding, eye contact was being made, smiles were emerging. I think everybody went home happier that evening.

Identification and desensitization

The first two parts of the course, identification and desensitization, were, for me, the most important.

I have an interiorized stammer. This means that, although I am continuously aware of my stammer inside me, it is rarely heard in my speech. The difficulty is insidious and subtle: the first step is to identify clearly what it is.

I have never wanted to admit to my stammer or to let it out publicly. A mixture of pride, shame and fear has made me suppress it. We learned that people with interiorized stammering are characterized as having strong negative emotions around their stammers. These negative emotions cause us to avoid stammering by substituting words and by staying away from circumstances in which speech is required. I had my tricks and I could see that they were, indeed, avoidance.

I thought a great deal about this. I have never felt myself to be a coward. But I realized that I needed to be courageous and to face my fears of stammering publicly. It was, for me, a moment of great revelation. I could see that I was going to need to learn to stammer openly, in front of anyone. I am not exaggerating when I say that this was terrifying.

Clearly I needed to toughen up. I had to learn not to care if I stammered. I had to develop the courage to stand in front of somebody and have my words r-r-repeat or perhaps not come out at all. I needed to desensitize.

We were sent out in pairs to do a survey about attitudes towards stammering. On a cold winter's night we went and accosted Londoners. 'P-please will you help with our s-survey about s-s-stammering?' Everybody helped. Everybody was nice. Nobody walked away, or mocked us or gave stupid answers. People were thoughtful and generous and seemed not to care at all if anyone stammered.

We were to practise letting our stammers out in public. At first to close friends and family and then to a wider circle. This has caused a few raised eyebrows. People who have known me all my life suddenly find me stammering. For them and for me a strange experience. And yet people have been very accepting. I struggle to think of a single adverse reaction.

Life continues

I now feel much more confident about stammering out loud. My use of avoidance techniques is greatly reduced; my speech and face are more relaxed; I gesticulate less. I believe that I am slightly less fluent than when I started the course, but a better communicator.

I am still toughening up. I continue to stammer out loud in order to make sure that I really am desensitized to it. There was a third part to our course, modification, which taught us how to modify our speech so as to reduce the effects of our stammering. I have deliberately held back on this to make sure that it doesn't turn into a subtle form of avoidance. I really want to make sure that I am completely comfortable with my stammer before I start modifying my speech.

It is difficult sometimes. I am trying to get used to stammering in business meetings or with people whom I have only just met. I am learning neither to apologize for my stammer nor to be defiant about it. These things come slowly. But it's definitely for the better.

John gives a vivid description of the exhausting effects of trying to keep stammering totally hidden. He goes on to talk about how hard it was for others to understand the nature of interiorized stammering when he did find the courage to 'come out'. Whilst he talks about it being 'strange' both for him and for others who know him to hear him stammering openly, he also says that others have been accepting. Most of our clients report that when they do start to stammer openly they realize it is much less of a 'big deal' for others than it has been for them. Finding his courage is a theme in the story as he makes the decision to start to reduce his avoidance strategies. As with Amanda, John identifies desensitization as the most important aspect of the therapy and we find this to be the case for most people with interiorized stammering.

Laurent Pariat – his story

Why speech therapy now?

I have been stammering ever since my teenage years, mostly in circumstances where I feel particularly emotional, whether it is because of the occasion or the people in front of me. I do like talking, however, and I often feel like my stammering is stopping me from expressing myself when I really want to, and from saying what I want.

The occasional stutter when ordering in a restaurant was annoying, but not something that would stop me from going out. However, the fear and stress that preceded having to introduce myself to an audience, as well as the pain after any instance of stammering were becoming increasingly difficult to bear.

Both myself and my partner sensed that I was being held back by my stammering. She suggested that it was something I might want to address, so I would feel better about myself. The thought had only ever crossed my mind, but I had always dismissed it as I imagined one-on-one sessions with a therapist, which I couldn't imagine helping in any way.

For that reason it was a while before I did my research and came across a group therapy course for covert stammerers. Reading the description convinced me that the course was what I needed, and in some way was the first time I realized that I wasn't alone living with a stammer that only manifests itself intermittently.

Early days of therapy

Expectations at the start of the course were as much about the other people there and how I would fit in the group as they were about the course itself and how it would help me cure my stammer.

From the first session it was obvious that the people there were all in a similar position – mostly very fluent and outgoing people, who for some reason all stammer with more or less frequency in situations which they've all come to dread.

It took a few more sessions to realize that stammering therapy does not pretend to 'cure' stammering (in the medical sense of the term) for good. And while techniques are available to help manage the stammering in everyday life, the main point is about learning to live with one's stammer and not letting it get in the way of day-to-day communication.

The most helpful aspect of therapy was the quick realization that my stammer wasn't going to go away, but instead that I had to accept it as part of me, and that it was down to me to work on it and around it.

Challenges, turning-points, changes and on-going issues

The most challenging aspect of therapy was disclosing my stammer, either through self-advertising or voluntary stammering. Like most people with a covert stammer, I have spent years hiding my stammer and denying its existence. Therefore, the idea of deliberately stammering or stating my condition to others are concepts that were completely alien to me, and which I wouldn't have dreamt of doing only a year ago.

One of the first turning points during the course was when a previous student came to share his experience of doing the same course a couple of years before us. His account of how he had learned to live with his stammer, particularly in his professional life, was enlightening. But more than anything else it was his ability to stammer freely and keep eye contact with an audience of complete strangers which caught everyone's imagination.

From a personal point of view, the main turning point for me was going to a meeting knowing that I would have to take my turn saying my name and my company's name and not feeling anxious about it, having accepted that I might stammer while doing so. From that moment I became curious about the mechanics of stammering and less afraid about when it might occur.

The main change for me is that I seem to take a more positive attitude towards my stammer, and I am more willing to tackle it head on rather than hide. For example, while I still dread going to work meetings and having to introduce myself, I'm also less inclined to come up with plans to avoid those situations. Every time the thought of not turning up to a meeting or arriving late crosses my mind, I now have strategies in place to help overcome the fear and the stress that arise in the hours or even days before the event that I dread. Simply, I remind myself that I have to be in control of my speech rate, and not have it imposed on me by other people or the circumstances. More importantly, I remind myself that I may eventually stammer and that it's not the end of the world.

Also, I find I am more comfortable in social situations and more at ease talking to a group as a whole, and less often taken by surprise when someone asks me to repeat something I've just said.

In many ways I feel I'm still not entirely willing to accept myself as a stammerer. I still see myself as mostly fluent and put all my effort in getting more fluent rather than 'embracing' my stammering self, and part of that effort consists in getting better at dealing with instances of stammering and managing my blocks.

The power of the group

Working as a group was one of the key aspects of therapy, as everyone was given the opportunity to share their experience and benefit from that of other participants in the group. This I think is particularly important for covert stammerers, and it was clear that most of us rarely had the opportunity to talk about our stammer before, or meet other people with similar experience. As a result, a sense of trust very quickly developed within the group and every single person was able to share their feelings and experience without fear of being judged.

In his account, Laurent starts off by stating how important it was to realize that there was help for someone like him. Again, there is the underlying theme of having felt like he was the only one. He describes the challenges involved in becoming more open, and his story shows that, whilst someone can have the early insight that acceptance is going to be fundamental to change, for people with interiorized stammering who can 'pass' as fluent, this work on openness and acceptance is often an ongoing process. Laurent writes about the power of the group and he identifies having had the opportunity to hear a previous client's story as a turning point in the therapy (see p.46 and p.72, Chapter 2). Interestingly, he also describes how becoming 'curious' about stammering helped him to work with his fear. Encouraging clients to be curious about their experience can be an important step in them confronting issues they have held at arm's length.

These stories are unique to the people they belong to. There are differences, but there are also powerful similarities that echo many of the other stories we have heard since offering this programme.

Analysis of assessment data

To complement the powerful accounts above, we are including data from assessments completed by nine clients who attended an interiorized stammering group in 2010/11. The assessments were the S24-scale (Andrews & Cutler, 1974) and the Wright and Ayre Stuttering Self-Rating Profile (WASSP, Wright & Ayre, 2000). The S24-scale is a measure of a person's attitude towards their communication skills, with a high score denoting greater negativity and a low score denoting greater positivity. The WASSP records how a PWS perceives his or her stammering at any one point in time, using five internally reliable sub-scales (behaviours, thoughts, feelings about stuttering, avoidance due to stuttering and disadvantage due to stuttering). The clients completed both assessments at three different time intervals:

Time 1: at the beginning of the course

Time 2: three months later at the end of the course

Time 3: six months after the end of the course.

A repeated measures ANOVA was conducted to compare the outcome measures scores between time points. The effect size was determined using partial eta squared. Results show significant differences across all measures between Times 1 and 2 and Times 1 and 3 with moderate to large effect sizes (Table 4.1).

Table 4.1 Descriptive statistics at the beginning of course, end of course and six months after end of course, (N=9).

Measure	Time 1		Time 2		Time 3		F value	P value	Partial eta^2
	Mean	SD	Mean	SD	Mean	SD			
S24	17.44	4.30	11.78	5.70	11.56	6.13	7.83	.004	.49
WASSP - behaviour	31.89	7.42	23.67	6.44	22.89	9.53	6.07	.011	.43
WASSP - thoughts	13.89	2.62	7.33	2.83	8.44	3.91	9.97	.002	.55
WASSP - feelings	25.33	6.40	11.89	4.70	12.67	6.26	23.44	<.001	.75
WASSP - avoidance	17.56	3.17	9.67	2.96	10.89	5.55	14.30	<.001	.64
WASSP - disadvantage	15.11	3.22	8.11	3.33	8.89	4.37	15.78	<.001	.66

These results show that, as a group, these nine clients had a significantly more positive attitude towards their communication at the end of the course, and that this change was maintained six months later. Similarly, they experienced different aspects of their stammering (behaviours, thoughts, feelings, avoidance of stammering and disadvantage due to stammering) as significantly improved.

A measure of percentage syllables stammered was not used. The rationale for this is that this client group come to therapy with high levels of fluency and therefore we do not consider a measure of overt stammering to be a relevant marker of change.

Closing remarks

The literature review illustrates how little has been written on interiorized stammering and we hope that this chapter will help this area of work to be more widely recognized and engaged with. We find that therapists on training courses are often particularly apprehensive about working with covert stammering. Our experience is that therapy with these clients can be deeply rewarding as they often make and maintain significant changes. For many, it is the first time they have sought out therapy and they bring a level of maturity and motivation that can greatly assist the therapy process. It is notable that the three clients who write above are in their 30s or 40s. It is clear that, for many, the group aspect of the programme is of vital importance and we are aware that many therapists will be unable to gather enough people to form such groups. It may, however, be possible to bring together two or three clients who are generally seen individually to meet occasionally to share experiences and recognize that there are other 'people like me'. It is also the case that advertising therapy for this specific group leads people to realize that there is therapy on offer for their particular type of stammering. Our clients often say that until they read about our programme they had no idea that help was available.

We hope that the stories and comments above illustrate what is central to the approach. It is rare for people to say that speech techniques are the most important aspects. Gradual shifts in openness and acceptance are identified as key. In his story, John talks about 'having to learn not to care'. Our sense is that what is generally most helpful for clients is starting to care less about stammering and to move forward in their lives, whilst allowing themselves to be people who stammer. This can be a truly liberating experience and resonates for us personally.

We would like to thank Amanda, John and Laurent for collaborating with us on this chapter and Steve Davis for his help with analysing data.

References

Andrews, G. & Cutler, J. (1974) S-24 Scale – Stuttering therapy: The relations between changes in symptom levels and attitudes. *Journal of Speech and Hearing Disorders, 39,* 312–319.

Andrews, G. & Harris, M. (1964) *The Syndrome of Stuttering.* Clinics in Developmental Med., No. 17. London: Spastics Society Medical Education and Information Unit in association with W. Heinemann Medical Books.

Beck, J.S. (1995) *Cognitive Therapy: Basics and beyond.* London: Guilford Press.

Doran, G.T. (1981) There's a S.M.A.R.T. way to write management's goals and objectives. *Management Review, 70*(11), 35–36.

Douglas, E. & Quarrington, B. (1952) The differentiation of interiorized and exteriorized secondary stuttering. *Journal of Speech and Hearing Disorders, 17*, 377–385.

French, S. (1994) Dimensions of disability and impairment. In: S. French (Ed.) *On Equal Terms: Working with disabled people*. London: Butterworth-Heinemann, pp.17–34.

Greenberger, D. & Padesky, C. (1995) *Mind over Mood: A cognitive therapy treatment manual for clients*. New York: Guilford Press.

Hayes, S.C., Strosahl, K.D., & Wilson, K.G. (1999) *Acceptance and Commitment Therapy: An experiential approach to behavior change*. New York: Guilford Press.

Hood, S. & Roach, C. (2001) I've got a secret – and it's scaring me to death (the story of a covert stutterer). Available at: http:www.mankato.msus.edu/dept/comdis/isad4/papers/hood.html

Kabat-Zinn, J. (1996) *Full Catastrophe Living*. London: Piatkus.

Kelman, E. & Nicholas, A. (2008) *Practical Intervention for Early Childhood Stammering*. Milton Keynes: Speechmark.

Kroll, A. (1978) The differentiation of stutterers into interiorized and exteriorized groups. *I.A.L.P. Proceedings Copenhagen 1977*, Specialpaedagogisk forlag, pp.137–157.

Levy, C. (1987) Interiorised stuttering: A group therapy approach. In: C. Levy (Ed.) *Stuttering Therapies: Practical approaches*. London: Crook Helm.

Pound, C., Parr, S., Lindsay, J., & Woolf, C. (2000) *Beyond Aphasia: Therapies for living with communication disability*. Milton Keynes: Speechmark.

Sheehan, J. (1970) *Stuttering: Research and Therapy*. New York: Harper & Row.

Simmons-Mackie, N. & Elman, R.J. (2011) Negotiation of identity in group therapy for people with aphasia: The aphasia café. *International Journal of Language and Communication Disorders, 46*(3), 313–323.

Rotter, J.B. (1966) Generalized expectancies for internal versus external control of reinforcement. *Psychological Monographs, 80* (1, Whole No. 609).

Ssikorsky, J.A. (1891) *Uber das Stottern*. August Hirschwald.

Thomas, C. (2004) Developing the social relational in the social model of disability: A theoretical agenda. In: C. Barnes & G. Mercer (Eds) *Implementing the Social Model of Disability: Theory and research*. The Disability Archive UK website www.leeds.ac.uk/disability-studies/archiveuk/

Tuckman, Bruce W. (1965) Developmental sequence in small groups. *Psychological Bulletin, 63*, 384–399.

Van Riper, C. (1973) *The Treatment of Stuttering*. Englewood Cliffs, NJ: Prentice Hall.

Wright, L. & Ayre, A. (2000) *Wright and Ayre Stuttering Self-Rating Profile*. Bicester, Oxon: Winslow Press Ltd.

5 Stammering therapy

An integrated approach

Rachel Everard

This chapter is dedicated to Catherine Montgomery, whose intelligence, warmth, generosity of spirit and charisma inspired people who stammer and clinicians alike.

Introduction

As practising clinicians working in the 21st century with adults who stammer, we are very fortunate: we have a wide range of different approaches to draw upon when deciding with our clients[1] what type of therapy route to take, best suited to their needs. Without a shadow of a doubt, stammering is highly complex, varies from individual to individual and within an individual and can be resistant to change. It makes most sense, therefore, to work holistically with adults who stammer and, just as there are many different aspects to stammering, there are equally as many therapy approaches: block modification, stammering management, fluency shaping, cognitive behaviour therapy, solution-focused brief therapy, mindfulness meditation – to name but a few (Guitar & McCauley, 2010; this volume, 2013). The ability to integrate these ways of working in such a way as to make sense to and benefit the client requires knowledge, skill and practice.

This chapter aims to describe a fully integrated course for adults who stammer as practised at City Lit, an internationally and nationally recognized centre of excellence in adult stammering therapy based in London, UK. Reflective accounts from people who stammer (PWS) who have experienced

---

1 Throughout this chapter, the term 'clients' is used consistently for ease of reference. We normally prefer the term 'students' or 'learners' in the context of City Lit, a college of adult education where emphasis is placed on the learning experience and people who stammer taking responsibility for their own learning.

the therapy will form a central part of the chapter. Clinician and clients will describe the highlights and challenges of this particular therapy journey.

The integrated approach in context

To set this particular approach in context, I would like to look back briefly at the history of integrating different therapy approaches and also to refer to other integrated ways of working currently being used.

In my opinion, it is clear from Gregory's seminal work *Controversies about Stuttering Therapy* (1979) that back then most clinicians belonged to one of two therapy models. Those who believed that a 'stammer-more-fluently' approach was more helpful focused on identification and desensitization work, with possibly some modification of stammering. Others who believed that a 'speak-more-fluently' approach would yield better results focused on fluency shaping with the expectation that increased fluency would bring about reduced anxiety for the client. However, even then it is interesting that clinicians were experimenting with combining the two approaches and this trend has continued up to the present day when a range of comprehensive stammering therapy programmes is on offer. The current position is neatly summarized by Yairi and Seery (2010):

> "The sharp contrasts between the stuttering management and fluency-shaping approaches have not prevented clinicians from realising potential advantages in combining elements of both into unified eclectic therapy programs. … we hold to the position that a comprehensive approach that also includes early work on facing the stuttering, identification and attending to the emotional aspects increase the likelihood of success in subsequent speech-oriented stages of therapy involving either stuttering modification or fluency management."

(Yairi & Seery, 2010, p.297)

They go on to describe a number of integrated therapies including their own. A programme devised by Yairi is briefly described which balances the cognitive-emotional and speech domains of stuttering and combines work on identification, desensitization, fluency-facilitating strategies and stuttering modification. At this point, Yairi and Seery raise the interesting question on the order of teaching the fluency work and stuttering modification – which should come first? The conclusion is that it ultimately depends on the individual's needs. In Seery's approach to integrated therapy, the fluency shaping and stuttering management techniques are taught concurrently and used according to the client's stammering pattern.

Guitar (2006) offers a highly detailed and accessible description of his own integrated approach with the following rationale:

> "Because the complex patterns of advanced stuttering involve behaviours, emotions, and cognitions, treatment is most effective if it targets all of these areas. These patterns are so deeply etched into the brain that treatment is best if it is intense, long-lasting and provides long-term maintenance. My approach to treatment is a brew blended from many sources. I have tried to integrate these procedures so that clients reduce their negative emotions and avoidances and learn to respond differently, with more fluent speech to old cues that have always triggered stuttering."

(Guitar, 2006, p.392)

He makes explicit the long-term fluency goals for his clients: differentiating between 'spontaneous fluency', 'controlled fluency' and 'acceptable stuttering'. Spontaneous fluency is the fluency of so-called 'normal' speakers where no or little attention is paid to maintaining fluency, but is something that happens naturally. In our experience at City Lit, participants on an intensive course, working for a concentrated period of time on different aspects of their stammering, frequently enjoy an increased amount of spontaneous fluency because of reduced communicative pressure. However, it can be short-lived as once they re-enter their everyday world former fears will naturally re-emerge.

Controlled fluency, by contrast, is characterized by relatively high levels of fluency where the PWS is actively working to produce this level of fluency. Acceptable stuttering is when they have chosen not to implement a fluency technique, but instead are using stammering modification tools as and when stammering occurs. At City Lit, we question the term 'acceptable stuttering' as it suggests that some types of stuttering are to be tolerated more than others, and this does not sit easily with becoming more accepting of stammering overall. Instead, we prefer the term 'easy stuttering or stammering' which indicates reduced levels of tension and reduced struggle behaviours. In this way, we are encouraging PWS to move away from the uncompromising standpoint that 'stammering is bad' and 'fluency is good' (and, therefore, stammering must be eliminated at all costs), and towards a less judgemental view where each individual who stammers chooses how to work on it. Offering PWS alternative ways of viewing stammering and, thereby, changing their way of responding to it relates closely to the social model of disability as described by Harris (2013, Chapter 1 in this book). Harris describes how the social and cultural stigma of stammering can affect a person's sense of self, and then outlines the possibilities for rehabilitation of their self-identity.

Another highly influential, well-researched and documented example of an integrated approach is the Institute for Stuttering Treatment and Research Comprehensive Stuttering Program (Kully, Langevin & Lomheim, 2007). Based on earlier programmes that used prolonged speech to induce fluency, the approach has been refined to integrate elements of fluency work, stuttering management, cognitive behaviour therapy and self-management. The programme begins by teaching participants very slow prolonged speech, with stuttering management introduced at a later stage as rates of speech increase and there is an increased likelihood of stammering occurring. Cognitive behaviour techniques are subsequently taught to help clients use their techniques in public, to reduce avoidance and to deal with residual stuttering.

Manning (2001) has also strongly influenced clinicians in their choice of therapy approach. He describes a therapy approach which usually begins with identification work (looking at both stammering behaviours and the choices PWS make because of their stammering) followed by desensitization, variation and modification. His aim is to help clients to take responsibility for the stammering moment. Fluency shaping follows to further enhance the smoothness of their speech. Manning varies the order at which he presents the various elements of therapy, to best suit his client's needs. He emphasizes that his desired outcome for treatment of adults is not stutter-free speech, but a reduction in the handicap caused by stuttering.

Montgomery's programme at the American Institute for Stuttering in New York is another example of a comprehensive integrated approach, combining not only stuttering modification and fluency shaping, but also inclusion of work on the emotional, physical and cognitive aspects of stuttering (Montgomery, 2006). Interestingly, she initially came from a more fluency shaping school (Webster, 1977) and then came to the realization that, for clients to make long-lasting changes, work on identification and desensitization was all -important; whereas we have made a similar journey but in reverse, coming from a staunchly stammer-more-fluently approach.

The above is not intended to be a comprehensive description of the many integrated programmes available today; instead, it demonstrates the different ways respected clinicians around the world have risen to the challenge of providing therapy which is flexible, relevant and individually tailored to the client's needs

Adult stammering therapy at City Lit and the course

Since the late 1950s, City Lit has offered a wide range of therapy approaches, mirroring to a certain extent worldwide trends. During this time, speak-more-fluently approaches have included syllable timed speech and slow prolonged speech, with stammer-more-fluently work (block modification) remaining a constant. We currently offer a range of 18 courses for adults who stammer, of varying length and content. Five of these courses are categorized as intensive, taking place on consecutive days (10am to 5pm), with the first part of the course (normally two weeks in length) followed by a short break before the final part of the course (normally lasting three to five days). These courses are intended for people new to our particular approach. The focus of this chapter 'Stammering therapy: An integrated approach' is one such intensive course, offered twice a year.

To this day we continue to be strongly influenced by Van Riper (1973) and Sheehan (1975) as their teachings are very much in line with our beliefs. We believe that stammering results from a complex interaction of attitudes, thoughts, feelings and behaviours, with avoidance of stammering being viewed as a key factor in maintaining stammering. In our view, it is therefore essential in therapy to address emotional, attitudinal and avoidance aspects of stammering as well as the speech itself. For the last 20 years, we have remained fiercely loyal to a stammer-more-fluently approach, developing our programme by introducing cognitive behaviour therapy skills, mindfulness meditation and acceptance and commitment therapy as well as by offering a variety of topic-based workshops, important as follow-up therapy.

Against this background, the decision to develop an integrated approach with the introduction of a fluency technique was a momentous one and resulted from a number of reasons:

- Naturally we continually question what we do and are open to new ways of working. Attending presentations by Montgomery (2006) and Kully et al. (2007) at ASHA 2001 clarified how integration could work in practice. Subsequently, we visited the American Institute for Stuttering and spent time with Catherine Montgomery, observing her integrated programme in action. We returned from the USA feeling optimistic about bringing together what we had previously felt to be distinct and opposing approaches.

- Many of our clients express, understandably, a desire for more fluency and although we believe this is possible using stammering management, for some of our clients with more severe stammering this is difficult to achieve. We believed that this group would benefit from more focused fluency work.

- We are very much of the opinion that, as Gregory (1979) suggested, there are different subgroups of people who stammer and, therefore, different approaches are required.

- The success of alternative stammering therapy programmes such as the Starfish Project (see website) and the McGuire programme (2003) demonstrated the appeal of direct fluency work within the stammering population.

Although we were comfortable with the idea of integration *per se*, introducing a fluency technique into our programme raised many questions for us. As mentioned above, we had a strong belief and commitment to stammer-more-fluently approaches and the importance of addressing the psychological aspects of stammering. We were less sure of the underlying neurological arguments, namely the centrality of laryngeal involvement justifying the fluency work (Montgomery, 2006). We also wondered whether integration was truly possible and had concerns about putting too much focus on fluency training. By doing this, we wondered whether PWS would take away the message that stammering is unacceptable and whether they would focus only on the fluency work, to the detriment of the other key aspects of the programme. We also wondered whether we would be colluding with their hopes for a cure, which could then lead to false expectations.

We addressed these concerns to some extent in a small research study, the results of which will be reported later. One on-going issue is the weight given to each element of the therapy and how to integrate the elements in such a way that they complement one another and make sense to the client. This is a theme to which I and the clients will return.

Stammering therapy: An integrated approach

'Stammering therapy: An integrated approach' is a three-week intensive daytime programme (90 therapy hours). Each participant is seen beforehand for an advisory session and their suitability for this approach evaluated. Generally speaking, people with moderate to severe overt stammering, the desire to learn a fluency technique and the ability to work in a group are accepted onto the course. The first two weeks of the course are followed by a break of about a month, after which the participants return for the final third week. The rationale for the break is to give them the opportunity to put what they have learned into practice in their everyday life and then to report back on their experiences. This encourages skills maintenance and transfer to the real world as well as developing self-directed learning.

Our overall aims for people attending the course are: greater knowledge of their own stammering pattern, reduced sensitivity to and increased acceptance of their stammering, and to gain the ability to use a range of skills to manage their stammering, whether that be managing moments of stammering or employing a fluency technique. We also give participants the opportunity to set their own aims at the start of therapy, which they review regularly and adapt as their knowledge of their own stammering and therapy increases.

The intensive nature of the course gives participants a concentrated amount of time to work on their stammering; this is particularly important with regard to the learning of the fluency technique, vocal fold management (VFM), which we believe requires consecutive periods of focused practice.

What follows below is an outline of each week, illustrated with comments from one of our clients. As our therapy model is largely based on Montgomery's integrated approach (Montgomery, 2006), the reader is encouraged to read her detailed description of therapy for a fuller account.

Week 1

Week 1 begins with two self-report assessments, the S24-Scale (Andrews & Cutler, 1974) and the Wright and Ayre Stuttering Self-Rating Profile (Wright & Ayre, 2000), explanation of therapy and eliciting hopes and fears. The first stage of the therapy process, identification, is introduced and participants have the opportunity to see themselves on video, to practise identifying moments of stammering, known as 'tallying' (Montgomery, 2006), and to give and receive feedback on their overt stammering behaviours. Exploration of thoughts and feelings associated with stammering follows, often a powerful experience for the group. Further identification work involves looking at avoidance in a structured way (Sheehan, 1975) which leads naturally onto avoidance reduction work and the setting of individual avoidance reduction aims. Alongside this work, the group is introduced to mindfulness (Cheasman, 2013), as well as key aspects of cognitive behaviour therapy (Beck, 1995). The avoidance reduction work is complemented with other desensitization tools such as self-advertising, voluntary stammering, carrying out a survey and regular videoing throughout the course. Stammering management techniques are introduced during the first week, including prolongations and pull-outs with opportunity to practise in a variety of settings. At the end of the week, the initial stages of learning the fluency technique, vocal fold management (Webster, 1977; Montgomery, 2006), are introduced.

As can be seen, the focus of the first four days is on identification, desensitization and modification, with the fluency technique, vocal fold management (VFM), introduced on the fifth day, before the weekend. This contrasts with other integrated approaches where the fluency technique is taught before any kind of modification (Kully et al., 2007). We believe that desensitization work is of fundamental importance before introducing any kind of stammering management or fluency work. Unless a PWS is starting to view their stammering differently and to respond differently to moments of stammering, it is very unlikely that they are going to be able to make any significant speech changes in the long term. We also believe it is important for people to be given the opportunity to work on developing an easier pattern of speech (described by Guitar (2006) as 'acceptable stuttering') before learning an all-encompassing fluency technique. Modifying individual moments of stammering follows on naturally from the identification work and gives clients practical strategies to use early on in the course.

Andrew's experience of Week 1

What follows are extracts from a personal learning journal written by one of our clients, named Andrew to protect his identity, as he was attending the course, interspersed with therapist reflections.

> "It was good and interesting to thoroughly consider my own stammering behaviours and write them down. Rather daunting to see that there are so many of them to confront. It

was painful to watch my own video, during which I displayed many learned stammering behaviours and demonstrated that I was not communicating effectively. I engaged fully with the suggestions and techniques and took criticism and comments constructively."

Andrew describes vividly here the necessary and difficult process of becoming more aware of stammering behaviours and his willingness to engage fully with this process. In our experience, this commitment to therapy is essential for change.

"Today, I built on yesterday's work by consciously reducing the avoidance behaviours/tricks I have been using to try to conceal stammering. This has resulted in unmasking my 'raw' stammer which is often slow in rate with multiple repetitions and drawn out sounds. An element of backtracking is persistent. It is difficult and perhaps painful to expose this raw speech, but the group is supportive of my work. I am assured that removing the coping strategies (which are often ineffective anyway) will be the best way to lay a foundation for applying new techniques to modify the stammer later in the course. I have to trust in the programme and give it a go.

It was interesting to consider all of the different types of avoidance and list those that I exhibited. I realized that I was not comfortable taking on the 'role' of a person who stammers. This is somewhat paradoxical as I often openly stammer despite struggling desperately not to do so at work or socially and so tell people that I stammer in order to explain it away and confront it, thereby hopefully disarming the situation. However, in my mind I still view myself as a fluent speaker, or rather wish to be so, seeing the role of a person who stammers as one of disadvantage and ostracization. I feel in my heart that being a fluent speaker is the only acceptable way to exist within society so that I must strive with all of my being to make myself

so. Perhaps this is wrong and I am approaching this from
the wrong angle?"

Andrew is quick to appreciate the importance of reducing his avoidance
behaviours and shows himself ready to trust the therapy process, even though
at times it is highly challenging. He movingly describes the inner conflicts he
is experiencing as he confronts his overwhelming desire not to accept himself
as someone who stammers, compounded by his perception that stammering
is not acceptable in society. This is consistent with some of the literature as
St Louis, Yaruss, Lubker, Pill and Diggs (2001) have shown that stammering
is as much or more stigmatizing than a wide variety of other problems that
people may be dealing with in their lives. However, even at this early stage,
Andrew's attitude towards stammering is starting to change.

> "I got on well with the voluntary stammering, finding that I
> could achieve a level of fluency by voluntarily stammering
> on every word and this was commented on by other group
> members. I was able to apply voluntary stammering on
> the street when asking for directions and it didn't feel too
> bad. However, the overall aim is to hopefully reduce the
> frequency and prominence of stammering so this will
> not be the key tool for my future fluency, but may be of
> use in some situations. I was anxious to start trying the
> stammering block modification techniques in case I could
> not use them or they were unsuccessful. I see this aspect of
> the course as very key to my progression. I did not feel that
> I made much progress with prolongations or pull-outs in
> the limited amount of time available in the afternoon and
> I was rather tired at that point too. Whilst I feel that I am
> doing well with my speech modifications so far, I will need
> to maintain a focus on my avoidance behaviours.
>
> Reducing avoidance is very new and difficult in itself, so
> I may need particular help to reinforce this. I haven't yet
> understood how block modification techniques can be
> utilized whilst in the midst of 'raw' stammering. It seems
> rather counterintuitive to me at this stage."

The fact Andrew finds voluntary stammering helpful in reducing stammering is a common experience amongst clients (Turnbull & Stewart, 2010). We frequently emphasize that its main purpose is to assist with desensitization work, not as a fluency technique. He is keen to start learning techniques, a desire frequently expressed by PWS and which can pose a challenge for us as therapists as we recognize the need for avoidance reduction work and a change in attitude before techniques can be realistically put into practice. Fortunately, Andrew recognizes this and his progress up to this stage has been rapid, due to his commitment to the therapy process and his readiness to take risks. He comments that the time spent on learning stammering management strategies, such as prolongations and pull-outs, seemed brief. We revise these strategies on future occasions during the course and are constantly aware of the challenge of balancing individual needs with the overall needs of the group, given the course time constraints.

> "Towards the end of the week, I was looking forward to more opportunities to practise my new speaking techniques within a small group. I have made a decision to refer to my 'real' stammering episodes as 'natural stammers'. I think that this fits with the concept of the stammering phenomenon being an internal neurological process that is sometimes out of my voluntary control. This helps me to think of occurrences as shameless, blameless and not to be hidden. When I let a stammer happen, I can choose to modify it, but I cannot/must not try to stop it entirely. Whilst I find it a delight to experience fluent, stammerless speech in a small group speaking exercise, it is perhaps unhelpful because it gives little opportunity to work on block modification techniques. I included some fake stammers in my speech so that I could work on them regardless, although it is less beneficial than modifying the natural stammers.
>
> I have also made up my mind to refer to my condition as a 'stammer' and refer to myself as 'someone who stammers sometimes'. I think this is more beneficial than calling it a 'speech impediment' as this implies that the condition is stopping one from doing or achieving something. A person who stammers must reach the realization that a stammer need not impede their involvement and success in everyday life.

Later, we were asked to venture out into the local streets in pairs and verbally interact with the public again. The aim of this exercise was for each person to ask five members of the public a short questionnaire about stammering. I had heard somewhere that this exercise was a part of the course and had felt quite apprehensive about the idea of doing it. However, I have really surprised myself how my attitudes and internal monologue are changing so dramatically and I was, in fact, actually quite keen to get out and give it a go. We found, along with other members of our group, that the general public were easy to talk to and were understanding of stammering, often having known a person with the condition before."

Andrew's decision to use the term 'natural stammers' demonstrates his ability to make sense of therapy and his understanding of stammering as a natural phenomenon that becomes easier to manage once he lets go of the attempt to control it. It is often the attempts at control that exacerbate the physical struggle within individual moments of stammering. He is starting to enjoy more spontaneous fluency, but realizes the necessity of practising modification as often as he can. His use of language to describe his stammer interestingly reflects the journey he is making, becoming more accepting of his stammer and recognizing that it does not have to be a barrier. His changed attitude becomes even more apparent when carrying out the survey.

"On the last day of the first week we started to experiment with vocal fold management (VFM). The necessity to start to learn the technique slowly means that we had to repeat single syllable sounds using no intonation. This was difficult to do at first because it really does sound quite funny and there was a period of adjustment as we became more comfortable attempting and practising the sounds. I had to keep faith with the programme and take the exercises at face value, hoping that more practical benefit could be gained in later stages.

I also reflected that if I am to truly accept the role of a person who stammers and overcome my fears and anxieties I will logically need to have a frank discussion with my close friends and regular colleagues/acquaintances about this fact rather than avoiding it. To that end, I even told my girlfriend that I was attending a course for stammering management and received a positive response."

Andrew's initial response to the speak-more-fluently element of the course, VFM, is slightly sceptical which is not surprising, given the focus on identification, desensitization and stammering management up to this point and the fact that VFM in the early stages sounds unnatural. He is clearly coming to the realization that being open about stammering is key, something we stress throughout the course. Confiding in his girlfriend about having therapy, rather than keeping it secret, seems to be a turning-point for him.

Week 2

Week 2 focuses on deepening participants' understanding of the connections between the different strands of therapy introduced in Week 1. To this end, we return to each element of therapy, encouraging development of their skills, whether it be gaining a deeper understanding of their stammering pattern; working with their negative thoughts and beliefs associated with stammering; becoming less sensitive about stammering; and progressing their stammering management and fluency shaping skills. At key points, clients are encouraged to assess their own learning and to reflect on the functioning of the group and whether this can be improved. A significant part of the week is dedicated to developing use of VFM as our aim is for participants to have gained sufficient expertise and confidence to practise it in chosen situations by the end of the week. We return frequently to both desensitization and stammering management work and integrate this with the cognitive behaviour skills we have introduced in Week 1. For example, we encourage clients to carry out behavioural experiments to test out their hypotheses about listener reactions when they are more open about stammering or are using their stammering management or fluency shaping skills. Another example of integration is when we return to the importance of self-advertising and how being open about speech aims can facilitate the use of VFM in situations where participants feel relatively comfortable. By the end of Week 2 they have decided which aims to work on over the forthcoming break. To help them in this work, they pair up into buddies, with the aim of contacting each other regularly over the next four weeks and to offer motivational support.

Andrew's experience of Week 2

> "Over the weekend break I tried to concentrate on my
> speech aims, but caught myself slipping back into old traps
> of sound avoidance, pausing and grunting. I was initially
> hard on myself, but reflected that I had made improvements
> so this was not a total failure and was at least some progress.
> Of course, I tended to focus on the negatives and episodes
> of stammering rather than the episodes of fluency. I have
> to remember that new skills take time to develop and that
> old habits may die hard."

The weekend between Weeks 1 and 2 is an important time for people to start
implementing changes into their everyday life and Andrew's experience of
returning to previous avoidance behaviours is not an uncommon one. His
recognition of being unnecessarily critical of himself is to his credit and this
self-awareness will support him in the long term.

> "As I have been introduced to the VFM techniques I have
> been impatiently trying to see how they would be applied to
> my regular speech patterns and have been experimenting. I
> find that sometimes I can use the VFM to some considerable
> positive effect and achieve comfortable and flowing speech
> with few noticeable/prominent dysfluencies. Most of the
> 'foreseen' dysfluencies can be tackled with VFM, but some
> sounds remain difficult and these probably include some
> plosives and fricatives. I have also noticed that if I have not
> been specifically practising VFM exercises in the recent past,
> my speech reverts to old dysfluent patterns even though I
> am consciously trying to use VFM. It is as if I have forgotten
> how to do it. This has emphasized to me the reality that I
> will need to practise VFM exercises regularly in order to
> become more familiar with the speech patterns/techniques.
> In this way, I hope that they will become more natural to
> me. Once again, I should realize that I am maybe being
> too hard on myself and that the therapy team don't even
> expect me to be using VFM in my regular speech yet. So
> let's just stick with it and see how it goes."

Andrew's comments on VFM reflect his desire to understand the technique and his frustration at not being able to use it across all situations. At this early stage in the learning process we would not expect clients to apply VFM to speaking situations outside of the classroom so in this respect Andrew is being overambitious. He recognizes that continuous practice is essential and this is something we emphasize again and again. This applies not only when learning a fluency technique, but also to stammering management strategies. In this regard we have been much influenced by Manning (2006) when he talks about the need to practise a skill rigorously and accurately before it becomes spontaneous. Even so, some people finish the second week with an expectation that they will be able to put all the techniques into use spontaneously in easy situations without the necessary regular practice. This is an important issue for us as therapists and we address it in a number of ways:

- We offer ample opportunities during the sessions for practice.

- We introduce the concept of hierarchies (Turnbull & Stewart, 2010) to enable clients to structure their work in a meaningful way.

- We ask clients to set home practice aims at the end of every day and to report on progress the following day. If someone is struggling to work on aims outside of clinical time, we explore with them the reasons for this in a supportive way.

- We encourage the group to support one another by setting up a buddy system.

- We stress the need for follow-up therapy as a means to continue the work they have done.

"The second week of the course seemed to go by quicker than the first for me. We revisited some of the themes of Week 1 and started to practise the techniques more.

I experienced an element of frustration as my speech fluctuated over the course of the week. I tried to give myself more time and have patience with myself. There was somewhat of a contradiction between accepting my open stammering in the first week and then trying to eliminate or minimize it in the second week through the use of techniques. I concluded that it would be necessary to accommodate a mixture of personal attitudes to my stammering in the early stages as I experimented with new speech patterns and techniques."

Here Andrew highlights the apparent paradox of emphasizing the importance of acceptance of stammering while at the same time teaching different strategies to manage it more easily. The paradox is less obvious when teaching stammering management tools as they support the 'stammer-more-fluently' message (the underlying message being: It's OK to stammer and you can do so more easily), but becomes more apparent when teaching a fluency technique alongside acceptance (the underlying message being: It's OK to stammer and now we're going to teach you to be more fluent). Clinical practice has demonstrated that teaching a fluency technique in itself is not enough without the accompanying work on becoming more desensitized to stammering (Manning, 2001). A PWS can often master a fluency technique within the therapy context, but needs to be psychologically ready to practise the technique in a range of real-life situations. Otherwise, they are likely to revert to former stammering behaviours, particularly in times of stress. The term 'acceptance' can be interpreted in a variety of ways; at City Lit we would define acceptance of stammering as 'letting the stammering be' rather than fighting against it, which in most cases is counterproductive. Acceptance is not about having to like or want stammering, but recognizing that it exists and from that position being prepared to make changes. Conveying this message clearly and accessibly to our clients can be challenging to us as therapists.

Kully et al. (2006) highlight this issue too, demonstrating the importance of combining fluency work with acceptance of stammering:

> "It is imperative that clients do not use fluency skills as a way to hide stuttering. We focus discussions on being open about stuttering and using fluency skills – how, when, and who to be open with; and perceptions of listener reactions to stuttering and fluency skills."

(Kully et al., 2006, p.225)

Andrew's experience of the break

"Upon returning to work the next week, I found myself

again thrust into the busy world of medicine amongst my peers. I was particularly struck by the speed with which everybody was speaking and the scrutiny that we were all under both from colleagues and the patients. Despite these pressures, I was pleased to slowly develop my VFM in the workplace during the first week of the break and to feel that I was making some noticeable progress with my fluency. I had good feedback from a few colleagues and from my family.

As the days passed and I was put under increasing pressure at work with different clinical environments and increasing workloads with time pressures, dealing with members of the public in tense situations, I began to suffer. The memories of all my hard work in therapy began to fade as the intense realities of my work life began to take over. I began to forget about my speech aims and my block management technique. VFM became impossible to perform under pressure, in spite of my best efforts to use it. My fluency and effectiveness as a communicator and an individual surely diminished and I was left exhausted and somewhat despairing.

Having reflected on my loss of fluency and more prominent stammering, I think that I may have got carried away with my early successes. This may have caused me to get too used to fluency. I had found that I was able to get through most of my blocks by using the techniques of VFM (which I might even suggest be renamed 'laryngeal speech') and prolongations. I had even somewhat looked forward to experiencing my spontaneous blocks so that I could actively use these techniques and further prove to myself that I could do it. As time passed, I lost sight of my aims and techniques because I didn't get to practise them formally. I may have begun to revert back into a form of avoidance behaviour, again strongly desiring to disguise any moments of stammering to maintain my new-found fluency. Perhaps it is this which has quickly led to my reverting to old speech patterns and habits.

A key turning-point for me was when I called another group member and explained that I had reverted to my old speech habits, but that I had re-listed my aims and needed to practise them. I selected a couple of aims – reducing pauses before a feared word and reducing backtracking. This, almost by definition, unmasks my stammer in its most raw form and I hoped by confronting it in this way, I would get used to it and slowly learn to consciously, actively apply modification techniques to individual episodes. We spoke for one hour and I applied these aims throughout. I found that by the end of the conversation, whilst I wasn't stammer free, I was speaking more fluently and easily. My aim was now to practise this more in the coming days and weeks, developing my ability to modify the raw stammering in order to produce easier speech."

Andrew's account of the break highlights some commonly-occurring themes. The sudden return to real life with all its stresses and strains can often affect a person's ability to maintain the changes made within the safety of the therapy room and group context; Andrew initially was able to manage, but then experienced increasing difficulties in his busy working life. This follows a pattern where clients, after such an intense period of therapy, leave on a high, but then everyday demands take over. A key learning point for him is his realization that his desire for, and success in, achieving fluency has on some level been counterproductive, and that he needs to revisit the earlier work on desensitization, particularly avoidance reduction. He is then in a position to apply stammering management techniques. This seems a logical progression and clearly helps him get back on track, with the support of a fellow student.

Week 3

We consider the month-long break between Weeks 2 and 3 a crucial part of the therapy as it enables participants to put into practice what they have learned into their everyday life and to experience the reality of doing so for themselves. The aim of the third week is to explore any difficulties they encountered, to provide ample opportunities for revision where necessary and further practice both in and outside of therapy.

At the start of the week, each person reports on progress with their aims, the highlights and low points of the break and how the buddy system worked out for them in practice. We then revise systematically the different elements of the course, including identification, desensitization, stammering management, cognitive behaviour therapy ideas and VFM, and discuss how these different elements can be integrated. For example, talking about the course openly to friends and family (which we encourage during the desensitization phase of therapy) can facilitate the use of stammering management strategies and/or VFM. As in Weeks 1 and 2, integrating these skills is practised in the safety of the therapy room and then outside. With regard to VFM, a previous student is invited to talk about his experiences of using a fluency technique which motivates and inspires the group. It is at this stage we emphasize the necessity of carrying out a 20-minute VFM practice three times a day in the first few months after the end of the course.

There is also opportunity during the final week to include work on time-pressure, presentations (including a session on Speaking Circles (Glickstein, 1999)) and to introduce the challenge and support model (Sanders, 2011) which encourages clients to reflect on the challenges they face and the level of support they have in place. This model can be usefully applied to the maintenance and progression of their attitudinal and speech changes, in addition to other areas of their life.

During the final week each group member has an individual session with one of the therapists, the purpose of which is deliberately open-ended so that clients can set the agenda; the only item we add is their access to follow-up therapy once the course has finished, which we believe is vital for maintenance and continuing progress.

The final day of the course is spent reassessing each person's progress. Overt changes are reviewed through the use of video recordings: we record clients one final time and they have the opportunity to view this recording alongside the video recording made the first day. We emphasize the fact that this only records overt changes and does not reflect the attitudinal changes they have made; we also make it clear that both videos are merely a snapshot of their speech at a particular moment in time. With these provisos in mind, we find people are often encouraged by the progress they have made, can see the changes for themselves and can reflect on further work for the future. Covert changes are assessed by readministering the S24-Scale (Andrews & Cutler, 1974) and WASSP (Wright & Ayre, 2000) and participants have the opportunity to compare the results from Day 1 of the course. Finally, the group takes part in an activity called 'tips and appreciations' where they share with each other particular pieces of advice (speech-related or more general) and what they have liked/valued about each person. This is a fitting way to complete three weeks of intensive work as it highlights the supportive nature of the group and the work for individual members to focus on.

Andrew's experience of returning for the final week of the course

"I had been looking forward to returning to City Lit because I had felt that four weeks was too long to be without any formal support. I had been struggling to understand the complexities of my own speech patterns and to analyze the new strategies that I had been trying to implement in the high stress work environment. On the Monday I found myself somewhat struggling to choose a speech technique to apply to my stammering speech. When I started to stammer in the class I felt as though I may have failed in some way and my efforts had all been in vain. I became frustrated as I tried to speak without dysfluency and failed. I became impatient with myself and I know that I am guilty of setting myself goals that are perhaps unrealistic for a lifelong developmental stammerer. However, it took a good deal of self-reflection and support from other group members to help me to come to this realization. I had become frustrated and confused as I tried to apply one speech strategy to my speech, failed and then tried strategy after strategy without success. Should I be openly stammering through my sentences, using block modification or even VFM?"

Here, Andrew clearly describes a low point in his therapy journey, where he becomes discouraged by his seeming inability to put into practice any of the strategies he had learned and is confused about which strategy to use. Although one of the strengths of the programme is the teaching of a range of 'tools', it is important for participants to come to their own understanding of what will be useful for them in particular situations and this understanding takes time to develop. It is useful at this point to refer to the cycle of change model (Prochaska & DiClemente, 1992) where minor slips and relapse are considered an integral part of the change process; this model was introduced to him and the other group members to help normalize their experiences of returning to previous behaviours.

The more impatient Andrew becomes to speak fluently, the more difficult it is for him to achieve fluency – an important learning point. Here, the power of the group is demonstrated by the support they give him at this stage. Andrew received his individual session on the following day and by that time he reported that he was making more sense of the different elements and could once again work on managing his stammering more easily.

> "The opportunity to experience the speaking circle was very welcome. I appreciated having the opportunity to speak and practise my speech aims/techniques in front of an audience. I was generally happy with my performance despite a few moments of dysfluency and stammering. I am learning to go easy on myself and accept that this sometimes happens. I would certainly consider attending a speaking circle in order to develop my confidence and skills. It is striking to notice and acknowledge the progress that people have been able to make. I can't help but compare my progress to that of others in the group, sometimes favourably, sometimes not."

By Wednesday of the final week, Andrew's frame of mind has improved and he benefits from the Speaking Circle session which reaffirms that it is OK for him to stammer. He also shows himself to be aware of the progress of other group members. This can be a drawback of group work and a challenge for us as therapists. We actively try to counteract this by explaining very early on that everyone moves at their own pace and that therapy is not about competing against one another.

Post-course reflections: Andrew's experience

Attending this course is an intense experience, and participants often leave confident about the future. In order for them to maintain the attitudinal, emotional and behavioural changes they have made, we believe it is vital for them to access follow-up therapy.

Since completing the course, Andrew has reported ups and downs and was actively searching for follow-up therapy, which was not available to him locally. Although his employer was prepared to fund some therapy out of area, the logistics of organizing this took so much time that he was unable to take this up before moving to a different area. This is how he describes his experiences:

> "Eight months or so on from leaving City Lit, I regret that I have been unable to access follow-up therapy before again having to move geographically. I think that follow-up with a specialist therapist who is familiar with the work that I had done would have been invaluable to me as an individual. I know that I was advised to practise VFM alone on a daily basis, but this has proved difficult to do. Living in multi-occupancy accommodation I have been too self-conscious to perform these vocal exercises in case other people were to overhear me and think me strange.
>
> Telephone sessions with other group members have had some benefit, but can lack structure. This is why it would have been so beneficial to access a regular therapy session, where dedicated time could have been spent on my speech aims and techniques, guided by a therapist in a structured way in a safe environment.
>
> As time has passed, I have become aware of myself reverting to old speech habits with avoidance behaviour of varying sorts and the usual full house of associated secondary stammering behaviours. This is difficult to accept, thinking back to my first video in City Lit and my awkward appearance. I hate to think of other people viewing me in this way. I have probably built up a psychological wall to pretend to myself that what people are seeing when I stammer isn't too prominent. This is somewhat subconsciously done, in order to enable myself to cope with the distressing experience of stammering, but in my heart I must know that it looks rather awkward and makes my listener feel uncomfortable."

Andrew's heartfelt comments demonstrate the importance of ongoing therapy provision and the frustration he feels at not being able to access it, despite exploring all avenues. His experience also illustrates the undesirable current situation with regards to National Health Service funded provision for adults who stammer within the UK. In many areas of the UK there is no service for adults who stammer and, therefore, people in this situation have the option of either returning to City Lit for follow-up therapy or seeking independent help if they are able to afford it.

I am pleased to be able to report that at the time of writing Andrew is at long last receiving follow-up therapy within the NHS.

Post-therapy reflections

The success of any therapy clearly depends on the long-term outcomes. Here Chris and Liz reflect on what attending the course meant for them one or two years afterwards.

Chris Mackintosh

Chris attended the course in January 2010 and this was his first experience of therapy as an adult.

> For me, attending the three week very intensive course called 'Stammering therapy: An integrated approach' was, metaphorically speaking, like being rescued from a desert island.
>
> At the age of 60 I came late to this sort of speech therapy, but redundancy had liberated my time so I could now face my stammering demons and address some of the issues that had become entrenched in my thinking over many years.
>
> I had lived in my own little stammering world since the age of 6. Nobody else stammered, only me. I built many defences, personal strategies to try and hide my stammer, but they never seemed to work for too long. I was alone in this, but somehow I muddled through. I sometimes feel that I have lived my life as two people leading two separate lives. One life, my inner self, the stammerer in denial, a fluent and articulate speaker. The other, my outer self, who tries to reflect the inner, but mostly fails miserably at every opportunity.
>
> If I'm honest, I didn't really fully appreciate what the integrated course fully entailed, but I realized it was going to be well outside my comfort

zone. It had to be that way or otherwise what would have been the point? So I became one of ten students who were thrown straight in the deep end from day one, and what an eye-opening experience this was to become. As a stammerer with wavering levels of self-esteem I don't think my expectations from the course, before I started, were very high, but I really was determined to give it my best shot.

I soon found out that my feelings about stammering, which I thought were personal only to me, were not. All of us on this course surprisingly shared the same fears, all had shared the same experiences and were all here together as a group of 'like-minded' individuals trying to do something positive about our stammers.

We were taught how to analyze our own stammer and examine our feelings towards it. The group quickly became a safe place to talk, to learn, to explore without embarrassment, humiliation or any of those other negative feelings associated with stammering.

An important aspect of the course was desensitization, where we again analyzed our feelings, became more open about our stammers and tried to reverse some of the negativities that we had started to believe were truths. We approached this from many different angles and it became the foundation on which everything else would be built. I started to realize that self-pity and resentment were very toxic feelings and should be avoided at all cost in the quest for more fluent speech.

The desensitization process slowly made me feel much better about myself and it became obvious that trying to present myself as a fluent speaker actually made my speech worse. The inner tension that it produced was totally counterproductive.

Stammering management was also an ongoing thread throughout the course. Here we learned many tools to help manage moments of stammering more effectively. One tool I became very enthusiastic about was 'prolongations'. If I thought I was going to stammer on a word I could prolong the first sound of that word and the rest would normally come out crisply and at a normal rate. Absolute magic. All of us developed favourite tools and this one in particular worked and still works well for me.

Then vocal fold management was added into the mix. I think everyone was a little confused as to where this was going to lead, as we started off with slow and exaggerated voice exercises. However, all soon began to make sense when we realized that this was about coordination between speaking and breathing, simple for most people, but not always to a stammerer. I eventually found this technique very beneficial and still practise the exercises today, over a year since the course ended. I also regard them as a work-out for my vocal cords (or folds) which need exercise just like any other muscle.

It's very important for me to keep the course alive in my mind every day. I learned more about myself and my stammer than I could ever have imagined. I still have to work at my speech, because my old habits are hiding around the corner waiting to ambush me if I let them, but my stammering state of mind has changed completely and many inner tensions seem to have vanished.

To say this experience has changed my life would be an understatement. I feel better as a person and being able to have more control over my speech is a great boost to my self-confidence, which sadly has always been lacking. I'm putting myself in positions I would have steered clear of before, saying 'Yes' to requests I would have said 'No' to before and enjoying a freedom that I always knew must exist, but always seemed out of my league.

I now regard myself as somebody who sometimes stammers, but can be much more fluent than he ever has been before, thanks to a greater understanding of stammering and self.

So, to continue the desert island theme where I started, I now know that my speech is not the 'shipwreck' that I always believed it to be."

Here Chris describes the different elements of the course (identification, desensitization, stammering management and VFM) and what sense they made to him. It is interesting to note his recognition of the importance of desensitization and how this links with his ability to change his speech pattern, changes he maintains through regular practice. (The discipline required to carry out this regular practice can prove challenging for some people, as illustrated in Andrew's account above.) Chris also highlights the significance of attitudinal change and how this has impacted on his life.

Liz Stanford

Liz's therapy journey is very different from Chris' in that she had attended a number of City Lit courses , as well as NHS and private speech therapy sessions, prior to joining this programme in July 2010. She was therefore already very familiar with the block modification approach and was intrigued by VFM.

I was very keen to attend this course as I had been introduced to the technique of VFM by my NHS speech Therapist in Somerset. I wanted to find out more and undertake a more sustained course in it, as I had heard of the excellent results that had been achieved with it. In addition, having already been on various other speech therapy courses at City Lit which had proved to be life-changing, I wanted to attend a refresher course for those elements of the course that I had done before. I felt that the integrated approach would prove particularly useful as stammering is a complex issue that can be addressed in a variety of ways and using numerous techniques.

I found it very helpful to go over some aspects of therapy that had been covered in previous courses, such as identification, desensitization and stammering management. Working on these aspects in conjunction with VFM was particularly beneficial and ensured that we were prepared for every eventuality. The emphasis was placed on stammering more easily and fluently, rather than trying not to stammer, which I found particularly helpful and realistic when transferring these skills into the outside world. I found the regular practice required outside the course quite difficult at first, although I strongly believe this was incredibly helpful in progressing.

I found that, towards the end of the course, when I was becoming more confident and comfortable in using VFM there had been a marked improvement in the fluency of my speech and, more importantly, in how I was feeling about my stammer. I felt much more in control and that I had all the tools necessary to deal with more difficult speaking situations. This has carried on since the course and in general I feel much happier about my stammer and more in control and better able to deal with it. Attending the course at City Lit was definitely a huge part of this change, as were some sessions of Solutions Focused Brief Therapy which I have attended since the course ended. The latter have been particularly useful and have worked really well in conjunction with the integrated therapy and VFM. I would recommend incorporating this into the integrated therapy approach as it seems to lend itself well to this. In addition, I am undertaking a rigorous MA course which involves a lot of presentations which have proved to be challenging yet rewarding and has ensured I have regular practice in using the techniques, which I think is vital.

Although I have noticed a marked and positive change in my stammer, at times I do still have problems and find that I can't use VFM and the techniques in some very difficult situations. Therefore, although I now avoid words and situations much less, I still feel there is some way to go and there is still room for improvement with my speech. However, I do not expect things to be perfect as I know and have accepted I will always have a stammer and am much more open and happy to talk about it. I now feel that rather than defining me, my stammer is just a part of my personality – I am a person who just happens to have a stammer, rather than a stammerer.

Liz's description highlights the value of ongoing opportunities to return to therapy, to maintain, and add to, the different ways in which she manages her stammering. It also illustrates her understanding of the complexity of stammering and the need for a variety of approaches to address it. She is able to build on her existing skills and knowledge, effectively incorporating her use of VFM into the mix. She recognizes and accepts that there are times when it is difficult to make use of her strategies; her realistic attitude and acceptance of stammering will stand her in good stead in the future.

Results of study

As well as including individual accounts of therapy, it is also useful to consider more quantitative results from a small-scale research study focusing on a cohort of clients who completed the course in 2004. We took fluency measures at the beginning and end of the course as well as six months afterwards and administered the S24-Scale (Andrews & Cutler, 1974) and WASSP (Wright & Ayre, 2000) at these time points, as well as a questionnaire (see Appendix) in order to obtain more qualitative data.

The results for percentage of stuttered syllables for speaking and reading at three different time intervals are illustrated in Figure 5.1. There is a reduction in percentage of syllables stuttered both in speaking and reading at the end of therapy. That percentage rises slightly six months after for speaking and reduces slightly for reading. The changes in speaking are approaching significance and the changes for reading are significant.

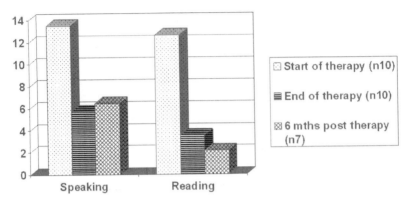

Figure 5.1 Percentage of syllables stuttered (means).

The results for the S24 assessment reflect a similar pattern (see Figure 5.2): again there is a reduction in scores between the start and end of therapy (which is statistically significant), with a slight rise six months after. This slight rise means that the change in scores at the beginning of therapy and six months after is no longer significant.

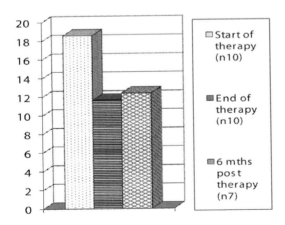

Figure 5.2 S24 results (means).

For the WASSP results we analyzed the results by calculating the total score for each subtest for each client and then working out the mean for each subtest (see Figure 5.3). The results are illustrated on the graph; the means for each subtest follow a similar pattern.

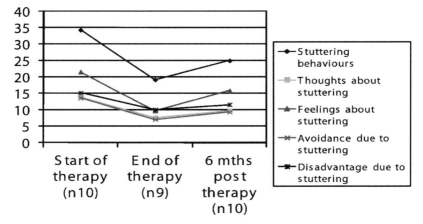

Figure 5.3 WASSP results (means).

There is a dip at the end of therapy and then a slight rise six months after. On each subtest these changes are statistically significant, except for the 'disadvantage due to stuttering'.

From these results and those from the questionnaire, we believe that our fears about introducing a speak-more-fluently aspect to the programme, where people might focus on the fluency aspect to the exclusion of everything else, have not been realized. This is clear from their comments; when we asked what elements of the course were most useful, desensitization and modification were the items most frequently cited.

In fact, our experience reflects what Montgomery (2006) describes as client choice; the idea that people are introduced to a range of strategies within a conceptual framework that emphasizes the holistic nature of stammering and that they can then make choices:

> "Clients can ultimately choose to manage their speech using one approach or combine aspects of both approaches, which moves us away from the notion that these approaches are incompatible."

(Montgomery, 2006, p.170)

We also asked participants what changes they have made as a result of attending the course and the majority talked about increased confidence and greater openness.

Introducing a fluency technique, VFM, was a significant change for us. Our experience so far has shown that our clients feel that they now have something they can do – whether they use it or not. We find that VFM brings an added bonus when it comes to working on modification as it gives people a greater awareness of their vocal tract and helps to develop their proprioceptive feedback.

It would be very useful to carry out a larger-scale and longer-term research study along the same lines as the one described above to supplement and extend the data we have so far collected.

Summary

From our experience so far, integrating the different elements of the course is possible. We continue to experiment with the amount of time we allocate to each part of the course, in particular identification, desensitization and modification, and with communicating our rationale for working in this way to our clients. The course is continually evolving and ultimately we hope to balance the various strands more optimally.

The changes we have made when introducing this course have been challenging, particularly with regard to teaching VFM. Coming as we do from a primarily stammer-more-fluently background, focusing on a fluency technique has required a different approach. I believe that introducing this behavioural way of working is particularly useful for people with severe overt stammering, one of the reasons for developing this methodology in the first place. Achieving a certain level of fluency can be immensely liberating and empowering, but clearly needs to be balanced with the essential desensitization work.

I believe that the success of this particular approach depends on a person's readiness to change, to engage with the therapy process and to make sense of the message, 'It is OK to stammer and I can manage my stammering in a variety of ways'.

Overall, the decision to introduce an integrated course into our programme has been a positive one and we will continue to develop it over time in light of clients' feedback, our own experiences and the latest developments in stammering research.

I would like to thank Andrew, Chris and Liz for collaborating with me on this chapter and Steve Davis for his help with analysing data.

References

Andrews, G. & Cutler, J. (1974) S24-Scale. Stuttering Therapy: The relations between changes in symptom levels and attitudes. *Journal of Speech and Hearing Disorders, 39*, 312–319.

Beck, J. (1995) *Cognitive Therapy: Basics and beyond.* New York: Guilford Press.

Cheasman, C. (2013) Mindfulness meditation. In: C. Cheasman, R. Everard, & S. Simpson (Eds) *Stammering Therapy from the Inside.* Guildford: J&R Press, p. 227-265.

Glickstein, L. (1999) *Be Heard Now: Tap into your inner speaker with ease.* New York: Broadway.

Gregory, H.H. (Ed.) (1979) *Controversies about Stuttering Therapy.* Baltimore, MD: University Park Press.

Guitar, B. (2006) *Stuttering: An integrated approach to its nature and treatment.* New York: Lippincott Williams and Wilkins.

Guitar, B. & McCauley, R.J. (2010) *Treatment of Stuttering: Established and emerging interventions.* New York: Lippincott Williams and Wilkins.

Harris, S. (2013) Self advocacy for people who stammer. In: C. Cheasman, R. Everard, & S. Simpson (Eds) *Stammering Therapy from the Inside.* Guildford: J&R Press, pp.13–36.

Kully, D.A., Langevin, M., & Lomheim, H. (2007) Intensive treatment of stuttering in adolescent and adults. In: E.G. Conture & R.F. Curlee (Eds) *Stuttering and Related Disorders of Fluency*, 3rd edition. New York: Thieme Medical Publishers.

Logan, J. (2002) An integrated treatment model for effective stuttering management. *Speaking Out,* 2002.

Manning, W.H. (2001) *Clinical Decision Making in Fluency Disorders.* San Diego, CA: Singular.

Manning, W.H. (2006) Therapeutic change and the nature of our evidence: Improving our ability to help. In: N. Bernstein Ratner & J. Tetnowski (Eds) *Current Issues in Stuttering Research and Practice*, Mahwah, NJ: Lawrence Erlbaum, Inc., pp.125–128.

McGuire, D. (2003) *Beyond Stammering.* London: Souvenir Press Ltd.

Montgomery, C. (2006) The treatment of stuttering: From the hub to the spoke. In: N. Bernstein Ratner & J. Tetnowski (Eds) *Current Issues in Stuttering Research and Practice.* Mahwah, NJ: Lawrence Erlbaum, Inc., pp.159–204.

Prochaska, J.O. & Di Clemente, C.C. (1992) Stages of change in the modification of problem behaviours. In: M. Herson, R. Eisler, & P. Miller (Eds) *Progress in Behaviour Modification.* Sycamore, IL: Sycamore Publishing Company, pp.184–218.

Sanders, P. (2011) *First Steps in Counselling*, 4th edition. Ross-on-Wye: PCCS Books.

Sheehan, J. (1975) Conflict theory and avoidance-reduction therapy. In: J. Eisenson (Ed.) *Stuttering, A Second Symposium.* New York: Harper & Row.

Starfish Project, http://www.starfishproject.co.uk/

Turnbull, J. & Stewart, T. (2010) *The Dysfluency Resource Book*. Oxford: Winslow Press.

St Louis, K., Yaruss, J., Lubker, B., Pill, J. & Diggs, C. (2001) An international public opinion survey of stuttering: Pilot results. In: H. Bosshardt, J. Yaruss & H. Peters (Eds) *Fluency Disorders: Theory, research, treatment and self-help*. Proceedings of the Third World Congress on Fluency Disorders, Nyborg, Denmark, pp.581–587.

Van Riper, C. (1973) *The Treatment of Stuttering*. Englewood Cliffs, NJ: Prentice-Hall.

Webster, R. (1977) *The Precision Fluency Shaping Program: Speech reconstruction for stutterers – clinician's program guide*. New York: Communications Development Corp.

Wright, L. & Ayre, A. (2000) *Wright and Ayre Stuttering Self-Rating Profile*. Oxford: Winslow Press.

Yairi, E. & Seery, C.H. (2010) *Stuttering: Foundations and clinical applications*. Boston: Pearson.

Appendix

Please answer the questions below as best as you can. There are no right or wrong answers! We have only just started running this particular type of stammering therapy course (Stammering therapy: an integrated approach) so it will be very helpful to have your feedback.

General questions about the course

What were you expecting from the course?

Did the course fulfil your expectations? If not, in what way?

What most sticks in your mind about the course?

What were key aspects of the course for you?

What have you been actively working on since the course finished?

What has been most useful to you?

What has been least useful to you?

What aspects of the course haven't you used?

What have been the difficulties you've experienced since the course?

What changes have you made as a result of attending the course?

Looking back, would you suggest that we change anything about the way we deliver the course or the content of the course?

Specific questions on vocal fold management

Do you use vocal fold management in your everyday life?

How helpful is vocal fold management?

How easy or difficult has it been for you to combine vocal fold management with desensitization and stammering management?

Do you carry out formal practice sessions?

If you would like to use vocal fold management but are finding it difficult for whatever reason, do you know what would help?

6 The teens challenge:
Stammering therapy, learning and adventure

Claire McNeil

Introduction

Working with young people has always been a privilege. Adolescence is a time of transformation and opportunity, when new learning can have a powerful effect. Young people who stammer may find it hard to access the support needed during what is often a challenging stage of development. To ensure a future free from the potential constraints of stammering, specialist therapy is required. Working with young people who stammer has helped me to develop new ways of working which have proved to be both challenging and fun.

The focus of this chapter is the Teens Challenge course, specifically designed for adolescents aged between 13 and 17. This course has evolved over the last 15 years as I and my colleagues have gathered insight from the course participants (who I will refer to as 'students'). The students have led the way in showing us and their parents what makes a difference, what works well and what is less helpful.

We have sought to develop a course that is relevant and inspiring and will provide a lasting, positive impact on how the young person chooses to manage their stammering and live their life. The course enables us to work intensively in a residential group environment that provides a dynamic context for change. One of the unique features of the course is the integration of outdoor activity and stammering therapy.

The intention here is to provide an overview of the course structure and aims, elaborate on the particular needs of young people, and share the unique aspects of the therapy approach. At the same time, we put at centre stage the thoughts and views of a number of students who have attended our courses, through regular use of verbatim transcripts. All students who contribute in this way are aged between 13 and 16 years old. Reference will be made to the

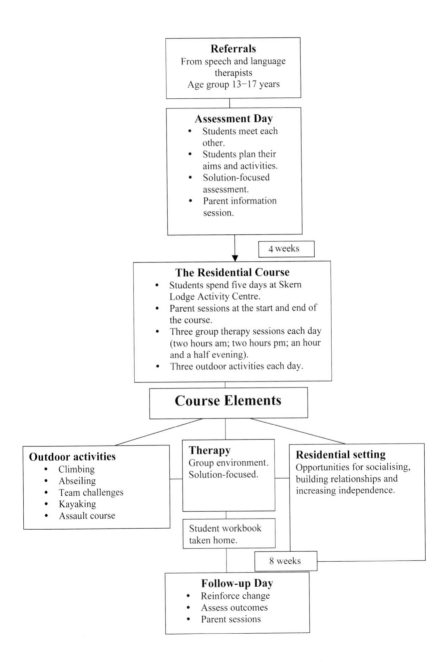

Figure 6.1 The Teens Challenge: Course structure.

therapy experience of one student in particular, Jack, at different points in the chapter.

The course

Course structure

The structure of the course is shown in the flow chart (Figure 6.1) and has evolved following feedback from clients and their families. Assessment and follow-up days take place at weekends and the residential course and outdoor activities during the school holidays. Referrals are taken from speech and language therapists, who receive a detailed report after the course and provide follow-up support if needed. Training courses on our therapy programme are available for speech and language therapists.

Course aims and assessment

The course has the following group aims:

- To develop confidence in communicating
- To develop a more positive attitude towards speaking and decrease sensitivity to stammering
- To develop strategies for managing stammering in a positive way
- To develop problem-solving, solution-building and self-help skills
- To develop positive thinking skills.

Having a shared purpose increases group cohesion, mutual support and motivation. Personal aims are also identified at the assessment day. The use of solution-focused questions (see 'The use of questions in solution-focused work', below pp.213–215) enables the students and parents to define their best hopes for the course, how they will know that the course has been a beneficial experience for them and detail what life will look like when these hopes have been achieved. Some students may express the wish to stop stammering, in which case it is important to validate this response rather than to express the view that this may not be possible. The therapist can ask, 'If you did stop stammering, what difference would this make for you?' This can potentially lead to more specific, personally-relevant life goals.

Students and parents come to us prepared to make positive changes. From our first meeting with the group and their parents, we acknowledge the useful aspects of their attendance rather than focus upon the problems that have brought them together. Most of the students will not have met before this session and having the courage to attend is a significant first step. Students and parents have made a commitment to the course; therefore, from the start we assume there is an expectation of change.

The assessment day is also an opportunity to identify pre-session change. It is often the case that, having made the decision to come on the course, the student has already made positive changes, and therapists will take the opportunity to identify and amplify these.

Adolescence and stammering

Adolescence – A time of change

When providing therapy for teenagers it is important to address the developmental factors of adolescence and the changes taking place at this stage in their lives. Weisz and Hawley (2002) discuss how many treatments for this age group are adaptations of adult therapy and do not address the biological, psychological and social dimensions of adolescent development.

We believe that the Teens Challenge course makes a difference because the content and structure enable adolescents to engage in therapy. At this stage of development, the student could have mixed priorities, and attending sessions at a local clinic or in school might not be appealing. Despite wanting desperately to improve their speech, they are often unable to commit to conventional therapy, so may try to hide the problem through the use of avoidance strategies.

Holmbeck et al. (2000) argue that the biopsychosocial changes of adolescence make this a developmental period in which intervention can have especially lasting impact. Change is a defining feature of adolescence, which creates increased opportunities for influencing a system that is already in a state of flux. Holmbeck believes that at this time a young person's future development can be dramatically altered in a positive or negative direction. The Teens Challenge course has been developed to give the students a strong, positive experience that can act as a springboard for further ongoing change. The evidence that we have collected so far indicates that the course increases confidence and optimism for future change. Eighteen months after attending the course, Jack commented:

> "I came on the course in search of something to help me handle stammering. The course gave me loads of ways to handle it. I felt that I could do it. From the course I knew I could do it because it had happened on the course."

Developing independence

The residential nature of the course means that the students have an opportunity to leave behind the constraints of their family and school. Separating from parents is appropriate and desirable at this stage of development. Students are congratulated on taking the courageous step of coming on the course, bearing in mind that many will not have met anyone else who is attending before the assessment day. They will have formulated their own personal aims and spent time deciding which outdoor activities they would like to do when they are at the centre. They have some control of the course from the start, and throughout the week they are encouraged to make their own decisions with regard to what they choose to work on. They are treated as young adults, to increase their sense of self-respect and to help them understand they are responsible for change.

> "The course gave me a feeling of independence I couldn't have at home or school because I relied on my friends and family." Jack

> "The assessment day was good. There were people like around my age group sorting out the course, sorting out the activities we wanted to do and meeting people." Tom A.

> "The instructors and you guys kind of treated us as independent people. I think that made a big difference." Jack

A buddy system is put in place at the beginning of the course, giving each student responsibility to look after another course participant. The identity of the buddy is kept secret until the end of the course. This helps the students to be vigilant in noticing support and increases the sense of trust that the group members will watch out for, and take care of, each other. It is also meant to add intrigue and fun for the students who, at the end of the week, guess the identity of their buddy.

The students are given time to talk together in the privacy of the centre dormitories and rest rooms in the knowledge that they can find us if needed, thus having the chance to share experiences and have fun as a group.

Therapists have responsibility for the students at nighttime and it can sometimes be a challenge to get the students to go to sleep. One group insisted on chatting into the night, but it became apparent that they were talking about their experiences of stammering and actually doing their own desensitization work.

Peer relationships

The development of peer relationships becomes increasingly important and influential during adolescence. It is necessary to form and enjoy new peer relationships in order to disengage from parents. Influence is shifting away from parents, and peers have an increasingly important role in shaping thoughts and beliefs. Relationships formed on the course often continue afterwards, and with the ability to communicate via popular social internet sites, it is easy for the students to continue to provide support for each other. The students' desire to develop relationships is often one of the motivations for change, as illustrated by Tom's comments:

> "The year leading up to the course was awful. I was introverted. I felt it was really hard to meet people cos you couldn't introduce yourself. No one really knew you, they knew of you, but they didn't know you because you couldn't explain. I was isolated from the world, I really wanted to go out and meet new people, but there was this thing kind of holding me back. After the course I now enjoy talking to new people and meeting new people, which was something I held back on, but now I just go out and speak to someone and speak to some random person, start talking and not having to worry and know that if he or she finds out [that I stammer], I don't really care. Of course it still affects me, but it's not a huge thing in my life, it is just something that is there." Tom A.

Initially, another student, Jack, stated that his goal was to achieve fluency. It then became apparent that extending his circle of friends was also important. At the follow-up day, Jack's main emphasis was that he was pleased that he had met a whole new set of friends. This, and being able to communicate in a variety of situations, became more important than achieving total fluency:

> "I have reached that point that at lunch break, I'm probably in four different social circles which is a really big difference to the one social circle I had before the course." Jack

Developing a positive self-image and hopeful future focus

During adolescence, it is important that individuals have the opportunity to build security in sharing their ideas with peers. It is through peers reflecting the individual's achievements and acknowledging their ideas that a positive self-image is formed (Grunebaum & Soloman, 1987). In the group sessions we are not looking for specific answers, but rather encourage the students to develop their own point of view. Debate and negotiation are encouraged in therapy and in activity time. Seeing how others in the group tackle a task and trying new activities provide opportunities for experimentation and learning more about what works for the individual.

Positive changes in confidence are often reported by students and parents. There seems to be a shift in self-belief with the locus of control becoming internalized (Rogers (1959) cited in Craig & Andrews, 1985).

> "I look at different situations in kind of different lights because before the course there were some things I wouldn't think of attempting and after the course, and now, I'll think about them, consider them and most of the time I'll probably attempt them. It's raised my confidence. Whilst I still have ups and downs with my stammer, I have the means to actually deal with that. I can probably deal with it by myself." Jack

When asked where that belief came from, Jack commented: "*I didn't have that before the course, so probably the course.*"

We have found that past students can contribute to the forward thinking of present course members, so we provide opportunities for the students to see how previous group members have progressed. Each year, a mentor from the previous year returns to provide information and support to the new group. This has been very beneficial in forming positive hopes for the future, as students can see how progress can be continued:

> "Jack is a great example of someone who has beaten his stammer and really overcome the negative aspects of stammering. From sharing a room with him, I've seen all the fluency techniques in perfect motion." Matthew

Opportunities to practise future challenges, such as interviews or presentations, provide a view of possible success with these tasks. Building positive experiences and reflecting on the outcome enable students to broaden their view of success with the focus shifting away from stammering:

> "I noticed I could talk more than I used to. I could go out and talk to people that I didn't know and in school talk to people I was afraid might think I am weird. I could talk to them. I could do it in class, I could ask questions. I've become active in lessons." Gakondi

Becca's mother commented via email three months after the course:

> "The course has given Becca not only techniques to manage her stammer but, of equal importance, has given Becca the confidence to speak regardless of her stammer. Becca is a confident and intelligent 15-year-old who happens to have a stammer rather than being a self-conscious teenager who rarely contributed to conversation. Becca still stammers, but it's an easy stammer that seems to be becoming less obvious. Since the course she has decided that she doesn't want any more speech therapy and will manage her speech herself."

Supporting parents

Supporting a young person who stammers can be a challenge for parents. Our workshops, prior to and after the course, enable parents to understand the developmental issues of adolescence and identify opportunities to foster their child's growing independence. We help parents to recognize the importance of developing peer relationships, a positive self-image and a hopeful view of the future. Using solution-focused questions creates a window to a positive future. With this in mind the family can identify possible solutions that will fit with their circumstances.

An example of a question we use in the parent workshop is: 'Suppose you are looking back at this time, and you recognize that you did a good job in supporting your child through this stage of development. What will tell you that you achieved this? What will you have done to achieve this?' Parent responses to this have included:

1. That they will:

- feel comfortable with their child's speech

- have given time to talk about the issue

- have given time for their child to express themselves

- have encouraged their child's strengths.

2. That their child will:

- be taking responsibility for their speech

- have a level of acceptance of any stammering that remains

- be expressing themselves

- know their strengths and be moving on with what they want to do in their lives.

Key aspects of the course

What follows is a description of the key aspects of the course, which provide the foundations for the overall approach and structure.

The importance of group work

The success of group treatments has been supported by literature reviews such as Bendar and Kaul (1994). Specific studies relating to the treatment of young people who stammer have also supported positive changes as a result of group therapy (Laiho & Kilippi, 2007). Yalom (2005) has identified a number of curative factors of group therapy, and ongoing research suggests that the most potent of these are catharsis, interpersonal learning, cohesion and self-understanding. Further research is needed to observe and describe the specific treatment elements of group therapy that create positive change.

We communicate to develop relationships with others. Manning (2001) states that 'if the goal of treatment is to help the speaker to change both the fluency of his speech as well as his understanding of himself and his interaction with others, group treatment is essential' (p.297).

I am in no doubt about the power of the group experience, as our students consistently comment on the fundamental importance of meeting others who stammer and working together:

> "To actually meet people who had the same problem and probably been through the same experience as me. Because up until the course I hadn't spoken to anyone else about the speech problem. There was no one else, I felt I was isolated, like I was the only one." Tom A.

> "It helps having friends who are in the same boat with you." Lloyd

As Yalom (2005) states: '…members of a homogeneous group can speak to one another with a powerful authenticity that comes from their first hand experience in ways that therapists may not be able to do' (p.8).

> "I thought it [the course] would help me with my stammering and I would get to meet new people like me, who stammer and they would understand what I am going through." Gakondi

Becca's mother comments:

> "The assessment day in June was the first chance that Becca had had to meet other people of her own age with the same problem. It was a revelation for her! To meet and hear from others of a similar age about how they managed and coped with a stammer was really enlightening for her."

The need to belong and to interact with others is a fundamental human trait. Sullivan's early work on interpersonal theory (quoted in Yalom, 2005) suggests that personality can be highly influenced by interaction with other significant human beings. During adolescence, peers are potentially the most important influence on each other (Grunebaum & Soloman, 1987), so the development of supportive and open relationships during the course may not only facilitate growth and change, but also be helpful to students when they return to their individual peer groups. The group environment on our courses provides opportunities to experience the support of others, including peers and members of the team (therapists and instructors), during challenging speaking situations, such as carrying out a survey about stammering with members of the public.

> "I was nervous before the assessment day because I was expecting that no-one would know me and no-one would talk to me, so I was quite nervous and stressed. But afterwards I got to know people and what I was expecting just didn't happen at all, it was the opposite of what I thought." Gakondi

> "You can practise things, and if they go wrong, then they go wrong and there is no backlash. I'm in a carefree environment, in such a relaxed way." Tom B.

The power of peer support was clearly brought home to me when I arranged for a student to carry out a survey about stammering with a member of the staff team rather than with the public on the street, as I thought this would be easier for him at this stage. He struggled severely with this task. We then met up with his peers, who had gone on to ask members of the public the questions. He went back out with two other students and performed the task successfully.

Group members not only learn from their own experiences within the group, but also by witnessing the experiences of others. Seeing other students face fears and challenges and succeeding can increase motivation. Providing support to others increases self esteem:

> "The strange thing was, there were people on the course who had more difficulties than me, and they are not bothered about it so I shouldn't be. What I particularly liked about the course was the mixture of the people and the therapy, cos everyone's experiencing the exact same things, so you

can see everyone's speech improving as well as your own." Tom A.

"I'm really enjoying it, because it means loads of new friends and I like seeing how everyone is improving their stammer, like myself, and like today I was so happy I read out, even though I didn't want to. I'm glad I did cos it proves to me that it's not always going to be bad for me. I just think I'm more positive." Chloe

The impact of the residential setting

As previously mentioned, the residential nature of the course means that the students have an opportunity to leave behind the constraints of their family and school. Having the time and space to talk while sharing everyday tasks can add to the learning experience (Barrett & Greenaway, 1995).

"It kind of felt like I was on holiday. I think that's what helped me feel more relaxed because I was away from everything." Jack

"It made a big difference because in our spare time we got to know each other, we talked, had games, we had fun, everyone got along and I think that made a difference." Gakondi

Students often comment that the free time provided more opportunities for practice and carryover of techniques as well as time to reflect on what was helping:

"In the dormitory, we are just talking about the techniques and they have worked, just to do them and the easy stammering and the slide as well, it really helps, like in the dormitory we were just like using the techniques, we were just helping each other out." Luke

"It was a really nice place. It was nice to hang out in the evenings. It was a chance for everyone to bond as well." Tom A.

Ultimately, our aim for the students is that they feel confident, competent and responsible for managing their stammering in their everyday lives. In order to achieve this there is a need to feel independent and self-reliant. The fact that students are away from home can bring a sense of release from pressures and for some a challenge:

> "It was a mixture of being slightly nervous because of leaving home for a week to go and have some therapy, and I suppose I was quite excited for the same reason, because I was leaving home and going to have therapy which was good." Tom A.

> "I was hoping to meet new people, make friends and hopefully have fun and forget about everything that was happening at home and just enjoy myself, like the whole world wasn't there, that was my hope." Gakondi

The influence of the outdoor activities

Outdoor activity courses have been shown to influence self-esteem and socialization, and encourage an internalization of the locus of control (Barrett & Greenaway, 1995). Such courses have been used to build self-confidence, develop self-awareness and enhance interpersonal relationships. Through combining therapy with outdoor activities, the course can have a very positive role in the development of the students' self-image. This is a unique aspect of the course. Strengths and skills are highlighted throughout, both in the therapy time and during the activities. The environment balances challenge and support to create new opportunities for learning. The outdoor activities are varied and there is a chance for each individual to discover where their strengths lie. Positive feedback is encouraged between group members both in and out of the therapy time.

> "I am finding out about other people's weaknesses and strengths and that is what really helps with this. For example rock climbing, people were scared and they helped each other and it was a lot of fun. I think it has helped me to speak more openly in the group." Sam

Self-reflection is also encouraged by the use of solution-focused questions when new tasks are achieved:

"How did you manage to climb the wall?"

"What did it take for you to overcome your fear of heights and get up to the top?"

This might be a new experience for the students who may have been accustomed to noticing when things have gone wrong rather than focusing and reflecting on achievements.

The way the outdoor activities are presented fits with experimental learning. Students are encouraged to set themselves a personal target with an activity and then to have a go at achieving it. Similarly, in therapy students are encouraged to try out strategies and persist with those that work for them.

Carrying over skills acquired during the course into everyday life is helped by the fact that, between each therapy session, there is an outdoor activity and a chance to put the skills into practice, during climbing, kayaking or carrying out a team activity. The activity centre's instructors observe some group sessions to be aware of the aims of the course and the therapy which takes place. We have the same instructors throughout the course, and over the past five years we have had the same lead instructor who chooses to work with our group. He has commented that he finds the group rewarding as he can reinforce the work we do and see the students change. At the end of each day we share our observations of how students are progressing. If a student has struggled in a therapy session we let the instructors know, so they will be aware of this in the next activity session. The instructors will then make a particular effort to recognize that student's skills in the activity session. This could be in the physical activity itself, in supporting others in the group or in demonstrating leadership skills. They will then give positive feedback to ensure that students recognize their success.

Students have highlighted a number of positive effects of combining outdoor activities with speech and language therapy, including respite from the intensity of therapy, time to think, time to cool down, have fun and forget about stammering. The activities encourage group cohesion and provide opportunities to practise skills learned in therapy:

> "Team work can apply to the speech lessons as well as the activities, cos you get support and you have got to think positive." Chloe

> "The activities make the course not as intensive as it could be with constant therapy. It kind of bonds you with everyone

else and increases your friendships, but it lets you practise, doing like we've been working on, like communication skills and supporting people and pausing, breathing and sliding." Tom B.

Carryover of therapy skills to everyday conversations takes place during the activities, immediately after the therapy session and continually through the day.

"It's tiring, but good fun. It's a contrast, it helps you relax a bit between therapy sessions and you can sort of practise the therapy in the activities, like the assault course. I just find it easier doing something active." Luke

"Communicating with others, like the assault course, was a good way of doing that, so you could take things on board and then kind of use them." Becca

The activities provide an ideal opportunity to use positive thinking skills and to see the effect of these as students confront some of their fears:

"Like today on the high ropes, I thought I'm never going to be able to do that, it's really, really high. Then I saw Tom doing it and I did positive thinking. I thought if it was on the ground, it would be easy. You can get through one challenge that looks really hard at first and then you can get through the speech you think you'll never be able to get it better or do it." Josh

Succeeding at the outdoor activity allowed Josh to see that he could succeed with his speech as well.

"Some [activities] are scary and some challenging and it helps, that was really hard, but like now speech is nothing to abseiling." Lloyd

Students can instantly see the effect of challenging and changing their thinking. The process can then be used for challenging speaking situations, for example, giving a group presentation:

"If I felt positive about doing an activity well, I would keep

those positive thoughts in my head when I went to the speech
therapy and still feel positive in doing well." Chloe

The comfort/stretch/panic zone model (Figure 6.2, derived from Sanford's 1962
challenge and support model), is introduced during the course to help students
learn how to make decisions about the level of challenge that is appropriate
for them. Developing their confidence in their decision-making with regard
to the outside activities helps them to make decisions about how and when
they will challenge themselves in speaking situations.

"My fears were heights and water, [bridge] jumping, that I
could not do, and also that pole we had to climb. That was
intense, but once I'd done it, I just wanted to do it again. I
enjoyed that." Gakondi

This student was comfortable using the ideas of comfort, stretch and panic
zones to judge whether he wanted to carry out an activity. Both in the therapy
assignments and in the outdoor activities students are encouraged to move
out of their comfort zone to their stretch zone where most new learning will
take place, while recognizing that moving into their panic zone is not helpful
as it leads to reduced risk taking in the future.

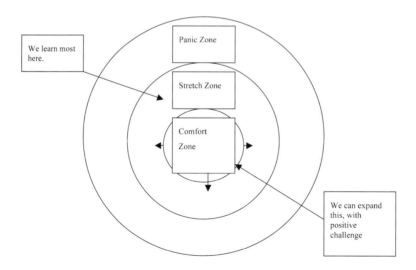

Figure 6.2 The comfort/stretch/panic zone model.

Gakondi commented on his decision not to do the bridge jump:

> "I think that worked OK because I knew that was going to put me in my panic zone. Most of the activities kept me comfortable."

Jack commented that he found the activities more of a challenge than the therapy, which he described as fun. He was aware that the activities affected his comfort zone:

> "It probably expanded my comfort zone not only in my speech, but in another way."

It is often noticed that students are more fluent while doing the outdoor activities and this can help with recognizing what helps and what is possible.

One of the speech and language therapists always takes part in the outdoor activity with the group. This strengthens the relationship with the group and provides opportunities for the therapist to see the group interacting in a natural setting. It is possible to see what is working for each student and what specific difficulties they face.

The activities can also provide motivation to keep going and perhaps, for some, even encourage them to come on the course. Once the student is engaged in the therapy and begins to experience positive changes they maintain the motivation to continue the work needed to succeed:

> "By Monday afternoon after the zip wire session I started to get into it, and to think it may be worth sticking to it and putting as much as I can into it. Since then I have been doing that and I have enjoyed it a lot more and found I am getting quite a bit out of it." Tom B.

The importance of solution-focused practice

The theory behind the practice

Solution-focused brief therapy is a future-focused, goal-directed, strength-based approach which is respectful, positive and hopeful. It was developed by Insoo Kim Berg, Steve de Shazer and their colleagues and clients at the Milwaukee Brief Family Therapy Centre in the early 1980s (de Shazer, 1985, 1988). It is now widely used in counselling, therapy and social care. It has been proven to be effective in working with adolescents and in producing positive changes in self-efficacy, reducing the intensity of negative feelings and in changing behaviours relating to interaction with others (Kvarme, Helseth et al., 2010; Daki & Savage, 2010; Kim & Franklin, 2009). It is increasingly being used by speech and language therapists (Burns, 2005).

In solution-focused brief therapy, the belief is that change is constant, with the focus on what the individual wants to achieve rather than on the problem. Questions are used to develop recognition of strengths and resources, exceptions to the problem and moments when success is evident. In this way, the student constructs a detailed, concrete vision of what they would like for themselves: the 'preferred future'. They are encouraged to explore their preferred future detailing when, where, with whom and how pieces of that preferred future are already happening. Small signs of success are noticed and built on.

Success in solution-focused therapy is defined and achieved by the student. As self-generated solutions are achieved, it is evident to the individual that they can create positive changes. This helps with the development of an internal locus of control, where the individual perceives that events are a consequence of his or her thoughts and actions. An internal locus of control has been identified as important in achieving long-term changes following therapy (Craig & Andrews, 1985; Rogers, 1959).

The Teens Challenge course encompasses the principles of solution-focused group work identified by Sharry (2006, p.17). These are:

1. Focusing on change and possibilities.

2. Creating goals and preferred futures.

3. Building on strengths, skills and resources.

4. Looking for 'what's right' and 'what's working'.

5. Being respectfully curious.

6. Creating cooperation and collaboration.

7. Using humour and creativity.

As mentioned above, adolescence is a time of great change, which makes it a perfect time to focus on strengths and to highlight any signs of developing skills. From small changes others follow. Focusing on positive change already occurring can create new optimism, increase motivation and build further momentum. Just as therapists notice positive differences in behaviour as the course progresses so they also notice differences in attitudes.

In solution-focused work, there is a belief that it could be easier for individuals to act their way to a feeling than to feel their way to an action (Walter & Peller, 1992). When an individual does something differently (for example, makes a stammer easy rather than adding tension) this leads to a change in attitude. As students develop their solutions to deal with their stammering, so their beliefs and feelings about their stammering change. This shift in attitude might lead to the problem being reframed. Evidence of this emerges in the comments from the students as they view stammering differently. Students begin to show a sense of humour about their stammering and some can see a few advantages of stammering. Former course students have commented that stammering can 'get you noticed' in a good way and that stammering can be attractive, 'the cute factor' (SPEAK DVD, The Fluency Trust, 2008).

How a person solves a problem might have little to do with the problem itself, but will be connected with the individual's strengths and resources. One student who had a severe stammer and a significant specific learning disability discovered his physical abilities during the course as he excelled in the outdoor activities. After the course, he went on to be involved in mountain boarding, which enabled him to form friendships and take his life forward in a direction that felt meaningful for him. His stammering remained, but eased as his confidence grew. An individual's self-healing potential and capacity to move forward has long been recognized (Rogers, 1959). Throughout the course, the focus is on noticing the students' strengths, skills and resources, amplifying these and encouraging the students to begin to notice these in others and, most importantly, in themselves. For example, when a student has managed a stammer differently the therapist may comment, 'How did you move through that word so easily?' or emphasize positive changes in a student's ability to manage situations by asking, 'What did you notice about the way you tackled that task?'. Compliments and positive feedback are given both in the therapy sessions and during the outdoor activities.

The use of questions in solution-focused work

Solution-focused practice uses questions as the primary therapeutic tool. Questions are used in goal setting, developing each student's preferred future and recognizing positive changes. Examples include:

'What are your best hopes for coming on this course?'

'Suppose you achieve your hopes, what difference will this make for you?'

'What will you be doing in your everyday life?'

'What will be the first tiny sign that you are moving towards your goal?'

Questions are also used to highlight what is working and the strengths, resources and skills that support these preferred behaviours. Asking about exceptions to the problem directs attention away from the problem and towards existing strengths and solutions.

Another procedure that is used to develop a sense of progression towards the preferred future is the use of rating scales (Berg & de Shazer, 1993). This flexible framework encompasses all aspects of the solution-focused approach. What is wanted, the preferred future, is at the top of the scale at 10. Every strength, resource, achievement and action which is keeping the student from 0 is then identified. The directions for this procedure follow the following format: 'If 10 is that you have achieved your best hopes and 0 is the opposite, where are you now?' 'How have you got that far up the scale?' 'What have you done to get there?' 'What would be the first signs that you have moved up one on your scale?'

We use scales at the assessment day, and scaling questions are used throughout therapy to emphasize positive changes and facilitate further movement towards personal goals.

Questions can be used to help forward movement when a student feels stuck or is experiencing a difficult time. If a group member puts themselves at 1 or 0 on their scale, coping questions can help put the focus on strengths. It is clearly important to also give space for sharing difficult experiences and to provide opportunities to discuss problems. It is possible to use coping questions to re-focus towards the student's current positive ways of dealing with the problem. It is also possible to highlight achievements despite the problem. For example:

'How did you manage to find the courage to come on this course at this difficult time?'

'Although you are struggling with your speech at the moment you are still sharing your views. How do you manage to do this?'

It can appear that using solution-focused questions is simple, and indeed the process does have a clear framework. However, every question needs to be based on the student's previous response and carefully worded using language that is relevant to the student and which reflects an understanding of their unique situation.

Solution-focused practice in action: Jack's experience of therapy

A good example of a student who has benefited from solution-focused therapy is Jack. It was immediately apparent from Jack's referral form that he and his parents had qualities that would make it likely that this approach would work well for him and his family.

Jack, aged 14, was described by the referring speech and language therapist as having a severe stammer with part-word repetitions, blocking and a high level of tension. He was reported to speak in half sentences in order to avoid difficult words, and was showing high levels of frustration and anxiety due to stammering. He had stopped accessing individual therapy as he felt he was not seeing change happen quickly enough and it interfered with school attendance. He intermittently attended a support group. Jack's confidence and fluency were reported to be deteriorating. He had had difficulties with ADHD as a younger child, but this was no longer causing concern. He was making good progress in school, but he was aware that his speech was holding him back. He was asking friends to respond to questions for him and failing to contribute in class. He said that his stammer was controlling his life and stopping him from enjoying himself. He described himself as discerning, good at sport and maths, well-behaved and good with small children. He said he thought he had low confidence and self-esteem:

> "My stammer will often seem to me to be out of control until I feel better for a few days, then it will go back to feeling bad. The stammer makes me feel forced into withdrawing and becoming sad and upset. There are times when I feel depressed and wanting to do anything to stop it."

Jack's parents reported that he had spent years overcoming low self-esteem resulting from ADHD and that now his stammering had presented him with another battle to fight. They described him as becoming withdrawn, speaking less, very anxious, frustrated and getting very angry when he got stuck.

Discussion with Jack and his parents revealed he had strengths and resources which, potentially, would enable him to make the most of the course:

he had overcome previous difficulties, he could recognize his strengths, he supported others and he was motivated to make changes. These strengths and resources became apparent during the assessment day. When Jack's parents were describing their preferred future for Jack, they mentioned their desire that he would feel able to ask for things in a shop rather than depend upon others to do this. As this was discussed, Jack's father remembered that recently Jack had gone into a shop and bought a card without asking for help. Jack's father had noticed this and gave Jack positive feedback for achieving this. It was therefore evident that Jack was already making changes and that his parents were not only able to notice this, but were also providing positive feedback. This was highlighted so that both Jack and his parents were able to recognize that they were already moving forward and finding positive solutions.

Jack's mother subsequently reported that when they came to the assessment day Jack was feeling very negative and she thought that he would not stay or agree to go on the course. When she returned at the end of the day, after Jack had been interviewed and met the other students, she reported that he was a totally different person and was very happy to have secured a place.

Jack's own comments on his memories of the assessment day were:

> "My biggest fear was that the course wouldn't help me. I saw the film [SPEAK, 2008] and it proved it would help. Because I was in that place where there wasn't much hope, the assessment day really lifted my spirits."

When Jack was asked about his best hopes for the course, he said, 'Do you mean results I dream of or results that are suitable?' He was asked to express what he dreamed of and Jack expressed his hopes as follows:

> "I know that it isn't going to happen, but I would really, really like to go, come on, come off the course and not have a stammer. That's obviously up there, but at the very least, I'd really enjoy to come back and have increased confidence in myself and to be on top of my stammer and to stop being in the dumps, to accept the fact that I have a stammer."

It was agreed with Jack that his hopes were suitable, even his dream of not stammering could be held onto, as although this might not happen right now, it could remain a future possibility. My belief is that we cannot know each individual's abilities and the unique way in which they will deal with the difficulties they face, therefore a range of outcomes is always possible. What that outcome looks like is up to the individual.

When asked to elaborate on his best hopes, Jack was able to give a detailed view of how he would recognize positive changes. He could identify a range of specific behaviours, including answering questions and reading in class, speaking more to family and friends and expanding his circle of friends by talking to new people. Developing this picture of his preferred future would help Jack to recognize these things as they began to occur.

Jack was aware that he often avoided words he found hard to say and he needed this avoidance to get by in the school environment. As his skill in managing his stammering progressed he was gradually able to reduce his avoidances. Using solution-focused questions, Jack was able to choose for himself how and when he made these changes, as he gradually increased in confidence. The types of questions used include:

'Sometimes you choose not to avoid a word and you get through it. How do you manage to do this?'

'When you do this, does it feel right for you?'

'What difference does it make when you tackle a word and work through it successfully?'

'What will it take for you to keep going with this?'

As therapy progressed, Jack was able to make good use of rating scales. His best hopes (identified as 10 on his scale) were: increased confidence, being on top of his stammer and accepting stammering. Zero was when his stammering had been at its worst. At assessment he identified that he was currently at 4.5. When asked why he was there and not lower he said that he was happy to try and would not give up, he sometimes felt confident and he had some good days. He identified his first 'tiny signs of progress' as taking more risks and starting to talk to people:

'Maybe if it is only a 'hi' in the corridor, it's something.'

Stammering therapy

The stammering therapy component of the course is an integration of approaches. We include sessions on the following:

- What we know about stammering

- Speech production

- Communication skills

- Helpful ways of thinking about stammering and communication

- Identification of individual stammering patterns

- Desensitization to stammering

- Modification of stammering behaviours.

As these aspects of therapy are well known, I will focus on the adaptations we have made on our course specific to working with young people.

The iceberg task (Sheehan, 1958; Stewart & Turnbull, 2007) is used to identify both overt and covert aspects of stammering. We have modified the original concept to include a solution-focused dimension, which is drawn around the iceberg and contains things that melt it away. The focus is shifted away from the problem of stammering to what the individual is already doing that is helpful. Figure 6.3 shows Justin's iceberg, giving his ideas about what

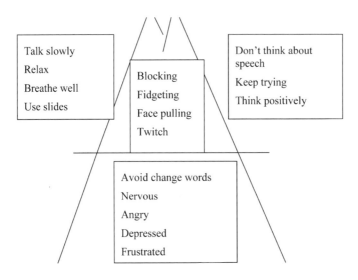

Figure 6.3 Justin's iceberg.

he is already managing to do that is helpful and beginning to melt his iceberg. Recognizing from the start of the course how each individual is successfully managing their stammering encourages the sense that they have the ability to deal with the difficulties themselves.

The process of drawing up a stammering iceberg provides the students with an opportunity to identify and share strategies they are already using to communicate successfully. The notion is reinforced that each person already has the skills to manage their stammering, which exerts a subtle change in their attitudes towards themselves and their stammering. Identifying changes that have taken place over time gives students an opportunity to reflect on good phases and the possibility of further change.

Some of the principles of Van Riper's (1973) 'stammer-more-fluently' block modification approach have been adapted with the recognition that easy stammering does not impede communication. My colleagues and I believe that an important part of learning how to manage stammering is to feel in control of the choices made about which strategies to use. We encourage experimentation and signs of positive solutions are noticed. We will comment and check with the student as they explore strategies. For example:

> 'That was an easy stammer, how did you keep it easy?'
>
> 'What difference did that make for you?'
>
> 'Did that feel OK?'
>
> 'Could you do that again?'

Modification of stammering behaviour is introduced as the week progresses. The focus remains on each person using what works for them to keep stammering easy and enable them to speak out and have their say. Students develop the skill expressed by Manning (2006, p.129) that 'it is possible to stutter and, by doing it well, to become a very good communicator'.

I have the view that each student may achieve fluency, but that this is not necessary for hopes to be fulfilled. The saying: 'Shoot for the moon – if you miss you will land amongst the stars' (Lester Louis Brown, 1928) illustrates the point that it is fine to aim for fluency, but it is also fine to stammer. The important thing is for each individual to live their life in a way that feels right for them whether they continue to stammer or not.

As therapy progresses, group identity strengthens and a collective view emerges that it is all right to stammer. Students begin to challenge the view that fluency is the answer to their problems and they challenge negative views towards stammering:

> "I can just go out and speak to some random person, start talking and not having to worry and know that if he or she finds out [that I stammer] I don't really care. Of course it still affects me, but it's not a huge thing in my life, it's just something that's there." Tom A.

When carrying out a questionnaire about stammering with members of the public, feedback begins with, 'What were you pleased to notice about how you carried out this task?'

> "At first I was nervous because I was so scared, but after I'd done it and was doing it I felt I was enjoying it quite a lot. I know I can go and ask people questions without worrying that they are going to feel that I am a bit weird or anything." Gakondi

Part of the evening therapy session is set aside to complete a large mind map of what has been covered during the course that day. This demonstrates to the group what they have achieved and gives opportunities to see links between the therapy tasks and the outdoor activities. Evening sessions also focus on developing positive thinking skills. We use the ideas of Anderson (1993) to help students identify their 'junk' and 'cool' thoughts, learning to challenge and change their negative thinking. Justin, for example, used these ideas to reflect on his thinking when giving a presentation. He changed 'I am going to look like an idiot when I'm stammering' to 'I will try my best and get my point across'. Toby changed his thought about his speech, 'I'll never get any better' to 'I barely stammered today, it was just some easy stammers'. Students often comment at follow-up sessions that these skills have continued and helped when dealing with any setbacks.

Telephone reviews six months after the course indicate that different aspects of the therapy are useful for each individual. This is to be expected, particularly with this age group, as individuals could be at different stages of development and what works for one person might not work for another. Although we follow our course programme, each individual can select from this what particularly helps them; they can dip into their toolbox of ideas and select different options at different times.

"My stammering has become more easy using the sliding, if I know that I will get stuck I slide it." Georgina

"The booklet helps, reading and stuff, I use the slow breathing one." Jake

"The positive thinking has definitely stayed with me. I normally don't use my techniques that often, but sometimes I'll be really tired and I'll use sliding or soft contacts, but mostly the two most useful things are positive thinking and slowing down." Jack

Measuring change

Talking with the students and their parents after the course and during a telephone follow-up 18 months later has consistently shown that the Teens Challenge course makes a positive difference. How to measure the changes remains a challenge. A range of questionnaires are completed by the students and their parents at assessment, post-course and at the follow-up day. This includes a progress questionnaire, in which changes related to the course aims are rated, a situation questionnaire and the pilot version of the Adolescent Wright and Ayre Stuttering Self-Rating Profile AWASSP (Ayre & Wright, 2008). The progress questionnaire is also sent to families for completion six months after the course, in order for us to see if changes have been maintained.

The solution-focused scales, started at the assessment day, highlight personal goals. Signs of progress towards these goals are detailed on the scale as students recognize important changes in their behaviour and thinking. The speaker's perceptions of changes in their stammering experiences are important and Manning (2006) suggests they can be a more reliable indication of progress than many other outcome measures.

Successful therapy should lead to positive changes in the everyday life of the individual. Identifying small specific changes in the way a young person interacts with others as they go about their daily life is important. Bernstein Ratner and Tetnowski (2006) refer to this as the social validity of a treatment and recommend the documentation of changes so that this area is included in outcome measures. Using solution-focused scales provides information on changes taking place as students progress towards their best hopes.

As previously mentioned, Jack's best hopes prior to the course were: to feel confident, to be on top of his stammer, and to accept his stammer. These were at the top of his scale. At assessment he rated himself at 4.5 on the scale. In detailing his preferred future (i.e. what he would notice when he achieves his best hopes) he described that he would be speaking more, asking for things in shops, reading aloud in class, answering questions in class, taking an active part in class discussions, sticking up for himself if teased and meeting and talking to new people. At the follow-up day he rated himself at 8.5 as he was able to recognize that he had achieved many of the things he previously detailed in his preferred future.

Jack knew what success meant for him and, as he went about his daily life after the course, he was able to see his success growing as he did the things he had described. Jack's parents saw the progress he was making as they had also detailed their own scale of their hopes for him.

These outcomes are illustrated below:

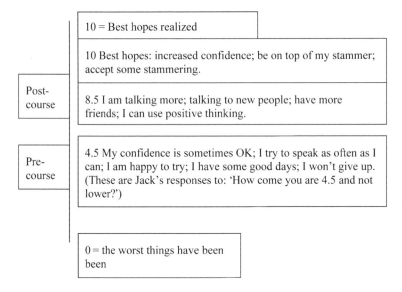

Jack's scale

Scales provide a simple format for both students and their parents to see what progress has been made. Using a range of outcome measures means that changes in both attitude and specific behaviours can be identified.

Another important way of measuring change is by hearing how students have changed their lives after attending the course. For example, one of the students quoted in this chapter, who attended the course in 2006, has recently qualified as a speech and language therapist. Prior to the course he had dropped out of studying his A-levels due to the difficulties he faced with his speech. After the course he went back to college, completed his A-levels and went on to study speech and language therapy. He is now returning to help us to run the course.

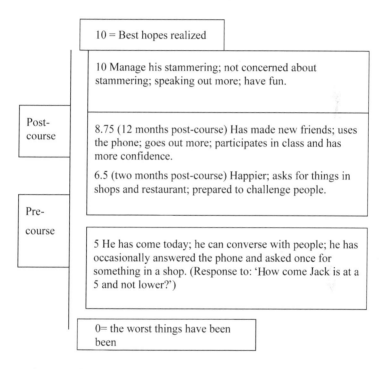

10 = Best hopes realized

10 Manage his stammering; not concerned about stammering; speaking out more; have fun.

Post-course

8.75 (12 months post-course) Has made new friends; uses the phone; goes out more; participates in class and has more confidence.

6.5 (two months post-course) Happier; asks for things in shops and restaurant; prepared to challenge people.

Pre-course

5 He has come today; he can converse with people; he has occasionally answered the phone and asked once for something in a shop. (Response to: 'How come Jack is at a 5 and not lower?')

0= the worst things have been been

Jack's parents' scale

What is the difference that makes the difference?

We expect students to gain positive outcomes from attending our course and feedback over the years has indicated that this occurs. What is it about the course that produces these positive outcomes? Is the fact that it is residential vital to change? Is a contributing factor the combination of outdoor challenge and therapy? Is it the solution-focused approach? Or is it a combination of all these factors?

We do not know the answer to these questions, but there are recurring themes which are continually highlighted by students as having a positive impact:

- The course provides an opportunity for students to meet and form friendships with others who have experience of living with a stammer.

- The course provides an environment of challenge, fun and learning, where new skills can be tested, shared and reflected upon with a group of people who matter.

- Future possibilities become evident to the students as they work together and learn from each other. They can begin to take risks, stepping out of their comfort zone to achieve new learning.

Jack clearly gained from attending the course and moved a long way towards achieving his best hopes. When he left the course, that same evening he ordered a drink for himself in a restaurant, something he had not previously done. Jack returned the following year as a mentor and, 18 months post-course, he reported that he remained confident and content with his ability to communicate. Stammering was no longer dictating what he did or said.

Jack's parents described the course as a life-changing experience for him. They felt that he had achieved the best hopes they had for him in that he now had confidence in himself and that he could control his stammer rather than his stammer controlling him.

I could have predicted positive outcomes for Jack as he clearly had the strengths and resources to move forward and received excellent support from his parents. His school responded positively to the course report and he was able to access local speech and language therapy if he needed it. He actually declined further therapy after the course as he felt he could manage his stammering himself, but he did have access to a support group and chose to attend this occasionally.

Solution-focused practitioners have the belief that everyone has the strengths, skills and resources to overcome any problem. Over the years, students have constantly surprised me by their ability to meet the challenges they face and begin to live their life on their terms. The views expressed here by many of the students seem to indicate a shift in their thinking towards life beyond the problem of stammering. Perhaps at this stage of development, more than any other, young people need to be able to get on with living their lives, with the focus on possibilities rather than problems. The Teens Challenge course sets them on the path to achieving this goal.

Writing this chapter has helped me to reflect on all the different elements that combine to make the Teens Challenge course unique. We do not know the influence of each element and we do not know how much the process of this experience has on the individual. A solution-focused approach has helped me to appreciate that an intervention only needs to open the way to a solution, which enables the individual to lead a life that is satisfactory for them. Small changes can have far-reaching consequences. Working in this way means that we trust the individual students to find and choose their own solutions.

References

Anderson, J. (1993) *Thinking Changing Rearranging Improving Self-Esteem in Young People.* Portland, OR: Metamorphous Press.

Ayre, A. & Wright, L. (2008) Developing A-WASSP: An outcome measure for adolescents and young adults who stutter. Paper presented at the 8th Oxford Dysfluency Conference, Oxford, UK.

Barrett, J. & Greenaway, R. (1995) Why Adventure: The Role and Value of Outdoor Adventure in Young People's Personal and Social Development. A Review of Research. Foundation of Outdoor Adventure, www.englishoutdoorcouncil.org

Bendar, R.L. & Kaul, T.J. (1994) Experiential group research: Can the canon fire? In: A. Bergin & S. Garfield (Eds) *Handbook of Psychotherapy and Behavioural Change.* pp.631–663. New York: John Wiley & Sons Inc, pp.631–663.

Berg, I.K. & de Shazer, S. (1993) Making numbers talk: Language in therapy. In: S. Friedman (Ed.) *The New Language of Change: Constructive collaboration in psychotherapy.* New York: Guilford Press.

Burns, K. (2005) *Focus on Solutions: A health professional's guide.* London: Whurr Publishers.

Craig, A. & Andrews, G. (1985) The prediction and prevention of relapse in stuttering: The value of self-control techniques and locus of control measures. *Behaviour Modification, 9,* 427–442.

Daki, J. & Savage R. (2010) Solution-focused brief therapy: Impacts on academic and emotional difficulties. *The Journal of Educational Research, 103,* 309–326.

De Shazer, S. (1985) *Keys to Solution in Brief Therapy.* New York: Norton.

De Shazer, S. (1988) *Clues: Investigating solutions in brief therapy.* New York: Norton.

Grunebaum, M.D. & Soloman, L. (1987) Peer relationships, self-esteem, and the self. *International Journal of Group Psychotherapy, 37,* 475–511.

Holmbeck, G.N., Colder, C., Shapera, W., Westhoven, V., Kenealy, L., & Updegrove, A.

(2000) Working with adolescents: Guides from developmental psychology. In: P.C. Kendall (Ed.) *Child and Adolescent Therapy: Cognitive–behavioral procedures*, 2nd ed. pp.334–385. New York: Guilford Press, pp.334–385.

Kvarme, I.G., Helseth, S. et al. (2010) The effect of a solution-focused approach to improve self-efficacy in socially withdrawn children: A non-randomized controlled trial. *International Journal of Nursing Studies, 47*, 1389–1396.

Kim, J. & Franklin, C. (2009) Solution focussed brief therapy in schools: Review of outcome literature. *Children and Youth Services Review, 31*, 464–470.

Laiho, A. & Kilippi, A. (2007) Long and short-term results of children's and adolescents' therapy courses for stuttering. *International Journal of Language and Communication Disorders, 42*(3), 367–382.

Manning, W. (2001) *Clinical Decision Making in Fluency Disorders*, 2nd edition. San Diego, CA: Singular.

Manning, W. (2006) Therapeuetic change and the nature of our evidence: Improving our ability to help. In: N. Bernstein Ratner & John Tetnowski, (Eds) *Current Issues in Stuttering Research and Practice*. New Jersey: Lawrence Erlbaum Associates.

Sharry, J. (2006) *Solution Focused Group Work*. London: Sage.

Sheehan, J. (1958) Conflict theory and avoidance-reduction therapy. In: J. Eisenson (Ed.) *Stuttering – A Second Symposium*. New York: Harper & Row.

SPEAK The Fluency Trust (2008) www.thefluencytrust.org.uk

Stewart, T. & Turnbull, J. (2007) *Working with Dysfluent Children*. Milton Keynes: Speechmark.

Van Riper, C. (1973) *The Treatment of Stuttering*. London: Prentice Hall.

Walter, J. & Peller J. (1992) *Becoming Solution Focused in Brief Therapy*. New York: Brunner/Mazel.

Weisz, J. & Hawley, K. (2002) Developmental factors in the treatment of adolescents. *Journal of Consulting and Clinical Psychology, 70*(1), 21–43.

Yalom, I.D. (2005) *The Theory and Practice of Group Psychotherapy*. New York: Perseus Books.

Further reading

Macdonald, A. (2007) *Solution Focused Therapy Theriory, Research and Practice*. London: Sage.

Sharry, J. (2007) *Counselling Children, Adolescents and Families*. London: Sage.

7 A mindful approach to stammering

Carolyn Cheasman

> "…the only time that any of us have to grow or change or feel anything or learn anything is in the present moment…"

Jon Kabat-Zinn (1995)

Introduction

My first encounter with mindfulness came when I attended a weekend introduction to mindfulness-based stress reduction for health professionals. On this course I learned about a Masters programme on training to teach mindfulness at Bangor University .This was a life-changing event for me – it seemed almost too good to be true – to be able to complete a programme that could enhance my professional work and also help me personally. I have subsequently gone on to train to become a mindfulness teacher.

From the beginning, I saw the clear relevance of mindfulness work for people who stammer (PWS) and I started to introduce mindfulness practices into the mainstream group stammering therapy programmes we run at City Lit. I have since gone on to run 8-week evening class programmes in mindfulness-based cognitive therapy (MBCT) (Segal, Williams & Teasdale, 2002) adapted for PWS and have developed a 2-day training workshop for speech and language therapists. My intention in this chapter is to explore what mindfulness is, to identify possible mechanisms of change, discuss their relevance to stammering and to outline some of the mindfulness interventions I now use in my work. A key aspect of the chapter is the inclusion of personal narratives from clients who have experienced some of these interventions.

My view of stammering

I have always believed that for speech and language therapists (SLT's) to work effectively with PWS they need to have developed their own way of making sense of stammering. Hopefully, therapists do what they do because it makes sense to them in relation to the way they see the particular difficulty they are working with. If clinicians do not gradually evolve their own way of understanding stammering they will merely follow others' guidelines or programmes as they might work their way through a recipe book. I have been drawn to mindfulness professionally because it connects with how I see stammering.

My ways of making sense of stammering in older children and adults come from my own experience as a PWS and as an SLT. There is an observable behavioural component which may present as blocking, repeating or prolonging sounds. There are also significant covert, internal aspects including thoughts, feelings and avoidance-related behaviours that develop over time. I have always been drawn to Sheehan's (1970) iceberg metaphor as a vivid way of describing the stammering experience. The stammering iceberg has a smaller, observable tip composed of speech behaviours and an often larger, hidden part composed of thoughts, judgements, feelings and avoidances. Avoidance is a central feature of most chronic stammering.

Van Riper (1982) describes the vast majority of stammering behaviours as reactive and defensive, being used to hide, avoid or escape from stammering itself. Avoidance behaviours also manifest through word substitution, staying silent and not entering situations. Whilst there is now growing evidence that organic factors are involved in the onset of stammering (Yairi & Seery, 2011), I still see Johnson's (1959) belief that stuttering is what PWS do when they try not to stutter as containing much wisdom in helping us to understand how secondary stammering features develop.

I am also drawn to the cognitive model of psychological difficulty which describes avoidance behaviours as coping strategies. For me, this takes away some of the judgement that can be inherent in the term 'avoidance' and rather describes what is a natural and understandable human desire to cope with aversive experience through turning away from it. However, most PWS and therapists who try to help them will know that usually the long-term disadvantages of avoidance as a coping strategy outweigh the short-term gains. I know this to be true for myself as a PWS and I observe it in my clients. I see avoidance as a coping strategy as being at the heart of the stammering dilemma.

As a clinician, I know that, whilst there are many ways to work with PWS, no single approach has been found to be 'the solution'. Stammering continues to be a capricious and fascinating challenge for therapists and researchers. PWS can become more fluent under a variety of conditions, but maintaining this change is often enormously challenging. Clients can struggle to apply speech techniques in the 'real world' outside of the therapy situation and often report difficulty being **aware** enough to consciously modify their speech whilst at the same time talking, thinking and interacting. Perkins (2001) describes this as a virtual impossibility. Many clinicians, including Van Riper (1982) and Plexico et al. (2009b), have identified the importance of clients developing a more accepting stance towards themselves as PWS and I too see this as a key aspect of therapy for many. Again, this can be easier in the therapy environment than in the outside world, where there is real and/or perceived negative judgement about stammering. In some therapies, clients also have to grapple with what they may perceive as an intrinsic dilemma of being encouraged to develop more acceptance of their stammering whilst at the same time learning techniques to 'not do it' or 'do it less'. I do not see these two approaches as incompatible; whilst I do teach speech management techniques, I view helping people to develop more acceptance of their stammering and reduce avoidance-based coping strategies as fundamental to the change process.

What is mindfulness?

> "Mindfulness is paying attention in a particular way: on purpose, in the present moment and non-judgementally."

> (Kabat-Zinn, 1994, p.4)

Mindfulness is a central aspect of a range of ancient spiritual traditions, including Buddhism. In the West, it is now being widely taught in a secular fashion in a broad range of contexts. It can be a pathway both to understanding suffering and the causes of suffering as well as a means whereby suffering might be alleviated. It can also assist a process of 'waking up to' and appreciating a mass of ordinary everyday experience, so increasing the richness of life. In a clinical context, mindfulness-based approaches (MBAs) are seen as being part of the 'third wave' of behavioural and cognitive therapies which are characterized by a focus on awareness and acceptance of thoughts, feelings and behaviours.

Mindfulness can be cultivated in two key ways: through formal meditation practices and through informal practice. Formal practice involves developing the 'muscle of the mind', i.e. training awareness of when the mind has wandered and gently but firmly reconnecting with present moment experience. Depending on the practice, this could be bringing the mind back to sensations in the body, the breath, movement, sounds or thoughts. Mindfulness can also be developed more informally through consciously bringing present moment awareness to everyday experiences, such as taking a shower or washing a cup.

Research studies in support of mindfulness

Meditation can be viewed with scepticism and seen as a not particularly scientific or evidenced-based approach to change. However, there is an exponentially increasing database of scientific evidence demonstrating its efficacy in clinical populations, for example: in preventing relapse of major depression (Segal et al., 2002); eating disorders (Fairburn, Cooper, & Shafran, 2003); attention deficit hyperactivity disorder (Zylowska, Ackerman, Yang, Futrell, Horton et al., 2008). In nonclinical populations, MBAs have been associated with reduction in the intensity and frequency of negative affect (Chambers, Llo, & Allen, 2008), more adaptive responses to stress (Davidson., Kabat-Zinn,. Schumacher, Roserkranz, Muller et al., 2003) and decreased negative self-focused attention (Murphy, 1995). I see these latter three studies being relevant to work with PWS where negative affect, non-adaptive responses to stress and negative self-attention can be central in feeding the stammering dynamic.

Some studies focus on mindfulness and brain function. I am highlighting one of these (Davidson et al., 2003) which is interesting in the context of stammering. The authors describe how right prefrontal activation is generally associated with avoidance, whilst left-sided activation is linked to approach behaviour. People have what is called a 'temperamental set-point' which relates to the ratio of alpha brain wave activity between prefrontal regions of the two hemispheres and this set point was felt to be relatively unchangeable. However, the study showed that after only eight weeks of mindfulness training, the experimental group (a nonclinical group of employees wanting to reduce stress) demonstrated a significant increase in left-sided brain activation in the prefrontal region. These changes in brain activation might indicate that people are more likely to approach experience than pull back from it as a result of mindfulness training. I see this as relevant to stammering as some widely-used therapies, including block modification (Van Riper, 1982) and avoidance reduction therapy (Sheehan, 1970) encourage approach behaviours. The chapter will return to this research later (page 244). Aside from the outcomes, the study is important in that it focused on a group of people who had a relatively short exposure to mindfulness meditation.

Whilst there are no published outcome studies on the use of mindfulness with PWS, there are a few documented instances of MBAs being used with this population. Montgomery (2006) incorporated meditation work in her intensive programme and Curtis and DiGrande (2006) also use aspects of mindfulness-based stress reduction (MBSR), including the raisin exercise, body scan and mindfulness of breathing. More recently, Beilby, Byrnes and Hart (2010) describe using acceptance and commitment therapy (ACT), a mindfulness-based approach (see Chapter 8), in their work with PWS. Plexico, Manning and Levitt (2009a) identify mindfulness as a way of supporting clients to acknowledge and confront stammering. They see this acknowledgement as central to people becoming their own agent of change. Boyle (2011) is one of the first to publish a paper dedicated to exploring the relevance of mindfulness in stammering therapy. He summarizes his findings thus:

> "Mindfulness practice results in decreased avoidance, increased emotional regulation, and acceptance in addition to improved sensory-perceptual processing and attentional regulation skills. These skills are important for successful long-term stuttering management on both psychosocial and sensory-motor levels."
>
> (Boyle, 2011, p.122)

A very contemporary addition to the literature comes from Silverman (2012), an SLT who stammers herself, who gives an in-depth and personal account of the value of mindfulness practice for PWS.

Key concepts

Whilst mindfulness needs to be practised and experienced to be fully understood, I believe it is helpful to have some insight into underlying theoretical concepts. There is now a large body of background theory and I will be highly selective here in selecting a few key concepts to aid understanding for those new to the field.

Automatic pilot

I am often struck by how straightforward, direct and apparently simple definitions of mindfulness are, yet I know that being more mindful can be enormously challenging as we have a strong tendency not to pay attention on purpose. On the contrary, our minds spend much of the time wandering and are often on what is described as 'automatic pilot' (Kabat-Zinn, 1996). Whilst on automatic pilot we "look but we don't see, we hear but we don't listen, we touch but we don't feel, we eat/drink but we don't taste" (Centre for Mindfulness Research & Practice (CMRP) University of Bangor, handout). Our attention is often far away from the present moment as our mind pulls our awareness back into the past or propels us into the future. We may be taking a shower or walking to work yet our minds are somewhere else entirely – daydreaming, fantasizing, turning over something that happened earlier on or worrying about something yet to happen. In relation to Kabat-Zinn's definition (page 229), not only are our minds often not in the present moment but they are frequently judgemental, dividing our experience into what we like and dislike. All of these powerful tendencies of the mind can be linked to the creation and maintenance of suffering (Kulananda, 2003).

Automatic pilot is a key concept in understanding mindfulness and describes the frequently occurring mind state when we "act without conscious intention or awareness of present moment sensory experience", (Crane, 2009, p. 21). The fact that we can do this is adaptive in that it enables us to carry out a whole range of complex tasks, such as walking and driving, more effectively. However, it also means that we can miss a huge amount of the inherent richness in our everyday experience of life – we sometimes do not even see the roses, let alone smell them.

In relation to our mental health, being on automatic pilot means that not only do we miss out on the richness of life but it can also be a risky state to be in with regard to emotional aspects of our experience. For example, we can be drawn into habitual negative patterns of thinking which can quickly escalate without us being aware. Recent research links the wandering mind to increased unhappiness:

> "A human mind is a wandering mind and a wandering mind is an unhappy mind. The ability to think about what is not happening is a cognitive achievement that comes at an emotional cost."

(Killingsworth & Gilbert, 2010 p.932).

Cognitive therapy describes how automatic negative thoughts trigger negative feelings/mood states and associated behavioural coping strategies

(Beck, 1976). I believe that it can be illuminating to look at stammering as occurring on automatic pilot. Behaviours are highly habituated and people are often caught up in a blur of negative emotion and cognition during the actual moment of stammering and so are not in touch with the direct 'in the moment' experience.

Williams (2005), writing about the brain's attention system, describes how conscious attention can be 'caught' or 'directed'. Importantly, this ability to direct attention can be developed through mindfulness training. Through practising mindfulness we can 'wake up' to our experience and step out of automatic pilot.

Doing and being mind

The distinction between two states of mind, 'doing mind' and 'being mind', is important in understanding the power of mindfulness. Segal et al. (2002) describe the **doing mode** of mind as occurring when the mind sees a discrepancy between *how things are* and *how it would like them to be*. It tries to reduce this gap through thinking, analyzing and attempting to 'sort it out'. Doing mode tends to be past or future focused. Whilst this mode of mind is useful for many tasks and the ability to plan has enabled the human species to accomplish so much, it is seen as profoundly unhelpful when it comes to trying to sort out emotional difficulties. We can rarely plan or think our way out of negative feeling states. In fact, these coping strategies often exacerbate and add layers to the negative emotions.

Mindfulness practices help to develop the **being mode** of mind. In this state of mind we:

- experience the world directly and are in the present moment
- can see thoughts and feelings as simply events in our awareness (as opposed to facts)
- are aware of ourselves and our actions
- accept what *is* rather than constantly striving to be somewhere else

[adapted from CMRP University of Bangor handout].

Being mode is about allowing and accepting and it enables the present to be fully experienced. Cultivating this being mode enables us to stay more easily with the uncomfortable or aversive. When we kick and struggle against things we can often feed the difficulty. In contrast, allowing what we are experiencing to 'be here' can lead to the possibility of finding more skilful ways of responding to difficulty. In line with this, Segal et al. (2002) cite Rosenberg who says, "sometimes the best way to get from A to B may be to be more fully at A" (p. 138). This paradox is central to the power and the challenge of mindfulness and it will be familiar to those of us who are experienced in working with stammering. I believe that often the attempts to not stammer (point A) and to try to be fluent (point B) make change harder. Doing mind is often to the fore as people anticipate stammering and make plans to avoid it. There is usually little willingness to 'be with' the experience of the moment. A mindful approach supports us in being at point A in a *different kind of way*, a way that is about openness and willingness to experience whatever is going on. I see this as a key way that mindfulness can support traditional desensitization approaches to stammering therapy.

Acceptance

The processes of becoming both more aware and more open to and accepting of our experience are at the core of being mode and mindfulness. This increased acceptance is not the same as being passively resigned to 'what is' and it can be a subtle distinction to communicate. Acceptance involves an **active** response to experience through **allowing** and **letting be** rather than immediately trying to 'fix'. This allowing of experience to be in awareness opens up the possibility of **choosing** how to respond. Resignation is very different, implying qualities of passivity and giving in/up.

'The Guest House', a poem by Rumi, a medieval Sufi poet, goes to the core of this idea and illustrates how radical an approach is being advocated. It is often read in mindfulness training:

> "This being human is a guest house
> Every morning a new arrival
> A joy, a depression, a meanness
> some momentary awareness comes
> as an unexpected visitor.
> Welcome and entertain them all!..."
> (Translation by Barks et al., 1995)

Often PWS and their therapists believe that having greater acceptance of stammering can facilitate change. For me, the ways in which mindfulness training can support acceptance of challenging experience are central to its relevance to stammering therapy.

Mechanisms of change

It is clear from the literature that MBAs are powerful in bringing about change and I believe it is valuable to have some understanding about **how** these changes might come about. This section explores mechanisms of change and why these mechanisms might be relevant to PWS.

Broadly speaking we can see mindfulness as a process of:

- awareness and insight – I can see clearly now
- acceptance – I can accept and be open to 'that is how it is for me right now'
- choice – I can see another way I might relate to this difficulty/another way I might behave [adapted from CMRP University of Bangor handout].

These points highlight the fundamental paradox of how fully engaging with experience, whilst simultaneously stepping back and 'allowing', can lead to change. Mindfulness is about 'non-doing' and this is what can make it so enormously challenging. We humans seem compelled to 'do' much of the time, especially and most understandably when we are suffering. Again, Segal et al. (2002) give some insight into what we might mean when we talk about acceptance, summing the paradox up thus:

> "...the easiest way to relax is, first to stop trying to make things different. Accepting experience means simply allowing space for whatever is going on, rather than trying to create some other state."

> (p.226)

I have identified the following central aspects of MBAs as being of value to PWS:

- development of in-the-moment, non-judgemental awareness
- development of greater acceptance
- kindness and compassion
- development of greater states of calmness and relaxation.

The following sections include comments from people who have attended the 8-session MBCT programme for PWS, to support some of the more theoretical thinking with the direct 'lived' experience of course participants.

Mindful awareness

Awareness is seen as central to the power of mindfulness to alleviate suffering. It is the particular quality of non-judgemental, present moment awareness that opens up possibilities of change.

First and second darts

A useful concept here is what Buddhists call the 'first and second darts' (Stone, 2006). We have a difficult experience due to, for example, anxiety, pain or stammering. These are the 'first darts'. Whilst first darts are painful, Buddhism distinguishes between pain and suffering and views our suffering as essentially coming not from the first dart but from the layers we add to this core experience – the 'second darts'. So, we have a bad back and we quickly start to worry that we will not be able to go to work, we will then miss an important meeting, will be out of the loop and will be vulnerable to losing our job. Negative thoughts, second darts, can escalate in microseconds. We often see this happening in stammering. There is the core experience, the block or repetition, followed by the second darts in the form of negative thoughts such as, 'this person won't like me, won't respect me, will think less of me in some way'. The thoughts trigger a whole range of negative emotions and often increase physical struggle behaviour. It is important to note that most of this activity occurs on automatic pilot, out of conscious awareness. A key aspect of mindfulness work is starting to see how we increase our suffering through adding these layers. This is the first stage – awareness and insight. Without awareness we are likely to continue to be lost in our old reactive patterns.

Responding versus reacting

Through becoming more aware and more open to our experience, we can open up the possibility of choice. Choice is at the heart of change. Kabat-Zinn (1996) describes this clearly in relation to stress as he introduces the concepts of *reacting* and *responding*. When we are on automatic pilot and confronted with something we find difficult, we tend reactively to try to find a way to escape from the difficulty. However, if we can bring some mindful awareness to the experience, we open up the possibility of responding rather than reacting. We may choose to act or behave in a different way or we may choose to 'be with' the difficulty in a different way. Mindfulness training is thus about opening up and increasing the possibilities of wiser choices or more skilful responses to the challenges that life throws at us. Awareness begins to open up the option of choosing so that we are less at the mercy of our grooved, automatic and habituated reactions. This is highly relevant to stammering where many of the behaviours, both core stammering behaviours and avoidance-based behaviours, can be viewed as automatic reactions to strongly conditioned thoughts and emotions. For example, a wiser choice for someone who stammers could be to 'stay with' the stammering moment long enough to respond by using in-block modification rather than struggling against it.

Cognitive awareness

Mindfulness can help us to become more aware of behavioural, emotional and cognitive aspects of our experience. Cognitive aspects are frequently important where suffering is concerned and many have identified the importance of addressing this area in relation to stammering (Fry, 2005; Plexico et al., 2005). Segal et al. (2002) developed mindfulness-based cognitive therapy (MBCT) and I think it is useful to understand areas of overlap and difference between MBCT and cognitive behaviour therapy (CBT). Both approaches emphasize that thoughts are 'just thoughts' as opposed to facts. The key difference is that in CBT there is often a focus on working with the **content** of thoughts. MBAs, however, emphasize the **relationship to** and **process of** thinking. Through mindfulness practice we come to know the 'patterns of our mind', for example our judging mind, our impatient mind, our planning mind. Change comes about not through **trying** to change these patterns but rather through recognizing them and, with more compassionate eyes, seeing them for what they are.

When we meditate, we start to notice how our attention is often being 'pulled' into streams of thinking and how we can get quickly 'hooked' by some particularly 'sticky' thoughts. A crucial early learning is that we become **aware of how unaware we are** of much of this activity. We start to notice that just as sounds come and go, so thoughts come and go and as we become a little more skilled we begin to notice that we can step back and see our thoughts as just thoughts. Boyle (2011) describes this as a mechanism that disrupts the literal interpretation of words and thoughts. It is a core mindfulness skill that Segal et al. (2002) have termed **decentring** – having the ability to step back and have some space between us and our thinking. Kabat-Zinn describes the therapeutic power of this clearly:

> "…it is remarkable how liberating it feels to be able to see that your thoughts are just thoughts, and that they are not 'you' or 'reality'… the simple act of recognising your thoughts as thoughts can free you from the distorted reality they often create and allow for more clear sightedness and a greater sense of manageability in your life".
>
> (1996, p.69)

Crane (2009) describes how decentring arises **implicitly** during the learning process in CBT. In contrast, MBAs have an **explicit** focus on developing this skill.

Cognitive therapy is being used increasingly in stammering therapy interventions and clients are asked to develop the skill of noticing and recording negative automatic thoughts (Menzies, O'Brien, Onslow, Packman, St. Clare & Bloch, 2008; Fry, Chapter 9 in this book). Specific mindfulness practices which help develop the awareness of the **processes and patterns of thinking** are clearly relevant to PWS where cycles of strong negative emotion and struggle and avoidance behaviours can be seen as being driven by negative thoughts. Segal et al. (2002) describe some thinking in people who are depressed as being like "propaganda directed against themselves" (p.245) and we can often observe this particularly harsh, judgemental thinking in PWS. If we can decentre and just notice a particular stream of thinking, we have the experience, even if only momentarily, of no longer being totally identified with or lost within it. So the PWS may move from thinking 'that person thinks I'm stupid because I've stammered' to an experience of 'I'm noticing I'm having the thought that that person thinks I'm stupid because I've stammered'. Identification with thoughts leads to being swept along with them, whereas having a mindful and decentred awareness leads to the possibility of responding in a different way.

> "Thoughts are now seen in a different way. New perceptions are forming that have a truth and integrity about them. I have greater awareness and greater clarity."
>
> (MBCT participant)

Body awareness

There is a focus in mindfulness training on increasing awareness of the body through developing sensory-perceptual processing. Throughout many of the meditation practices there is specific guidance to bring awareness to sensations in the body. Why might this be important and helpful? Welwood (2000) describes the body as being the most accessible ground of our present moment experience. Until I started to practise mindfulness I did not appreciate the degree to which emotions are directly experienced as body sensations. When we are in our heads we are frequently far away from the present but sensations in the body are always present moment experiences. The body is a rich source of wisdom and a guide to what is going on for us, but it is a guide that we are frequently not in tune with. As Crane (2009) says:

> "all of our thoughts, emotions, speech and action are (whether we are **aware** of it or not) guided by background felt meanings, which are expressed through our experiencing in the body."

> (p.49)

The body can be seen as a "window to the mind" (Segal et al., 2002, p.175) and it can provide a different vantage point from which to experience thoughts and emotions. When we are carried away on streams of thought we are totally identified with the thinking and so can get lost in it. Coming to the body can help us to see from another place. Kabat-Zinn (2005) sums this up thus:

> "…to come to our senses, both literally and metaphorically … we first need to return to the body, the locus within which the biological senses and what we call the mind arise."

> (p.10)

Stammering is clearly a bodily experience at one level but PWS are often disconnected from this as they are carried away on automatic pilot. Van Riper (1982) describes the importance of cultivating proprioceptive awareness throughout his block modification therapy programme. Proprioceptive awareness is very much linked to felt body awareness. In mindfulness practices, there is an ongoing invitation to 'just notice' and open up to sensations in the body. On mindfulness courses the meditation practices are followed by a teacher-led inquiry process. One aspect of this is that the teacher helps participants to explore how thoughts and emotions may be experienced in the body. For example, someone might say they felt anxious at a certain point and is asked, 'Were you aware of this feeling in your body at all?' It is striking how often people are out of touch with this key aspect of experience. For PWS, starting to bring a gentle and kindly awareness to the body could be a crucial first step to stepping out of the old reactive patterns.

Mindful awareness and stammering therapy programmes

I believe that developing the ability to cultivate 'in the moment' non-judgemental awareness is relevant to various aspects of stammering therapy programmes. Clients are often taught to identify moments of stammering and are then taught techniques to modify them. Some PWS are unaware of moments of stammering. Many are hyper-aware but this awareness is often accompanied by high levels of anxious anticipation, negative judgement and a strong desire to avoid the experience. These emotional and cognitive aspects often obscure the awareness of the actual behaviours, and mindfulness practices which help to develop awareness of body sensations could be helpful here. Developing a basic stance of non-judgemental and friendly curiosity, as described by Kabat-Zinn (1996), can help PWS raise their awareness of moments of stammering in a constructive manner. Introducing the concept of first and second darts during identification work could help increase awareness of some of the processes that drive stammering.

PWS often report how difficult or impossible they find implementing techniques learned in therapy in the 'real world'. This may be partly because of wanting to avoid stammering, but it also relates to the challenge of being both aware and calm enough in the moment to modify speech behaviour, whilst also engaging in the complex process of communication with another person. Developing the skill of moment-to-moment awareness and being able to step out of 'automatic pilot' can be helpful in both identifying and modifying moments of stammering.

> "I am more able to 'catch' stammering moments and choose how to manage them rather than trying to push through."

> (MBCT participant)

"It helped me with the moment of stammering and seemed to enable me to slow my rate of speech down."

(MBCT participant)

Mindfulness training increases attentional control (Chambers, Lo & Allen, 2008). In line with this, Goldin and Gross (2010) demonstrated increased activity in brain areas related to attentional deployment and regulation. Much stammering therapy requires clients to have the ability to direct attention towards specific events and yet few therapy approaches give any time or skills training in this area. Furthermore, Starkweather and Givens-Ackerman (1997) discuss how increased attention to stammering-related experiences, whether cognitive, emotional or behavioural, can reduce the tendency for denial and suggest this may have implications for reducing relapse after therapy.

Acceptance – cultivating a different relationship to difficulty

"...I find it easier to accept my stammer as part of me – I feel whole and don't feel I am dragging my stammer around like a troublesome appendage."

(MBCT participant)

Most people come to mindfulness work because they want to feel better, reduce suffering or in some way improve the quality of their life. This is a natural and understandable desire. However, one of the key challenges of mindfulness training is to let go of wanting things to be different. Mindfulness recognizes the ancient wisdom and paradox that change can come through letting go of trying to change or trying to fix and instead moving towards allowing and letting be. Buddhist philosophy sees craving (wanting more of what we want) and aversion (wanting what we do not like to go away) as being the sources of suffering. Batchelor (1997, p.68) alludes to this natural tendency as follows:

"So, I set out on the absurd agenda of reordering the world to fit my agenda. I try to create a perfect situation, one in which I have everything I want and nothing I don't want ... in doing so I find myself at odds with the very presence of things."

Attempts to avoid aversive experience are seen as the first steps in a negative cycle of reactivity. As we tense up, resist and brace against what is, we can trigger cycles of thoughts, feelings, body sensations and behaviours that tend to perpetuate the difficulty. In mindfulness meditation we start to become aware of our tendency to react reflexively to what we do not like.

It has been hypothesized that mindfulness practice increases exposure to experience and this might be one of the core mechanisms responsible for its beneficial effects. MBAs have been shown to lead to increased acceptance through reduced experiential avoidance (Roemer & Orsillo, 2008). Baer (2003) discusses how mindfulness facilitates exposure to internal and external events that are usually avoided. The non-judgemental observation of thoughts and emotions is identified as a way to weaken the fear response. Increasing a basic stance of approach or 'turning towards' can reduce old reactive patterns of tensing and negative cycles of thoughts, feelings and behaviours which stem from a desire to avoid a difficult experience.

Crane (2009) describes how "reactions to unpleasant experience will often be accompanied by impulses of urgency, or by contraction, bracing and tightening" (p.116). It is not hard to see the relevance to stammering behaviours which are typically characterized by urgency, contraction, bracing and tightening. Through staying with and being with our experience we increase the approach gradient and reduce avoidant behaviour. Sheehan (1970) describes the importance of this in relation to stammering therapy; and mindfulness practices can be a **means whereby** people learn to approach aversive experience. So, alongside increasing awareness there is much space given in mindfulness training to cultivating acceptance. Indeed, an essential aspect of the work can be seen as being about **developing a different relationship to difficulty**.

Avoidance-based coping strategies can be seen as the behavioural correlates of a non-accepting stance towards a difficulty. Starkweather (1999) refers to stammering as a process of self reference, i.e. a process which operates on itself: "in stuttering, it is the disorder creating the disorder" (p.233). This process can be seen as lying at the heart of the stammering paradox. When people are asked to stammer on purpose they frequently become more fluent and conversely they often stammer most when this is least desirable to them. Van Riper (1973) describes avoidance as "fuelling the pump of fear" (p.285) and sees fear in turn fuelling stammering. He documents a comprehensive desensitization programme designed to help PWS become more open and accepting of stammering. Both he and Sheehan (1970) rely on largely behavioural means to bring this about. Plexico et al. (2005) describe how people who no longer identify stammering as a problem include acceptance as a key factor in their recovery. Manning (2012) says for PWS:

> "…learning how to accept that they are a PWS provides the opportunity to learn and often leads to higher levels of fluency."

My belief, based on clinical and personal experience, is that reducing avoidance could not only lead directly to greater fluency in time but also enables speech modification strategies to be applied more effectively. However, it is important not to underestimate the enormous challenge of this work. MBAs with their explicit and implicit focus on acceptance of **all** experience could be most relevant here and, as said, could be a means whereby people are helped to develop greater openness to stammering. Segal et al. (2002) describe this vividly in relation to depression: "it is the continued attempts to escape or avoid unhappiness, or to achieve happiness that keep the negative cycles turning" (p.91). I have written elsewhere that we can substitute the words stammering and fluency for unhappiness and happiness and the quotation will still make perfect sense (Cheasman, 2008).

In a similar vein, Kabat-Zinn (1994) says, "to let go means to give up coercing, resisting, or struggling, in exchange for something more powerful and wholesome which comes out of allowing things to be as they are" (p.53). This is a description of the power of **non-doing** or **being** and I see it as highly relevant in the stammering context where so many PWS believe they have to **do** in order to change. The inherent variability in stammering feeds this belief as it reinforces the thought, 'If I can speak fluently some of the time then with effort or training surely I could speak fluently more of the time', i.e. **doing** must be required. This in turns feeds the desire to 'try to get rid of it'. Stammering therapy, which often focuses on teaching speech control techniques, can collude with this belief. Whilst techniques can be helpful (Ingham, 2003), I would assert that they are most helpful if they are approached in an 'allowing' or 'letting be' mode as opposed to a 'striving to control' mode.

This perspective is in line with Kabat-Zinn (2005) who talks of the importance of "being willing to turn toward and work with whatever arises in our experience" (p.142). He goes on to describe mindfulness meditation as a "radical non-doing, inviting a counterintuitive inward stance of acceptance and opening rather than fixing or problem solving" (p.436). It is interesting that Manning (2004) also describes the power of counterintuitive strategies when working with PWS. The most obvious of these is voluntary stammering.

Segal et al. (2002, p.74) describe being mode as involving:

> "…a greater ability to tolerate uncomfortable emotional states without immediately triggering habitual patterns

> of mental or physical action in the attempt to escape or ameliorate these states."

Whilst coming from a different field entirely, this echoes much of Van Riper's (1982) rationale for desensitization work. I have observed that often clients, and sometimes therapists, approach desensitization as a process which is about **not feeling** negative emotion. Whilst the long-term aim is for people to have less stammering-related negative emotion, I now believe that the process is essentially about being **willing to experience the feelings**. It is important not to underestimate the challenge of working on increasing acceptance and openness. I see mindfulness training, with its explicit focus on opening up to and approaching negative emotion, as being highly supportive here.

Silverman (2012, p.44) writing about this aspect of mindfulness work describes the process vividly,

> "standing toe-to-toe with the fears and the physical unpleasantness of stuttering from which we have fled much of our lives we apply our courage and curiosity to examine them"

There is evidence that PWS tend to have more sensitive or reactive temperaments (Anderson, Pellowski & Conture, 2001; Guitar, 2003). Gray (1987) describes a 'behavioural inhibition system' to account for individuals' responses to fear or frustration. He suggests that the more reactive people are the more they are likely to react with freezing, flight or avoidance responses when experiencing fear. Guitar (2013) discusses the link between right hemisphere activity, temperament and avoidance in stammering and describes research identifying a high level of right hemisphere activity in PWS. He hypothesizes that speech in PWS is more lateralized in the right hemisphere and is therefore more vulnerable to emotions that accompany avoidance and withdrawal. Davidson et al.'s (2003) work described earlier (p.218) shows how even relatively brief periods of mindfulness training can increase activity in regions of the left hemisphere associated with approach behaviours. This could clearly be helpful to PWS seeking to increase the approach as opposed to the avoidance gradient. In line with this, Williams (2005) discusses how learning to "recognise the subtle signals that the avoidance system is being activated" and "a means to shift our attention so that the alternative pattern of the brain was activated instead" can leave us less at the mercy of our emotions. For me, seeing links between these different strands of research is exciting and further evidence of just how relevant mindfulness training could be for PWS.

Kindness and compassion

Mindfulness work also emphasizes the importance of cultivating greater kindness and compassion towards both ourselves and others. Much of the guidance in mindfulness practices explicitly invites us to notice our experience with a kindly and compassionate stance. This is all part of learning to relate to ourselves and our difficulties in a different way and provides a contrast to the habitually judgemental and self-critical attitude that often prevails. It says something essential about the **flavour and spirit** of acceptance. As Crane (2009, p.54) says:

> "...the spirit we bring to the process of acceptance is important. It has an open quality, which is part of the attitudinal stance of willingness to be available to our experience. We learn to be tender, gentle, kindly, compassionate and respectful towards ourselves and our experience."

In addition to fostering this general attitudinal approach of greater gentleness, mindfulness teaching can also include specific kindness and compassion practices.

The development of self-compassion is now viewed as one of the healing mechanisms in therapy. Bueno (2011) reports that preliminary studies suggest that teaching people to develop self-compassion can reduce shame. Gilbert (2010) describes how compassion-focused therapy can help clients to connect more at an emotional level and so address the 'head-heart' lag that can be experienced in CBT approaches. Rather than the benefits coming from directly challenging thoughts and feelings, change is increasingly being seen as arising from developing a new relationship to them. Germer (2009, p.31) describes this relationship as:

> "...less avoidant, less entangled, more accepting, more **compassionate** and more aware. Leaning into our problems with open eyes and an open heart – with awareness and

compassion – is the process by which we get emotional relief."

In my experience, fear, shame and negative self-judgement are often at the core of the lived stammering experience. Buddhist psychology views kindness and compassion as the antidote to fear and Salzburg (2009) talks of the true development of self-compassion as being the basis for fearlessness. Germer (2009, p.99) describes the mechanism for this and sees compassion as underlying the development of greater acceptance and increased self-esteem:

> "…freeing yourself from the trap of destructive thoughts and emotions through self compassion can boost your self-esteem from the inside out [and] reduce anxiety and depression."

I do not remember hearing the words 'kindness' and 'compassion' during my training as an SLT. I think these terms are still rarely used in contemporary training courses. It is not that there is an intention for therapy to be 'unkind' or 'uncompassionate' but simply that these qualities do not fit into more medical-model, impairment-based approaches to change. Compassion can help us to turn towards our emotional pain. I believe that for PWS to break free from some of the imprisoning bars of stammering, they need to be able to turn towards their own challenging emotions.

Helping PWS to carry forward the benefits of therapy once sessions have ended is recognized as being a major challenge. This is also true for clients in counselling and psychotherapy. Therapists who incorporate mindfulness work in their practice see helping people to have more self-compassion as being a key to enabling the benefits of therapy to be more portable. Mindfulness teachers see self-compassion as being a trainable skill.

> "Since attending the course I am kinder to myself all round."

> (MBCT participant)

Relaxation and stress management

Whilst there is clear evidence that mindfulness-based interventions can lead to reduced anxiety and stress (Kabat-Zinn, 1992; Shapiro, Schwartz & Bonner,

1998; Davidson et al., 2003), this is generally described as a by-product of greater states of awareness and acceptance. Relaxation is seen to develop more as a result of **dwelling with what is** as opposed to arising from attempts to **try to** relax. Relaxation therapies have been used in work with PWS but outcomes are viewed as questionable. Bloodstein (1975) says that whilst relaxation therapies have been widely used in work with PWS, considerable dissatisfaction has arisen amongst clinicians, commenting that "most authorities either do not advocate the use of relaxation or employ it only in certain special forms in conjunction with other types of therapy" (p.305). However, many PWS identify stress as a factor in precipitating dysfluency. Whilst I do not see stress reduction as the key benefit of mindfulness work for PWS I would argue that having an increased ability to manage stress could be helpful .

> "I can focus on one thing at time now which reduces the levels of stress in my head – this has had a positive effect on my speech. I am just calmer all round."
>
> (MBCT participant)

> "…it has helped me to remain calm within myself and focus on the moment and not dwell on habitual negative thoughts."
>
> (MBCT participant)

Teaching mindfulness to PWS

Since training as a mindfulness teacher I have developed an 8-session (20 hour) mindfulness-based cognitive therapy (MBCT) course for people who stammer and I also integrate short mindfulness practices into mainstream stammering therapy programmes..

MBCT for people who stammer

The programme

The MBCT programme I teach is based on MBCT for depression which is described in detail by Segal et al. (2002). The same core mindfulness practices are taught: the bodyscan, mindful movement, awareness of breathing, sitting meditation and the 3-minute breathing space. Home practice is a vital part of the process and participants are given CDs to listen to daily.

Each session follows a similar pattern, starting with a longer meditation practice (c.35 minutes), followed by discussion of the week's home practice. There is a theme to each week (see below) which is explored through an activity or discussion along with additional didactic content. Sessions conclude by setting up the following week's home practice and a shorter practice. Much of the learning takes places through inquiry into participants' experiences of the session practices and home practice. The inquiry process requires skill on the part of the mindfulness teacher as participants are helped to explore their 'noticings'. In time, the teacher will start to make links between participants' growing awareness of the activity of the mind and body and underlying theory either about mindfulness in general or the specific difficulty that has brought people to the course, in this case stammering. The group is a powerful vehicle for learning, in part because the underlying tendencies of the human mind to wander and judge are normalized.

The themes of the sessions are:

Session 1 Automatic pilot

Session 2 Dealing with barriers

Session 3 Mindfulness of the breath

Session 4 Staying present

Session 5 Allowing/letting be

Session 6 Thoughts are not facts

Session 7 How can I best take care of myself

Session 8 Taking the learning forward

I have adapted some of the content to make the course more stammering specific. Some of these adaptations, described below, relate to the didactic content and some involve modification of the mindfulness practices.

MBCT adaptations for PWS

In Session 3 of MBCT for depression, there is specific content on and exploration of the nature of depression. I have replaced this with discussion on the nature of stammering using Sheehans's iceberg analogy as a framework (Sheehan, 1970). This highlights the view that stammering is more than just a physical behaviour and vividly illustrates the importance of thoughts, feelings and avoidance-based coping strategies.

In Sessions 4 and 5, I incorporate information on the stress response and stress reaction (Kabat-Zinn, 1996) because of the role of stress in stammering variability.

During the sitting practice in Session 5 (theme 'acceptance and allowing/letting be'), participants are invited to bring to mind a difficulty and explore its effects on body and mind. This includes explicit guidance on opening to the experience. A similar practice is led in Session 6 and at this point I suggest that people may want to bring to mind a stammering-related difficulty and work directly with this.

In Sessions 2 and 3, participants are asked to complete pleasant and unpleasant events calendars where they record their observations of thoughts, feelings and sensations. I have developed this to include a stammering events calendar in Session 6. Participants are invited to be aware of a stammering event **at the time it is happening**. They then record their answers to the following questions: What was the experience? Were you aware of any feelings **while** the event was happening? How did your body feel, in detail, during this experience? What moods, feelings and thoughts accompanied this event? What thoughts are in your mind now as you write this down? (see Appendix 1).

Session 2 includes a classic CBT exercise to demonstrate how thoughts and interpretations of an event affect our emotions and behaviour. This is developed in Session 6 to show how our thoughts can in turn be affected by our emotional state. This activity has been adapted to be stammering specific (see Appendix 2). The intention is to show that our thoughts are consequences of many influences, including past and present mood states. Discussion continues to explore the underlying theme of Session 6 that "just because our thoughts are compelling does not make them true" (Segal el al, p.257).

Since so many PWS bring high levels of negative judgement to themselves and their stammering I have chosen to include a kindness practice in the programme. Crane (2009) states that developing a sense of compassion and friendly curiosity to experience helps to change avoidance mode into approach mode. So, in Session 7, I lead a breath-and body-based acceptance and kindness practice.

Session 7 includes a 'stress signature' activity involving participants noting down their own personal stress cues/warning signs. There is then discussion about unhelpful and helpful ways of responding to these cues. I have elaborated this to include a 'stammering signature' component so that, as well as identifying stress indicators, participants also note down how they might become aware of when they are in an unhelpful place in relation to stammering (e.g starting to pull back, tense, brace, avoid speaking or situations, catching themselves getting hooked into well grooved negative thinking patterns). They then go on to list unhelpful and helpful ways of responding to these indicators. Helpful ways might include taking a breathing space, using some voluntary stammering, contacting a speech buddy, etc. This is usefully done as a group activity.

Client accounts

The following are reflections from two people who have attended the 8-session programme.

Amy Leggatt

I was drawn to the mindfulness meditation course as I already had some experience of meditation, and after reading the course summary, I could see how mindfulness could be applied to manage my stammer and my feelings around it more effectively. I had previously had some speech therapy, but enrolled on the course with the hope of picking up some extra tools that I could use to help me with my speech.

We established that mindfulness meditation involved aiming to pay deliberate attention to the present moment rather than running on 'autopilot', and we explored how this could be useful with regards to stammering. Through the aid of meditation we learned that by raising our awareness of any negative thoughts or feelings that may come up in moments of stammering, and accepting their presence as opposed to pushing them away, we are then able to look for skilful ways to help ourselves at these times. The theory was that with heightened awareness and acceptance of our thoughts, feelings and behaviour, it is then easier to choose appropriate action, such as using stammering modification techniques or practising non-avoidance. It was said that having the self-awareness to be able to choose helpful ways of dealing with challenging speaking situations, or life in general, contrasts with allowing difficult feelings to unconsciously drive our behaviour in potentially counter-productive ways, for example not making a phone call to avoid any feelings of anxiety associated with stammering. By accepting the presence of our thoughts and feelings, they do not have as much power to control our behaviour as they would do if they were pushed out of our awareness, giving us more choice over how we deal with situations, stammering related or otherwise.

The type of meditation practices we used to achieve this self-awareness included body scans and breathing meditations. These meditations helped us to tune in to our moment-to-moment experience, such as bodily sensations, thoughts, and sounds. In order to benefit as much as possible from the meditation techniques, we were given several CD recordings of various guided meditations, and were encouraged to use these on a daily basis. We were also given events calendars in which to record our experiences of pleasant and unpleasant events and our accompanying thoughts and feelings. This was another useful way of focusing our awareness on the details of our experiences as they were happening, and identifying any unhelpful thought patterns or behaviours. For me, this increased awareness of thoughts, feelings and their interconnectedness gives me more sense of choice about what I do with them. It may be about continuing to think along the same lines and just accepting this or looking at potentially more helpful ways of thinking, for instance positive self talk or self support. I think this is a way in which mindfulness can support traditional CBT therapy.

Aspects of the course I have found most useful in terms of my stammer, as well as other situations, have been the shorter meditation exercises, as I can do them at any time, such as on the tube or before making a phone call. Even a couple of minutes spent tuning in to myself can help me to feel grounded and relaxed, and in this state, I am more able to identify what I do physically when I stammer, enabling me to manage it more effectively. This state of awareness, when accompanied by acceptance, also helps me to give my feelings space in moments of stammering, so they do not have as much free reign to dictate my behaviour. Additionally, apart from the speech-related gains I made on the course, I realised that I was beginning to notice more pleasurable sensations than I may have done before such as pleasant smells and tastes. I really felt that my experience of life was being enhanced and I attributed this directly to my meditation practice and subsequent heightened awareness.

A more challenging aspect of mindfulness has been that when I'm focusing on raising my awareness of my speech after a period of not doing so, my stammer can sometimes get worse. This could be due to the sudden direction of attention towards my speech, which might increase tension. Although initially this can be very challenging, it is usually only temporary, and with sustained meditation and fluency skills practice, my speech normally starts to improve and I am able to employ speech techniques with less struggle. I have also found maintaining the long home practice sessions challenging. It was suggested that in order to get the most from meditation, we should be meditating for at least 40 minutes a day. Although when I did manage to do the longer practice sessions, I definitely reaped the benefits in terms of my speech and by an enhanced experience of life in general, having an extremely busy lifestyle meant I began to resent spending so much time meditating. Once the course had ended, I eventually stopped doing the longer practice sessions, and opted instead for the shorter 10 and 20 minute meditations on the CDs, as well as what were known as 'breathing spaces' – short 3-minute meditations that can be done anywhere, at any time, in order to ground oneself and get present. Although I found the shorter meditations very beneficial, I did notice that my awareness wasn't as sharply focused as it was when I was regularly practising the longer meditations.

However, even taking into consideration the challenges that meditation can present for me, I believe that with regular practice, whether for longer or shorter periods of time, mindfulness has had a beneficial impact on me in several ways. Whether in relation to my speech or other life events, I feel it has helped me to raise awareness of, accept and therefore better process, my thoughts, feelings and behaviour and make more considered decisions. Additionally, I've found it enables me to feel more relaxed and grounded, and better able to enjoy the pleasurable things in life. Because of these benefits, I feel it is well worth working through the more challenging aspects and I shall continue to practise it for as long as I find it helpful .

Amy identifies a number of benefits including:

- Greater awareness leading to more sense of choice
- The functionality of some of the shorter practices enabling her to feel more grounded in everyday life
- Having a sense of an improved ability to use stammering management strategies

- A sense of space for challenging emotions

- A greater appreciation of life

She also touches on the challenges that increased awareness can bring and identifies one of the frequently raised challenges of mindfulness: finding time for practice.

Christine Simpson

I have done a range of speech therapy over the years and have also done some personal development courses aimed at everyone, i.e. with no stammering context, including some with meditation (which I found very hard). I chose to attend the mindfulness meditation course because I have felt for a long time that many of the manifestations of stammering were in my body (tensing shoulders, chest, throat, etc.). Speech therapy had concentrated on my head and my mental processes but not on the rest of my body.

Mindfulness meditation taught me to feel what is going on in my body, without putting the emphasis on relaxing. I have always found it very hard to relax, particularly when I was expected to. A key benefit is that I can now feel what is going on in my body when I am stammering. The practices develop the skill of tuning into each part of the body, along with the ability to imagine the breath moving through it. For me, being aware is the first step to making changes to what I do with my body when I stammer. I find that just taking a minute to focus on what I am doing with my body is really useful for when I have an important speaking situation and with daily practice I can do this more effectively – it is work in progress!

What I'm really pleased about is that I have learned to meditate. My mind does wander, ALL THE TIME, but I keep coming back to the meditation. It has been most helpful in allowing me to accept my mind racing about in ordinary life, particularly in a difficult speaking situation. I accept more readily that my mind will do this and it is OK. It has also taught me to sit in one place, without worrying about having to sit still, accepting my body as it is. Mindful yoga is also part of the course; I have really enjoyed doing this exercise and the gentle stretching has brought its own benefits. I know that I need to keep practising mindfulness to gain full benefit. I see mindfulness as being like exercise for the mind. I find that practising with CDs helps me with the challenges of daily practice.

I think the real benefit I have had from meditation is greater self-acceptance. It has allowed me to accept 'me as me', including me as a person who stammers, and to recognize that whilst I will probably never be a really calm person, I can get to a place I am happier with. I can now accept that sometimes I will stammer quite a lot and sometimes I will have quite a lot of fluency. A big challenge of stammering for me is the variability and acceptance of this variability has been really important. The concept of being rather than doing has helped here. Acceptance is not a fixed state, it ebbs and flows and can be challenged by certain events, e.g. recently starting a new job. One of the aspects I struggle to accept is the silence that goes with blocking and the feeling that the word will never come out. I can see how this feeds my urgency and can see how 'being with' the silence more can be really helpful. As I say, it is a work in progress.

Christine's account highlights some of the benefits of increased awareness of the body and how this was facilitated through not trying to relax. She also describes the power of acceptance of the fact that the mind does wander. I personally like the way mindfulness practices encourage this acceptance and it has enabled mindfulness meditation to be more useful for me than some other meditation approaches which can be less gentle in working with mind wandering. Christine's account closes with what I feel is a powerful description of the benefits and challenges of the process of self-acceptance and I have a strong sense of someone who is really engaging with these challenges. Mindfulness is indeed not a 'quick fix'.

Integrating mindfulness into mainstream stammering therapy courses

I believe that mindfulness can support both the desensitization and speech management work included in the 'mainstream' stammering therapy courses I teach. Whilst participants have been informed that the course will include some mindfulness, they are in a different position to clients who have enrolled on the dedicated mindfulness programme. As such, it is made very clear to them that they have a choice as to whether to participate in the practices. Most clients choose to 'give it a go' and there have only been a couple of instances when someone has opted out. I introduce mindfulness experientially through the raisin exercise (Segal et al., 2002).

The raisin exercise

Participants are invited to explore and then eat a raisin mindfully. As Crane (2009, p.101) says, it is an excellent way to introduce mindfulness as it "intentionally conveys the message that meditation is not about unusual or mystic experiences but about the ordinary in life". Whilst clients may find it strange that, within a few hours of coming on a stammering therapy course they find themselves eating a raisin, they generally engage with the experience. The inquiry process after the practice usually illustrates many of the key aspects of mindfulness including:

- the concept of automatic pilot

- experiencing the difference between mindful awareness and automatic pilot

- seeing how mindful awareness can reveal aspects previously unnoticed and can also transform the experience itself

- seeing the interconnection between sensory, cognitive and emotional experience

- noticing how mental 'time travel' can take us far away from the present moment

- the importance of bringing curiosity to familiar experiences

A simple rationale as to why mindfulness may be relevant to PWS flows naturally on from this.

Three minute breathing space

I lead short awareness-of-breath practices throughout the programme and then introduce the 3-minute breathing space as the courses progress. The breathing space was developed by Segal et al. (2002) as a 'mini-meditation' and is in part a vehicle to enable mindfulness to be brought into the hurly-burly of everyday life. It is influenced by cognitive therapy practice in that it is highly explicit and structured with three discrete stages.

1. Notice what is going on right now cognitively, emotionally and in the body and in so doing step out of automatic pilot.

2. Bring the attention to the breath so gathering the scattered mind.

3. Expand the attention to include the breath and the whole body.

This can be a way of 'taking a pause' or having some time out, but the wider aim is that, in time, people can use it intentionally to open to any difficulty as it presents itself in the here and now. In this sense it is not being used as an escape hatch, but as a method of practising a new way of being with difficulty. As such, it goes to the heart of mindfulness practice.

Support for desensitization work

I believe that mindfulness can support and enhance traditional desensitization work. Desensitization can become very outcome-oriented. For example, clients can quickly get into a mode of thinking, 'If I do voluntary stammering I will stammer less', or 'If I reduce my avoidance I won't have to feel painful emotions'. The strategies therapists introduce to support desensitization can rapidly become subverted to the 'I want to not stammer' agenda. I hope that mindfulness can help PWS to truly open to the experience and, in so doing, really get to the heart of the approach-avoidance conflict so vividly described by Sheehan (1970). For me, mindfulness has led to a shift in the way I approach desensitization work. I am explicit about encouraging clients to see it as a process which is about allowing themselves to feel whatever they are feeling as opposed to just aiming to feel it less. Yes, the long-term hope is that they will feel painful feelings less, but I see this as coming through becoming less fearful of experiencing anxiety, embarrassment or whatever emotion might be 'up' for them. This is what acceptance and commitment therapy describes as 'willingness' to experience emotion (see Chapter 8). In teaching mindfulness, I also have to be alert to the fact that this too can quickly become subverted into the 'not wanting to have something or feel something' desire. As humans, our urge to not feel pain is so strong that anything will be recruited in its service. Returning to the concept quoted earlier that says that sometimes the easiest way to get from A to B is to be more fully at A, the challenge is really being more fully at A as opposed to a more outcome-oriented stance which says I will be more at A because that will lead me to get to B.

The following is a reflection from a client who attended a block modification intensive course.

Lynn Jeffrey

I have to admit I had never heard of mindfulness before encountering it on a stammering management course at City Lit, London. My initial thoughts were, 'Well, this is meditation of some sort ... but how is that going to help me not to stammer' or, as I learned during the course – how was it going to help me stammer more easily?

So what have I learned about mindfulness as a stammerer? Having enrolled on the course – which incidentally was my first-ever therapy – I was willing and keen to learn techniques of any nature that would help me to become more fluent, especially in circumstances of fear – interviews, meetings with senior managers at work, unknown situations (new people), and so on. Starting off thinking it was meditation and nothing else, I tried to apply what I thought mindfulness was: just meditation, in other words – emptying my mind of everything, including my stammer. Now how was I going to do this in a classroom full of people who stammer, when all we've talked about for days is stammering?

I think this illustrates that I really had no idea what mindfulness is about. However, once I got over my lack of knowledge and understanding I really began to look forward to the various mini-sessions. We started off learning about some very simple techniques that helped us to learn how to focus on our breathing or being with any other distractions around us. Allowing oneself a few moments of time to focus on just breathing can be invaluable in learning to let go of all that 'busy' stuff going on in one's head.

Mindfulness is about being aware 'in the moment', and not making a judgement about that moment and that awareness. An example would be hearing someone in the group coughing and sneezing. An automatic reaction would be to become impatient or feel some sort of empathy or sympathy. Mindfulness means paying attention in the moment, and on purpose and without judgement. So, be aware someone is coughing or sneezing; be focused on what you're supposed to be focused on, be non-judgemental – and move on. Using mindfulness exercises has helped me to remain calm during tense situations and has also allowed me to prepare myself for conversation that can otherwise be quite emotional and full of stammering.

A sublime but simple exercise we did was to eat a raisin in a mindful manner. People might wonder how that might help. For me, it's all about bringing my mind to the sensations, the smells, the tastes, and the sights and sounds of eating. In other words, focus on the raisin – what does it look like, what does it smell like, what does it taste like, how do you eat it? If other thoughts come into your head, just notice them and then come back to focusing on the raisin. That way, you are present in the moment; in a purposeful and non-judgemental way. My automatic reaction was to think about Christmas – the smell, the taste – but Christmas was not the issue at that moment – the raisin was! Using this exercise, I was able to take away the knowledge that it is more beneficial to concentrate on what there is at the time and not let my mind wander in a different direction. I feel this is very important for a person who stammers. In my experience, and some may differ, people who stammer are so busy concentrating on what they're going to say after their next sentence or after someone else has finished talking, that they allow themselves to 'get worked up', and end up not being able to voice what they wanted to say in the first place.

It was really beneficial for me to focus on my breath, and my 'being' at the end of each day on the course. Over the duration of the course, with the help of the mindfulness exercises we practised, I slowly learned to appreciate myself for who I am and not worry about what I need to say next, and how people are going to react. The feelings of panic when speaking in public slowly began to melt away; and although I will never be completely 'cured', I know that I only have to refer back to my learning and the mindfulness exercises I have since learned to use, just to allay those feelings of panic and allow myself to be me.

I have also found that undertaking a specified mindfulness meditation the evening before an interview or a challenging situation like those described above has really helped me to remain calm, and just use the technique of putting myself in the moment – focusing on the present and not allowing judgement of happenings or other emotions to intrude on that moment. I almost sailed through a recent interview! I attended a first interview and had not made best use of the mindfulness CD I have and basically made a mess of it. None of my learning was applied. I attended a second interview, and made full use of my mindfulness knowledge which enabled me to remain calm during what was a somewhat stressful experience. I'm now in a high profile job in Central Government – so believe me, I use mindfulness at least twice a week to sustain my inner calmness!

I have not encountered too many challenges when using mindfulness, maybe because I am more open to natural support techniques than some. I would say that if there have been any challenges they have been more around other people's attitudes to mindfulness. It can be seen as quirky, alternative, and a little bit 'bohemian'. If you can get past other people's attitudes, the rewards are huge.

Lynn's account illustrates some of the assumptions and preconceptions that can be commonly brought to meditation. She also brings to life the power of the raisin exercise and goes on to describe how she has integrated mindfulness practices to help her cope with specific speaking challenges. I am interested that one or two comments suggest she may be trying to exclude judgemental thinking as opposed to just noticing judgement when it arises. This can be a common aspect of the learning process; participants would be encouraged to simply notice judgement, and if they find themselves being judgemental about being judgemental then again to just notice this with kindness and compassion as best they can.

Me as a therapist

It is considered important for those who teach mindfulness to have their own mindfulness practice (Segal et al., 2002). I believe that my personal practice and my training as a mindfulness teacher have influenced the way I work with PWS regardless of whether I am directly teaching mindfulness practices.

Kabat-Zinn (1996) describes the seven pillars of mindfulness which are the attitudinal qualities that underpin mindfulness practice. The attitudes are both consequences of the practice and also support its development. They are:

- non-judging – noticing without adding interpretation or judgement
- patience – allowing change to take place in its own time
- beginner's mind – bringing a lively curiosity to experience
- trust – developing faith in the validity of our experience
- non-striving – allowing things to be the way they are
- acceptance – developing a way of being with experience without struggling to change it
- letting go – letting our experience be what it is, accepting and so letting go.

Cultivating these qualities is very much a lifetime's journey and each one presents its challenges to me as a person and as a therapist. However, as I continue on the journey I am aware of some changes in my work. I increasingly hear myself encouraging clients to 'just notice' their experience, whether that be emotional, cognitive or behavioural. I notice myself inviting clients to notice their own judgements and to see if they can bring a little more kindness to themselves. I am more able to sit with a client's emotional distress without rushing to 'fix it' and I have a deeper, more felt understanding of why it may be helpful for people to 'be with' their own negative feelings. For many years I have talked of the importance of approaching techniques, such as in-block modification, in an 'allowing' as opposed to 'trying to control' way. Mindfulness has supported this stance. I invite people to be a little more curious about their experience in the hope that will encourage their 'beginner's mind'.

I see these attitudinal pillars as central to the benefits and challenges of mindfulness for both clients and clinicians and I believe that, for therapists, becoming more mindful will be valuable regardless of whether mindfulness practices are taught directly. Santorelli (1999, p.129) expresses this eloquently:

> "Our willlingness to begin with ourselves, embracing the fullness of our lives, whatever the landscape, is where practice begins. When such a practice becomes the core of the healing relationship, we encourage the same willingness in others. This is necessary if healing is to occur."

Conclusion

Inevitably, the way clients respond to mindfulness varies but I continue to be struck by how many people do engage with it. Some connect more at the level of seeing it as a relaxation technique, whilst others start to glimpse and experience other more profound aspects. It is a radical, paradoxical and challenging approach that can be introduced into therapy in a variety of ways. It has the potential to support and facilitate many traditional approaches to stammering therapy, whilst at the same time supporting the therapist's own being and ability to be with their clients who stammer as they both engage with their ongoing journeys.

I would like to thank Cathinka Guldberg and Walt Manning for reading a draft of this chapter.

References

Anderson, J., Pellowski, M., & Conture, E. (2001) Temperament characteristics of children who stutter. Paper presented at the Annual Meeting of the American Speech-Language-Hearing Association, New Orleans, LA

Baer, R.A. (2003) Mindfulness training as a clinical intervention: A conceptual and empirical review. *Clinical Psychology: Science & Practice, 10,* 125–145.

Barks, C., Moyne, J., Arberry, A.J., & Nicholson, R. (Translators) (1995) *The Essential Rumi.* San Francisco: Harper.

Batchelor, S. (1997) *Buddhism without Beliefs.* London: Bloomsbury Publishing.

Bloodstein, O. (1975) *A Handbook on Stuttering.* Chicago: The National Easter Seal Society for Crippled Children and Adults.

Beck, A.T. (1976) *Cognitive Therapy and the Emotional Disorders.* New York: International Universities Press.

Beilby, J.M., Byrnes, M.L., & Hart, M. (2010) Effectiveness of a mindfulness-based acceptance and commitment therapy approach to improve quality of life of adults who stutter. *European Symposium of Fluency Disorders,* Antwerp, Belgium.

Boyle, M. P. (2011) Mindfulness training in stuttering therapy. *Journal of Fluency Disorders* 36(2), 122–29.

Bueno, J. (2011) Promoting wellbeing through compassion. *Therapy Today,* June issue.

Chambers, R.H., Lo, B.C.Y., & Allen, N.A. (2008) The impact of intensive mindfulness training on attentional control, cognitive style, and affect. *Cognitive Therapy & Research* 32, 303–322.

Cheasman, C. (2008) Mindfulness and speech and language therapy. *Royal College of Speech & Language Therapists Bulletin (January).*

Crane, R. (2009) *Mindfulness-Based Cognitive Therapy – Distinctive Features.* Hove: Routledge.

Curtis, N. & DiGrande, A. (2006) personal communication.

Davidson, R.J., Kabat-Zinn, J., Schumacher, J., Roserkranz, M.S., Muller, D., Santorelli, S.F., Urbanowski, F., Harrington, A., Bonus, K., & Sheridan, J.F. (2003) Alterations in brain and immune function produced by mindfulness meditation. *Psychosomatic Medicine* 65, 564–570.

Fairburn, C.G., Cooper, Z., & Shafran, R. (2003) Cognitive behavior therapy for eating disorders: A "transdiagnostic" theory and treatment. *Behavioural Research & Therapy* 41(5), 509–528.

Fry, J. (2005) The cognitive model of social anxiety and its application to stuttering. Paper presented at the 7th Oxford Dysfluency Conference.

Germer, C.K. (2009) *The Mindful Path to Self-Compassion*. New York: Guildford Press.

Gilbert, P. (2010) *Compassion Focussed Therapy*. London: Routledge.

Goldin, P.R. & Gross, J.J. (2010) Effects of mindfulness-based stress reduction (MBSR) on emotional regulation in social anxiety disorder. *Emotion 10(1)*, 83–91.

Gray, J.A. (1987) *The Psychology of Fear and Stress* (ed 2) Cambridge: Cambridge University Press

Guitar, B. (2003) Acoustic startle responses and temperament in individuals who stutter. *Journal of Speech, Language & Hearing Research*, 46:233-240

Guitar, B. (2006) *Stuttering – An Integrated Approach to its Nature and Treatment*, 3rd ed. Baltimore: Lippincott, Williams & Wilkins.

Guitar, B. (2013) Stuttering: *An Integrated Approach to its Nature and Treatment* (4th edition). Baltimore: Lippincott, Williams & Wilkins.

Ingham, R.J. (2003) Evidence based treatment of stuttering: 1. definition and applications. *Journal of Fluency Disorders 28*, 197–207.

Johnson, W. (1959) *The Onset of Stuttering. Research Findings and Implications*. Minneapolis: University of Minnesota Press.

Kabat-Zinn, J. (1982) An outpatient program in behavioural medicine for chronic pain patients based on the practice of mindfulness meditation. *General Hospital Psychiatry 4*, 33–47.

Kabat-Zinn, J.(1994) *Wherever You Go There You Are*. New York: Hyperion.

Kabat-Zinn, J. (1995*) Healing and the Mind*, Volume 3. Healing From Within (DVD).

Kabat-Zinn, J. (1996) *Full Catastrophe Living*, London: Piatkus.

Kabat-Zinn, J. (2005) *Coming to our Senses, Healing Ourselves and the World through Mindfulness*. New York: Hyperion.

Kabat-Zinn, J., Massion, M.D., Kristeller, J., Peterson, L.G., Fletcher, K.E., Pbert, L., et al. (1992) Effectiveness of a meditation-based stress reduction program in the treatment of anxiety disorders. *American Journal of Psychiatry 149*, 936–943.

Killingsworth, M.A. & Gilbert, D.T. (2010) A wandering mind is an unhappy mind. *Science 330*, 932.

Kulananda (2003) *Principles of Buddhism*. Wisdom, UK.

Manning, W.H. (2004) Making clinical decisions with people who stammer. Presentation to Special Interest Group in Dysfluency.

Manning, W.H. (2012) Personal communication.

Menzies, R.G., O'Brien, S., Onslow, M., Packman, A., St Clare, T., & Bloch, S. (2008) An experimental clinical trial of a CBT therapy package for chronic stuttering. *Journal of Speech Language & Hearing Research 51(6)*,1451–1464.

Montgomery, C. (2006) The treatment of stuttering: From the hub to the spoke. Description and evaluation of an integrated therapy progam. In: N. Bernstein Ratner, & J. Tetnowski (Eds) *Stuttering Research and Practice. Volume 2: Contemporary Issues and Approaches.* Mahway, NJ: Laurence Erlbaum.

Murphy, R. (1995) The effects of mindfulness meditation vs. progressive relaxation training on stress egocentrism, anger and impulsiveness among inmates. *Dissertation Abstracts International: Section B: The Sciences & Engineering 55(8),* 3596–3604.

Perkins, W.H. (2001) *Tongue Wars.* Los Angeles: Athens Press.

Plexico, L., Manning, W.H., & DiLollo, A. (2005) A phenomenological understanding of successful stuttering management. *Journal of Fluency Disorders 30(1),* 1–22.

Plexico, L., Manning, W.H., & Levitt, H. (2009a) Coping responses by adults who stutter: I. Protecting the self and others. *Journal of Fluency Disorders 4,* 87–107.

Plexico, L., Manning, W.H., & Levitt, H. (2009b) Coping responses by adults who stutter: II. Approaching the problem and achieving agency. *Journal of Fluency Disorders 34,*108–126.

Roemer, L. & Orsillo, S. (2008) *Mindfulness- and Acceptance-Based Therapies in Practice.* New York: Guilford Press.

Santorelli, S. (1999) *Heal Thy Self.* New York: Bell Tower.

Salzberg, S. (2009) In: C.K.Germer (Ed.) *The Mindful Path to Self-Compassion.* New York: Guildford Press.

Segal, Z.V., Williams, J.M.G., & Teasdale, J.D. (2002) *Mindfulness-Based Cognitive Therapy for Depression.* New York: Guilford Press.

Sheehan, J. (1970) *Stuttering: Research and Therapy.* New York: Harper & Row.

Silverman, E-M. (2012) Mindfulness and Stuttering. North Charleston, SC: Create Space.

Stone, M. (2006) *The Two Darts: Meeting Pain with Mindfulness Practice.* Washington: Heldref Publications.

Starkweather, C.W. (1999) The effectiveness of stuttering therapy. In: N. Bernstein Ratner & E.C. Healey (Eds) *Stuttering Research and Practice: Bridging the Gap.* Mahwah, NJ: Lawrence Erhlbaum Associates.

Starkweather, C.W. & Givens-Ackerman, J. (1997) *Stuttering.* Austin, TX: Pro-Ed.

Van Riper, C. (1973) *The Treatment of Stuttering.* Englewood Cliffs, NJ: Prentice Hall.

Van Riper, C. (1982) *The Nature of Stuttering.* Englewood Cliffs, NJ: Prentice Hall.

Welwood, J. (2000) *Towards a Psychology of Awakening, Buddhism, Psychotherapy and the Path of Personal and Spiritual Transformation,* Boston: Shambhala.

Williams, M. (2005) The nature of attention: How the brain does it. Unpublished chapter.

Yairi, E. & Seery, C.H. (2011) *Stuttering Foundations & Clinical Applications*. New Jersey: Pearson.

Zylowska, L., Ackerman, D.L., Yang, M.H., Futrell, J.L., Horton, N.L., Hale, T.S., et al. (2008) Mindfulness meditation training in adults and adolescents with ADHD. *Journal of Attention Disorders* 11(6),737–746.

Appendix 1

Stammering Events Calendar

Be aware of a stammering event *at the time it is happening.* Use these questions to focus your awareness on the details of the experience as it is happening. Write it down later.

Appendix 2

Scenario 1

You are feeling down because you've just had a meeting with your manager. They have said they are quite concerned about your speech and the impact it is having on your performance at work. Shortly afterwards, you make a phone call in your open-plan office and have some problems with your speech. You look round and see a couple of colleagues whispering. What would you think?

Scenario 2

You are feeling happy and upbeat because you have just had a meeting with your manager who has given you a very positive appraisal and said how confidently you are managing your stammering in work situations. Shortly afterward, you make a phone call in your open plan office and have some problems with your speech. You look round and see a couple of colleagues whispering. What would you think?

Stammering Events Calendar

What was the experience?	Were you aware of any feelings *while* the event was happening?	How did your body feel, in detail, during this experience?	What moods, feelings and thoughts accompanied this event?	What thoughts are in your mind now as you write this down?
Monday *Stammering while talking to my boss in a meeting*	*Yes*	*Heart beating fast and tightening in my chest*	*Anxiety, embarrassment 'they're going to think I don't know what I'm talking about'*	*'wish I had spoken differently there' 'maybe it wasn't as bad as I thought at the time'*
Tuesday				
Wednesday				
Thursday				
Friday				
Saturday				
Sunday				

Developed from the work of Segal et al, 2002

8 Embrace your demons and follow your heart

An Acceptance and Commitment Therapy approach to work with people who stammer

Carolyn Cheasman and Rachel Everard

Introduction

> **Katy Bailey: Acceptance and Commitment Therapy (ACT) in action**
>
> Before doing this ACT course, I thought I had reached the point in life where I could accept my stammering. On a theoretical level I was quite happy to see myself as a stammerer, and I really believed that stammering was OK. I hadn't chosen to do therapy for a long time; I thought Sheehan and Van Riper had got it about right and I was way beyond looking for a cure. However, as I spoke, I was still struggling and getting myself into violent blocks, recoiling away from my stammering like I couldn't bear to experience it. I really didn't want to struggle any more, but I felt like my body was still fighting.
>
> From the beginning of the course, the focus on struggle as the main problem made perfect sense to me; although this therapy was not designed with stammering in mind, I think the fit is remarkable. Acceptance is easier said than done; this course helped me to see that acceptance is an active and ongoing process, and that there are a lot of useful tools to help on the way.

The course made good use of metaphors when discussing struggle, with different examples making sense to different group members at different times. For me, the metaphors were powerful and there were a number of 'penny dropping' moments, most notably with a metaphor imagining scary distracting passengers on a bus we were driving. We thought about whether we were able to stay on course. I realized I had got pretty good at keeping the passengers under control, but didn't know where my bus was going! This then linked to our discussion of values, probably the pivotal part of the course, and where this approach certainly goes deep. My family were quite shocked with the homework to (just) identify your main values in life! The homework was challenging, but very rewarding; I think it is easy to get separated from your values. I certainly had.

I learned a repertoire of skills to handle difficult thoughts and feelings, mindfulness-based exercises that we practised on the course. The mindfulness practices were realistically short and straightforward and I found that I could fit them into my busy life. These practices had an immediate effect which was striking; my inner life became more bearable straight away. I could tell this because I went home and no longer chose to have the radio on all the time; I had previously found silence uncomfortable.

Having a break between the first two days and the follow-up day worked well; some real-life issues to work through and a chance to see how the mindfulness practices fitted in at home. It was also good to let the concepts settle in before the last day because the challenge ramped up when we looked at excuses and what we can do when we realize we are not acting in line with our values. There were more straightforward practical exercises which made me feel I could take good steps with some difficult problems.

The discussions and practices about being 'in the moment' were particularly relevant to my stammering, and I think probably other people's stammering, too. My experiences of recoiling from my stammer felt a lot like not being able to 'stay in the moment' and I realized that focusing on accepting those physical feelings as they happened, and the thoughts and memories they brought up, might be a very valuable thing for me to work on. This has proven to be true. Since the course finished, I have started to develop a mindfulness practice of my own based on saying a favourite poem, noticing the feel of my speaking (rather than judging my fluency) as a way of practising staying in the moment while talking. I just move gently through any stammers that occur, using my previous work on in-block modification, and I sprinkle in some voluntary stammers just for the feel of it. At this point on the course, I was able to make a satisfying link back to speech therapy that had helped me in the past. I think the practical aspects of ACT fit very well with the desensitization and block modification approaches that I had found so useful, in that they give concrete skills to support acceptance once you feel ready to consider acceptance as an option.

As I expected, we finished with target setting, and it was clear and clever, especially in having a mini target to do within 24 hours. This helped to bridge the course straight into real life. The amazing difference with this course was that because it linked actions and goals to our own values it revealed to me the mechanism through which my motivation would be activated. I have felt excited at the end of a speech therapy course before, but this time there wasn't the worry about how long I could stay motivated, or when I would start feeling guilty for 'not doing enough practice'. This time, I had a freaky feeling that I couldn't help but be motivated, freaky but good!

The course was not overtly focused on stammering, which was a bit unsettling at first, but ultimately more useful because it allowed me to really look at how my stammering fits in with other aspects of my life. Only some of my aims were about my speech. I am also making useful changes in my home that are improving family life and I have got myself a job. Since the course, I am struggling a lot less with my speech and, in general, I feel more free to get on with life.

We hope Katy's account illustrates why we are so passionate about Acceptance and Commitment Therapy. Katy attended our three-day ACT workshop for people who stammer (PWS). Her opening paragraph describes someone who feels very ready for this kind of therapy; someone who has a real openness to a non-impairment-based approach. Whilst the story weaves together descriptions of both speech and non-speech related benefits, there is a strong sense that the impact of the course has been deep and wide-ranging. The idea of 'sprinkling in voluntary stammering just for the **feel** of it' indicates that this is someone who is really connecting with a mindfulness-based approach. As she picks up on the depth of values identification, she reminds us that this work is not to be undertaken lightly. It is a therapy that takes us to the very heart of what is most important to us and this can be both liberating and scary.

Our interest in ACT stemmed initially from Carolyn's training to become a mindfulness teacher. ACT is a mindfulness-based approach developed by Hayes, Strosahl and Wilson (1999). We both read *The Happiness Trap*, an ACT self-help book (Harris, 2008), and were immediately struck by how relevant it could be to PWS. More in-depth reading around how it had been applied in a variety of fields, including anxiety, depression and chronic pain, strengthened this initial impression. We could see its value either as a stand-alone programme or through being integrated into existing stammering therapy. In 2009, we attended the Second European Symposium on Fluency Disorders in Antwerp and were excited to attend a presentation given by Beilby and Byrnes on their application of ACT to work with PWS (see Beilby & Byrnes, 2012, for further information).

Here we aim to describe ACT, to explore its relevance to stammering and to outline how we have applied it to our client work. Central to the chapter are client commentaries, which illustrate how this radical and innovative approach has impacted on their lives.

Theory behind ACT

ACT (pronounced as one word 'act') has a strong and coherent theoretical basis and is seen as part of the third wave of cognitive and behavioural therapies. The first wave, prevalent in the 1950s and 1960s, was about encouraging overt behavioural change, using operant and classical conditioning principles with little importance placed on thoughts and feelings. The second wave in the 1970s emphasized cognitive interventions as a way of bringing about behavioural change, by challenging dysfunctional or negative thoughts and replacing them with more rational or positive thoughts. The third wave emphasizes the importance of acceptance and mindfulness, in addition to traditional behavioural strategies.

ACT has been described by one of its main theorists and practitioners, Steven Hayes, as 'a contextualistic approach that embraces elements of both traditional behaviour therapy and traditional cognitive behavioural therapy, but adds new elements that carry this tradition in a new direction' (Eifert & Forsyth, 2005, p.x). Harris (2009) usefully makes the point that it is not necessary to have a deep understanding of ACT's philosophy and theoretical basis to be a good ACT therapist, and compares practising ACT to driving a car. You can drive perfectly well without understanding the mechanics, but it can help to have some grasp of what is going on under the bonnet. For readers who would like more background theory, please see Hayes, Strosahl and Wilson (1999) and Harris (2009).

With its roots also in the human potential movement, which stresses the importance of values and meaning in life, ACT is inherently optimistic. One of its key messages is that we do not need to get rid of fears and anxieties before starting to lead the life we want to – we can get on with it right now. For PWS, the message is very clear – they do not need to 'sort out' their stammering (whatever that might mean) before moving towards what is important to them. This guiding principle fits in with our firmly-held belief that therapy which focuses purely on symptom reduction can be unhelpful. Helping PWS see the bigger picture and look beyond speech change can unlock the door to change.

Broad aims

The aims of ACT are implicit in its name – **accept** what is out of our control and **commit** to taking action that will enrich our life – hence the title of this chapter. It is about embracing our demons and following our heart. ACT is about doing what matters in life **with** whatever our difficulties are, whether anxiety, pain or stammering, as opposed to feeling that we have to get rid of our difficulties before we can do what we truly want.

ACT is a behavioural therapy in that it is about taking action, but a specific type of action, which is values guided. It is also about taking mindful action, i.e. action that is taken from a position of awareness and openness to experience. Unlike behaviour therapy, the aim is psychological flexibility as opposed to specific behaviour change or symptom reduction. When we are psychologically flexible, we respond to a difficult event with awareness, openness and focus and are able to take effective action guided by values.

ACT identifies two key processes – cognitive fusion and experiential avoidance – as being responsible for most psychological suffering.

1. Cognitive fusion (or fusion as it is generally described) occurs when we become totally 'caught up' in our thoughts, are entangled with them, and when they come to dominate our experience and behaviour. In states of fusion, our thoughts may be experienced as the truth, as commands to be obeyed or as threats to be got rid of as quickly as possible.

2. Experiential avoidance is the ongoing attempt to get rid of or suppress unwanted internal experiences including thoughts, feelings and memories.

We believe that that these two processes are highly relevant to stammering. The flip side of these processes, i.e. cognitive defusion and willingness to open to/be with difficult experience, are consequently viewed as central to therapeutic change.

Cognitive fusion and experiential avoidance are natural human responses and ACT therapists stress this throughout therapy. This normalization of these processes is seen as helpful and important.

The hexaflex – psychological flexibility

One of the joys of ACT is that it offers some very practical, concrete and powerful techniques to facilitate change. Underpinning these techniques is a model known as the hexaflex. This model has made a lot of sense to us both personally and professionally, so we will spend some time describing it. Six core principles make up the hexaflex. When these six principles are acting together, our psychological flexibility is greater. This means we can manage painful thoughts and feelings more effectively and go on to take committed action to help us lead rich, full and meaningful lives. These six core processes overlap and Harris (2009) invites us to view them as being like facets of one diamond, with the diamond as a whole being psychological flexibility (Figure 8.1).

Four of these principles – defusion, acceptance or expansion, contact with the present moment and self as context or the observing self – are based on mindfulness. Harris (2008) defines mindfulness as 'a mental state of awareness, openness and focus' (p.41).

Defusion (watch your thinking)

Defusion is about stepping back and watching our thoughts, which may present as words, images and memories. The idea is that instead of getting caught up in them (cognitive fusion) we are able to 'get some space' so that we can see that they come and go. A common metaphor is to view thoughts as cars going by our house. We start to see our thoughts for what they are – words and pictures – and to recognize that many of our thoughts are 'stories' about how we see life. ACT is not interested in whether the stories are true or false.

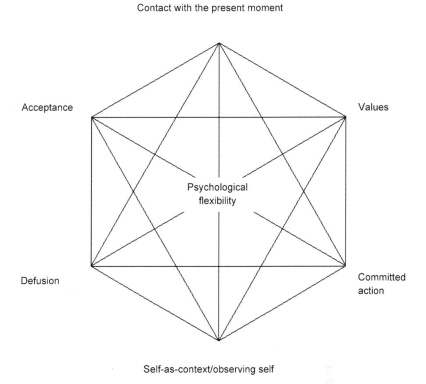

Figure 8.1 Psychological flexibility.

The important question in this type of therapy is: 'Does attending to these thoughts help me to lead the life I want?'

Harris (2008) gives a useful framework to discriminate between fusion and defusion. In states of fusion, the thought and the thing(s) it refers to, i.e. the story and the event, become stuck together. In this state, we react to a thought such as 'I'm stupid' as if we really are stupid. In fusion, it is as if thoughts are:

- Reality
- The truth
- Important

- Orders

- Wise

- (Can be) threats.

Conversely, in states of defusion we can see that thoughts are:

- Sounds, words, stories

- May or may not be true

- May or may not be important

- May or may not be orders

- May or may not be wise

- Never threats.

In ACT the story is not viewed as the problem, so the therapy is not about getting rid of or changing the story. In this way, it is very different to cognitive behaviour therapy. Fusion is seen as the problem and ACT includes a wide range of defusion techniques to help us notice thoughts and then go on to ask the question, "Does this thought help me to lead the life I want to lead?" Defusion is not about feeling good or controlling our thoughts, it is just about disentangling ourselves from these stories that can have so much power in our lives. PWS frequently fuse with negative thoughts that get in the way of them leading the life they want to lead. We believe that gaining some distance from their thoughts can be immensely liberating.

Acceptance (*open up*)

In states of acceptance we allow our thoughts and feelings to be as they are, whether we like them or not. We make room for them and let them be here. Acceptance is about creating space and letting go of struggle in order to allow difficult experiences to 'come and go' as they naturally do. In ACT, the aim of acceptance is to allow ourselves to have these difficult experiences if doing so will enable us to act on our values. It is a highly challenging process because, as human beings, our basic instinct is generally to try not to have experience we do not like. Terminology can be important as clients can confuse acceptance with resignation, 'gritting your teeth', tolerating or liking. So, whilst the concept is so central to ACT, the term 'acceptance' may not be widely used in the therapy process. Harris (2009) supplies a helpful list of phrases that can be useful to experiment with in therapy. These include:

- Being willing to have it
- Allowing it to be here
- Expanding around it
- Giving it permission to be where it already is
- Making peace with it
- Giving it some space
- Breathing into it
- Softening up around it
- Letting go of struggling with it.

So, acceptance is an **active** process. It is about actively making space for our difficult internal experiences; this is very different to passively tolerating a life situation. On the contrary, ACT is very much about us taking action to lead the lives we want to lead. A key aspect of ACT is about recognizing when experiential avoidance (the opposite of acceptance) is getting in the way of leading the lives we want, and so a therapist would try and help someone cultivate acceptance under two circumstances:

- When control of thoughts and feelings is limited or impossible
- When control of thoughts and feelings is possible, but the methods used to do this reduce the quality of life (Harris, 2009). We see many stammering-related avoidance behaviours as fitting into this category.

Many identify lack of acceptance as a key issue for PWS (Plexico, Manning, & DiLollo, 2005). In our experience, cultivating acceptance is a central therapeutic process as clients engage with therapy. The more we explored ACT, the more we could see its relevance in supporting this stage of the therapy journey. (For further exploration of acceptance, see Chapter 7.)

Contact the present moment (*be here now*)

This process is about being present, fully aware of 'in the moment' experience as opposed to being lost in thinking about the past or future. It may relate to being present to inner experience (thoughts, emotions, body sensations) or outer experience (noticing what we can see, hear, touch, taste or smell). Present moment awareness enables us to see what is happening and to make wiser choices about how to act. It can also give us a greater appreciation of ordinary, everyday events and so enrich our lives. "To find our way, we will need to pay more attention to this moment. It is the only time that we have in which to live, grow, feel, and change" (Kabat-Zinn, 1994, p.xv).

Mindfulness practices enable us to become more skilful at:

- Contacting the present moment

- Noticing when we are no longer in the present moment – when our minds have carried us to some other place or time

- Deliberately bringing our attention back to the present moment.

As well as being the means whereby we come into the present, mindfulness is also at the heart of practising defusion techniques and becoming more accepting of our experience. Whilst depicted as separate processes in the hexaflex model, the three aspects of acceptance, contact with the present moment and defusion actually merge and overlap. Present moment awareness also enables us to identify and connect with our values and to take committed action. If we are not in contact with the present moment we are much more likely to react automatically and may be less effective and less values guided in our actions.

In ACT sessions, clients are invited to bring attention consciously to present moment experience. So, they may be asked to 'notice what is going on in your body right now', 'notice what your mind is telling you right now' and 'notice your feelings – how are you aware of these right now?'. These strategies can be helpful to PWS in the context of broader stammering therapy programmes where present moment awareness can support key processes including identification and modification. Clients are also given CDs with guided mindfulness practices to help develop the skills of noticing present moment experience, noticing when their mind takes them away from the present and bringing their attention back to the present. ACT-based mindfulness practices are traditionally shorter than those taught in mindfulness-based cognitive therapy and mindfulness-based stress reduction (see Chapter 7). Often mindfulness is introduced through teaching an awareness of breath practice, but clients could equally be invited to participate in the raisin exercise (guided mindful exploration of a raisin – see Chapter 7) to introduce the concept.

The Dropping Anchor metaphor (www.thehappinesstrap.com, 2009) can be used as a grounding technique if someone becomes distressed or overwhelmed by experience. This involves noticing the feet contacting the floor, feeling the support of the ground, noticing sensations associated with the breath, directing the breath into the feet and noticing when the mind pulls awareness away and consciously bringing awareness back into the present moment. This can be useful both in sessions and in everyday life.

Self as context (the observing self)

> "The observing self sees things as they are, without judging, criticizing, or doing any of the other thinking processes that set us up for a struggle with reality. Therefore, it gives acceptance in its truest, purest form."

(Harris, 2008, p.179)

Self as context, commonly described as the observing self, refers to the place from which we notice our experience without getting entangled in it. It is also termed 'pure awareness' because it is our awareness of our own awareness. It refers to when we notice that we are noticing or when we are aware that we are aware. This is the fourth core process that is cultivated by mindfulness. Indeed, the concept of the observing self is implicit in all mindfulness teaching. Identifying and connecting with the notion of an observing self or a transcendent self can help to give us a sense of a safe, enduring and non-judgemental place that we can access in the midst of pain and turmoil.

The observing self can be a challenging process to describe in words and is best explored through experience. However, it is often first introduced in ACT through the sky and weather metaphor. Here, our thoughts and feelings are likened to the weather and the observing self is likened to the sky. The weather is always changing – it might be calm, bright, windy, rainy or stormy, but no matter how intense it gets, it cannot damage the sky. The sky endures and is always there, even if it is obscured, and crucially it has the space to accommodate all of the weather. Clients are also introduced to the concept through the ideas of the 'thinking self' and the 'observing self'. The thinking self is the part of us that thinks, plans, analyzes, daydreams, etc, and it is a part that, despite our best efforts, is not easy to control. The observing self is aware, but does not think; it simply notices and registers experience directly without intervening with thinking.

Values (know what matters)

Our values describe what truly matters to us and define who we want to be and how we want to live our lives. They are principles that can both guide and motivate us as we move through our lives. In ACT, work on identifying values may take place early on in therapy or after work on the mindfulness-based processes already described (see Harris, 2009, for a discussion on this topic). Values are best viewed as directions we want to move in and, as such, the compass metaphor is often used to illustrate this. Just as a compass can keep us on track, so do our values. Values can be likened to moving west in that it is always possible to keep moving west. If one of our values is to be a loving parent this endures. We do not suddenly wake up one day, tick it off the list and move on to something else. Goals, by contrast, are things which we can achieve and tick off the list. Using the compass metaphor again, goals can be likened to things we want to see/achieve/do on our journey west. In relation to the value of being a loving parent, tangible goals might include planning a memorable family holiday or spending regular quality time with our children.

Values are judgement free – they are not 'good' or 'bad', 'right' or 'wrong'. They are simply directions we identify as enabling us to live full, rich and meaningful lives. Harris (2009) identifies five key points that can be drawn out in therapy when identifying values:

- Values are here and now – in contrast to goals which are in the future
- Values never need to be justified
- Values often need to be prioritized
- Values are best lightly held, i.e. having our values as guides rather than rules
- Values are freely chosen.

Harris (2009) invites clients to consider success not as about achieving goals, but as living in tune with their values. This could clearly be liberating and motivating for many PWS who often describe success in terms of speech-related goals as opposed to whether they are doing what they truly want or behaving as the kind of person they want to be.

Values identification is about helping people contact their 'heart's truest desires'. For PWS, it can be enormously powerful as it can reconnect them with areas of their life they may have lost touch with through experiential avoidance. For example, someone who stammers might have being a supportive friend as one of their values. They may become aware that they have avoided speaking to a particular friend in need because they do not want to experience the fear of using the phone; re-connecting with this particular value may give them the impetus to go ahead and speak to the friend, being willing to make room for the fear. As such, this part of the work can help clients have other powerful reasons for working on avoidance reduction. Not just because the therapist says this will help them work on their speech, but because they will then start doing more of the things that make life truly worth living.

Committed action (*do what it takes*)

This process is about taking values-guided, effective and flexible action. It is where the therapy may be seen as more behavioural in nature and becomes goal-directed, in contrast to many other mindfulness-based approaches. What sets this apart from other behavioural approaches is that the focus on goals is guided by values and also that action, when it is taken, is supported by the four mindfulness-based processes. Taking mindful action in this way is, in our opinion, a refreshing and novel approach to goal-setting and can enable clients to take important steps towards what really matters to them.

Harris (2009) identifies four steps to taking committed action:

- Choose a domain in life that is a high priority for change
- Choose the values to pursue in this domain
- Develop goals guided by those values
- Take action mindfully.

Emphasis is placed on taking small steps: 'What is the next tiniest step you can take to help you move in this direction?'

Inevitably barriers are encountered. Challenging thoughts and feelings can arise as someone takes committed action and the mindfulness-based strategies can help to support them as they encounter these difficulties. Clients are encouraged to open up and allow space for these experiences to be here using processes such as acceptance and defusion. It might be that someone sets an impossible goal and it could be important to acknowledge that this is not going to be achieved any time soon, but that smaller goals are possible. Returning to values is important to try and identify what is underlying this desired change. Different ways to act on this value can be identified. The concept of 'willingness' becomes very important at this stage. The client is encouraged to be **willing** to experience a range of difficult experience in the service of values-guided action. This is more than just a verbal encouragement though, as clients have practised mindfulness processes to help them 'open up to' and 'be with' their difficult thoughts and feelings.

Yaruss (2010) describes the importance of linking therapy to the wider quality of life issues for people who stammer. We believe quality of life is addressed when we make space in therapy for clients to identify what is truly important to them through values identification and when we encourage committed action.

Psychological inflexibility

The core processes described above together create psychological flexibility. The opposite of these processes is psychological inflexibility (Figure 8.2) characterized by:

- Living in the past or future

- Experiential avoidance

- Cognitive fusion

- Attachment to the conceptualized self – a way of describing ourselves, which can be limiting; for example, 'I am a stammerer which means x, y and z'

- Lack of values clarity/contact – when what is important to us in our life becomes lost, neglected or forgotten

- Unworkable action – patterns of behaviour that keep us stuck in one place rather than moving towards our values.

These processes are closely interconnected; for example, a PWS asked to give a presentation may immediately think back to past experiences where they had difficulty talking in public, getting caught up with the thought, "I'm no good at

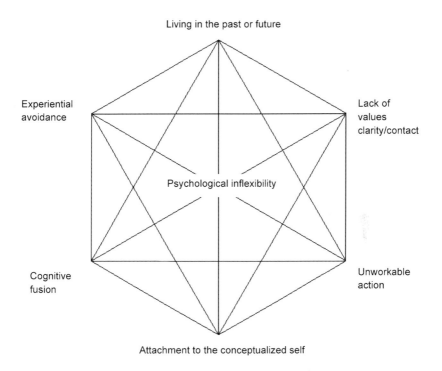

Living in the past or future

Experiential
avoidance

Lack of
values
clarity/contact

Psychological inflexibility

Cognitive
fusion

Unworkable
action

Attachment to the conceptualized self

Figure 8.2 Psychological inflexibility.

talking in front of others" (cognitive fusion) and the overarching belief, 'Because I stammer, I can't do things like that' (attachment to the conceptualized self). They may then choose to avoid giving the presentation because they do not want to experience anxiety (experiential avoidance), losing sight of the values they may have around their career development (lack of values clarity/contact). Subsequently, they may become 'stuck' if they continue to avoid challenging situations (unworkable action).

Applications of ACT and parallels to stammering

There are an ever-increasing number of studies (including randomized control trials) demonstrating the effectiveness of ACT in the management of conditions such as anxiety, depression, obsessive-compulsive disorder, social phobia, workplace stress, chronic pain, weight control, epilepsy, post-traumatic stress disorder and smoking cessation (Öst, 2008).

Although these studies did not involve people who stammer, there are parallels to be drawn between some of the conditions listed above and stammering. For example, Dahl and Lundgren (2006a, p.286) write:

> "The basic premise of ACT as applied to chronic pain is that while pain hurts, it is the struggle with pain that causes suffering."

The same can be said to be true of stammering; whilst the actual moment of stammering can feel physically uncomfortable, it is often the struggle with stammering and the accompanying thoughts and feelings that cause suffering. Moreover, whilst stammering is amenable to change, it can be seen as a chronic condition since the majority of adults who have stammered since childhood do not stop stammering altogether. Therefore, an approach that fosters acceptance and encourages values-based action can enable a person who stammers to move forward in their lives in a meaningful way.

Eifert and Forsyth (2005, p.8) make an interesting point when talking about agoraphobia:

> "When persons with agoraphobia avoid public places, they are not avoiding the places per se. What they are really avoiding is experiencing their thoughts and emotions associated with panic in such places."

Likewise, PWS might avoid moments of stammering as a way of avoiding experiencing the painful thoughts and feelings that accompany those moments. To us, it makes sense that ACT's emphasis on managing painful thoughts and emotions differently would be particularly helpful in the field of stammering.

Beilby, Byrnes and Yaruss (2012) describe and evaluate an ACT group intervention programme for PWS, the first of its kind to our knowledge to combine ACT techniques with speech and stuttering modification. The results of the programme are impressive, with statistically significant improvements in psychosocial functioning, preparation for change and therapy, utilization of mindfulness skills, and overall speech fluency.

The therapy sequence

As discussed, the aim of ACT is to cultivate psychological flexibility and in order to achieve this, the therapy process traditionally follows the sequence described below:

1. Confronting the agenda (creative hopelessness)

2. Control is the problem

3. Willingness is the alternative (defusion/acceptance/ contact with the present moment)

4. Self-as-context

5. Values and action (Harris, 2009).

The sequence of therapy is highly flexible and individualized to the client's needs. In addition, as all six core processes of the hexaflex interconnect and overlap with one another, it is likely that in any one session, whilst the main focus might be on one component, other aspects will also be touched upon.

Following a description of creative hopelessness, we will outline how we have integrated ACT into our work with groups of adults who stammer, and this will illustrate the therapy sequence described above.

Confronting the control agenda (creative hopelessness) is an optional part of the therapy process. It explores the ways a client might try to control unwanted experience as well as the outcomes of this 'control agenda'. This is similar in many ways to what speech and language therapists might already do in work with PWS as they explore the outcomes of avoidance strategies. It is also similar to some CBT work where vicious cycles are explored during the conceptualization stage of therapy. In ACT, this stage is seen as important when the client is strongly attached to the control agenda, and it can also highlight another key concept: workability. Harris (2009) describes the whole of the ACT model as resting on this concept, so it is important. The underlying idea is that if what we are doing is helping us lead the life we want, then that is fine – there is no need to change these strategies. However, if the way we are dealing with our experience is getting in the way of us leading the life we want, then it might be helpful to find alternatives. So, for example, if an avoidance strategy is not getting in the way of us leading the rich, full and meaningful life we want, then that is OK. However, more often than not, overuse of experiential avoidance does get in the way of us doing the things we want and this is what would be seen in an ACT framework as 'unworkable'. Exploring control strategies in this way is described as the 'creative hopelessness' process. However, therapists are advised not to use this term with clients. The central question in ACT is: 'Is what you are doing working to give you the life you want?' as opposed to 'Is this behaviour right or wrong/good or bad?' Such judgements are taken away.

The use of metaphors

ACT often involves the use of metaphors. Eifert and Forsyth (2005, p.103) comment on the power of metaphor:

> "Metaphors are nothing more than stories. Because they cannot be taken literally, they allow clients to make experiential contact with an aspect of their experience that may be frightening for them to contact directly. In so doing, they help create distance between the client and how they are approaching their anxiety, while also opening the door for new solutions to emerge. Studies have shown that figurative metaphorical language is emotionally more meaningful, and hence more likely to impact a person's overt behaviour, than straightforward rational-logical talk."

Clients are also encouraged to create their own metaphors; this is a powerful and highly personal way of getting in touch with their experience. Metaphors we have found useful in work with PWS are 'the quicksand', 'feeding the baby tiger' and 'the struggle switch'. These are described in more detail below.

Applying ACT to working with young people and adults who stammer

Whilst we will illustrate the application of ACT in adult stammering therapy in a group setting, ACT is widely used by psychologists in individual therapy. We can see great scope for integrating ACT principles into one-to-one stammering therapy. Speech and language therapists might also see the relevance to work with client groups other than PWS.

Integration of ACT into speech and language therapy programmes

We have started to integrate ACT principles into our stammering therapy programmes, which primarily take a block modification approach (Van Riper, 1973). We introduce mindfulness practices early on, starting with the raisin activity (Williams, Teasdale, Segal & Kabat-Zinn, 2007). This enables clients to experience first-hand what it feels like to relate to a common experience differently, to come into contact with the present moment and to notice how our thoughts often take us away from our direct experience. Subsequent mindfulness practices include awareness of breath and the three-minute breathing space (see Chapter 7 for further description of these practices).

When exploring the ineffectiveness and the costs of experiential avoidance (creative hopelessness), clients participate in an activity called 'Avoidance: the pay-offs and prices'. This helps them to reflect on both the benefits and costs of avoidance in all its myriad forms. This activity is described in more detail in Chapter 4. We find that most clients come to the conclusion that avoidance strategies offer momentary relief in the short term ('Thank goodness I got out of going to that meeting and having to introduce myself'), but in the longer term these strategies can have a detrimental effect on what they want to achieve. This level of exploration helps to give greater impetus to their work on reducing avoidance behaviours as described below.

The ACT model is formally introduced when starting work on avoidance reduction. This part of therapy can be highly challenging as these avoidance-based coping strategies are likely to be well-embedded and powerfully reinforced. Doing something different can therefore take determination and energy. Reducing avoidances might lead to increased stammering, a frightening prospect for many people. ACT can support this stage of therapy by helping clients to get in touch with what is really important to them, so increasing motivation to carry out what can be difficult work. The mindfulness practices already introduced can help clients to cultivate openness to and acceptance of difficult experience. By introducing the full ACT model at this stage, clients can see how developing mindfulness skills and identifying values could enable them to move in the directions they want.

The concept of values is introduced to the group and each client is encouraged to consider:

1. Their reasons for wanting greater ease in communication; identifying these reasons can help them move forward in therapy when it becomes challenging. Examples of reasons given by clients have included 'to express myself fully', 'to be myself', 'to say what I want when I want'.

2. Their values in life as a person (not just as a speaker). Clients are given four areas (Dahl & Lundren, 2006b; Harris, 2008) to consider as outlined in Table 8.1.

Table 8.1 Life values.

Area	May include	Questions for clients to consider
Work/education	Workplace, career, education, skills development	What do you value in your work? What would make it more meaningful? What personal qualities would you like to bring to your work? What sort of work relations would you like to build?
Relationships	Relationships with partner, children, parents, relatives, friends, co-workers	What sort of partner/ brother/ sister/son/daughter would you like to be? How do you want to behave in these relationship? What qualities would you like to bring to these relationships? How would you treat others if you were the 'ideal you' in those relationships?
Personal growth/health	Religion, spirituality, creativity, life skills, meditation, yoga, nature, exercise, nutrition and/or addressing health-risk factors	What ongoing activities would you like to start or take up again? What groups would you like to join? What lifestyle changes would you like to make?
Leisure/recreation	Activities for rest, recreation, fun and creativity	What sorts of hobbies or leisure activities do you enjoy? How do you relax/have fun? What sorts of activities would you like to do?

We then demonstrate how goals can be used to help them move towards their values, and how this relates to the work they are currently doing on avoidance reduction. To illustrate this point, we give the example of someone who values 'being an effective manager'. A goal which will help them to move towards this value might be to speak up more in managers' meetings on behalf of their team. This could be something that they have previously avoided because of their fear of stammering in front of their colleagues; however, by recognizing that this value is important, they might become more willing to experience that fear and give their point of view. Note again the concept of willingness, which we believe is very useful in supporting all aspects of desensitization work. By talking openly about being willing to experience negative emotions, such as anxiety or fear, in challenging speaking situations, we encourage our clients to be with these emotions rather than trying to reduce them.

One client commented on how he had avoided attending his children's parents' evening as he was anxious about school staff becoming aware of his stammering. However, he recognized that one of his key values was to be a good parent. Consequently, avoiding such meetings was not in the best interests of his children. He realized that it was important for him to be willing to experience this anxiety and to go ahead with attending such events. Another student identified that one of her recreation/leisure values was to enjoy nature and for this reason her goal was to join a walking club, something she had previously avoided because of her fear of meeting new people and what they might think of her because of her stammer. She reflected that by joining a walking club and being willing to experience that fear, her life would become richer.

ACT as a stand-alone course

Motivated by the novel approach offered by ACT and its obvious relevance to PWS, we decided to offer a three-day workshop. We targeted this at past and current clients who had already had some experience of therapy as, in our opinion, they were better prepared to look at stammering from a fresh perspective. Encouraged by the positive response, we now offer this workshop on a regular basis. Katy's account at the start of this chapter is based on this workshop.

The initial two days of the workshop are consecutive, followed by a break of four weeks before the final day. This format allows clients to gain a basic understanding of ACT and to start to apply it to their lives, setting short- and medium-term goals in line with their values prior to the break. Part of the final day allows space for reporting back on changes made and troubleshooting ongoing concerns. The topics covered on the course include:

- What is acceptance and commitment therapy?
- Letting go of the struggle
- The impact of avoidance
- Defusion – creating a distance between you and your thoughts
- Mindfulness
- Identifying valued life directions
- Goal setting.

Undermining the control agenda

We first introduce the topic of creative hopelessness (see 'The therapy sequence', p.283) through the use of the digging metaphor (also known as 'The Man in the Hole', Hayes et al., 1999):

> "Imagine you're put into a field, blindfolded, with a bag of tools and told to run around. Sooner or later, you fall into a hole and can't get out. In your tool-bag you find a shovel, so you start digging, but the more you dig, the bigger the hole becomes. There are no other tools, so you seem to have no other choice – although exhausted you keep on digging…"

This neatly illustrates that often our natural and instinctive response to a problematic situation can make things worse (Harris, 2009). PWS usually connect with this when they consider their natural reactions to stammering, which might include putting more effort into moments of stammering, using escape behaviours or avoiding speaking altogether. These ways of reacting to stammering can become subconscious over time, therefore increasing awareness is the first stage to change.

We encourage clients to consider their own control agenda by discussing how they have tried to manage certain behaviours and/or negative thoughts and feelings and what the consequences have been. We give them the option of focusing specifically on stammering or on other areas of their lives. Following their own real-life examples, we talk about the tendency for most people to keep on doing things that are not particularly helpful and the reasons for this. These include the fact that control strategies are often very helpful in the external world (for example, if your boiler breaks down, it makes sense to ask a heating engineer to fix it) but can be less helpful when dealing with our internal world of thoughts and feelings. Also, society in general can encourage emotional avoidance by giving out key messages such as 'put on a brave face' or 'you'll get over it'. In addition, as previously mentioned, avoidance control strategies offer short-term relief and this is a powerful reinforcer.

The main learning point here is that control can be the problem rather than the solution. With this in mind, we introduce other metaphors including struggling in quicksand (Harris, 2009): the automatic reaction of someone in this precarious situation is to struggle, which only decreases their likelihood of survival as the more they struggle the deeper they sink down. However, if they can remain calm, lie back, stretch out and distribute their weight evenly over the sand (a highly counterintuitive strategy), they stand a much greater chance of getting out alive.

Another useful metaphor at this stage is 'feeding the baby tiger', described by Eifert and Forsyth (2005) as 'feeding-the-anxiety-tiger metaphor'. It not only shows clients that it is hard to control anxiety (or any other difficult feeling) by trying to appease it, but also is a graphic description of how increasingly larger portions of our resources and life space can be consumed by efforts to control and avoid difficult feelings:

> "Imagine you're at home and you notice a baby tiger snapping at your heels, looking a bit fierce and very hungry. You go to the fridge to find some food for him to get him to go away. And it works – you throw him some food and he leaves you alone for a time. However, he's still lurking somewhere, growing bigger thanks to the food you've just given him. So the next time you see him, he's got bigger and bolder so you do the same thing – you throw him some food in the hope he'll go away again. This goes on for some time – you throwing him scraps of meat in the hope he'll disappear for good – until one day you look round and there's this enormous starving tiger looking you directly in the eye, ready to gobble you up."

When applied to stammering, this metaphor can help to vividly portray the attempts to control the fear of stammering by employing a whole raft of avoidance strategies. The more the fear of stammering is avoided, the more it grows and, if taken to extremes, this can significantly limit life choices.

Working through the hexaflex

Having introduced the concept of 'control is the problem', we talk through the hexaflex illustrating each aspect through practical exercises. We make it clear, as previously explained, that the six aspects of the hexaflex are not separate processes, but their combined synergy works towards achieving the same purpose: to help us lead rich, full, meaningful lives whilst managing the pain that life inevitably brings us.

Contact with the present moment: The raisin activity (Williams et al., 2007) helps participants to get in contact with the present moment, whilst noticing that their minds often take them away from the here and now. Participants are also guided through regular awareness of breath practices (Williams et al., 2007) and are given a CD for home practice.

Acceptance/opening up: As described above, the term 'acceptance' can have different meanings for different people; for example, for some people it might imply 'giving up'. The group has the opportunity to explore what the term means to them as individuals and we then offer a list of alternative terms, such as 'opening up to', 'allowing' and 'giving space to'.

We introduce a new metaphor, the 'struggle switch' (Harris, 2008). Put simply, the struggle switch is an imaginary switch at the back of our minds. When it is on, we struggle against any physical or emotional pain that comes our way to try and get rid of it. So, if we are feeling anxious, we might start to struggle and say things to ourselves, such as, 'Getting so anxious can't be good for me – why do I get like this?' which can lead to even more anxiety. When the struggle switch is off, whatever emotion shows up and no matter how unpleasant it might be, we do not struggle with it. We let our feelings and thoughts come and go and do not waste time and energy struggling with them. When we are not struggling, we experience what is called in ACT **'clean discomfort'** – a natural level of physical and emotional discomfort, which we all experience at one point or another. **'Dirty discomfort'** occurs when the struggle switch is on and we are struggling against it.

At this point we introduce the four steps to emotional acceptance, which are:

1. Observe: bring awareness to the feelings in the body

2. Breathe: take a few slow breaths

3. Expand: make room for these feelings – create some space for them

4. Allow: allow them to be here; make peace with them.

We also suggest it can be useful for clients to silently say to themselves: 'I don't like this feeling, but I have room for it' or, 'It's unpleasant, but I can open to it.'

The observing self: This is introduced through the use of the sky and weather metaphor (see p.277). The distinction between the observing and thinking self can also be usefully illustrated through the bad news radio metaphor (Harris, 2008). Our thinking self is similar to a radio, constantly playing in the background. It is unhelpful when it is the Radio Doom and Gloom show, broadcasting negative stories constantly. It reminds us of the bad things from the past, it warns us of the bad things to come in the future, and it gives us regular updates on everything that is wrong with us. It is hard to switch it off, but we can learn not to tune into it, just as we might have a radio playing in the background but pay little attention to it. A useful experiential exercise to introduce here is called 'Take your mind for a walk', which brings to life the distinction between the observing self and the thinking self, as described in the section 'Self as context' above. This is carried out in pairs, with Person A being their own observing self and Person B being Person A's thinking self. Person A's job is to feel, see, hear and smell whatever is happening around them, and to notice things they might not normally notice, whilst listening gently and compassionately to their thinking self. Person B as the thinking self chatters away. The point of the exercise is for Person A to realize that they are not their mind as represented by their thinking self, and that they can choose to tune into what their mind is saying or to tune out.

Defusion: We introduce a variety of creative and fun ways for clients to work on defusion as described by Harris (2008). The list of strategies is extensive and we have selected some examples:

> **Distancing ourselves from our thoughts**: this can be achieved by noticing a thought, e.g. 'This person will think I'm stupid if I stammer', and then acknowledging it by silently saying something along the lines of

'I'm having the thought that this person thinks I'm stupid if I stammer'. Further distance can be achieved by acknowledging the noticing, i.e. 'I notice that I'm having the thought that… .

'Thank you mind' and 'naming the story': Recurring thoughts can be acknowledged by thanking our mind for serving them up again and again: 'Ah, there's the thought again about how I'm going to stammer and make a fool of myself – thank you, mind!' Similarly, it can be helpful to name a particular theme or story: 'There's that 'I'm a failure' story.'

Helpful questions for unhelpful thoughts: As previously discussed, ACT's take on thoughts is that it is not important whether a thought has any basis in truth or not, but whether it serves us in any way. Once again, workability is key. It is therefore useful to question thoughts using the following prompts:

- Is this thought helping me at all? Does it help me to take effective action?

- Is this an old story that I've heard before?

- Do I feel better or worse when I have this thought?

- Am I going to trust my mind or my experience?

Clients are likely to connect to one or more of these exercises to help disentangle themselves from the thoughts that can have so much power over them.

Values: The Bull's Eye worksheet (Harris, 2009), which divides life into four domains (work/education, health/personal growth, relationships, and leisure), gives the client the opportunity to think about their values in relation to these four areas and consider to what extent they are living by them. This can be challenging as it could bring into sharp relief areas where clients are not living by their values. We ask them to focus on one or two values only, to make the work more manageable, and ask them to start thinking about goals that will move them in the right direction. It is at this point that the concept of willingness is brought to the fore and discussed. We talk about how many PWS are reluctant to use the telephone, but in an emergency they would be willing to experience the fear of using the phone in order to make a potentially life-saving call. Clients are asked to discuss what thoughts and feelings they would be willing to have when working towards their values.

Committed action: This is where the goal-setting process begins; participants choose a value they would like to work on and then set themselves immediate, short-term, medium-term and long-term goals. For example, one client chose as his value 'life long learning'; his immediate goal was to spend time reading an article he was particularly interested in; his short-term goal was to do some research on the internet on topics of interest; his medium-term goal was to explore evening/weekend courses; and his long-term goal was to work towards doing some teaching himself.

By the end of the first two days, our aim is for clients to have practical goals in place that they can work on in the next few weeks before returning for the final day. They can reflect on the progress they have made so far and consider some of the barriers which they may have experienced. To help them in this task, the concept 'reasons are not facts' (Harris, 2008) is introduced. This distinguishes reasons from excuses and reinforces the concept of willingness.

We also use the FEAR and DARE acronyms to identify what is getting in the way of committed action and how they can work on these barriers:

FEAR

F = fusion with unhelpful thoughts such as 'it's too hard', 'I'll do it later'; practising defusion helps with managing these thoughts.

E = excessive goals; the client might have set themselves unrealistic expectations, so breaking the goals down into smaller steps would be useful here.

A = avoidance of discomfort, such as fear or anxiety; practising mindfulness skills will help to open up to the experience and develop willingness.

R = remoteness from values; questions, such as 'what do I really care about?', 'what really matters deep in my heart', are useful here.

DARE, the antidote to FEAR

D = defusion

A = acceptance of discomfort

R = realistic goals

E = embracing values.

We have found it valuable to structure the course with a break between the first two days and the final day, as this enables clients to experience for themselves some of the barriers they might encounter when working towards their valued directions. By identifying these barriers (through FEAR) and finding ways forward (through DARE), participants are likely to be in a better position to work independently on their goals after the course has finished.

Outcome measures for the ACT stand-alone course

As well as receiving qualitative feedback directly from clients through their self-reflections, we also used the following assessments at the beginning and end of the workshop.

> **Freiburg Mindfulness Inventory** (Walach, Buchheld, Buttenmuller, Kleinknecht & Schmidt, 2006): This is a 14-item scale which assesses a person's experience of mindfulness. Using a four-point scale ('rarely' to 'almost always'), respondents rate how often they have experiences of being open and receptive to present moment experiences. Examples of items include: 'I sense my body, whether eating, cooking, cleaning or talking'; 'I accept unpleasant experiences', and 'I watch my feelings without getting lost in them'.

> **Stammering Acceptance Questionnaire** (adapted from Chronic Pain Acceptance Questionnaire, McCracken, Vowles & Eccleston, 2004): This is a 20-item scale which assesses a person's level of acceptance with regards to stammering. Using a six-point scale ('never true' to 'always true'), respondents rate their readiness to be with their stammering. Examples of items include: 'It's OK to stammer'; 'I need to concentrate on getting rid of my stammer', and "when my stammering increases, I can still take care of my responsibilities".

> **Wright and Ayre Stuttering Self-Rating Profile** (Wright & Ayre, 2000): Well-known to speech and language therapists, this profile records how a PWS perceives his or her stammering at the beginning and end of therapy, using five internally reliable sub-scales (behaviours, thoughts, feelings about stuttering, avoidance due to stuttering and disadvantage due to stuttering).

Fourteen clients completed each of these three assessments at the beginning and end of the course (an interval of five weeks) and the pattern of scores was similar across all the measures. There was a significant difference between the mean scores at the two different time points, indicating development of mindfulness skills, greater acceptance of stammering and a reduction in behaviours, thoughts, feelings, avoidance and disadvantage ratings. For a comprehensive breakdown of the results, see Table 8.2.

Measure	Pre		Post		F value	P value	Partial eta^2
	Mean	SD	Mean	SD			
Freiburg	31.36	4.92	37.57	4.94	15.27	.002	.54
Acceptance	65.76	17.66	77.89	15.83	15.10	.002	.54
WASSP – behaviour	27.21	5.55	22.79	6.07	12.59	.004	.49
WASSP – thoughts	12.07	3.41	9.00	3.53	14.20	.002	.52
WASSP – feelings	19.00	7.52	14.29	6.13	16.24	.001	.56
WASSP – avoidance	10.67	4.21	7.78	3.96	19.45	.002	.71
WASSP – disadvantage	10.33	3.35	8.00	3.57	17.82	.003	.69

Table 8.2.

We recognize the need for long-term data, but are excited by these preliminary results, particularly since they reflect both psychological and speech changes (there was no direct speech work included in the therapy). As described earlier, the course took place over three days (two consecutive days followed by a third day five weeks later). Since the second assessment point took place after the break in therapy, our preliminary results are encouraging and suggestive of maintenance of learning over time.

Our next steps include offering the workshop non-intensively, as a 10-session evening course, and collecting longer-term follow-up data.

Clients' stories

Amanda Littleboy– a turning-point in her life

In choosing the course, I decided I wanted something that wasn't specifically speech-based and which would look more into the emotional and psychological aspects of stammering. At the time, I was struggling with a number of negative feelings and stresses, relating both to my stammer (which had recently become more difficult to control) and other areas of my life, particularly work-related, all of which contributed to a great deal of emotional tension.

We were given opportunities to identify personal values, set achievable goals both long-term and short-term, share ideas and opinions with others, and participate in practical exercises on mindfulness. The mindfulness exercises, which we did as a group, were extremely helpful and it was also good to be able to go away and practise these alone on a daily basis, with the help of a CD. Being a particularly 'visual' person, I was able to become immersed in the images described. These exercises encouraged participants to experience and connect with the present moment, become aware of our senses, to let go of external distractions and concerns. I have personally made an effort to continue with the techniques I learned beyond the course and have found them to be a very useful tool in times of stress or fatigue.

The most challenging aspects for me were the defusion exercises involving separating, or detaching, myself from thoughts or feelings. Although able to visualize, I found it very hard to actually detach myself from the specific feeling in this way, especially when the thought or idea I was focusing on was a painful one. I did experience some distress during this process, but persevered and was able to accept the ultimate gain that came from it.

ACT proved to be something of a turning point for me. The course enabled me to feel much more empowered to handle difficult emotions and thoughts connected to my stammer in a positive way, to understand that I don't have to keep struggling and fighting against them all the time, but instead give them space and permission to be. I have experienced anxiety, chronic worry and depression in the past and have always battled hard to overcome them. I have fought and recovered, fought and recovered ... but only ever on a temporary basis. The underlying issues have always remained there, below the surface, and have merely been suppressed, often creating a vicious circle. This way they have continued to subtly damage my confidence and self-esteem. The idea that I no longer have to struggle all the time was something of a revelation to me and learning to regard negative thoughts and feelings in a new way has robbed them of their power and prevented them from becoming overwhelming. I am no longer so frustrated or self-critical and am learning to be kinder to myself. The resulting increase in self-confidence has in turn encouraged me to step forward in my life and take on new responsibilities and challenges which in the past I would have avoided. From now on, when times of stress present themselves, as they are bound to in life, I will feel much more equipped to deal with them.

Regarding my stammer, I cannot honestly say my level of fluency changed much through doing the course, although I am less despairing at times when my speech lets me down and have better coping strategies than before. But, as already stated, fluency was not my main aim in undertaking this training. If a person is looking for techniques to control their speech then this course may not be for them. If, however, they are more interested in the advantages that can be gained from learning new ways of dealing with the submerged part of the 'stammering iceberg' (in my opinion the most significant part) I would recommend ACT.

From the outset Amanda makes it clear that she was interested in working with negative thoughts and feelings, and that ACT gave her a new way to manage them more effectively. It is interesting to note that previous attempts to overcome strong negative feelings had failed for her and that ACT's emphasis on letting feelings be was empowering and liberating. In this way, she illustrates the effectiveness of letting go of the struggle, allowing her to move forward in her life. It is also interesting that she talks about learning to be kinder to herself as developing greater self kindness and compassion is often reported as a valuable outcome of mindfulness-based approaches.

John Collins– applying ACT to everyday life

I have been a stammerer for most of my life and have felt that stammering and the quest for fluency was a journey of inner exploration involving much more than focusing on speech alone. The very name, acceptance and commitment therapy, gave me a 'Wow! Let's explore this' response. Five months have passed since I did the course and for me there has been a real and meaningful integration of some of the principles.

The emphasis on a mindfulness approach of recognizing thoughts and feelings as they arise, giving them space and making time in your day when that skill is practised is, for me, spot on. Yet I find, like many other life skill learning experiences, there are many levels to 'getting it'. An example of a difficult but manageable situation is when I struggle with a few words in a shop and perceive the shop assistant's response to be patronising. In this type of situation I can observe my feelings and make choices about how to respond. However, in a heated conversation with my spouse when emotions are running high, being mindful can be much more difficult.

Another aspect of the course I found hugely stimulating was the concept of the 'happiness trap'. As ACT puts it, the happiness trap we can set ourselves is about trying to be happy and feeling good all the time, wanting things to always work out. But life's not like that and letting go of the need to be happy all the time can be strangely empowering. The idea that feeling down and miserable can be a perfectly human/normal response to a difficult situation and that feeling this way is OK, is something I knew about already, but the course gave me a way to handle difficult thoughts and feelings more easily. Sometimes, I can bring mindfulness to a situation and other times I can't and that's OK.

I also found the ACT approach stimulating and in some ways very obvious. I'm fortunate to work in a field I love, but I do know that fear of stammering and, more particularly, fear of how other people might judge me because of my stammering affects how I am with that work in the world. I've learned from the course that being willing to face discomfort when bringing my work to a wider more varied audience will be worth it as I'll be moving towards what's really important to me. Going through a process of identifying values which match my personality and then working on a plan to bring these values more into my life through action seems to be a recipe for a rich and meaningful life.

Since doing the course, ACT strategies have become part of my experience of reality and I draw on them regularly.

John's practical application of key ACT principles demonstrates the extent to which he is able to use what he has learned in his everyday life, highlighting the fact it can be easier to be mindful in some situations than others. His understanding and acceptance of ACT's premise that life inevitably brings pain is important, as it enables him to be willing to experience discomfort when working towards his values. He also illustrates the importance of action which is values-based.

Mercedes Oakley– improved quality of life

The three-day ACT course has helped me maintain a good level of fluency and also feel better about things generally. I had already attended a mindfulness course at City Lit and read Russ Harris' book *The Happiness Trap*, so I was familiar with the principles and wished to take this course to put them into practice. I liked how the ideas were explained and applied to stammering, although for me they also had a wider relevance beyond my speech.

I found the metaphors used in ACT very powerful, particularly the 'struggle switch' which has helped me to become more accepting of events and feelings. I often find it useful to visualize a big switch, like an electricity power switch, physically being switched off. This helps me to accept the issue and stops me going over and over it. Whilst, it doesn't work each and every time, I do find myself dealing with issues in a more relaxed manner. Now, difficult feelings pass more quickly even though I'm not trying to make them go away. I think of these feelings as being like storm clouds, they'll pass of their own accord: I don't like them, but wanting them to go away doesn't help, in fact it often makes me feel worse.

The idea of 'acceptance' is central to ACT. Before this course, it was a big issue for me and I had very strong views on how I thought things 'should be'. I'm still a bit like this but getting less so and it is easier for me to 'let things go' without getting so frustrated. The idea of expansion has been very helpful in accepting challenging feelings through making space for them, even if I don't like them and they're uncomfortable.

The mindfulness meditation is important – I don't practise as much as I would like to but when I do, I find it very beneficial. I am now more aware in everyday situations. The meditation makes me feel more grounded and gives me more 'head space' so I don't get wrapped up in overanalysing as much.

By completing the 'Bull's Eye' values exercise, I identified the areas of leisure and personal growth/health as the two values I wished to work on. I wanted to spend more time relaxing and engaging in creative activities such as drawing, painting, gardening, sewing and making, as well as getting fitter. Pursuing these values would help me gain more balance in my life and to enjoy it more by spending less time at work and more time on activities which make me feel more fulfilled. Working on those values through committed actions has had a very positive effect so far and has indeed helped me get more balance in my life and realize some of the actions I had wanted to pursue for a while ... My husband and I had talked about getting a dog for ages, and after the first part of the course, I took the initiative to actually do this. We now have a beautiful puppy – it's been hard work but very rewarding and has made a huge difference to our lives: we both come home from work earlier and go for regular walks. And we finally redecorated our house, which we'd been planning to do for years but had never got around to. Now I feel happier to have friends and family come and visit and it's a nicer environment in spend time in.

Here we have another account which explores both speech and non-speech related outcomes. Mercedes describes clearly the paradox of difficult feelings moving through more easily as she lets go of her attempts to control them. She identifies valued outcomes in the domains of leisure and personal growth, powerfully illustrating how ACT-based therapy can help improve quality of life.

Conclusion

Our experience and the responses we have had from clients have confirmed our initial thoughts that ACT as an approach has much to offer people who stammer. We are pleased with the outcomes of the three-day ACT workshop, and are keen to integrate more aspects of this way of working into our block modification courses. Whilst we have only used ACT in group work we anticipate it could have much to offer therapists who are working individually with clients and it can be adapted for work with children and older teenagers (Bowden & Bowden, 2010; Greco & Hayes, 2008). There is increasing focus now on quality of life when evaluating the outcomes of therapy. We hope that our description of the approach and the clients' reflections demonstrate how ACT can help people transcend their stammering and enable them to live their lives more fully.

We would like to thank: Katy, Amanda, John and Mercedes for collaborating with us on this chapter and Steve Davis for his help with analysing data.

References

Beilby, J.M. & Byrnes, M.L. (2012) Acceptance and Commitment Therapy for people who stutter. *Perspectives in Fluency Disorders*, American Speech-Language-Hearing Association Special Interest Group – Fluency and Fluency Disorders, *22*(1).

Beilby, J.M., Byrnes, M.L., & Yaruss, J.S. (2012) Acceptance and Commitment Therapy for adults who stutter: Psychosocial adjustment and speech fluency. *Journal of Fluency Disorders*, Online publication.

Bowden, T. & Bowden, S. (2010) I Just Want to be Me: Building Resilience in Young People. Wollombi, NSW: Exisle Publishing

Dahl, J. & Lundgren, T. (2006a) Acceptance and Commitment Therapy (ACT) in the treatment of chronic pain. In: R. Baer (Ed.) *Mindfulness-based Treatment Approaches – Clinician's Guide to Evidence Base and Applications*. New York: Elsevier, pp.285–306.

Dahl, J. & Lundgren, T. (2006b) *Living Beyond Your Pain*. Oakland, CA: New Harbinger Publications, Inc.

Eifert, G.H. & Forsyth, J.P. (2005) *Acceptance and Commitment Therapy for Anxiety Disorders: A Practitioner's Treatment Guide to using Mindfulness, Acceptance and Values-based Behaviour Change Strategies*. Oakland, CA: New Harbinger Publications Inc.

Greco, L. & Hayes, S.C. (Eds) (2008) *Acceptance and Mindfulness Treatments for Children and Adolescents: A Practitioner's Guide*. Oakland, CA: New Harbinger Publications, Inc.

Harris, R. (2008) *The Happiness Trap*. London: Robinson.

Harris, R. (2009) *ACT Made Simple*. Oakland, CA: New Harbinger Publications, Inc.

Hayes, S.C., Strosahl, K.D., & Wilson, K.G. (1999) *Acceptance and Commitment Therapy: An Experiential Approach to Behaviour Change*. New York: Guilford Press.

Kabat-Zinn, J. (1994) *Wherever You Go There You Are*. New York: Hyperion.

McCracken, L.M., Vowles, K.E., and Eccleston, C. (2004) Acceptance of chronic pain: Component analysis and a revised assessment method. *Pain 107*, 159–166.

Öst , L.-G. (2008) Efficacy of the third wave of behavioral therapies: A systematic review and meta-analysis. *Behaviour Research and Therapy 46*, 296–321.

Plexico, L., Manning, W.H., & DiLollo, A. (2005) A phenomenological understanding of successful stuttering management. *Journal of Fluency Disorders 30*, 1, 1–22.

Van Riper, C. (1973) *The Treatment of Stuttering*. Englewood Cliffs, NJ: Prentice Hall.

Walach, H., Buchheld, N., Buttenmuller, V., Kleinknecht, N., & Schmidt, S. (2006) Measuring mindfulness – the Freiburg mindfulness inventory (FMI). *Personality and Individual Differences 40*, 1543–1555.

Williams, M., Teasdale J., Segal, Z., & Kabat-Zinn, J. (2007) *The Mindful Way through Depression.* New York: Guilford Press.

Wright, L. & Ayre, A. (2000) *Wright and Ayre Stuttering Self-Rating Profile.* Bicester, Oxon: Winslow Press Ltd.

Yaruss, J.S. (2010) Assessing quality of life issues in stuttering treatment outcomes research. *Journal of Fluency Disorders 35*(3), 190–202.

9 Therapy within a CBT framework

A reflective conversation

Jane Fry

Introduction

The aim of this chapter is to reflect on 18 months of therapy undertaken by one client, Anya, with the author, using Cognitive Behaviour Therapy (CBT). CBT provided the overarching conceptualization of the work, guided the process and formed the basis for the majority of therapy tasks; however, some interventions, such as identifying and exploring signs of change, were drawn from Solution-focused Brief Therapy (de Shazer, 1988), and standard interventions for fluency management were also included. The chapter is based on transcripts of recorded therapy sessions and a series of reflective interviews arranged after the therapy described had taken place. Where Anya's comments are taken from session recordings they are identified as such in order to make their contemporaneous nature clear, with all other comments being sourced from the reflective interviews. The manuscript has been read and approved by Anya.

Overview of Cognitive Behaviour Therapy

Sources such as Beck (1995), Greenberger and Padesky (1995) or Westbrook, Kennerley and Kirk (2007) are recommended for a full description of CBT theory and clinical practice, but a brief introduction is provided here in order to contextualize the work described.

Beck (1976) proposed that cognitions, in the form of negative automatic thoughts, appraisals, images, assumptions and beliefs, are linked to, and help to explain, individuals' affective, somatic and behavioural responses to events.

He was particularly interested in the role that cognitions and behavioural responses have in developing self-perpetuating systems in which emotional vulnerabilities, unhelpful patterns of behaviour and negative beliefs are reinforced (Beck, 1976; Westbrook et al., 2007). These ideas are typically represented in a generic cognitive model (Beck, 1976) utilizing the concept of the vicious cycle. CBT is primarily concerned with understanding the role of cognitions, or the personal meaning that individuals give to events, and on working within this domain in order to achieve cognitive as well as behavioural change (Beck, 1995; Wills & Sanders, 1997).

In CBT, clients learn how to identify their cognitions, beginning with their negative automatic thoughts (NATs). Negative automatic thoughts are fleeting, unbidden cognitions in the form of predictions, appraisals, images and self-statements which have a negative impact on the individual's mood (Beck, 1995). They tend to be highly convincing and are often linked to negative core beliefs and assumptions. Clients practise identifying negative automatic thoughts using thought diaries, otherwise known as thought records (Beck, 1995). Clients are also invited to question their negative automatic thoughts and to test them out using behavioural experiments, to identify and question assumptions and beliefs, and develop problem-solving skills in order to enhance resilience and coping.

The style of CBT is collaborative, with the therapist aiming to work in partnership with clients and to help them clarify and explore their thinking through the use of guided discovery. It is also structured, focused on specific problems, time-limited and educative, encouraging individuals to understand their difficulties better (Beck, 1995; Westbrook et al., 2007).

CBT is based on a cognitive case 'formulation' which is a written-down, typically diagramatic 'map' of the client's problem that is developed by the clinician and the client together (Wills & Sanders, 1997). A formulation may focus on the dynamics that maintain the client's current difficulties and will, when this is the case, frequently use the concept of the vicious cycle to illustrate the links between the client's cognitions and their emotional, physiological and behavioural responses to events. It might also set out key aspects from the client's early experience, showing how negative assumptions and core beliefs have developed and demonstrating their role in contributing to particular emotional vulnerabilities. There are no rules about what a formulation should look like; however, the concept of reinforcing cycles often helps the clinician and client develop a clearer understanding of problems, and clarify the direction of therapy.

CBT and stammering

CBT, and in particular CBT for social anxiety, is now commonly referred to in discussions of chronic stammering. The role of anxiety about negative listener evaluation has been of interest for some time (Menzies, Onslow & Packman, 1999) and this has been supported by evidence that adolescents and adults who stammer score relatively highly on measures of anxiety which focus on the social domain (Craig, Blumgart & Tran, 2009; Kraaimaat, Vanryckeghem & Van Dam-Baggen, 2002; Stein, Baird & Walker, 1996; Messenger et al., 2004). CBT has been integrated with traditional therapy components such as speech restructuring and communication skills with teenagers who stammer (Fry, Botterill & Pring, 2009) and its effectiveness as a stand-alone component with adults who stammer has been explored and found to reduce social anxiety related to stammering, although not overt stammering behaviours (Menzies et al., 2008).

Cognitive models of social anxiety appear to have, with some caveats, the potential to shed light on the nature of the speech-related anxiety which is experienced by many individuals who stammer. A key difference is the well-documented context of social stigma and stereotyping that exists in relation to stammering, and care must be taken to validate the concerns of individuals who stammer and the experiences that they have encountered while also inviting them to explore other perspectives.

Overview of social anxiety

Clark and Wells' (1995) model of social anxiety proposes that socially-anxious individuals wish to come across well in social situations, but are uncertain of their ability to do so. This arises from past experiences of perceived or actual failure in social situations and the development over time of negative assumptions and beliefs, which make them more likely to view social situations as threatening. Socially-anxious individuals tend to anticipate that they will behave ineptly or inadequately in these situations, expect that they will be embarrassed or humiliated as a result, and that they will incur social penalties in the form of negative listener reactions and judgements.

As discussed by Clark & Wells (1995), socially-anxious individuals worry about problem situations before they enter them. This anticipatory thinking, or 'pre-event processing', focuses on past failures and tends to reinforce the anticipation of difficulty and contribute to an anxiety response being triggered.

Once activated, this results in heightened social self-consciousness and self-focused attention, and prompts the use of self-protective, safety-seeking behaviours, which the individual employs in order to avoid or minimize exposure to perceived threat. While implemented for this purpose, safety behaviours are counterproductive because they reinforce anxiety and maintain problems. For example, safety behaviours may make a feared event more rather than less likely to happen, which then reinforces the view that the situation is problematic, such as when concern about being noticeably nervous and shaky leads an individual to hold a glass more tightly resulting in obvious tremor. Alternatively, when avoidance-based, they prevent the individual from entering a situation and obtaining information which might disconfirm their fears, or finding out that they might have been 'OK', thus by default strengthening the anxiety associated with that event.

Finally, people with social anxiety tend to engage in extensive post-event processing or 'post-mortem thinking', during which events are reviewed excessively and with a negative bias. This further tends to confirm the individual's initial fears and perspective (Clark & Wells, 1995; Wilson & Rapee, 2005).

Key therapeutic tasks in CBT for social anxiety are therefore to help the individual identify and challenge the perceived threat, drop safety behaviours through graded exposure, shift self-focused attention, and to address negative biases in thinking such as post-mortem thinking.

Suitability for CBT

CBT is likely to be best suited to clients who seek help for a specific problem, who are able to access negative automatic thoughts in session, who feel that the model fits their experience, who see themselves as being responsible for changing their own lives, who are able to work collaboratively, and who have a degree of optimism about therapy (Safran et al., 1993). In the field of stammering it is likely to best suit those who are interested in psychological aspects of stammering and want to see change in that domain. However, it can be argued that CBT has a role when psychological work is not necessarily the main thrust of therapy, as demonstrated in the section 'Integrate CBT and fluency' work where the integration of standard fluency skills therapy and CBT with Anya is discussed.

Rationale for choosing CBT

> "I didn't initially know that I'd be having CBT per se, although I had read an article written by Jane about it which was on the British Stammering Association website and that had a huge impact on me. I just came to the Michael Palin Centre to receive expert help in whatever form that would take. Once we talked about CBT, and things like looking at the evidence, I thought it would be really interesting because I was aware that in certain situations I walk in with some pretty negative thoughts, and see people as guilty until proven innocent. I thought it would be good to explore what happens, looking at 'Is that really what happened?', and 'Is that really what they said?' I thought it would be useful and interesting, but I didn't realise just how useful and how interesting it would be."

In many respects Anya came across as an individual who would engage well with any therapy approach, demonstrating as she did from the start a proactive style and a readiness for change:

> "Starting therapy was part of a larger process of shaking things up. I had become aware of, and frustrated with, a pattern of playing it safe. I wanted to change my life, to shift things around and see what that would mean. I'd found a new job, and I'd asked to do a masters. It felt as though this therapy was part of a larger process of changing direction, shifting focus and sorting things out."

While Anya wanted help with motoric aspects of her stammer, and particularly the tremor that she experienced during speech blocks, she saw psychological aspects as important and she had already investigated, and rejected, a programme which she understood to be primarily fluency-focused. While coming across as a successful, dynamic and sociable individual, and an expressive and engaging communicator, she referred to the constant fear, stress and shame that she had experienced since starting to stammer at the age of 6, and the impact of being 'viciously teased' at school on her self-esteem and personality. Her stammer was her 'rawest nerve', sensitivity about which she effectively masked with an appearance of confidence.

Anya spoke about how changes in her thinking and perception had helped in recent years and this suggested that CBT in particular might be a good therapeutic fit. She had noticed that becoming more confident and calmer, finding out that things were not usually as bad as she anticipated, changing the way she thought about things and taking a broader perspective had all helped.

Her responses to specific CBT-based questions in her initial assessment underlined this. These questions probe for emotional reactions to anticipated or actual stammering, negative thoughts or images, and somatic and behavioural responses, in line with the cognitive model. The degree to which a client identifies and elaborates cognitions associated with stammering, the intensity of associated emotional responses and the centrality of these aspects for the client will suggest the extent to which therapy needs to address these domains. Anya spoke eloquently about the emotions associated with stammering (fear, 'wall of dread', nerves, 'blind, white-light panic'), her somatic responses (shaking, feeling physically sick), and her negative automatic thoughts both before the moment (I'll be teased, I'll be judged, people will be nasty, people won't talk to me, people will smirk, people will think I'm weird), and afterwards (I'm rubbish, I can't even speak). She was also quick to identify safety behaviours such as using shorter sentences, talking quickly, switching words and keeping quiet or avoiding situations that she adopted in high-risk situations. Finally, and most importantly, Anya responded positively to the cognitive model when it was discussed at her assessment, commenting that it helped her to structure her experience, and that the therapeutic direction that it potentially offered was both interesting and relevant.

Beginning therapy

Fears

Anya's decision to start therapy triggered anxiety which was linked to her anticipating that it might not be successful, and the consequences if that were to be the case:

> "I was completely terrified, and not very hopeful because my stammer seemed like an insurmountable problem. The fear wasn't about confronting my stammer, or about the process of therapy. It was about 'What if I get help and it doesn't help, then I've got no options left, nowhere left to go'. Having an untapped option made me feel weirdly

> comforted, but if I used that one option and it didn't help
> – that really terrified me."

The strong affective response accompanying the thought, 'What if it doesn't help?' suggested that this might be a key cognition which could reappear in therapy. Rather than exploring this before Anya was familiar with core CBT skills, an emphasis was placed on acknowledging her anxiety, and developing a positive therapeutic relationship that would enable her to experience therapy as a place where she felt understood, able to proceed at her own pace, and supported in dealing with challenges as they arose. Finally, in CBT, as in other therapeutic approaches, therapists notice and reinforce the client's coping strengths, and seek to integrate these into the work. Here, and throughout therapy, there were opportunities to reinforce Anya's natural, proactive coping style, which is demonstrated in her reflections on the period leading up to starting therapy:

> "There were loads of forums online that I looked at in the couple of years before deciding to have therapy and it felt like I was desensitizing myself, rather than looking for guidance or knowledge. I was thinking: 'I'm about to face this properly and I always feel completely rubbish about it, so I need to try and break down those walls so I'm more prepared for it, more open to it, and less sensitized about it generally.'"

Hopes

Anya recalled that her initial hope had been simply to be able to talk about stammering, and to be understood:

> "I had battled with my stammer alone for so long, so at first there was just a huge cavernous hole of definitely not wanting sympathy, but really needing empathy. My hope was that I would be able to talk to someone who understood and who could give me advice and comfort in quite general terms."

In her initial therapy session she identified two areas where she hoped to see change. One of these was her sensitivity about stammering, as she described at the time:

"I thought I'd have got over it more by now, but this massive sensitivity to stammering still just winds me. I want to be more accepting of it in myself, and find a way to be less hurt by other people's reactions."

However, having no substantial prior experience of therapy Anya also wanted to learn about fluency management strategies, as she also explained in session 1: 'I'd love to have input on how to control my stammer because I've never had any help with that at all.' This would not be a purely psychological therapy, and decisions would be made together about how to integrate psychological and speech work.

Anya was invited to explore her 'best hopes' in this first session by using a 0–10 scaling task, which is a commonly-used intervention in Solution-Focused Brief Therapy (Iveson, 2002). Her best hopes included having ways to control her stammer, but encompassed broader ideas as well, for example:

"…being more carefree, focusing on things that matter, listening to people more, enjoying people more, saying what I want to say, being more fun and easy going, being calmer and more considered, being less stressed all the time, enjoying life more, being more relaxed, making eye contact more, being less affected or hurt by people's comments (water off a duck's back), being less sensitive, not falling apart as often and being stronger."

When reflecting on therapy, Anya explained that this was a key turning point. While helping her to articulate her goals in terms of concrete signs of change, it also triggered a reconstruing of her self and decentralizing of her stammer at a core level:

"When I marked where I thought I was now on the scale that was a proper lightbulb moment. I'd always automatically thought of my stammer as a complete disaster – the bane of my life – so when I found myself pegging it at 6½ that totally flipped it on its head. I thought, 'I've actually done a lot of things, and I've got loads of lovely friends, and basically a really nice life.' It made me contextualize my stammer in a way that I hadn't done previously. Focusing on everything I've done in spite of it, in a structured, written-down way,

> helped to make it massively less painful. It made me think 'It's not what defines me.'"

This task also instilled a sense of optimism about therapy, which can be expected to augur well in terms of its effectiveness:

> "It was interesting to have it jump up to 8 after not many sessions. I felt I was in safe hands and I could see that this was going to be a really interesting, worthwhile and valuable journey, and that helped hugely."

Overview of therapy

> "What did I do in therapy? So much! A huge amount of time was spent ironing out all the muddle of negative emotions and experiences that had formed a very robust and painful set of beliefs which I carried with me everywhere. I've learned new techniques such as looking at evidence behind negative automatic thoughts and problem solving and the tools that I now have at my disposal are based on understanding the problem, and understanding it in relationship to my experiences in the past."

Anya received 23 hours of therapy over a span of two years with sessions taking place at 8am in order to minimize impact on her work schedule. The initial therapy plan, decided with Anya, was to arrange two blocks of therapy with the first focusing on CBT and the second on fluency management skills. However, in her early sessions Anya expressed an interest in bringing the fluency work forward and working on both simultaneously. The tense blocks and tremor that Anya experienced, her lack of previous therapy, and her anxiety about loss of control emerging as a theme in her thought records all suggested that this could be productive, although it could also, potentially, result in an unmanageable demand for her in terms of the time and emotional focus that work in each domain requires. A trial session of two hours rather than the standard one hour was scheduled, and Anya was introduced to a smooth speech model which she could practise at home and review in clinic.

Ultimately, Anya decided to concentrate on CBT alone at first. At the time, she reported that this was related to time management concerns; however, during the reflective interviews she also attributed this decision to a need to prioritize work on psychological issues, reflecting her increased awareness of the role these played:

> "There was a lot of painful and negative stuff that I needed to iron out before I could think about speech work in a positive way. So much of my belief system and my attitudes were so snarled up and in a mess that I needed to unpick those things first."

Anya's initial block of therapy was extended to 11 weeks. With the exception of the trial session on fluency techniques described above, these were primarily CBT-focused and at the end of these she wrote her first 'blueprint' or summary of her key ideas for self-management. Following this, Anya came in for sessions approximately once a month, with an additional session included at one point when she felt she was losing confidence and needed more input. She revisited her interest in fluency techniques and had a block of once-fortnightly sessions in which speech skills were explored, followed by six months when she requested a session approximately once every two to three months. Changes in the regularity of sessions was in response to Anya's other commitments, such as work or study deadlines, and her increasing confidence in self-management.

Core CBT tasks

Introduce the cognitive model and the 'vicious cycle' of stammering

The cognitive model was revisited in session 1 with the aim of exploring this in terms of Anya's experience of stammering and checking that this was a 'good fit'. The model was then used over time to develop simple, here-and-now formulations of what maintained her difficulties and, as she described it, 'entrapped' her. Simple formulations, such as those shown in Figures 9.1 and 9.2, captured the links between increased tension and stammering, and between fear of negative listener reactions and her own interpersonal behavior.

Anya explained in sessions that the cognitive model and the concept of the vicious cycle helped her to organize her experience, and also gave her a sense that she could deal with things differently.

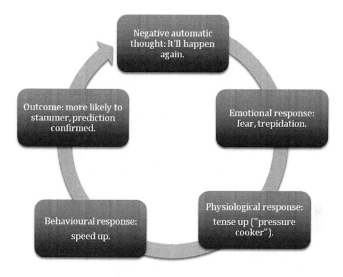

Figure 9.1 Vicious cycle formulation.

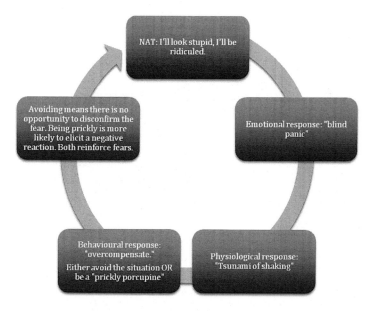

Figure 9.2 Vicious cycle formulation showing role of safety behaviours in maintaining anxiety.

"If I iron it all out so it's not this crumpled mess, I can see it all spread out more clearly, then I can draw a map through it and I can rationalize it and reason with it far more practically, rather than it being this scary mess in my head. If instead I think 'actually that bit's there and that bit's there and so what you need to do is that', that kind of reasoning would give me more control over how I feel about it, rather than this constant, incredibly sensitive, knee-jerk reaction which I do a lot."

She also noted that her behavioural responses, or safety behaviours, tended to be unhelpful, 'over-compensatory' and did not fit with her sense of self as she wished to be. The model thus offered a potential direction for therapy, namely to identify and work with the cognitions which were 'driving the system', and to experiment with dropping safety behaviours.

Identify negative automatic thoughts

One of the first skills that individuals learn in CBT is to identify their negative emotions and the negative automatic thoughts which are associated with these (Westbrook et al., 2007). The therapist uses questions to elicit negative automatic thoughts associated with particular experiences and introduces the client to thought records, which are used routinely in therapy. The practice of completing thought records helps individuals to access the cognitions associated with the negative emotions that they experience and gain an emotional distance, making it easier to then consider alternative points of view. Thought records also highlight high-frequency and high-intensity or 'hot' thoughts which are central and, therefore, key to work with. Finally, they can be used to track changes, in terms of the degree to which negative automatic thoughts are assumed to be correct and the intensity of the associated emotional response, both of which are recorded as percentage ratings.

The therapist uses questions to help the client identify specific negative automatic thoughts word-for-word and to explore implicit meaning which is less immediately accessible. The following session excerpt gives an example of this process.

Jane: So you've written 'she noticed'. What exactly were you thinking that Amanda noticed?

Anya: That I was stammering, having a tremor.

Jane: So your first thought when you were feeling frustrated was that you were stammering?

Anya: I'm blocking.

Jane: OK, [writing that down] and going back to that moment, what was the worst thing about blocking right then for you?

Anya: That I feel responsible for making other people feel uncomfortable.

Jane: It sounds as though you were expecting that Amanda would feel uncomfortable, is that right?

Anya: Yes, and I don't want her to feel bad, or feel anything really. I just want it to not be there and for her not to think anything other than about what I'm saying.

Jane: So I'll write 'Amanda will feel uncomfortable' and 'I'm responsible' in the negative automatic thought column. You also wrote down 'what my face looked like'. What were you thinking your face might look like at that moment?

Anya: That it would look strange and that I would look uncomfortable, and I wouldn't be able to maintain eye contact because that is the first thing that automatically goes away, and that it changes my behaviour and I get more wound up.

Jane: So let's write each of those down as a negative automatic thought [writing down: I'll look strange, I'll look uncomfortable, I won't be able to maintain eye contact, I'll get more wound up]. What do you notice we've done?

Anya: It's more individualized thoughts, writing down actually what I think right in that moment rather than describing it with hindsight.

The following week, Anya explained that, while it was difficult to complete thought records, they gave a helpful structure:

> "It was hard to articulate what I was thinking because normally if you're in a situation when you're feeling anxious, frightened or angry you're so focused on feeling that way, and wanting to not be feeling that way, that you're not

necessarily tuned in to what you're thinking. It was really interesting and also rewarding because I felt I was making sense of it."

She returned to this theme when reflecting on the therapy process as a whole:

> "It was helpful to compartmentalize things and I liked being able to visualize what I'm feeling rather than just going 'Gaaagh', which is normally how it feels. So instead of being panicked and flustered and out of control, it's been helpful to go 'right I'm feeling angry and anxious' and to put a label on things. I hadn't done that before."

Themes emerged which fitted with Clark and Wells' (1995) model of social anxiety: specifically, concern about performance as a speaker (I'll look uncomfortable, I'll lose control), negative listener reactions (They'll notice my stammer, He'll think I'm an idiot, He'll think 'what's wrong with her?', People will take a cheap shot), self-critical, post-mortem thinking (I'm rubbish, I can't even talk) and cognitions which suggested underlying negative beliefs about herself in respect to her stammer (I'm weak, I'm on the back foot, I'm at a disadvantage). As Anya started to identify her cognitions two things became apparent. First, it would be important to routinely explore images, as well as verbally-represented cognitions, as Anya referred to visual images either of her listener (i.e. her landlord 'looking confused') or of herself stammering. Secondly, her childhood memories were highly salient to her present experience of herself as a person who stammers.

Understand how the problem has evolved.

While formulations most commonly focus on the here-and-now (Westbrook et al., 2007) Anya's childhood experience of stammering was explored in response to material that she brought to session 3, and a formulation of her early experience and the impact of this began to be developed. While in the waiting area, she observed a family being welcomed on their first visit to the Centre. This chance experience of seeing a 10-year-old girl, surrounded by her mother, father, local therapist and two Michael Palin Centre therapists who were all gathered to help, contrasted with her own experience at the same age, and triggered highly-emotive memories and what she described as a profound sense of sadness.

Anya recalled that, throughout her childhood, her stammer was not talked about or acknowledged, and that as a result she had felt misunderstood and isolated, and unable to express the difficulty that she experienced. She did not remember receiving any help other than at one point being asked to practise reading aloud, and she had also been 'viciously' and 'ritualistically' bullied throughout school, and reprimanded by teachers who assumed that she was stammering to gain attention. These experiences left a 'resounding scar' and established a fear of being teased, humiliated and judged which underpinned her 'massive, massive' sensitivity about stammering. The remainder of the session focused on exploring these experiences and memories, and starting to build a formulation which would help her to understand her day-to-day, 'defensive, knee-jerk reactions' when she felt under scrutiny in the context of these early experiences. It was particularly relevant to start to understand why her 'defensive' reactions or safety behaviours were triggered, to help her view those reactions compassionately rather than critically, and also to examine how these reactions might reinforce problems. A key dynamic that emerged as therapy progressed was Anya's sense that many of her safety behaviours, such as being 'barky' or 'hard as nails', while triggered by anxiety ultimately reinforced her sense of being misunderstood as these ways of responding were not true to her nature.

For Anya, the process of talking about her past in therapy contrasted with her early experience of isolation and had a cathartic and therapeutic function.

> "My stammer was never really spoken about when I was a child, and all of this overwhelming pain, humiliation, fear and anxiety was never addressed or acknowledged, which made me feel as though it was all in my own head and my own fault. I carried so many unspoken, painful experiences with me for so long and this formed a huge part of how, on an everyday basis, I would react in all manner of situations. Talking about it, and understanding it, almost felt like purging it."

Challenge negative thoughts by checking the evidence

Once a client is able to identify their negative automatic thoughts they are invited to start working with re-appraising or challenging them. The therapist uses questions to help the client to mentally step back, consider evidence, explore other perspectives, consider the helpfulness of negative automatic thoughts, notice any patterns of unhelpful thinking or 'thinking traps' and engage in problem-solving. The aim is to develop a spirit of curiosity in which cognitions are seen as hypotheses to be tested rather than as statements of irrefutable fact.

> "The first thing about the work on negative thoughts was realizing that I made so many negative assumptions about what other people would first notice and what they thought of me. I kept people at arm's length with thoughts of *'They will be going away and talking to their colleagues and saying "Did you see her mouth?"'* or doing spiteful impersonations of me behind my back. I would assume things and write people off."

One way of working with negative automatic thoughts is to consider the 'evidence' that supports them, as well as that which does not or which supports an alternative view. Clients are helped to examine their cognitions more critically, record their line of thinking in a thought record, and check that they are taking all information into account before drawing a conclusion. It is expected that clients will overestimate threat and find that the evidence which unequivocally supports their negative automatic thoughts is less robust than first anticipated; however, it is important that this is approached with genuine flexibility, and that the therapist is not experienced as trying to persuade the client to adopt a particular view.

Where supporting evidence *is* found, alternative explanations are explored and, where necessary, problem-solving skills applied. Clients *will* experience non-ideal situations, there *will* be days when fluency is less secure, or when people *do* respond to their stammer in an unhelpful way. Giving due consideration to events which fit with the client's fears enables authentic, problem-solving-based conversations to be had about difficulties that are encountered, with the aim of increasing the client's resilience and sense of being able to cope with adverse events.

In one of her sessions Anya explored the negative automatic thought that she would not be respected if she stammered at work. Cognitions related to people 'taking a cheap shot' or ridiculing or humiliating her were recurrent and emotionally charged, and these 'hot' thoughts could be particularly understood in the context of her early experience of being humiliated at school.

To make the process more concrete and encourage use of observation rather than relying on a 'felt sense', Anya was first asked to identify what she would consider to be evidence that a person *is not* respected at work. This included the individual being publicly humiliated, set up to fail and criticized unjustifiably, and people being dismissive, talking about the person behind their back and 'taking the piss'. Evidence that a person *is* respected at work included the individual being given responsibility, being asked for their opinion, being asked to come back, being thanked, having clients phone for help, and people wanting to introduce them to colleagues. She noted that all of the signs that someone is respected were true for her, and while recalling one overtly negative comment being made about her stammer, minimized this by considering the importance of this in the larger scheme of things. Overall, she concluded that 'on the basis of the evidence, people may notice my stammer, but people do actually respect me and respect what I have to say'.

Anya's session feedback suggested that the process of working with her negative automatic thoughts promoted a sense of empowerment.

> "It's so fundamentally useful just in terms of the fact that it's a giant mountain in my head and I do have the power to bring that mountain down to more of a molehill size."

The structure and clarity afforded by thought records themselves was also helpful, as Anya reflected:

> "The way that my brain works is to be compartmentalized and structured, and writing things down helped me to think it through, and to just go 'you know what, I'm not that important, people probably aren't thinking about me and even if they do make a passing comment it'll be just that'. Being able to go back and reread it one month later also helped because the more I looked at things the more preposterous my thoughts seemed. It started to seem silly because people have got far more serious things to think about than me."

Anya reflected that learning to evaluate the evidence for negative automatic thoughts rather than take them as facts, and also to consider other explanations, was central to the process of change:

> "I'd say that looking at the evidence for NATs has seen the biggest change in my mindset. The other thing that helped was to construct a different reality to people's behaviour. If somebody did smirk, I used to automatically think that they were being cruel and mean and it never entered my head that perhaps my stammer just made them feel a bit awkward. I automatically jumped to the negative side."

Working with thinking biases

CBT helps individuals to identify particular biases in thinking which are unhelpful, such as focusing on negative information, making assumptions about what people think (mind-reading), or drawing conclusions prematurely (jumping to conclusions). Anya read CBT material related to thinking biases and identified with many of the patterns described, as she described in session:

> "I've realized I've got to be more willing to give credit where it's due and that has been incredibly positive. I've just felt happier thinking about 'Am I being a fair judge? Am I ignoring or minimizing positives?' It's been like 'No, I'm not being a fair judge and yes, I am minimizing things, I am blaming myself and beating myself up all the time, I am jumping to conclusions, I am thinking in all-or-nothing terms, I am doing all of these things and I need not do that, and it would be far more helpful and a far nicer way to live if I just didn't do it."

While confident in other domains, Anya tended to have a pattern of being highly critical of herself as a communicator because of her stammer. She referred to 'beating herself up', not understanding why her friends thought she was a good communicator and describing them as 'kind' when they complimented her on her skills in this respect. Several therapy interventions were used to address this, including: drawing attention to her strengths as a communicator, directly questioning the pattern itself (How helpful is that to you?, Is that a fair or balanced view, or are you being tough on yourself?), and working specifically with the topic of communication and Anya's underlying assumption that having a stammer ruled out being an effective communicator.

To encourage a more balanced view of herself as a communicator, which incorporated her strengths, Anya was first asked to list the skills that are involved in communicating effectively and construct a pie-chart, apportioning each skill a section of the pie in line with its importance. This enabled consideration of fluency within a wider context of communication skills.

> "Looking at communication skills was huge, and really interesting because it made me think that yes, the speech part is definitely part of it and that's not my strength, but it's only part of it and there are so many other things about the words that you use, and your facial expressions and your body language and the way you tell a story. I'd never thought about it like that. I'd always just thought 'I'm bad at communication because I can't talk properly'. I used to feel grateful to my friends and think 'thank god they are so patient', and that has stopped completely. They hang out with me because they want to, and they think I'm funny and interesting and not just because they think they have to look after me."

Testing cognitions through behavioural experiments

Behavioural experiments enable clients to test their cognitions in the real world. They are constructed in session with the therapist helping the client to define concrete and specific parameters for observations linked to a specific negative automatic thought. The client is helped to decide how to test their thought, and they then make a record of what they did and what they found out. While talking in clinic can be empowering, it is often the act of doing something differently and finding out that it is OK, or more OK than anticipated, which is most effective in challenging fears.

Anya took therapeutic ideas forward quickly and on several occasions began sessions by describing an experiment that she had conducted spontaneously.

"The huge difference was that I started to get really curious to see what people said and how they reacted to my stammer. So I started mentioning my stammer in passing and looking at what they actually did. That was a real lightbulb moment. There's been the whole gamut from people being incredibly matter-of-fact about it, saying things like, 'It really isn't that bad, now who wants a cup of tea?', to some people saying they haven't noticed it, which I still think is being kind, and every now and then someone being genuinely curious and asking about it. But there's been no judgement or malice or nastiness."

Anya also decided to watch herself stammer in order to see if her speech was 'as bad' as she anticipated. She had identified a negative automatic thought related to seeing herself (What if I'm so mortified that I withdraw socially, professionally and academically?), and had been invited to consider an alternative perspective (e.g.: I won't know until I try, I'd rather regret something that I've done than something I've not, it'll be empowering, I'll be pragmatic). She spontaneously filmed herself and watched this at home:

"I was really shocked by it and I got quite teary about it. My rawest nerve and extreme sensitivity had been that I didn't ever want to see what I looked like. I started to just think 'You know what, I don't really know what I look like because I've spent my entire life avoiding it like the plague and if I just listen to myself, and watch myself speak, and if I watch that back with my CBT, evidence-based, negative thought armoury, how bad can it really be?' So I did it one night and it was life changing. I had this total construct of me speaking with all sorts of hideous facial contortions and making weird noises, and in fact, yes, my stammer is there, it's pretty hard to miss, but there are other things going on too in terms of how I communicate and it's nowhere near as bad as I thought it would be."

This activity of practically testing cognitions is central to CBT. The spirit of enquiry fostered by CBT means that any information derived is seen as useful, even when adverse events are encountered, as problem-solving skills are then applied so that the client's resilience is developed in response to the real world that they encounter. Anya's sometimes spontaneous approach to initiating experiments, to facing things head on, was wholly in keeping with her nature and this was one of her strengths. A potential risk, particularly when watching herself stammer, which is normally facilitated in a therapy session, was that she might observe aspects of stammering that were unexpected or more severe than anticipated, which could potentially reinforce fears and erode tentative confidence. This did not occur but, if it had, the close timing of the next session would have provided the means to debrief and resolve any issues, and this opportunity to debrief and summarize what has been found out is a critical part of any behavioural experiment.

Experiment with dropping safety behaviours

People who stammer describe many strategies that they use to try to cope with stammering, and which can be thought of as safety behaviours, with the key criteria being that they are implemented as a means of avoiding, minimizing or escaping from perceived threat. Safety behaviours are often based on avoiding the feared situation, for example, deciding not to speak or join in an activity; however, they can take the form of other behaviours such as: talking faster in order to 'get it over with' which increases the likelihood of stammering, or putting one's hand over one's mouth to mask stammering which draws more attention to the speaker.

Anya identified a range of self-protective but 'over-compensatory' safety behaviours that she commonly adopted in response to her anxiety about listener reactions. These included: losing eye contact, putting a hand over her mouth, 'turning on the thesaurus' and avoiding words, using extra words, speeding up, being a 'prickly hedgehog', being scary and 'barky' ('so that people are less likely to have a go'), stating her views in a clipped or brutal way, being 'hard as nails', not listening to others and keeping people at a distance.

The first goal is to help clients explore why they use their safety behaviours, and contextualize their use in response to perceived threat or risk. Anya reflected that her safety behaviours were predicated on a sense of vulnerability and expectation of 'attack':

> "I built a shield around me because I always felt under attack. I would lead with this 'don't you dare', 'first rule of defence is attack' attitude, and give a quick remark that

would let people know that if they started to take the piss I would not be holding back in giving a vicious response. It was almost like laying trip wires."

Next, Anya was invited to consider the possible disadvantages of using safety behaviours:

"It was self-perpetuating because it would lead to me overcompensating, and then it would seem to me that I had been right and I would be glad that I had been on stand-by with my verbal armoury. But it's a really horrible way to be and it gets you nowhere, and it's totally exhausting and stressful and tense and the worst part is that it's not representative of what I'm really like. It comes across as being scary and aggressive but in fact it was because I was scared myself."

Finally clients are encouraged to experiment with dropping safety behaviours in a structured way and to consider the effect of this.

Anya was invited on a weekly basis to notice times when she dropped safety behaviours and to think about the impact of this. She started to report that she was looking at people more, listening more, being more considered in how she stated her views, being less 'barky', changing words less and avoiding talking less. A structured series of sessions in which audience and video feedback is used to help clients compare the effectiveness of both using and not using safety behaviours while giving a presentation, did not take place. Postgraduate course demands and other issues became a priority for her and sessions at this point became more periodic, taking place approximately once every few weeks or when Anya requested a session; however, when interviewed Anya also volunteered that a degree of avoidance may have been involved in this decision. Where it is clear that this is the case it is helpful to explore the situation from a CBT perspective, which involves exploring the fears attached to a task as well as considering more graded tasks that trigger less anxiety. For Anya and for most clients, monitoring and 'keeping safety behaviours in check' is an ongoing process as their use is a natural response to reduced confidence when a sense of increased risk or threat is encountered.

Integrate CBT and fluency work

Whilst wanting to learn about fluency techniques Anya also expressed anxiety about this. CBT therapists aim to notice changes in emotions and 'follow the affect', and the question 'What is going through your mind as we start talking about fluency work?' helped to unpack the nature of her concerns. Anya identified that her anxiety was, in part, related to a re-emergent cognition: 'What if I try it, and I can't do it, and it doesn't work, then I've got nowhere left to go?' This negative automatic thought revealed a fear of therapy failing, and a sense of helplessness were that to happen, which resonated with her initial anxiety about starting therapy. It also suggested that she was thinking about fluency work in dichotomous or 'all-or-nothing' terms. This pattern of thinking reduces options (fluency techniques either work or do not, she is able to use them or she is not), which in turn increases pressure on performance and fuels self-criticism when the desired goal is not met. Anya also identified that her anxiety was linked to the thoughts: 'What if it *does* work?' and 'What if it feels "not me"?' which captured a sense of fluency as something that would feel 'foreign' and suggested that the role of being a fluent speaker might in itself involve a change that could be challenging for her.

This highlights the degree to which therapists need to be ready to work at a psychological level, even when therapy is primarily targeting speech restructuring, as any therapy task which triggers high affect provides an opportunity to explore, acknowledge, and work with emotions and cognitions. Fluency work can activate negative predictions and conclusions about the skills involved (I can't, It doesn't help) and self-critical or 'should' based reflections (I'm rubbish, I should've been able to use my techniques), which add to pressure to perform and reduce confidence. It can also activate more core anxiety about change.

Negative automatic thoughts about fluency work can be addressed directly by the therapist's use of questions (What is the effect of thinking that way for you? Does that help or make you feel worse? Is there another way of viewing this?), and indirectly through the style of the therapy itself. For example, with Anya an intentionally low-key approach was used, with an emphasis on 'having a go' with a range of techniques, and discussing options and choices about levels of desired fluency, rather than using a programme in which a certain level of fluency was required in order to 'progress'. It was hoped that this would discourage her from viewing fluency management in terms of a success–failure dichotomy. Anya was also invited to reflect on her experience of being 'fluent sometimes' to help her integrate the idea of being fluent into her sense of self, using a drawn scale or 'continuum'. Continuum work, supported by a written scale and the therapist's questions, aims to enable clients to explore the 'shades of gray' in experience, and identify and express subtleties and exceptions to the rule that can be missed when ideas are initially expressed in relatively black-and-white, or 'all-or-nothing' terms. In this case, it allowed Anya's experience of being fluent 'sometimes' to be acknowledged and thus provide an alternative view to her initial sense that fluency was foreign:

> "It was really free-ing to play around with the speech tools that we used here but without pressure, not having to be x,y,z fluent by this deadline to progress to the next level. Instead the phrase was 'play around with it'. I could think 'OK, I'm going to try this out in a shop where it's pretty safe because chances are I won't see that shopkeeper again', and start to do that more and more and realize that I did have tools that didn't take a huge amount of hard core practice, and did make a huge difference. There was a variety there, too, which counteracted the fear of 'what if it doesn't work' because 'it' then turned out to be various different things to try, rather than one thing that I needed to master or it was game over."

Introduce problem solving

Anya also talked about the unreliability of fluency and fluency control, describing it as being like a puppy which suddenly slips its leash, being 'on thin ice' or 'hitting an oil slick'. It is likely that clients who choose to experiment with fluency techniques will encounter times when it is difficult to apply them. While it can be helpful to work with the fears that trigger anxiety in high-demand situations, problem-solving contributes by increasing the individual's sense of being able to cope with difficulties when they arise. Anxiety is reduced when individuals have a stronger sense of being able to cope with anticipated difficulties and is increased when they do not have a 'contingency plan'. Having more options would also counterbalance Anya's fear of being stranded with 'nowhere left to go' when it was difficult to use fluency techniques.

In order to access and reinforce the positive coping skills already in her repertoire, Anya was asked to identify what she would normally do in other domains of her life when something she was trying did not work perfectly. Her responses included to adopt an 'It is what it is' attitude, try harder, and carry on. Standard problem-solving steps were also introduced; namely, generating a range of ideas before considering, selecting and prioritizing the most useful, in order to establish a contingency plan.

> "This was really interesting even just purely from a visual point of view. You look at this piece of paper and think 'Well, there's quite a few ways here', so as a visual aid it's about all is not lost."

Work with core beliefs

Recurring themes in Anya's negative automatic thoughts and in her discourse suggested beliefs, arising from her early experience, about being vulnerable, not belonging and being disadvantaged because of her stammer. She made references to being exposed, weak, a 'wounded animal', 'on the back foot', and 'easy prey', although this was nuanced and related to extreme sensitivity rather than weakness as a person. Her negative thoughts also expressed her experience of not belonging or of being 'the black sheep', and of being 'held back' or being unable to reach her potential because of her stammer.

> "As I got older and I was able to demonstrate that I was actually quite bright and did have strings in my bow, it made it worse because I thought 'If only I didn't have this massive anvil that I drag with me.'"

Anya reflected at the end of therapy that her attitudes and beliefs had changed and that this had been an important part of the process. While therapy was not specifically directed towards core beliefs, Anya took the work to this level herself, beginning with her talking about her childhood experiences in session 3. Anya later reflected that for some time in her life she had tried to 'just carry on' without looking at her stammer, and it is apparent that, for her, entering into this process of telling the story of her experience, or 'purging', and of making the links between her past and current experience, was an important catalyst for change in itself. Anya reflected that she spontaneously applied CBT skills, for example evidence-checking, to her core beliefs, and that this gave her emotional distance and reduced her sense of hurt.

"Now when I look back, it's more out of reflection, curiosity and acceptance than before. It no longer feels as though I'm lighting a stick of dynamite within me when I think about it. Now I think 'I was singled out by teachers – well, who isn't?' But I don't think I could have that reaction without all the work on NATs."

She also reflected that it was natural for her to approach these core areas quickly because that fitted with her personality: 'That's how I live – let's get straight to the good stuff! I had a clear sight of where things stem from and I didn't want to beat around the bush but go straight to the heart of it.' This would not always be the case in CBT and for many clients the approach to working at core beliefs is gradual and explicit, being introduced after essential CBT skills are securely established and applied to less emotively powerful cognitions. Equally, however, many clients will naturally apply the concepts of CBT to the areas of their life that they are most interested in exploring and therapy is, ultimately, led by the individual.

Keep change going and deal with setbacks

CBT aims to strengthen the individual's sense of empowerment and ability to self-manage the problem that they brought to therapy. Each session, clients are invited to summarize the 'message in a bottle' that they will take away, and to periodically construct a 'blueprint' of the key things to remember, together with an action plan with concrete steps for ongoing self-management. Questions such as 'What have I found out so far?', 'What is particularly important for me to remember?' and 'Why is that important?' or 'How does that help me?' enable clients to distill key ideas and develop their self-management skills. It is expected that setbacks will be encountered and by preparing for and normalizing them they can be experienced as less catastrophic or even as learning opportunities.

Anya encountered times when she noticed that she was avoiding more, 'going into her shell' and losing confidence. Reflecting on the ease with which this could happen she drew on both her own awareness of the need to 'get back on the horse' and the support of occasional additional sessions to get 'back on track'. Anya explained that these setbacks became less problematic over time. The feelings engendered by difficult experiences resolved more quickly, and she likened these moments to more like 'tripping up and grazing a knee' rather than 'catastrophically falling and crashing'.

Anya's initial blueprint and action plan included: 'read notes and remind myself, notice when my comfort zone is constricting and keep a check on avoidance'. She initially reviewed her notes on a regular basis, as she explained approximately six months after starting therapy:

> "It's been really key to refer back to all this stuff. It's incredibly useful because when I think 'That was a bad day', or 'I don't really know why I had such difficulty talking with my nan last night', then I just look through things and somewhere in there I will read something that will make me feel that I haven't gone right back to square one again."

This shifted over time, as stammering became a less central concern for her, as illustrated in her reflections one year after starting therapy:

> "I haven't been here [the Michael Palin Centre] for a while now and in that time I've found that I haven't been thinking, 'I must do thought records or read about x, y or z' and I haven't looked back through our ream of paperwork. I used to refer back to that quite regularly as a reminder and a pick-me-up, and I haven't for the last few months. It was all brilliant and invaluable and I will come back to it, but it's been profound to park it and say, 'I just want to live my life' and see how it feels to have this amazing new backdrop that's there. I just give less of a shit now, and that's brilliant. So I've liked realizing that now it's not a project I'm working on. I just haven't really thought about it as much."

Her final reflections also suggest that the perspective and skills acquired in therapy became internalized: 'This is part of my everyday life, to the point of being subconscious. It's like something that I wouldn't leave the house without.'

Anya's final reflections

On expectations at the start

"Originally I thought I would have to do lots of speech exercises and be videoed, and I would have to put up with the fact that I would have to look and feel stupid. But that hasn't been remotely what it's been like – it's been a really nice process. What I hadn't thought for a moment was that I'd have the amazing opportunity, with so much support and tools, to really get a grip on how I feel about my stammer, and that's what's been such a massive surprise to me. I always thought that I would stammer less and would therefore feel less bad about it, not that I'd feel less bad about it and then it wouldn't matter as much. That's absolutely the biggest surprise because I'd say I stammer every bit as much, in fact probably sometimes more, but I just care so much less about it and now I sometimes think just 'that's a bit rubbish' rather than 'I have to go and curl up in a corner and die'. That's what has been so surprising for me and absolutely the biggest gift. So this entire process has completely surpassed my expectation a thousand times."

On turning points and lightbulb moments

"Therapy has felt like such a journey and there have been so many 'lightbulb' moments. Using the 0–10 scale in the first session, and realizing that I'm not defined by my stammer, was huge. Watching myself stammer and realizing that my speech – while noticeable – is a small part of how I communicate and how I come across to people, was profound. It's not what people notice first about me and it's not all that they see when they see me. If someone wants to hang out with me or hire me then it won't be because of how fluent my speech is but for a thousand different reasons. That was a massive shift in my self-perception, but I don't think I would have had the courage to do that if I hadn't had the months of digging deep and unpicking things first, because the more I unpicked it the more I got curious about my stammer and started to think the whole thing was really interesting!"

"Another lightbulb moment was learning that there's nothing wrong with the physical speech mechanism – everything is all in place and works perfectly well, but there are genetic and neurological aspects to stammering and the mechanism misfires. That was a real eye opener because I had linked the entire thing to emotional disturbance. It started when my little sister was born, and I had just started school, and mum had post-natal depression. My world felt turned upside down and so I'd always put it down to emotional trauma. I still think that those things probably exacerbated it, but I think that I was predisposed to it anyway. Learning things like that was actually quite liberating, and also realizing that everyone's stammer is unique. I hadn't ever looked into it before because it was too painful and I didn't want to know, but now I think it's really fascinating!"

On what has changed...

"It feels like literally everything has changed. I am far more accepting of my stammer as just being part of who I am rather than it being the thing that ruled my life. I can talk about it more and I am generally less fearful and anxious, and more self-confident now, although that's not in a way that other people would necessarily notice because people always think I'm pretty confident even though I haven't always felt like that."

"My physical reaction, when I approach a situation when my stammer might trip me up, has lessened. I shake less, my heart doesn't pound as hard and I've learned the huge power of taking a breath and slowing my speech down instead of trying to get it over with as quickly as possible or cutting it short."

"I used to be constantly on guard, on alert, for anyone taking the piss. I felt as though I was constantly under attack and I would be hurt by something as little as someone looking at my mouth rather than my eyes. It was as if I had these ultra-sensitive feelers out and they would be jarred so frequently. I felt like I had no real perspective on it, no objectivity about it, and no control over it. Whereas now, this large part of my mind that was constantly riddled with negative, hurt and paranoid thoughts has either evaporated off or distilled down but it's just not there any more and I've been able to focus on other stuff that really matters."

"I've learned that I give myself a horribly hard time and that I need to cut myself a lot more slack. I used to think I was a control freak who had to have everything all mapped out, but now I know that I was like that because my whole approach to life was about assessing the risk in every situation and trying not to look like an idiot. I'm more willing to play things by ear now."

"At first I would probably have said I wanted people to notice a marked difference in my stammer and that's really shifted, because I don't really mind as much what other people think now. It's neither here nor there, really."

"I've been surprised that I've been able to let go of so much deeply rooted, incredibly painful and long-lasting childhood stuff. It was very real for a very long time, but with the work that we've done I've just let go of it, like those Chinese lanterns that you light. It feels like I've lit some Chinese lanterns of pain and hurt and sensitivity and they've just floated off, and now I can't even remember how it felt to live with it all."

"There's been a radical change in how I think about my stammer. At first, I described it as a box of cut glass that

I was carrying around that hurt me all the time. Then it morphed into one of those platypus water bottles that you wear on your back – not so much at the forefront any more, softer and not as painful but still very much there, but I haven't even felt like that for a while. Now it's more like the nice witch from the 'Wizard of Oz' who's in that floating bubble, and every now and then it floats in and I'll say 'that's a pain in the ass' and then it floats away again. It's a bit inconvenient and a bit rubbish but it's far more transient and it's not spiky any more and I don't react to it now. I notice it, and observe it, almost with interest or in a fond and laugh-y way, and it's just an inconvenience that needs acknowledging."

"I have different perspective on it all now. In a nutshell – it is what it is, and it isn't that bad, and it doesn't matter anyway."

...and what helped this happen

"My stammer felt like this snarled-up muddle that I didn't know what to do with. Talking it through and thinking it through so I could see what I needed to work with was at least 80% of what helped. It was a very emotional process initially as it felt like I was sweeping away emotional baggage and turning my innermost fears inside out. The first sessions were extremely raw and there were lots of tissues, but I also felt incredibly safe and understood, and as though I could really say how it feels, warts and all, without any judgement or negativity. It really helped to vent all that stuff. There was a balance, though, between me saying what I really wanted to get out, and being gently guided back to a question so that the sessions were always really valuable."

"It also helped that there was flexibility built in rather than it being a prescriptive set of sessions irrespective of what I was feeling or what was going on my life. It was the opposite of that. We did whatever I needed, I went at my own pace, and the open discussions about how it was going and what I needed were incredibly comforting."

"On a practical level, the CBT tools that we've covered in therapy have helped. I've been able to change the way that I look at myself, my behaviour, my beliefs and my outlook – all for the better. Trying things and realizing that they actually do help has been absolutely critical!"

On what *hasn't* changed…

"There are some situations, like public speaking, that I don't automatically volunteer for and will never be easy. But you know what, I should just do it because what's the worst that can happen? I have no doubt that if I tried it I would probably be quite pleasantly surprised."

…and what *didn't* help

"I decided that I didn't want to spend so much time on speech techniques. It's not that I didn't find them helpful, in fact I'm going to revisit them, it's more the order and timing of the things that was important to me."

On the process as a whole

"Therapy has been incredibly valuable and life-changing! What surprised me was I had this vision that I would have a course and then I would be discharged and it would be hard to come back and there would be a huge waiting list. But at the Centre it's felt like 'If you need us we're here' and that's been extraordinary. So if I have a blip or a day when I seem to be verbally wrapping myself around a tree then I know that I could phone or email if I needed to – and I haven't needed to, but knowing that I could has really helped."

" I do have a sense of regret and loss that I spent most of my life to date consumed by, and fighting with, my speech and having it control most aspects of my life, but ..."

"...most importantly, now I just feel that there's no point in looking back."

Jane's final reflections

CBT is an evidence-based therapy and outcome measures were completed at initial assessment and at intervals throughout the following 18 months. The two measures used were *The Overall Assessment of the Speaker's Experience of Stuttering (OASES)* (Yaruss & Quesal, 2010), which measures the impact of stammering in terms of emotional reactions, ability to communicate in everyday situations and quality of life, and *The Wright and Ayre Stuttering Self-Rating Profile (WASSP)* (Wright & Ayre, 2000) which measures the client's perception of physical, affective, behavioural and cognitive aspects of stammering. For both measures, a downward direction in scores is desirable. A Solution-Focused Brief Therapy rating scale from 0–10 where 10 is 'best hopes' and 0 is 'the opposite of best hopes' was also used. Assessment results, which are shown in Table 9.1, show a substantially reduced impact of stammering as measured by the OASES, with this remaining stable. WASSP scores similarly reduced while Anya's ratings using the 0–10 scale increased beyond her initial desired 'good enough' goal of 8.

Anya came to therapy with considerable skills and strengths as a person and she engaged in therapy with commitment, courage, honesty, optimism, creativity, humour and an 'in for a penny, in for a pound' attitude. These, and her many other qualities as a person, made the process of working with her and seeing her make changes in her life a great pleasure and a rich experience for me as a therapist. One of Anya's goals was to learn speech techniques, and this had its place; however, the most significant changes occurred in the realm of her thinking, her assumptions about the ability to communicate effectively as a person who stammers and her deeper beliefs about herself. While assessment scores capture a sense of change, it is Anya's description of therapy which particularly illuminates her experience.

Table 9.1 OASES scores, WASSP scores and Brief Therapy (BT) ratings.

	T1 (20/08/09)	T2 (26/04/10)	T3 (08/01/11)	T4 (21/06/11)
OASES total*	76.5	40.2	42.8	41.2
WASSP total	112	70	74	68
BT ratings	6	8	8.5	9

*OASES Impact rating: Mild (20.0–29.9); Mild–moderate (30.0–44.9); Moderate (45.0–59.0); Moderate–severe (60.0–74.9); Severe (75.0–100).

During the time that this chapter was being prepared, Anya's shift in her beliefs about herself and about the nature of having a stammer was further reinforced by her successfully obtaining her 'dream job' in which she now feels able to fully demonstrate her skills and fulfill her potential.

I would like to thank Anya for agreeing to contribute to this chapter, which describes key aspects of therapy but which inevitably cannot capture the whole. Specifically, I would like to thank Anya for participating in several hours of reflective interviews, giving permission to use excerpts from session recordings and for her additional comments on the manuscript.

I would also like to thank Frances Cook for her comments on the manuscript and acknowledge the work of the Michael Palin Centre team in striving to deliver the best possible care to the children, young people and adults who come to us.

References:

Beck, A.T. (1976) *Cognitive Therapy and the Emotional Disorders*. NY: International Universities Press.

Beck, J.S. (1995).*Cognitive Therapy: Basics and Beyond*. London: Guilford Press.

Clark, D.M., & Wells, A. (1995) A cognitive model of social phobia. In R. Heimberg, M. Liebowitz, D.A. Hope & F.R. Schneier (Eds), *Social Phobia: Diagnosis, Assessment and Treatment*. New York: Guilford Press.

Craig, A., Blumgart, E., & Tran, Y. (2009) The impact of stuttering on the quality of life in adults who stutter. *Journal of Fluency Disorders 34*(2), 61–71.

De Shazer, S. (1988) *Clues: Investigating Solutions in Brief Therapy*. NY: Norton.

Fry, J., Botterill, W., & Pring, T. (2009). The effect of an intensive group therapy programme for young adults who stutter: A single subject study. *International Journal of Speech-Language Pathology, 11* (1), 12–19.

Greenberger, D. & Padesky, C. (1995) *Mind Over Mood: A Cognitive Therapy Treatment Manual for Clients*. NY: Guilford Press.

Iveson, C. (2002) Solution-focused brief therapy. *Advances in Psychiatric Treatment, 8*, 149–156.

Kraaimaat, F.W., Vanryckeghem, M., & Van Dam-Baggen, R. (2002) Stuttering and social anxiety. *Journal of Fluency Disorders 27*(4), 319–331.

Menzies, R.G., Onslow, M., & Packman, A. (1999) Anxiety and stuttering: Exploring a complex relationship. *American Journal of Speech-Language Pathology 8*(1), 3–10.

Menzies, R.G., O'Brien, S., Onslow, M., Packman, A., St Clare, T., & Bloch, S. (2008) An experimental clinical trial of a cognitive-behaviour therapy package for chronic stuttering. *Journal of Speech Language and Hearing Research 51*(6),1451–1464.

Messenger, M., Onslow, M., Packman, A., & Menzies, R. (2004) Social anxiety in stuttering: Measuring negative social expectancies. *Journal of Fluency Disorders 29*(3), 201–212.

Safran, J.D., Segal, Z.V., Vallis, T.M., Shaw, B.F., & Samstag, L.W. (1993) Assessing patient suitability for short-term cognitive therapy with an interpersonal focus. *Cognitive Therapy and Research, 17*(1), 23–38.

Stein, M.B., Baird, A., & Walker, J.R. (1996) Social phobia in adults with stuttering. *American Journal of Psychiatry 153*(2), 278–280.

Westbrook, D., Kennerley, H. & Kirk, J. (2007) *An Introduction to Cognitive Behaviour Therapy: Skills and Applications.* London: Sage.

Wills, F. & Sanders, D. (1997) *Cognitive Therapy: Transforming the Image.* London: Sage.

Wilson, J.K. & Rapee, R.M (2005) The interpretation of negative social events in social phobia: Changes during treatment and relationship to outcome. *Behaviour and Therapy 43*(3), 373–389.

Wright, L. & Ayre, A. (2000).*WASSP: Wright & Ayre Stuttering Self-Rating Profile.* Bicester: Winslow.

Yaruss, S. & Quesal, R. (2010).*Overall Assessment of the Speaker's Experience of Stuttering.* San Antonio: Pearson Education.

10 Stammering, imagework and self-esteem

Debs Plummer

> Early in my life, my self-esteem was hindered by an egotistical father who could not at all see my strengths but only my weaknesses. It was not until I reached the age of 20 that I 'accidentally' discovered I had strengths, and focusing on these helped me have more confidence to live more wisely and happily with my weaknesses. Only when I realized I was made of **many** parts – some strong, some weaker – did I overcome self-degradation, underachievement and instability. Self-esteem is so much more than just what one thinks of oneself. Rather, it is the multifaceted measure from which one estimates one's ability to perform tasks and engage and interact in relationships. It corresponds almost directly to personal happiness and wellbeing. It is knowing our strengths and playing to them and also living and acting wisely towards our weaknesses.
>
> **H. E.**

Note: The scenarios used to illustrate the various concepts outlined in this chapter are based on the combined experiences of several people who stammer (mostly, but by no means exclusively, male) and students (mostly female) who have joined with me in the exploration of self-esteem and the use of imagery as part of their training or therapy. For this reason, I have used the pronouns he and she interchangeably throughout. Details of the images have been altered in order to maintain confidentiality.

Introduction

This chapter explores the idea that the experiences of a person who stammers (PWS) are intimately associated with his personal perceptions of self-esteem. For this reason, supporting the growth and/or maintenance of healthy self-esteem is seen as a necessary consideration in any therapeutic encounter, as well as it being a crucial part of personal development for PWS and therapists alike. In fact, I believe that awareness of self-esteem issues is so pivotal to the effectiveness of therapy, whatever the goal might be (fluency enhancement, controlled stammering, stress management and so on), that PWS will undoubtedly be engaging in the exploration of self-esteem issues whether they are consciously aware of it or not. Outside of the therapy process, a PWS may also find himself exploring levels of self-esteem and how these contribute to his understanding of himself in relation not only to dysfluency, but also to other aspects of life. Similarly, and very importantly from my perspective as a tutor, students and qualified therapists alike often face their own self-esteem demons through the process of learning and through working with others.

There are two main strands inherent in the approach that I have developed during my years as a therapist and a lecturer. The first comes from my ongoing learning in relation to the concepts and complexities of self-esteem; the second comes from a passionate interest in the potential of the creative unconscious and the use of Imagework (e.g. Glouberman, 2003) as a way of exploring this invaluable resource. Although I can only give a 'flavour' of this approach here, I hope that it will encourage readers to explore the ideas further. Please also see my own books and website and the works cited in the bibliography for further information.

Understanding self-esteem

Self-esteem is one of the most widely studied (and heatedly debated) areas of psychology. American psychologist Nathaniel Branden, one of the most prolific writers in the field of self-esteem, considers this aspect of our lives to be an absolute necessity: 'It is a basic human need that makes an essential contribution to the life process; it is indispensable to normal and healthy development; it has survival value' (Branden, 1992, p.9).

Despite the strength of such claims, there has been considerable discussion over the last two decades about the nature of self-esteem and its relevance in both teaching and therapeutic contexts. Sea changes in academic and popular psychology have heralded the self-esteem movement and a subsequent self-esteem backlash, noted by psychologists such as Chris Mruk (1999). Indeed, there are still many theorists who believe that focusing on building self-esteem leads to unrealistic expectations, detracts from other important issues and denies people the opportunities for experiencing the 'buzz' that comes from achieving a challenging goal. However, as Mruk points out, this backlash appears to have arisen because of a fundamental misunderstanding of what self-esteem is; a misguided belief that it relies almost totally on feeling good about oneself, possibly fostering a narcissistic tendency to the detriment of others. This is not, of course, what healthy self-esteem is all about. A person who has developed a healthy sense of self-worth is, in fact, more likely to be able to cope with life's inevitable difficulties and failures. He will be able to weather the occasional storm and regain his equilibrium more readily; he will be more able to make informed decisions. He will usually be more willing to try new ways of doing things, learning from mistakes and building confidence for future challenges. He will be able to recognize and develop his specific strengths and cope with changes successfully. All of these aspects are invaluable in terms of progress in therapy and in self-help and personal development. My starting point with many PWS has often, therefore, centred on a discussion of self-esteem as an important concept in the process of change. There are a few key points that I think are particularly relevant to include as part of this discussion.

Self-evaluation

Research suggests that an important aspect of healthy self-esteem is the way in which individuals evaluate their *self-concept*, usually in comparison with an *ideal self*. This evaluation is both global (e.g. 'I am a worthwhile person') and specific (e.g. 'I am a good communicator'). The differences between a person's evaluation of his self-concept and his perception of his ideal self can give an indication of his levels of self-esteem. The extent to which his self-esteem in different areas of life affects his global sense of self-worth will also depend on the level of importance he places on each area at any one time. A PWS could, for example, place very little emphasis on stammering per se, envisioning his ideal self as a person who copes successfully with moments of stammering (rather than someone who is constantly controlling fluency). If his evaluation of his self-concept is close to this ideal, then he is likely to have healthy self-esteem in terms of communication, despite any fluctuations in fluency. He may also evaluate himself in a positive light in other specific areas of life and in terms of his overall ideal. For example: 'Because of my stammer, I have heightened sensitivity to the difficulties of others, I am a hard worker and I have great determination.'

In contrast, a person who sees his self-concept as being intimately tied up with speaking fluently might find that fluctuations in fluency, or experiencing difficulties in social situations because of stammering, affect not only his self-esteem in relation to communication, but also his global sense of self-worth and self-efficacy.[1] If such a person has created an unrealistic image of his ideal self, the gap between how he has constructed his self-concept and the self he strives for can appear insurmountably huge and lead to further anxieties and loss of self-esteem, as if the plug has been pulled on the entire self-esteem 'pot'.

Fluctuations in self-esteem levels are normal

Changes in self-evaluation occur naturally in different situations and at different times. These may be due to our stage of life or occur because of major life experiences, such as the loss of a loved one. Fluctuations can also occur simply because of the type of task that we are undertaking, our mood at the time or the attitude of the important people in our lives. Most importantly, the way in which we self-evaluate is also related to our *perceptions* of how people react to what we do and say. Someone who is fully aware of this and who evaluates their self-concept favourably in relation to their ideal self may accept fluctuating levels of self-esteem with equanimity and work to boost their feelings of self-worth within various domains. They are likely to recognize their competencies and have a moderate to high level of self-efficacy which will allow them more choice and a greater sense of control in life

Self-esteem levels can be stable or unstable

The interplay between self-concept and self-evaluation affects not only the levels, but also the stability of self-esteem – the more that we invest our feelings of self-worth in 'everyday outcomes' (such as experiencing difficulty in a familiar situation which we consider should be 'easy' for most people) and the less well developed our self-concepts, the more unstable our self-esteem is likely to be (Greenier, Kerris, & Waschull, 1995, p.67).

---

1 Albert Bandura defined self-efficacy as the *belief* that we are capable of doing something and that we can influence events that affect our lives (e.g. Bandura, 1977). Bandura suggested that people who have perceptions of high self-efficacy often do better than those who have equal ability but less belief in themselves; they are more likely to persevere with difficult tasks and to use more effective problem-solving strategies; they also have a tendency to set themselves more demanding goals and to focus less on the possible consequences of failure.

Healthy self-esteem is both a primary motivator in effective change, and also a necessary enabling factor

One of my earliest realizations as a trainee specialist in dysfluency was the importance and value of healthy self-esteem in the process of change. It was evident that those who were self-aware and able to evaluate themselves realistically, not just with regard to communication skills, but also in other domains, such as relationships, work and academic abilities, were much more likely to make long-lasting changes in their relationship with their stammer. It was also clear that the prospect of change through the process of therapy can be daunting for many people, however 'healthy' their levels of self-esteem might be. Therapy will almost certainly be even more of a challenge for someone who has low self-esteem, particularly as this is invariably related to low self-efficacy.

The process of change can affect self-esteem in surprising ways

Even though a PWS may feel ready and able to make the changes required in order to control or to live with his stammer more successfully, such changes can sometimes have unsought for and surprising repercussions on levels of self-esteem in many other areas of life. In some instances, this can be as far-reaching as a reconfiguration of the whole self-concept ('Who am I when I don't stammer?') while for others it may simply involve a deeper understanding of their relationship with their stammer and perhaps lead to 'a quiet pleasure in being one's self' (Rogers, 1961, p.87).

A self-esteem approach to personal development

As I explored the complex relationship between self-concept and ideal self, and between self-concept and stammering, I began to formulate a self-esteem approach to therapy which I introduced into my work with both children and adults who stammer. Subsequently, I have developed the approach into a more integrated model of wellbeing, informed by my work as a lecturer in health studies and in speech and language therapy (see Appendix for an outline of the model; see also *Helping Adolescents and Adults to Build Self-Esteem*, 2005; *Helping Children to Build Self-Esteem*, 2007a; *Focusing and Calming Games for Children*, 2012).

This model acknowledges the interplay between the physical, social, emotional and spiritual aspects of our lives. It is firmly embedded in the concept of 'mutuality' (i.e. a balance between healthy connectedness with others and personal autonomy (Harter, 1999, p.295)) and recognizes the importance of actual and perceived competence, and a strong sense of self-efficacy.

Within this model there are eight *foundation elements* which I believe to be vital components of self-esteem. I have used terminology related to the 'self' to distinguish each of these elements:

1. Self-knowledge

2. Self and others

3. Self-acceptance

4. Self-reliance

5. Self-expression

6. Self-confidence

7. Self-awareness

8. Beyond self.

Please see the Appendix for a full description of how I conceptualize each of the elements (see also Plummer, 2007a, 2007b, 2011, 2012).

These eight elements act as the bedrock for sets of *core abilities* (such as the ability to imagine) and *specific skills* (such as the skill of monitoring personal thoughts). Examples of core abilities and specific skills are also given in the Appendix.

For me, one of the important considerations in developing and using this model (and one of the challenges) was the recognition of the interconnection between the different parts. Whichever area we are working on – specific skills, core abilities or foundation elements – we will see repercussions in the other two aspects as well. So, for example, if we can identify current efficacy in one or more of the *foundation elements* (such as self-knowledge and self-reliance) and consciously develop other foundation elements (such as self-expression), this will support us in learning and sustaining *specific skills* (such as self-monitoring of unhelpful thoughts); if we learn *specific skills* then we can directly affect our perceptions of our *core abilities* and of our strengths within the *foundation elements*; and if we identify and further develop *core abilities* (such as the ability to use the imagination constructively) we will be 'feeding' the *foundation elements*.

Similarly, there are interconnections *within* the three different aspects: when working in the domain of one of the foundation elements we will invariably see effects in other elements too; core abilities will develop alongside each other; and working on developing and improving specific skills will lead to the enhancement of others.

The interconnectedness between different aspects of the model can be illustrated by looking at how a person might cope with stress (such as the potential stress experienced by someone who stammers). For example, in order to be able to make effective choices and increase our resilience to stress, we will undoubtedly need to have a well-developed level of self-awareness (foundation element 7) and self-confidence (foundation element 6). Self-knowledge and self-acceptance (foundation elements 1 and 3) and self and others (foundation element 2) would also be important exploration points, since our choice of coping strategy is strongly influenced by personal temperament and past experiences, and also by environment and social support.

The core abilities of control, adaptability and effectiveness will all facilitate our use of appropriate coping strategies but, within different foundation elements, we may choose to develop specific skills to enhance the process (such as learning a particular stress management technique).

Masten, Best and Garmezy (1990, cited in Garmezy, 1994, p.14) highlight the role in stress management that is played by other personal 'protective' factors, such as 'manifest competence and perceived efficacy' (foundation elements 3 and 4, self-acceptance and self-reliance would relate to this), and what they refer to as 'planfulness and aspiration' (related to foundation element 6, self-confidence). These personal factors interact so closely with other stress-buffering factors, such as supportive social relationships, that the efficacy of one may be highly dependent on, or certainly relate to, the degree to which another is present (Gore & Eckenrode,1994). This, again, adds weight to the idea that we need to explore and strengthen relevant foundation elements in order to more fully understand our relationship with self-esteem and with stress.

A self-esteem approach to managing the stress of a communication difficulty is certainly not then simply about boosting feelings of self-worth through positive thinking. Within this approach, I see the task of the therapist and client as being to jointly establish the nature of the intended change; discover which foundation elements are most vulnerable and which ones the client might, therefore, particularly want to strengthen (e.g. self-reliance, self-confidence); find out which core abilities the client is already capitalizing on and which ones he would like to develop further (e.g. self-control, adaptability);

and decide what specific skills will be used and developed in order to reach a successful outcome (e.g. assertiveness skills, problem-solving skills).

This is still not the full story, however! In the very early stages of creating this therapy approach I was in the midst of rediscovering myself in quite a dramatic way through the process of Imagework (see later) and it was this experience that eventually led me to 'flesh out' the approach to one that is also based on the use of images and metaphors. As an illustration of this, my personal way of conceptualizing the self-esteem model, outlined above, is as an image of a building (see Box 10.1). This has proved to be useful for some of the clients and students with whom I have worked and so I will share it here.

Box 10.1 An image of the self esteem/wellbeing model.

Imagine that you and I have been invited to join a new community of wellbeing. We are offered adjoining plots and told that we can build a home within this plot, containing eight rooms (each of these rooms represents one of the self-esteem/wellbeing foundation elements).

We are told that we can have walls between the rooms or we can have a more 'open plan' design if we like, with rooms flowing into each other.

In order to complete our new homes to our desired specifications we will be given help from the current inhabitants of Wellbeing Town (representing ideas gained from reading self-help books, attending courses, talking to friends, engaging in therapy, etc.). We also need some 'core abilities', such as the ability to imagine, the ability to observe and listen effectively, a degree of self-control and the ability to adapt to different environments. The furnishings and fixtures of our two homes are likely to be different although we might naturally share some items in common. The furnishings and fixtures represent the specific skills that demonstrate and enhance our core abilities.

We can also have any number of windows and doors to facilitate views and access to and from different rooms and to and from the outside world. These represent our levels of self-efficacy and mutuality.

We each construct our homes, and move in as soon as possible. Soon, I notice that you appear to be having a lot more fun than me in your new home! You help me to realize that two of my rooms need changing. 'Beyond self' is small and sparsely furnished and the adjacent 'self-reliance' room looks more like a fortress than the relaxing, comfortable space that I would like it to be. You help me to recognize that different rooms serve important functions at different stages in our lives. I knock down a wall, shift a bit of furniture, add some comfortable floor cushions (develop a new skill) and, lo and behold, I have a meditation room, large enough for friends to use as well.

Adapted from: *Focusing and Calming Games for Children* (Plummer, 2012, p.49)

Following a training session in which I presented this image to a group of students on a health studies course, 'S' chose to draw her own version of the image in her personal log (see Figure 10.1). With her permission, the notes that she made to accompany her plan are given below with my comments and descriptions of her drawing given in brackets:

I found the wellbeing [self-esteem] model really interesting, especially the idea of drawing a house with rooms related to the different aspects ... The first thing to notice is that it [the exercise] ended up working, and that it definitely represents me and my life at the moment ... It highlighted to me that although I have quite a lot of self-confidence, I do not necessarily have the skills to portray my confidence to others ... **Self-knowledge** [large room with a representation of a family tree in it]: My family tree is my life story and facilitates my self-knowledge. **Self and others** [small room containing a large X, interconnecting with rooms of self-expression and self-reliance]: I have difficulties with friendships, making this room small. My **self-acceptance** varies, sometimes it is high, other times it is low [represented by a wavy line]. I am very **self-reliant** but do not let others in [the self-reliance room has a thick wall], [this room is] linked with 'self and others' because I want to let others in. **Self-expression:** very, very small. I find it difficult to express who I am, linked with difficulties in self and others. **Self confidence:** I am confident, but do not have the skills to use this confidence [an empty room]. **Self-awareness:** the only room where everything is good [contains shapes of different colours]. I am self-aware and have the skills to facilitate this. **Beyond self:** I am mindful that I need to alter different areas of my self.

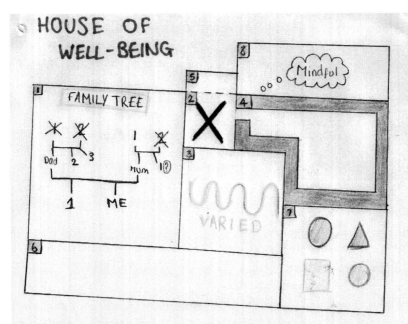

1 – Self – knowledge.
2 – Self + others.
3 – Self – acceptance.
4 – Self – reliance.

5 – Self – expression.
6 – Self – confidence.
7 – Self – awareness.
8 – Beyond self.

The first thing to notice is that it ended up wonky, which definitely represents me and my life at the moment.

1 – My family tree is my life story and facilitates my self-knowledge.

2 – I have difficulties with friendships, making this room small.

3 – My self-acceptance varies, sometimes it is high, other times it is low.

4 – I am very self-reliant but do not let others in, linked with self + others because I want to let others in.

5 – very very small, I find it difficult to express who I am, linked with difficulties in self + others.

6 – I am confident but do not have the skills to use this confidence.

7 – Only room where everything is good, I am self-aware and have the skills to facilitate this.

8 – I am mindful that I need to alter different areas of my self.

Figure 10.1

In this example, 'S' wanted to strengthen her 'self and others' and self-expression elements (see Appendix). She might, perhaps, do this by further developing the core ability of adapting to new situations and by developing specific self-monitoring skills. Although she felt that she is self-confident, she identified that she would like to enhance her skills so that she could convey this confidence to others. Identification of these skills, as she sees them, could be a potential starting point for change.

Whatever our self-esteem/wellbeing homes look like at any given time they will inevitably continue to alter, sometimes in subtle ways, sometimes more dramatically as we cope with life's ups and downs.

Imagework: A personal journey

As the image of the house perhaps illustrates, imagery is a very natural way of thinking for me, but it was several years after qualifying as a speech and language therapist before I discovered the power and potential of imagery as a self-help tool. When I took on the post of clinical lead in dysfluency over 25 years ago I was very soon aware that my counselling and support skills, although seemingly adequate to begin with, were in fact very basic. The experiences and feelings of the children, young people and adults who were seeking help were often complex and I knew that I needed further training. I duly signed up for a two-year part-time introduction to psychodynamic counselling and followed this with forays into personal construct psychology (e.g. Kelly, 1991), transactional analysis (e.g. Berne, 1964), neurolinguistic psychotherapy (a therapeutic version of neurolinguistic programming) and solution-focused brief therapy (e.g. Berg & de Shazer, 1993). But in fact, as is perhaps often the way, the turning point in my therapy approach came about through my engagement in a personal journey of self-discovery when I enrolled on an introductory 'Fundamentals in Imagework' course in London. I had never heard of Imagework, but I was attracted by the notion of being able to use images from my unconscious to understand myself and to be able to make more informed choices in life.

The experience was not, however, the 'walk in the park' that I had expected it to be, but was more akin to a full-scale expedition to the ocean depths and up again! It was revelatory in a profound and life-changing way. Of all the various types of training that I had signed up for, this was the one that most appealed to my way of thinking. Interestingly, it also incorporated many aspects of the various approaches to counselling that I had already studied. I decided to do the full training, undertaking firstly the diploma and subsequently the Imagework teaching certificate. I then began to offer it as part of the therapy process for a few clients, gradually increasing the scope and extent of the exercises and strategies that I felt would be useful. Eventually, I was able to fit these into the self-esteem approach that I have already outlined so that there was a logical structure to the explorations.

What is Imagework?

Imagework is a term created by psychotherapist Dr Dina Glouberman to denote a way of working with personal images from the unconscious. It involves 'developing the receptive ability to tune into the images that guide us, and the active ability to create new images that enhance our health, happiness, and creativity' (Glouberman, 2003, p.6). Imagework is applicable to all areas of life and is not a specific 'therapy'. It helps us to befriend a problem rather than make an enemy of it and in this sense it is basically a solution-focused, rather than a problem-focused, approach. Imagework, and particularly Imagework within a self-esteem framework, is one of many therapy and self-help tools. It will not suit everyone's way of thinking, but there is enough evidence in its favour for me to confidently advocate its usefulness in stammering therapy and as a self-help tool.

The process requires the ability to focus on a particular problem, dilemma, puzzle or question and then to enter a period of relaxation, allowing images to 'emerge' from the unconscious which somehow represent the issue to be explored, without any attempt to consciously construct them. The imageworker (client) and the guide (therapist) then work with the images to gain a better understanding of their meaning and relevance in the imageworker's life. The interactions are structured in such a way as to facilitate insight without muddying the waters with presuppositions and prejudices. In other words, as with other forms of active imagination, Imagework starts from the premise that the unconscious has its own wisdom, so, although the person is consciously engaged in the process (i.e. it does not involve deep hypnosis), she allows her imagination to flow where it wants and then works with whatever images arise. Imagework allows us to explore our present reality from the *perspective* of our images; to experience the image by 'stepping into it' or 'becoming it'. The image is further expanded and deepened through active dialogue and, where appropriate, it may be transformed or replaced.

"...the images that come in this way have a powerful ability to sum up with a telling metaphor the basic structure of whatever it is you are asking about. The metaphor tends to be so accurate that the more you explore it, the more it can be seen to correspond on every level and in every detail not only with the specific problem but even with your life as a whole. The implicit becomes suddenly explicit, the complexities of the problem become streamlined into a simple structure, the history of the situation becomes obvious, and suddenly a resolution emerges where it seemed impossible before."

(Glouberman, 2003, p.91)

So, for example, if I ask you to allow an image to emerge that somehow represents how you are feeling right now, each reader will of course see, hear or sense something different (images do not have to be visual). As I am writing this, I am sensing a baby dragon trying to stretch its wing – I have a pain in my shoulder that is aggravating me and I am finding it difficult to write. When I allow myself a moment to step into being the baby dragon I am keen to tell my 'self' (Deborah, sitting at the computer) that, although I am just a baby pain, I have the potential to cause aggravation to others by becoming more dragon-like unless I am soothed. I know immediately that this is not just about me dealing with discomfort before it gets worse. I can get very 'tetchy' and breathe fire when I am tired or in pain! I have a short talk with the baby dragon. I tell it that I am going to take a break in a few minutes and I make a note to take my awareness of potential 'tetchy-ness' with me so that I do not allow it to affect my interactions with my family. I sense the baby dragon settling into a more relaxed state – still there, but more calm.

Each person's imagery is unique. It represents our own personal way of relating to ourselves and the world, our own personal way of thinking. There is no right or wrong way of perceiving an image and, even if two people have the same image, they may *experience* it very differently.

The idea of working with images from the unconscious is not new, of course. It played an important part in the healing traditions of many ancient cultures and has been particularly well-documented in the work of Austrian psychoanalyst Carl Jung (1978), and in the subsequent work of psychotherapists such as Robert Johnson (e.g. Johnson, 1989) and James Hillman (e.g. Hillman,

1990). The exploration of personal imagery is now an established basis of many forms of therapy and counselling.

The richness and creativity of our unconscious mind and the abundance of images available to us means that we not only have the opportunity to understand ourselves more fully and make more informed choices in life, but also to create new images that will work for us. These can replace or outweigh old stored images, formed through past experience, that are no longer useful for our self-development. Carl Jung, for example, described the unconscious as:

> "... a living psychic entity which, it seems, is relatively autonomous, behaving as if it were a personality with intentions of its own ... Completely new thoughts and creative ideas can present themselves from the unconscious – thoughts that have never been conscious before. They grow up from the dark depths of the mind like a lotus and form a most important part of the subliminal psyche."

(Jung, 1978, p.25)

Robert Johnson describes how, by talking to our images and interacting with them, we will invariably find that 'they tell you things you never consciously knew and express thoughts that you never consciously thought' (Johnson, 1989, p.138). Time and time again, when I have introduced Imagework to students and clients, including those who are sceptical and feel that they 'won't be able to get an image', the subconscious processes reveal themselves in all their glory. Sometimes this manifests in very obvious metaphors, sometimes in ways that require further exploration in order to contribute to a more meaningful experience.

Hillman suggests that we do not necessarily need to interpret the images that arise, but that the image itself is more important, more inclusive and more complex than what we have to say about it (see, for example, 'Imaginal Practice' (Hillman, 1990)). This means that we should also never try to interpret images for someone else. In other words, images demand respect, not analysis! The guide can, however, ask questions in order to help the imageworker come to their own understanding, and certainly once an image or set of images have been worked with for a while, it is often possible for the imageworker to make a tentative mapping onto actual life. She may then experience an 'aha' sensation ('that feels right') which leads to a shift in perception and opens up possibilities for movement and change.

One of the first exercises I used with a small group of adults who stammer was 'image as life metaphor'. The full version of this, devised by Dina Glouberman, takes the person into the realm of the unconscious to 'find' an image that somehow represents who she is or what she needs to know at that moment in time (and is, therefore, a useful exercise for exploration of self-knowledge (foundation element 1). For some of the group this proved to be a revelatory experience, but for others it was something they could not immediately connect with. They said to me afterwards that if I had asked them to allow an image to emerge that somehow represented their stammer, they could perhaps have engaged with the exercise more successfully.

This focus on stammering rather than the person as a whole was something that I had tried to steer away from, but in fact, for some people, it is exactly the right thing to do in order to introduce the concepts of Imagework. Becoming the image of the stammer and having a dialogue with it can be remarkably 'healing':

'P' saw his stammer as a spiky ball, 'out there', floating in front of him (It's always 'in my face'). When he stepped into being the ball it felt quite menacing. If this had been me I am sure that I would have wanted to shout at the image and tell it to get out of my face! But he was interested in getting to know more about it, and developing more control over it – so that it floated near him, not in front of him where it obstructed his view of the world ('It will always be around, but it doesn't have to dominate my life').

On completion of an Imagework activity, the process is often recorded through drawings, movement, poetry or story. By chance, I met 'P' again a short while after writing this part of the chapter. He told me that he still has the picture that he drew following our session together (several years ago) – a reminder of the power of images and the importance of making a record of their impact: 'Once we have entertained an image, it is always potentially present to our gaze ... This is the basis of art therapy or journal-keeping: making a home for certain images that have been transforming' (Moore, 1992, pp.64–65).

Imagework and the self-esteem model

Below are further examples of Imagework sessions with suggestions as to how these might be incorporated into a self-esteem approach.

The expert

This is an exercise that I have used with groups when looking at foundation element 2: self and others and also foundation element 6: self-confidence. It is adapted from an exercise on health and illness by Dina Glouberman (2003, pp. 226–227), in which the imageworker finds his inner expert on relationships or the expert on assertiveness, the expert on friendships and so on.

'R' explored her image of assertiveness in her house of relationships. She found that her expert was a disliked teacher from her childhood, who appeared to be aggressive, rather than assertive. At first, she found it very difficult to relate to this image. She rejected it and wanted to search for an alternative image in the house. However, when encouraged to stay with her original image and to step into 'being' the teacher she realized that one of the barriers to her own expression of assertiveness was the fear that people would react to her as she had reacted to this teacher – with strong dislike – even though she was fully aware of the difference between assertiveness and aggression. She gained valuable insights from this 'inner teacher' – an expert in how not to do it!

'C' told me that her father had never seen a speech and language therapist but had 'solved' his stammer by analyzing the physical aspects of his speech in minute detail and gradually altering the patterns of muscle movements. She remembered him pacing around the room, repeating words over and over again and having a succession of 'aha' moments as he made each new discovery about what was happening. This strategy was not one that she felt she could use when tackling her own stammer – she had tried and 'failed'. During an Imagework exercise in which she explored 'expert' status, she was able to acknowledge that her strengths lay more firmly in engaging with why she was stammering in some situations and not others. Her self-esteem was boosted when she realized that she did have successful problem-solving abilities – they were just different to those of her father. Her father's support and her own ability to set goals and to aspire to greater achievements were also prime motivators and important factors in the success of the therapeutic process.

The saboteur

One of the many images that could be explored in the context of self-reliance (foundation element 4) is the image of the internal saboteur – that part of us which appears to thwart our attempts at change. The following illustrates one of those 'aha' moments experienced by a client during this imagery.

'M''s saboteur image was a mischievous little girl who would go to great lengths to 'trip up' 'M' and prevent her from trying new things in life. When 'M' became the little girl and explored her relationship with this saboteur she discovered two important aspects. Firstly, this was a little girl's best attempts at self-protection, and secondly there was a positive 'playful' side to the image which could be utilized in a different way, allowing 'M' to play with trying new approaches and new experiences without so much fear of making mistakes or failing.

Decisions and dilemmas

There is an Imagework exercise that I use during exploration of self-confidence (foundation element 6) which is similar in its aims to the ABC-model of decision making (Tschudi, 1977). Tschudi's model is described as being 'useful in exploring the reasons behind not moving from one pole of a construct to another apparently more attractive one, or for examining difficulties in making a decision between two alternatives' (Dalton & Dunnett, 1990, p.89). In Imagework, the idea is to access some of the unconscious elements at work in the evident dilemma through imagery. This can be done in many different ways, but one which I have found particularly useful involves leading a person through a series of questions to the point where they have identified a *feeling* associated with the decision/dilemma. They then allow an image to come to mind that somehow represents this feeling. They imagine themselves 'holding' this image in one hand and describe its shape, size, colour, texture and so on, elaborating the image as much as possible. They next allow an image to come to mind that somehow represents the opposite of that feeling. This they hold in the other hand. This exploration alone can often bring insight, but it can be taken one step further by inviting the person to bring both images together and to see what emerges when they are combined. This exercise can work equally well for almost any construct that a client would like to explore.

'T' wanted a high degree of control over his life and his stammer. His opposite pole to 'control' was 'chaos'. The two images that emerged were a neatly pressed blue suit for control and a ball of crumpled up newspaper which left black ink all over his hands for chaos. When he merged the two images he 'saw' a blue ball, which he associated with play. This led him to make small steps towards allowing a bit of untidiness in his life (and perhaps speech?) in the spirit of play – enabling him to consider the possibility of increasing his tolerance of life's natural inconsistencies and unpredictability.

Future possibilities

The miracle question, which is often used in solution-focused brief therapy (SFBT) can also be adapted for Imagework. It can be used as a way of exploring several of the self-esteem foundation elements, and I have found it particularly useful in exploration and development of self-reliance (foundation element 4) and self-confidence (foundation element 6). The aim in SFBT is to help clients to create sensory-specific internal representations of what they want (as opposed to what they do not want).The question to the client might be something like:

> "Imagine tonight while you are asleep that a miracle happens
> and your hopes from coming here are realized, but because
> you are asleep you don't realize that it has happened. What
> are you going to notice that is different about your life?"

From an Imagework perspective the client is encouraged to imagine that they are experiencing the day as if it is currently happening, strengthening the experience by engaging with all the main senses: 'What are you doing now? What can you see? What can you hear?' And so on. Alternatively, the person can imagine that they have reached the end of the day and they are looking back on what happened. Relevant questions then might be, 'What is the feeling that you have now? What did you do/not do to contribute to this feeling? What attitude got you here? What decisions did you make?'

The idea of projecting yourself forward in time to explore a positive outcome is well known in sports psychology – athletes are trained to visualize themselves making the perfect high jump, for example, so that when they come to compete they have a 'memory' of having already achieved their goal. Another way of doing this is to allow an image to emerge that somehow represents 'you when your hopes have been realized'.

Conversational Imagework

Yet another way in which we can engage in Imagework is through heightening our awareness of metaphors used during conversations. A person may, for example, talk about the experience of stammering as being akin to being in a cage or a cave. Rather than just exploring the fact of being trapped, imagining becoming the image of the cave or cage can lead to a deeper understanding of the relationship between the person and his speech.

'P' referred to the sudden onset of his stammer as like falling into a deep hole. The hole was muddy and slippery; he could not haul himself out of it. When he imagined **being** the hole he experienced a feeling of 'protection' – the hole was serving to protect 'P' during his recovery from a trauma, but quite clearly there was light and hope above. 'P' felt that he was trying too hard and making matters worse. This image exploration helped him to accept a more gradual recovery than he had at first aimed for.

Images and associative sensitivity

Hillman (1983) talks of the therapy process that occurs between therapist and client as being most successful when there is 'collaboration between fictions, a revisioning of the story into ... a more imaginative plot ...' (pp.17–18). A well-developed therapeutic imagination can also lead us to be so in tune with another person's story and their way of imaging that we could find ourselves entering into a shared space, where what is happening is no longer simply a function of 'their imagination' and 'my imagination' as separate processes, but is instead an interactive and dynamic experience which results in the emergence of new and often deeply meaningful images. So, for example, a therapist may be engrossed in a client's telling of her personal story about stammering and find that an image comes to mind which at first does not seem to be connected to the words that the client is actually using. Taking the step to share this image can have a profound effect. The other person may have an immediate and deep sense of 'being heard' – 'Yes, that's *exactly* how it is' or 'I hadn't realized, but that makes so much sense to me'.

This phenomenon has been extensively described by Cox and Theilgaard (1987) who refer to this level of attunement as a form of 'associative sensitivity'. Although working in the field of psychotherapy and psychiatry, they suggest that such sensitivity is not confined to the clinical field alone:

> "… Indeed it enhances all deep human encounters. We found that an image could safely hold experience which was too painful, too brittle, or too broken to be firm enough to tolerate analysis. Such patients enabled us to see that the image, activated by metaphor, could be the location of exploration or the fabric of support."

> (Cox & Theilgaard, 1987, p.xiii)

I have observed this sensitivity and attunement to others many times amongst groups of people who stammer to the extent that sometimes a group member will say with great conviction, 'I think I have someone else's image' and, sure enough, they do!

Challenges

Although Imagework is evidently unsuitable for people who are not firmly grounded in reality, it is perfectly possible to engage with imagery and the workings of the unconscious at a level that 'makes sense' without delving into the depths that might perhaps be explored between a psychotherapist and his or her clients. This is not about uncovering buried traumas and defences, but rather about facilitating those 'aha' moments that help people to move forward with their understanding of themselves and with their aspirations. It can be an incredibly powerful and life-changing process. As with any therapeutic tool, participants need to experience safety and understand the images *as* metaphors – they represent the truth for us *as we see it at the time*, within the story that we are telling ourselves – they are not fixed entities.

Another challenge of working in this way relates to the importance of choosing the appropriate strategies at different stages of change in order to continue to promote a sense of self-efficacy and self-esteem and, therefore, continued motivation. Carefully-chosen Imagework exercises can be utilized to strengthen and enhance the process. For example, in the early stages of change, Imagework could be used to explore 'future self' and to look at outcome possibilities, or we might work with images of 'barriers' to change. During periods of relapse (or 'lapse') Imagework can help in the exploration of times when we have previously been successful in achieving goals and overcoming obstacles or can be useful in discovering or rediscovering our own internal expert – that part of us that already 'knows' at some level what is needed.

Summary

The self-esteem approach to stammering therapy that I have proposed here is constantly evolving in response to my own learning and experiences and in response to discussions with others. Yet, despite the organic nature of this model, there are certain underlying principles which have endured. These principles might already be familiar to therapists and to people who stammer in an array of different contexts; I offer them here as encapsulating the essence of a self-esteem approach based on Imagework:

- Self-esteem is a complex, multi-faceted aspect of life.

- Supporting someone in building and maintaining healthy self-esteem ultimately involves *a way of being* rather than a procedure with an end product, or something we do to make people 'feel better'.

- A self-esteem approach using Imagework is based on collaboration between an imageworker (client) and guide (therapist); it is supportive, rather than confrontational, and seeks to capitalize on existing skills and strengths.

- When we engage with others in building and maintaining healthy self-esteem through Imagework we should do so with mindfulness, integrity and respect for each person's unique images.

- When we are able to be in tune with the other person's concerns and dilemmas to such an extent that we can tentatively offer new and creative images, then we have potential to strengthen rapport, build trust and increase the possibility for long-lasting change.

Certainly every one of us has greater potential to grow and develop if we are more aware of the different aspects of our own self-esteem and of the different levels of consciousness within which we operate.

Appendix

A self-esteem model of support

A. The foundation elements of healthy self-esteem

1. Self–knowledge

Development of this foundation element contributes to the building of an 'awakened' relationship with the self. It involves:

- Developing a sense of security in terms of a strong sense of self: an understanding of who 'I' am and where I fit into the social world around me.

- Understanding differences and commonalities – for example, how I am different from others in looks and character, or how I can have an interest in common with others.

- Knowing that I have many aspects to my personality.

- Developing and maintaining my personal values – my guiding principles in life.

- Developing a sense of my personal history – my own 'life story'.

2. Self and others

This involves:

- Understanding the joys and challenges of relationships: learning to trust and to negotiate and cooperate with others; being able to see things from another person's perspective (empathy) and developing an understanding of how they might see me; learning respect and tolerance for other people's needs and views.

- Developing and maintaining my own identity as a separate person while still recognizing the natural mutuality and interdependence inherent in relationships.
- Developing a sense of my family/cultural 'story'.

3. Self-acceptance

This involves:

- Knowing my own strengths, recognizing what cannot be changed and recognizing areas that I find difficult and may want to work on.
- Accepting that it is natural to make mistakes and that this is sometimes how we learn best.
- Developing the capacity to recognize and accept feedback from others in terms of my progress.
- Feeling OK about my physical body and enhancing positive body awareness so that I can, for example, let go of unwanted tension or focus on calm breathing.

4. Self-reliance

This involves:

- Knowing how to take care of myself, both physically and emotionally.
- Building a measure of independence, emotional resilience and self-motivation; believing that I have mastery over my life and can meet challenges as and when they arise.
- Reducing my reliance on other people's opinions and evaluations.

5. Self-expression

This involves:

- Understanding that my interactions reflect my beliefs about myself and about others.

- Building and maintaining a sense of enjoyment and effectiveness in the act of communication.

- Developing creativity in self-expression and recognizing and celebrating the unique and diverse ways in which we each express who we are.

6. Self-confidence

This involves

- Developing a strong sense of self-efficacy (see foundation element 4)

- Knowing that my opinions, thoughts and actions have value and that I have the right to express them.

- Developing my knowledge and skills so that I feel able to experiment with different methods of problem-solving and can be flexible enough to alter my strategies if needed.

- Feeling strong enough to accept challenges and make choices.

- Feeling secure enough in myself to be able to cope with the unexpected.

7. Self-awareness

Self-awareness is the cornerstone of realistic self-evaluation. It involves:

- Developing the ability to be focused in the 'here and now' rather than absorbed in negative thoughts about the past or future.

- Recognizing my feelings as they arise.

- Understanding that emotional, mental and physical changes are a natural part of my life.

- Being aware of the normal fluctuations in how I feel and how these link to my thoughts and behaviour; recognizing that I have choices about how I think, feel and behave.

- Knowing what I am capable of, and learning to set realistic yet challenging goals.

- Developing and maintaining emotional intelligence.[2]

8. Beyond self

This involves:

- Deepening my awareness and engagement with other people, with life and with my inner self. This might manifest in a number of ways such as a strong sense of connection with music, art, or the wonders of the universe; or a transpersonal/spiritual element to our lives which may or may not be based in religious beliefs.

- Developing an ability to focus and reflect upon realities beyond 'the self'.

- Acceptance of living with a degree of uncertainty and 'not knowing' in life.

- Developing my ability to imagine.

B. Control, adaptability and effectiveness

Within the self-esteem model there are five sets of core abilities: self-control, adaptability, effective observation, effective listening and imagination. As with the foundation elements, these abilities are, in fact, fairly generic and are central to a number of different aspects of wellbeing (see, for example, Plummer, 2012). They not only involve actual competency or mastery of skills, but also positive perception of self-efficacy.

Self-control

This includes the ability to have some control over our feelings and thoughts and

---

2 Daniel Goleman suggests that emotional intelligence involves the ability to recognize and understand our own emotions and those of others, the ability to manage our emotions effectively and the ability to motivate ourselves (Goleman, 1996 pp.43–44). Emotional intelligence within this model of self-esteem, therefore, also includes self-reliance (foundation element 4) and links with foundation element 2: self and others.

the ways in which we express them, the ability to tolerate waiting and manage impulsivity, the ability to consciously switch attention from one stimulus to another by choice, and the ability to persevere with difficult tasks.

The ability to maintain focus, through self-awareness and self-control leads to concentration. Effective concentration contributes to perseverance, which in turn will increase the likelihood of successfully completing a task.

Adaptability

This involves the ability to adapt to new situations and changes in contexts; the ability to monitor and adjust actions, feelings and thoughts according to realistic assessments of personal progress, and the ability to adapt to obstacles and challenges, such as a demanding listening environment. Adaptability not only enables us to move from one focus of attention to another appropriately, but also allows us to attend to more than one stimulus at the same time. This divided attention often consists of a mixture of an internal stimulus (e.g. a memory) and an external stimulus. For example, we can link a current challenging event with the memory of a similar past experience that we handled well in order to feel confident about coping with it effectively again this time.

Effective listening

This includes the ability to really hear what others are saying and to reflect on what is heard. Effective listening inevitably includes self-control, for example the ability to focus on what is being said by others without allowing our own thoughts to dominate.

Effective observation

This includes the ability to observe, and to reflect on, details within our environment, non-verbal aspects of interactions and our own behaviour. It also includes the ability to expand our contextual awareness of the object of our attention.

Imagination

The ability to imagine is an important aspect of learning, creativity and problem-solving. It is also vital for empathy: the ability to see things from another person's point of view and to be aware of others' needs. Imagination allows us to be more effective in directing our attention both internally (to images, feelings and thoughts) and externally. Imagination is the key to effective change.

C. Specific skills

Specific skills refer to the behaviours which, in effect, demonstrate the core abilities. The key concept here is *appropriateness* – the application of skills in an appropriate way. For example, in relation to the core ability of being able to *control* impulsivity I may need to develop skills of:

- Self-rewarding

- Making appropriate choices

- Monitoring physical sensations

- Monitoring my internal 'chatter'

- Pausing and focusing on a specific stimulus (for example, focusing on my breathing).

Acknowledgements

The description of images and Imagework is adapted from Chapter 3 of *Helping Adolescents and Adults to Build Self-Esteem* (Plummer, 2005), published by Jessica Kingsley Publishers.

References

Bandura, A. (1977) Self-efficacy: Toward a unifying theory of behavioural change. *Psychological Review 84*, 191–215.

Berg, I.K. & de Shazer, S. (1993) Making numbers talk: Language in therapy. In: S. Friedman (Ed.), *The New Language of Change: Constructive Collaboration in Psychotherapy*. New York: Guilford Press.

Berne, E. (1964) *Games People Play. The Psychology of Human Relationships*. New York: Ballantine Books.

Branden, N. (1992) *The Power of Self-Esteem*. Deerfield Beach, Florida: Health Communications Inc.

Cox, M. & Theilgaard, A. (1987) *Mutative Metaphors in Psychotherapy. The Aeolian Mode*. London and New York: Tavistock Publications.

Dalton, P. & Dunnett, G. (1990) *A Psychology for Living. Personal Construct Theory for Professionals and Clients*. Self-published: Dunton Publishing.

Garmezy, N. (1994) Reflections and commentary on risk, resilience, and development. In: R.J. Haggerty, L.R. Sherrod, N. Garmezy & M. Rutter (Eds) *Stress, Risk, and Resilience in Children and Adolescents: Process, Mechanisms, and Interventions*. Cambridge: Cambridge University Press.

Glouberman, D. (2003) *Life Choices, Life Changes: Develop Your Personal Vision with Imagework* (revised edition). London: Hodder and Stoughton (first published by Unwin Hyman, 1989).

Goleman, D. (1996) *Emotional Intelligence: Why it can Matter More than IQ*. London: Bloomsbury.

Gore, S. & Eckenrode, J. (1994) Context and process in research on risk and resilience. In: R.J. Haggerty, L.R. Sherrod, N. Garmezy & M. Rutter (Eds) *Stress, Risk, and Resilience in Children and Adolescents: Process, Mechanisms, and Interventions*. Cambridge: Cambridge University Press.

Greenier, K.D., Kernis, M.H., & Waschull, S.B. (1995) Not all high (or low) self-esteem people are the same. Theory and research on stability of self-esteem. In: M.H. Kernis (Ed.) *Efficacy, Agency, and Self-Esteem*. New York and London: Plenum Press.

Harter, S. (1999) *The Construction of the Self*. New York: Guilford Press.

Hillman, J. (1983) *Healing Fiction*. Putnam, Connecticut: Spring Publications, Inc.

Hillman, J. (1990) Imaginal practice. In: T. Moore (Ed.) *The Essential James Hillman: A Blue Fire*. London: Routledge.

Johnson, R. (1989) *Inner Work: Using Dreams and Active Imagination for Personal Growth*. New York: HarperSanFrancisco.

Jung, C.G. (Ed.) (1978) *Man and His Symbols*. London: Pan Books (first published by Aldus Books Ltd, 1964).

Kelly, G.A. (1991) *The Psychology of Personal Constructs, Vol 1: A Theory of Personality*. London: Routledge, in association with the Centre for Personal Construct Psychology.

Moore, T. (Ed.) (1990) *The Essential James Hillman: A Blue Fire*. London: Routledge.

Moore, T. (1992) *Care of the Soul. How to Add Depth and Meaning to your Everyday Life*. London: Piatkus.

Mruk, C.J. (1999) *Self-esteem Research Theory and Practice*, 2nd ed. London: Free Association Books.

Plummer, D.M. (2005) *Helping Adolescents and Adults to Build Self-Esteem*. London and Philadelphia: Jessica Kingsley Publishers.

Plummer, D.M. (2007a) *Helping Children to Build Self-Esteem* 2nd ed. London and Philadelphia: Jessica Kingsley Publishers.

Plummer, D.M. (2007b) *Self-Esteem Games for Children*. London and Philadelphia: Jessica Kingsley Publishers.

Plummer, D.M. (2011) *Helping Children to Improve their Communication Skills*. London and Philadelphia: Jessica Kingsley Publishers.

Plummer, D.M. (2012) *Focusing and Calming Games for Children*. London and Philadelphia: Jessica Kingsley Publishers.

Rogers, C. (1961) *On Becoming a Person: A Therapist's View of Psychotherapy*. London: Constable.

Tschudi, F. (1977) Loaded and honest questions. In: D. Bannister (Ed.) *New Perspectives in Personal Construct Theory*. London: Academic Press

Further reading

Burns, R.B. (1979) *The Self Concept in Theory, Measurement, Development and Behaviour*. New York: Longman.

Coopersmith, S. (1967) *The Antecedents of Self-Esteem*. San Francisco, CA: W.H. Freeman and Company.

Plummer, D. (1999) *Using Interactive Imagework with Children: Walking on the Magic Mountain*. London and Philadelphia: Jessica Kingsley Publishers.

Rayner, E. (1993) *Human Development: An Introduction to the Psychodynamics of Growth, Maturity and Ageing*. London: Routledge.

Rutter, M. (1994) Stress research: Accomplishments and tasks ahead. In: R.J. Haggerty, L.R. Sherrod, N. Garmezy & M. Rutter (Eds) *Stress, Risk, and Resilience in Children and Adolescents. Process, Mechanisms, and Interventions*. Cambridge: Cambridge University Press.

11 Feelings and stammering – Finding a way forward

Peter Cartwright

Introduction

In January 2004, Carolyn Cheasman and I planned and delivered a course called 'Feelings and stammering – finding a way forward'. It was part of the range of stammering therapy courses offered by the speech therapy department at City Lit in London.

Having successfully collaborated before on planning and delivering courses for people who stammer, we thought there was much to offer by developing this new course. In particular, we considered that the difficult and painful emotions associated with stammering are often the most distressing part for those who stammer. Also, these emotions often seem to inhibit people from benefiting from stammering therapy approaches, like desensitization. Therefore, helping people to cope better with these emotions seemed highly relevant.

It is important to note that whilst Carolyn is a speech and language therapist, I am a Gestalt counsellor. I am, therefore, writing from that perspective. My intention is to offer an alternative view of stammering and how to cope with it, as well as to offer ideas for how Gestalt theory and practice might be integrated into stammering therapy, through describing the course.

The chapter includes the reflections of Lisette Wesseling, who participated in the course.

Overview of the course

The course offered adults who stammer an opportunity to explore their emotions, become more aware of and make better sense of them, and experiment with new ways to cope emotionally. This took place in a supportive group of others who stammered, including both facilitators, myself and Carolyn.

As it was a new course there was no specific research or evidence base within the field of speech and language therapy. However, the underlying ideas we drew upon were respected and well-established ways of working in the field of counselling.

Theoretical foundations of the course

Underlying the course were three theoretical approaches: relevant ideas from Gestalt counselling theory and practice (Joyce & Sills, 2001), the concept of emotional literacy (Goleman, 1996) and aspects of cognitive behavioural therapy (CBT, Greenberger & Padesky, 1995). These three approaches were integrated together to form the course's theoretical foundation.

Later in the chapter, I explain the relevant aspects of Gestalt and emotional literacy. As CBT is described in greater depth by Fry (2013, chapter 9 in this book), I have only provided a brief description of the relevant concepts.

The course structure, content and delivery

The course took place over 10 two-hour sessions. Initially, participants were introduced to the CBT cycle, the concept of emotional literacy and the Gestalt idea of experimentation (developing new ways of living by experimenting with different behaviours which appeal to someone). In this way, they started to develop skills to increase their own awareness, make sense of their emotions and begin to change. They next explored the emotions of fear, shame and anger, and were encouraged to experiment with different ways of coping. The course developed participants' abilities to support themselves emotionally and offered the Gestalt idea of 'internal conflicts' with suggestions on how to reconcile these. In the final session, participants had the opportunity to reflect on their learning and how they would continue their personal growth.

The course was primarily experiential with the amount of didactic teaching kept to a minimum. We believed that people learn better this way and that the course would be more stimulating. Therefore, a minimum of key information was presented, combined with exercises so that participants could experience personally what was taught. They would then reflect upon this experience to raise their awareness, make sense of their emotions, identify ideas they wanted to experiment with and subsequently try them out. To facilitate this personal growth, people kept a journal to record key ideas, their growing self-awareness, strategies they tried and whether they were helpful or not, and to celebrate their successes.

A Gestalt view of stammering and associated emotions

As noted above, I believed a Gestalt view on stammering and the associated emotions would offer something potentially new and innovative. The following describes relevant aspects of Gestalt counselling theory which I then apply to my own stammering to illustrate how I consider I started to stammer, the way it became habitual and how I then became more fluent. This perspective informed me throughout planning and delivering the course.

Gestalt counselling theory

The term 'Gestalt' as used in this chapter refers to an approach to counselling and psychotherapy (Joyce & Sills, 2001), rather than other uses of the term, such as Gestalt psychology. The theory and practice have developed much over the years. As I see it, contemporary Gestalt counselling, the foundation for the course, integrates a wide range of influences to create a unique, coherent and highly effective theory and practice.

The word Gestalt is German; it does not easily translate, but broadly means 'pattern' or 'whole'. 'Pattern' means that Gestalt counselling is curious about the patterns of how we live, the habitual ways we do things. In particular, Gestalt theory proposes that each episode of living begins to emerge when we need, want or have an interest in something. We organize ourselves in a particular way to complete that episode, which is potentially healthy and satisfying to us, or not. Then another need, want or interest emerges and so on. Each of these episodes of living is called a 'Gestalt' (Korb, Gorrell, & Van De Riet, 1989, pp.4–6), another use of this word which also picks up on the idea of pattern referred to earlier. At any one time we have many active Gestalts, although our attention is often focused on just one or two at any one moment. An example of a Gestalt is you reading this chapter and as a Gestaltist I would be curious about *how* you are doing that.

'Whole' means taking a holistic approach. Therefore, Gestalt theory is interested in the whole person and aims to integrate all aspects of our selves, rather than parts of us being undeveloped, denied or in conflict with each other. For example, as a Gestalt counsellor I am interested in how all of you approach reading this chapter, not just the part of you that believes 'I should read this for work', but also other parts, such as you possibly also saying, 'but I'd rather be watching the telly'. 'Whole' also includes being interested in the constantly changing context of our lives; therefore, how we relate to and are influenced by others and the world around us. For example, you might read this chapter after struggling with a client who stammered and hope this will help you.

Another important aspect of Gestalt theory is the idea that human beings are essentially organisms (Crocker, 1999). Like other animals, we have within us the innate capacity to maintain life and to grow, which happens through a continual process of interacting with others and the world around us to get our needs met.

Bringing these three ideas together, Gestalt theory views our lives as an active, lived experience, involving our whole being and our interaction with the environment around us. Healthy living is the flexible and creative formation of Gestalts that respond to what is happening for us right now, so we get our needs met. With one Gestalt satisfactorily completed we can then live the next one and so on. Ill-health occurs when Gestalt formation is not effective at meeting our physical, psychological or social needs. The process may be interrupted, performed ineffectively or not completed.

One key way in which Gestalt formation becomes unhealthy is as a result of insufficient support in our childhood environment to form healthy Gestalts. As children we then have to adjust how we live to still meet our needs as best we can, and this is called a 'creative adjustment' (Joyce & Sills, 2001, p.63). If this keeps on happening, or occurs through a traumatic experience, this creative adjustment typically becomes habitual and a fixed way of being is created that tends to stay with us whether or not it is relevant to our lives now. These are referred to as 'fixed Gestalts' (MacKewn, 1997, p.22–27). They can be observed in the way we live our lives now, from our habits that no longer seem relevant or appropriate. For example, someone who experienced repeated hunger in childhood might now eat very quickly or hoard food, even though it is no longer necessary. To put it another way, a fixed Gestalt is living by habit from the past, rather than as is necessary in the present. It is important to recognize that fixed Gestalts were the best way we could find when they were formed. They served us well, even if now they are potentially unhealthy. Lastly, a fixed Gestalt is not always unhealthy; being able to tie up our shoe laces every morning from habit is much more helpful than having to create a new way every day!

A Gestalt perspective of stammering

Using this theory, I now offer an interpretation of my own experience of stammering. I stammer only in certain circumstances, such as when I am with another person who I perceive as being in authority. My stammer varies over time and I stammer much less than I used to. To me, this implies that it is not an innate aspect of myself, like the ability to speak. Rather it is something that is dependent upon the context I find myself in and is, at least in part, something I unintentionally learned to do.

I believe several interconnected themes combined to create and then maintain my stammering, until it became a fixed Gestalt. From the outset I did not speak fluently, tending to stutter on sounds such as 'b' and 'm'. Obviously, such dysfluency can often occur as speech is acquired. At that time, my parents were not concerned as they assumed that I would grow out of stammering as my speech developed. This did not happen because of particular influences in my life that I describe next.

My older brother, Michael, and I have always been very close; we were the same height and could be seen as peers. However, there was 21 months' difference in age and, crucially, Michael learned to speak easily. I believe this may well have led me to try and speak beyond my developmental ability, thereby reinforcing my stammer.

As a toddler I was very energetic, uninhibited and noisy. This is partly my temperament, but was also a way to get attention and express my anger at not having enough of it. This occurred as I was squeezed between my older brother and Clare, a new baby sister who is 21 months younger than me. Then the birth of Thomas, just over three years later, probably exacerbated the situation. See how I had 'creatively adjusted' to get my needs met. At that young age this would have happened more through an innate capacity to survive and grow rather than through a deliberate choice made with self-awareness. Perhaps an unintended side-effect of wanting attention was to put pressure on myself to speak beyond my capability reinforcing my stammer? Also, it is possible that I felt further pressure to be fluent when younger siblings had no difficulties.

My parents reacted by wanting me to contain my energy because I would smash things (although they see now that I also needed more space and attention). By the time I went to school, aged five , they seem to have succeeded as I had become a 'good boy'! This was another 'creative adjustment'. I learned that, through being good, I would not get into trouble and would also get my parents' approval, both vital to a developing child. This meant holding in and repressing my impulses, which Gestalt terms 'retroflection' (Joyce & Sills, 2001, p.114). I consider this had an unintentional effect on my speech: by inhibiting I learned to trap all my excited energy within myself as I had become anxious about expressing it. Gestalt theory views anxiety as 'trapped excitement' (Perls, Hefferline & Goodman, 1972, p.128), as the dread we feel at the prospect of daring to do something which we assume will be risky. If we believed there was no risk then we would feel excitement and our energy would flow. A physiological effect of this process is a tendency to freeze. It is my belief that trapping the impulses to be myself and the associated freezing inadvertently encouraged stammering.

Once I began interacting with people outside my family, at playgroup aged four and then at school, I began to learn that stammering was best avoided as it resulted in teasing by other children and the concern of teachers. At such a young age I was unable to consider their reactions and choose whether I wanted to believe them. I had 'introjected' these ideas, which is where 'an opinion, an attitude or an instruction is unquestioningly taken in from the environment as if it were true' (Joyce & Sills, 2001, p.125). A useful way to think of an introject is to see it like a virus that has been introduced into a computer and starts directing how things are done.

This internalizing of others' reactions led to me telling myself that I should not stammer. A consequence of this was my assumption that the slightest negativity I perceived in others meant that they thought stammering unacceptable, whether in reality they did or not. For example, I misunderstood my parents later asking if I wanted help as evidence that stammering was 'wrong'. I had become acutely sensitive to stammering and was projecting my unhelpful beliefs about it on to others. Gestalt theory would suggest that I had developed both 'sensitivity', which is an 'overload of sensory stimuli' (Joyce & Sills, 2001, p.119), as well as 'projection', which is assuming that others are as we believe them to be, without realizing that those assumptions are our own (Joyce & Sills, 2001, p.123). Note how I had again creatively adjusted, this time to protect myself from feeling embarrassment and shame as there was not enough support in my environment to be fully who I was (see the section on shame below). By the age of seven, I had learned to avoid stammering as best I could. This was another 'creative adjustment': to avoid, or 'deflect' away from an aspect of myself that felt shameful. Gestalt calls this way of being 'deflection' (Joyce & Sills, 2001, p.116).

It is important to make the following observations. First, I would like to draw attention to the importance of other people's influence on the development of my stammering and how I creatively adjusted to cope with it. I made these adjustments through being influenced by others, which Gestalt terms 'co-creation' (Joyce & Sills, 2001, p.47). The way that relationships shape what happens to us, and thereby, influence who we become, is central to the Gestalt theory view of human development. Much of how we influence each other is unintended and many of the consequences are unintentional, as is the case of others' influence on my stammering.

Second, the beliefs I introjected and the creative adjustments I made became a fixed, habitual part of who I am. I had developed a 'fixed Gestalt' that enabled me to speak whilst also avoiding the difficult, painful and excruciating emotions associated with stammering, as best as I could. Like any fixed Gestalt, it is a way of living created for circumstances in the past. It gets triggered now by the perception that the present is somehow like the past. It includes regressing into a childhood emotional state of fearing stammering and of others' reaction, of the embarrassment and shame of doing it, and then the self-loathing and upset of having done it. It is useful to recognize just how complex this fixed Gestalt is: obviously there is the actual stammering and it also includes my whole being and interaction with others.

Last, and most significantly, an intrinsic aspect of the fixed Gestalt is that I stammer more, not less. When I live this way I am self-conscious, afraid of stammering, tense, believing I should not do it, all of which make stammering more likely. So, paradoxically, my old way of coping with stammering actually increases the likelihood of it. Therefore, it is not unlike a panic attack, where the fear of it can escalate into having one. This unintended consequence was beyond my awareness or understanding for years. Thus, my way of coping, my fixed Gestalt, was both useful and ultimately self-defeating. Such paradoxes are widely recognized in counselling. Clearly, I needed a new way of coping with stammering, i.e. to create a new Gestalt. Much of this change did not occur through having Gestalt counselling, but the theory and practice still apply and give a counselling perspective to changing stammering.

Gestalt theory proposes that change is 'a natural process of growth' (Joyce & Sills, 2001, p.37), which is typically complex, nonlinear, repetitive, and interconnected with other aspects of ourselves and those around us. For me, there were several Gestalt ideas occurring in parallel, which produced this growth over many years. My innate capacity to grow, combined with having developed enough inner support, led me to begin speech and language therapy at City Lit, aged 29. This helped by desensitizing me through challenging my assumptions about stammering. Therefore, I began to reject my old introjects and create new, more helpful, adult beliefs, such as 'I can communicate effectively'. Another significant change for me was becoming aware that stammering meant more to me and evoked greater emotion in me than it did for those I spoke to, especially if I could stay calm and stammer fluently. Therefore, I began to recognize that a different 'co-creation' was possible, and one over which I had significant control.

I had begun developing a new Gestalt. At first, this needed to be self-consciously evoked, which felt awkward. The old fixed Gestalt was still much more how I was. However, gradually new habits formed, which I could trust and which automatically happened alongside the old fixed Gestalt, so I could both stammer and cope better. Over the years, the new Gestalt has become the way I am most of the time.

I also began to undo my creative adjustments and began moving from 'deflection' to facing my stammering; from 'retroflecting' my energy to being more spontaneous again; from 'projecting' my unhelpful beliefs to owning them and not assuming how others saw me; and lastly, from being sensitive about my stammering to becoming more desensitized. Change does not occur in isolation, but is part of, and interconnected with, the rest of our lives (Joyce & Sills, 2001). Therefore, as I had girlfriends and developed my career I gained confidence and stammered less. Lastly, this growth required supporting myself to repeatedly risk experimenting with being different and, thereby, finding my own way forward. Through this I discovered for myself what had been discussed in speech and language therapy: when I stopped avoiding and began accepting that I stammered I paradoxically stammered less. The way 'self-support' and 'experimentation' led to such 'paradoxical change' are three key Gestalt concepts, which I cover below when relating theory to the course.

I am now 49, much more fluent and when I do stammer I do so 'fluently' and without the awkwardness I used to have. I no longer have strong emotions when stammering nor do I dwell on it afterwards. I am therefore easier to be with when I stammer, which in turn helps me to stammer less. I now see stammering as just another aspect of who I am, not as defining who I am. However, it can still be a mild irritation, provoke anxiety, and is 'work in progress'.

Obviously, other people's stammering is different, although I expect there would be broad similarities in the inter-personal origins, in the kind of creative adjustments, the way stammering is inadvertently maintained and the process of change.

The course

Gestalt counselling, emotional literacy and CBT were integrated together to produce the theoretical foundation of the course. I now explain these ideas in more detail, describe how they were used on the course and comment on how effective they were for the participants.

Gestalt theory and practice

I was keen to integrate five Gestalt concepts into the course.

Awareness

A cornerstone of Gestalt theory and practice is the importance of awareness.

> "Awareness is a form of experience which can be loosely defined as being in touch with one's own existence, with *what is* ... the person who is aware knows *what* he does, *how* he does it, that he has alternatives and that he *chooses* to be as he is."
>
> (Yontef, in Joyce & Sills, 2001, p.27)

Put another way, awareness is the 'here and now' sensing and knowing of our own experience. There are clear links to the concept of mindfulness described elsewhere in this book.

Raising participants' awareness was a key theme running throughout the course. To enable this, we introduced the CBT cycle (as described below) at the start because we thought it would be helpful for participants to be able to differentiate their awareness between thinking, emotions, internal bodily experience and behaviour.

Various ways of raising awareness were used through the course, including: experiential exercises such as using mindfulness practices; 'homework' to notice and pay attention during the week to a particular emotion, thought pattern or behaviour; completing a handout for each emotion to describe the experience of thinking, emotions, internal bodily experiences and behaviours; and recording significant experiences, insights and awareness in their journals.

This work on awareness seemed to be relatively straightforward for the participants. I believe there are two reasons for this: the first is the explicit focus on and repetition of awareness throughout the course. Second, the importance of awareness was explained at the start: namely, when we are aware, we can then choose between how we tend to be from habit (a fixed Gestalt), or to experiment with being different (so form the Gestalt in a new way) and change (Joyce & Sills, 2001). Knowing this increased participants' motivation to become more aware.

Experimentation

'Experimentation' is creating something new that we feel drawn towards and want to do, and then 'having a go' at it. So it is not doing what others say, following a prescriptive path, trying to do something we believe is good for us that we do not really want to do, nor forcing ourselves when too anxious to risk having a go (MacKewn, 1997, p.131). Additionally, it is important to recognize that we can only make this choice 'here and now'. However much we wished we had been different in the past or want to be in the future, we can only be different 'here and now' (Clarkson, 1989). Therefore, awareness and choosing to experiment can be enough to change (Houston, 2003). This formed another key idea that was shared with participants at the start of the course.

As each emotion was being covered, time was given to introducing and sharing ideas for participants to experiment with at each stage of the CBT cycle, i.e. creating new beliefs, coping with emotions, working with bodily experiences and experimenting with new behaviours. Participants were then encouraged to experiment with what attracted them and record what happened. Examples of what participants found helpful are given later in the sections on fear, shame and anger.

Sadly, though, change is not always this straightforward. We want to be different and do not seem able to change. We get stuck. Gestalt theory recognizes two basic ways in which we do not change despite seemingly wanting our lives to be different, both of which are highly relevant to stammering. First, we might try to improve, usually by following an introjected idea, whilst believing deep down we are unable to do it or just do not want to do it. An example of this might be when a person who stammers strives to voluntarily stammer (deliberately choosing to stammer as a way of becoming less sensitive and anxious about stammering) but believes it would be too difficult to do. Second, we scare ourselves into inactivity for fear of risking being different and of what we imagine will happen; for example, fearing that using the phone and thereby risking stammering would be too catastrophic to even attempt (Korb, Gorrell & Van De Riet, 1989).

It was important the course addressed these two potential pitfalls. We chose to begin this when covering the first emotion, fear, by asking participants to identify the negative automatic thoughts or 'NATs' (Greenberger & Padesky, 1995) that lead to them feeling fear. We then asked participants to 'catch the NAT' during the week and just notice whether that was enough to change or not. The following session some participants reported that being aware, or 'catching the NAT', had been enough to change and cope better with their fear, and others had been aware but unable to change. Having had those experiences, the group was ready for these two ideas about how we prevent change, as well as the Gestalt concept of internal conflicts that I cover next.

Internal conflicts

Gestalt proposes that striving to change, or trying to be what we are not, fails because a psychological conflict gets set up within us. These internal conflicts are seen as a fight between a 'top-dog' and an 'under-dog' (Joyce & Sills, 2001, p.104). The top-dog contains beliefs that are introjected, i.e. learned and unquestioned, so often begin with 'I should/ought/must...'. The under-dog contains what is more innate and what we want to do. The top-dog tries hard to prevail and is often punishing of the under-dog. Change is often achieved for a while as the under-dog is kept down. However, the under-dog usually wins out, often in subtle ways, because it knows what we really want to do, not what we should, ought or must do. We can invest a lot of time and psychological energy in being stuck in these internal conflicts, often out of our awareness.

I can illustrate this from my own stammering. I had learned about the use of voluntary stammering in speech and language therapy. However, when it came to actually trying it out, I never did it. I had taken in the belief I should stammer voluntarily, that this would be good for me, and part of me saw the sense in it too. Pitched against this was a lifetime's experience of fearing how I felt when I did stammer, so I really did not want to voluntarily stammer. Here was a classic top-dog/under-dog conflict: 'I should voluntarily stammer' versus 'I don't want to'. However hard my top-dog tried to make me stammer voluntarily, and occasionally succeeded, my under-dog would subtly and cleverly resist doing it. Within a few weeks of ending speech and language therapy I had stopped altogether. My top-dog would then often criticize the rest of me for not doing it, leading to guilt and regret that I had failed. As is so often the case with internal conflicts, see how my top-dog and under-dog were both potentially helpful and unhelpful to me: my top-dog knew about the usefulness of voluntary stammering, but could bully me into doing it before I was ready, and my under-dog knew how to prevent me from feeling ashamed of stammering, but deprived me of using a useful therapy tool.

Internal conflicts need to be resolved if we are to grow and feel at ease with ourselves. Gestalt theory and practice propose that this is done by accepting how we are (as anything else is not our reality); separating, owning and becoming more aware of the two parts, including acknowledging both their usefulness and limitations; then with this new awareness rising above the conflict and choosing a way forward, whatever that may be. To be successful this way forward needs energy or 'wanting' behind it, thereby getting away from trying and doing what we 'should' do. Note that this resolution includes our considering whether we might want to follow the top-dog's belief. If we consider we do and really integrate it into who we are, then we are more likely to follow that belief.

Exactly how internal conflicts are resolved is beyond the scope of this chapter. However, an example of resolving a conflict is my own internal conflict over voluntary stammering. I have become much more aware of this struggle and developed the ability to step back from it and choose what seems best for me at any one moment, rather than 'ping-pong' back and forth between my top-dog and under-dog.

Participants were introduced to this way of viewing internal conflicts and readily related to it. They were then given an opportunity to reflect on their own 'top-dog/under-dog' conflicts in relation to stammering and record this. I was keen to then demonstrate how Gestalt counselling works with internal conflicts to bring the idea alive. One participant, Lisette, volunteered to do this and she describes her experience of our work in her reflections later.

This was an entirely new approach for those on the course. It was insightful and potentially very helpful. However, their conflicts remained largely unresolved due to the limitations of time. I noted that counselling would be an ideal way for participants to continue this work and suggested that internal conflicts are resolved through stepping back from them and making a choice based on awareness.

Supporting ourselves

As noted above, the second way we can struggle to change is when we feel fearful because we see change as too challenging. This phenomenon is well recognized in Gestalt, so great emphasis is placed on self-support which is seen as 'the necessary basis for all healthy functioning' (Joyce & Sills, 2001, p.83).

For the course, 'support' meant anything that helped participants cope with the difficult or painful emotions associated with stammering. For example, if someone notices themselves tensing, clenching their jaw and beginning to feel anxious because they fear they will stammer, they can then support themselves in a variety of ways, including calming themselves by breathing more deeply, saying to themselves something like "I can still communicate well enough and if I say I stammer people usually understand", and loosening clenched jaw muscles.

To help participants identify the support they had and to consider whether this was enough to cope with their difficult and painful emotions they were introduced to the 'support pyramid' (Kuykendall, 2001). This proposes that support comes from four sources:

1. From within ourselves, such as celebrating our achievements; breathing in a calmer, less anxious way by slowing down the rate and using the diaphragm as well as the rib cage; talking to ourselves in a helpful and compassionate way.

2. Emotional support from other people, such as talking to people who care about us when we find life difficult or painful; being with people who encourage us and enjoy our successes; someone who we can discuss a problem with.

3. Distractions provided by other people, such as going to the pub or cinema; people who make us laugh; or someone we regularly do something with like an evening class.

4. Organisations who offer support, such as stammering therapy at City Lit; the British Stammering Association's website.

Evenings out to cinema with Andy and Beth.
Having a laugh with colleagues at work.
Art class on Tuesday evenings.

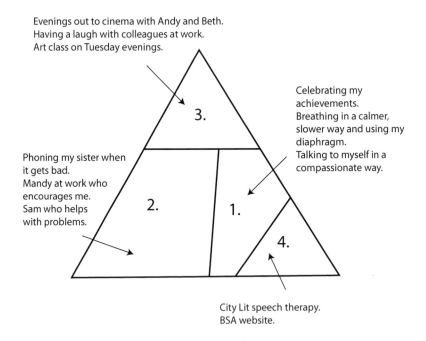

Celebrating my
achievements.
Breathing in a calmer,
slower way and using my
diaphragm.
Talking to myself in a
compassionate way.

Phoning my sister when
it gets bad.
Mandy at work who
encourages me.
Sam who helps
with problems.

City Lit speech therapy.
BSA website.

Figure 11.1 Example of a support pyramid.

So healthy self-support entails recognizing when to provide for ourselves and
when to use the support of others. This means having awareness of when we
need to support ourselves, then being able to either provide for ourselves or
ask others for support, and lastly being willing to let ourselves have what we
need and do so without self-judgement.

Participants were asked to produce two support pyramids. The size of
the first pyramid represents all the support they have and is divided into four
parts, each representing the proportion of support from the four sources noted
above (Figure 11.1). They then listed on their drawing the actual support they
had in each of the four parts.

Their assignment for the following week was to draw a second pyramid, similar to the first, but this time representing the amount of support they considered they needed to help with their emotions about stammering. In the following session, they compared their two pyramids and considered how to develop their support so that it matched the second one more closely.

Participants found two aspects of this exercise particularly helpful: the idea of deliberately choosing to help themselves when experiencing difficult or painful emotions, and the actual ideas they felt drawn to and experimented with to support themselves.

The paradoxical theory of change

What underlies all of the above is how Gestalt theory proposes that meaningful, lasting change occurs. Change is viewed as a process of personal growth (Joyce & Sills, 2001). It tends not to occur when we try to impose on ourselves an idea of self-improvement, or try to be who we are not. The failure of New Year's resolutions is a typical example of this phenomenon.

Change as personal growth entails staying where we are now, becoming aware of how we are, and accepting what we find. This is potentially challenging and when someone is able to do this that is often a change in itself (and an example of the paradox). Note that awareness without accepting what we experience is of little use, as not accepting our reality is self-deception. Through awareness and acceptance we can discover, create and realize our own potential. As self-trust develops we gradually become more fully and authentically who we are. This is a paradox as change occurs when we stop trying to be different. An example of this is my stammering: when I became aware of and accepted that I would not be fluent, I paradoxically stammered less.

Lastly, Gestalt theory recognizes that there is still a place for the way people tend to believe that change happens, i.e. 'deliberate, thought-out or wished-for change that needs determination and courage' (Joyce & Sills, 2001, p.39). However, Gestalt theory proposes that for this kind of change to work it 'requires it being freely chosen, with real wanting, in full awareness so not just a cultural or social pressure to be different' (Joyce & Sills, 2001, p.39). This is still consistent with the paradoxical theory of change, as it is a choice made with awareness of who we really are. This kind of change is not a quick fix, does not occur along an orderly, linear path of continual improvement, neither is it easy. It does require a moving towards and curiosity of what is disliked and feared in ourselves. It means losing unrealistic hopes and expectations. It requires a commitment to the sometimes painful process of growth. This paradox was not explicitly taught on the course, although it remained implicit throughout and informed the way I delivered the course and related to participants.

Cognitive Behavioural Therapy

This approach is covered in more depth elsewhere in this book, so the following is a brief description of the two CBT ideas used on the course.

CBT proposes that thoughts, emotions, internal physical responses, and behaviour are connected in a cycle (Greenberger & Padesky, 1995). The idea is that, when something happens, our perceptions of that event are processed by the brain, leading to our giving it meaning and understanding. This then produces emotional and internal physical responses, which then influence behaviour. Typically, this process becomes a cycle with new cognitions following our behaviour, then further emotional and internal physical responses, and so on. For example, in the past I have stammered with some managers. When meeting them I would be thinking that I was going to stammer, but I might not have been aware of this thought. This then led to my feeling anxiety, to tensing muscles in my jaw, and then stammering and losing eye contact.

The second CBT idea we used was that of negative automatic thoughts or 'NATs' (Greenberger & Padesky, 1995). These are the immediate automatic cognitions that occur when experiencing something, and which are unhelpful or unhealthy, for example, 'Oh no, I'm going to stammer'. Becoming aware of these as they occur, or 'catching the NAT', can help us not to react to them automatically.

We chose to use these ideas because they integrate neatly with Gestalt as they help to raise awareness and take a holistic view of human experience. Participants found them easy to understand; could separate out the different aspects of their experience; and could recognize the way that their cognitions led to emotions.

Emotional literacy

Emotional literacy is the ability to: name each emotion as we experience it; make sense of why that emotion arose at that time; gauge how much we feel it; understand what the emotion is for; and then to have ways of expressing, coping with and/or acting on that emotion which are effective. In this way, there is less risk of us becoming overwhelmed, confused by, or distanced from our emotions. This concept, also referred to as emotional intelligence, has been popularized by Goleman (1996) amongst others.

A key idea is that emotions are of use to us, if only we can make sense of them and mobilize our capability to use them. Emotions serve us in three ways: they provide important information, they urge us to act in a certain way, and they convey to others what is happening for us. Emotions evolved to enable us to survive, enhance our existence and to reproduce.

An example from my own experience of stammering can illustrate how emotional literacy is helpful. Imagine I need to phone a company which has failed to deliver a package. As this idea forms in my awareness I become anxious. I know I am anxious from being aware of myself: the feeling of dread as I anticipate stammering, a rise in muscle tension in my jaw and shoulders, becoming busy with things other than the phone call, etc. I make sense of being anxious: I am assuming I shall have difficulty in getting what I want because I will stammer, so my anxiety is telling me this could be risky so be ready for a fight, it urges me to take care and conveys this to others through my facial expression and posture. I notice I am only moderately anxious. I am aware that by having the experience of anxiety I am expressing the emotion, moving through it and thereby opening the possibility of another experience. I cope with it by loosening my muscles, breathing deeper, reminding myself that I can still make the call despite feeling anxious, and that I can communicate effectively enough to get what I want. I then successfully make the call. I consider it important to draw attention in this example to how my emotional reaction is an old habitual one. I believe that a key aspect of stammering is this regression into a younger emotional state.

There have been various attempts made to categorize emotions. Goleman's (1996) idea of five groups of emotions can usefully be related to stammering. His five broad groups are fear, anger, shame, sadness and happiness. The concept of emotional literacy was introduced to participants at the start of the course and it formed a core theme throughout. We considered that the emotions typically associated with stammering are fear, shame, anger and sadness. Regrettably time constraints meant the course could not cover all four in the necessary depth. Sadness was the one left out as in my opinion it is probably the one that interferes less than fear, anger and shame when coping with stammering in everyday life.

Fear

Using the idea of emotional literacy, fear can be seen as the emotion that comes in anticipation of what we believe will be risky or unpredictable. Note how the thought leads to the emotion. It prepares us to take care over something which is going to happen. Our fear is conveyed to others by our body language and facial expressions.

Fear covers a wide spectrum of emotions from mild apprehension, through anxiety, to fear and even terror. It is a primitive emotion found in many life forms and aids survival by providing an instant powerful internal signal to take care when faced with danger or threat – the 'flight or fight' response. However, in our relatively safe modern world fear's signal is usually more powerful than it needs to be. The build-up of this response in our bodies is what we know as stress.

Stammering is typically greatly feared by those who do it. Williams (in Gregory, 1979) suggested that there are four fears which people who stammer may have:

1. Fear of the stigma associated in being found out as a person who stammers.

2. When starting to stammer a fear of not being able to finish a word, or at least fear about how long it takes to get a word out.

3. Fear that if stammering happens once then an avalanche of stammering will follow, making it hard to finish what is being said.

4. Fear of feeling out of control of our behaviour, with the associated embarrassment.

Also particularly relevant is Gestalt's view of anxiety as 'trapped excitement' and how this can encourage stammering as covered earlier, i.e. the dread we feel at the prospect of daring to do something which we assume will be risky.

These ideas about fear and stammering were presented to participants. Much attention was given to raising their awareness of how their fears about stammering actually happen. From this they were asked to notice their 'negative automatic thoughts' (Greenberger & Padesky, 1995) which led to fear.

The ideas for coping better with fear that appealed most to participants were as follows: Firstly, they found it useful to 'catch the NAT' and then ask themselves 'What's the worst that could happen?', rather than following their habitual responses. Secondly, the idea of supportive self-talk or imagining 'hearing' what a trusted person might say to calm and reassure was helpful. This 'evoked companion' could be a parent, therapist or friend. Thirdly, it was useful to calm their bodily reaction to fear by slowing their rate of breathing, using the diaphragm more than the rib cage, and gently stretching tense muscles. Lastly, participants were encouraged to choose either to move away from what is fearful or, if feeling supported enough, to 'feel the fear and do it anyway', the idea behind a self-help book of that title (Jeffers, 1989).

Shame

The emotion of shame occurs if we believe that we are intrinsically unacceptable, worthless or defective as a person. We feel an excruciating sense of self-consciousness, look embarrassed, possibly feel hot and flushed, our eyes look down or we turn away, we want to hide, and imagine others see us as unacceptable too. Shame, therefore, tells us when we see ourselves as unacceptable, it urges us to hide away or be different, and our shame reaction is a powerful signal to others about how we see ourselves.

I believe it is necessary to say how shame is different from guilt. Shame occurs when we believe our whole self is somehow not good enough or defective, whereas guilt is felt for a particular act or behaviour. For example, someone can feel guilty for breaking a law and feel ashamed of being a criminal. A recognized phenomenon in counselling is that clients usually know when they feel guilty, but typically need their counsellor to name the experience of shame.

Shame can be seen as an emotion that helps to maintain social cohesion. This happens by us internalizing unwritten 'rules' about what is unacceptable. Society needs us to have basic respect for each other and to cooperate enough or else we become too individualistic and selfish, resulting in a breakdown of social cohesion. Therefore, to feel ashamed we first need to believe that we are unacceptable in a particular way. What is considered unacceptable is usually decided by those with power in society or by the power of the majority. Some of these beliefs are widely accepted and unchallenged, such as believing that criminality is unacceptable. However, other socially-constructed beliefs are less clearly beneficial to society and are unhelpful, even dangerous, for individual citizens. For example, racist or homophobic beliefs can lead black and gay people to feel ashamed of whom they are, through their unquestioning internalization of those beliefs. Note the Gestalt idea of introjection again.

Therefore, a socially-useful emotion can sometimes work in damaging ways. I see stammering as another area where unhelpful shame can develop: society assumes that people are fluent, so those who stammer are somehow defective, or even to be ridiculed. Such beliefs are introjected in childhood by people who stammer when there is not enough support in their environment to affirm this aspect of who they are. My own experience described earlier illustrates how this can happen. However, as adults we can challenge our beliefs and develop new ones that are self-affirming, such as, 'I stammer and I'm still equal to others'. Over time, it is possible for old beliefs to wither and new ones to develop as automatic thought.

Given the powerful effect shame can have, the way we are often not aware of feeling ashamed, and how we can withdraw when ashamed, this was an important emotion to cover for people who stammer. We were keen to create a safe environment in which participants could feel affirmed, name the experience of shame, offer a chance to learn how shame happens and then work on their shame-inducing beliefs. This involved explaining how shame worked, focusing on becoming aware of the experience of shame and making sense of how their beliefs lead to and maintain feelings of shame.

One thing that helped convey the way cognitions lead to feeling shame was suggesting to participants that if they believed stammering made them better than others they could feel pride. Participants had time to consider whether they wanted to continue following their old beliefs or to begin creating new self-affirming beliefs to lie alongside their old negative ones. Lastly, as holding different beliefs to mainstream society is potentially risky, we also wanted participants to know they could choose whether to reveal they stammered or to conceal it, as circumstances made necessary.

Naming the experience of shame and challenging underlying beliefs was new, insightful and empowering for participants. However, in the time available people could only begin to create new beliefs about stammering to challenge the deeply self-critical and self-shaming beliefs they might have had.

Anger

Anger covers a range of emotions from mild irritation, to annoyance, frustration and anger, through to murderous rage. It is a tricky emotion to express safely and effectively. At its best, anger tells us that we have lost control in some way, find it difficult to accept how things are, or that we are being threatened. It then provides the energy to deal with or to put right what is wrong. Also, others around us know we are angry by our behaviour and body language, facial expression and raised volume of voice. However, our anger is potentially dangerous to us and to others. Therefore, many unwritten social 'rules' have developed, inhibiting anger and reducing these risks. We typically introject these when children and then might develop beliefs such as 'people who are angry have lost it'. This fear and shame about anger can lead us to modify what we do with it, with potentially unhealthy consequences, such as becoming unaware of anger, not expressing it effectively, or misdirecting it. Anger can also mask other feelings such as hurt, fear and shame. There is usually some hurt behind anger.

We considered that stammering evoked anger in two ways. First, what I see as the unhealthy turning inwards, the 'retroflection' of anger, such as through frustration at stammering or, worse, self-loathing for being someone who stammers. Underpinning this are the same unhelpful social beliefs that provoke shame, i.e. believing that stammering is wrong, that we are unacceptable. Second, what I see as a more healthy turning outwards of anger towards others, such as frustration felt towards people who patronise, judge, or ridicule. I believe this second way can help cope with fear and shame about stammering, by providing the energy to act and assert ourselves. Indeed, from a Gestalt perspective, 'aggression' is the essential energy for healthy living (Perls, Hefferline & Goodman, 1972, p.70). It is not seen as damaging or abusive, but instead as an assertive energy, or life force, to act to help ourselves.

I therefore wanted participants to know that anger is an acceptable, normal and potentially helpful emotion, and that it was empowering to be able to assertively direct their anger outwards in an effective and safe way. I demonstrated how to be assertively angry and how that was different from being aggressive or passive, including appropriate body language, and volume and tone of voice, as well as what to actually say. Key to this is saying how we feel and what we want in a firm, serious and self-respectful way, whilst also maintaining respect for the other person. Participants then had an opportunity to practise expressing their anger at others in the safety of the course. The idea of expressing anger assertively, rather than bottling it up inside, was exciting, a bit scary and new to most of the group.

Two other ideas that appealed to participants were: first, transforming anger's energy into something constructive, such as becoming active in the British Stammering Association; second, being curious rather than self-critical when frustrated with themselves for stammering, and then finding compassion, forgiveness and acceptance for how they were.

Sadness

Whilst we recognized at the outset that the course did not have time to cover sadness I still want to mention it here. Sadness is the emotion that follows losing, or anticipating losing something of value. For example, we feel sad when we lose someone or when things turn out worse than expected. Therefore, sadness tells us that we have lost something of value and can slow us down to be introspective and adjust to not having what we have lost. Sadness comes with particular facial expressions, body language, crying and sometimes deep distress. These reactions invite others to care for us at a time when we are vulnerable.

I consider that people who stammer have usually lost a lot. There is the obvious loss of fluency and the disappointment of stammering when not wanting to. I believe that there are often secondary losses that occur as a result of stammering, such as unfulfilled potential at work and difficulty in forming relationships.

Had there been another two sessions of the course then sadness could have been covered in much the same way as the other emotions, by teaching emotional literacy ideas about sadness; inviting participants to become more aware of their sadness associated with stammering; enabling them to make sense of that sadness; and allowing and acknowledging the grief for their losses. Lastly, time could have been given to seeing losses as unmet needs and considering how they might still be able to meet those needs.

Reflections from a student

The following is an account by Lisette Wesseling of her experience of the course and its impact on her life.

The Feelings and Stammering course really changed my perspective on stammering, and opened up a new world for me to explore. I have a lifetime of hiding my stammer, which meant that there were long periods of time in which I denied to myself and others that I stammered. This, plus my previous experience with stammering therapy, had led me to believe that feelings were my enemies and would stand in the way of progress. Fear, I thought, made me stammer more, and so I should ignore the fear and pretend it wasn't there, just like my stammer. If I didn't feel the feelings, I wouldn't stammer, and the fluency technique I had been previously taught would work. If I didn't admit to being afraid, sad or ashamed about my speech, I wouldn't be, and I could continue to pretend I did not really stammer at all. My speech was incredibly fast, and often I would half say something but never finish the idea for fear of exposing my stammer. If anybody tried to talk about my stammer, I would either deny it outright or go quiet and change the subject. It would leave me feeling upset and ashamed, with the idea that I should not show these feelings so as not to admit I had a problem.

Through other City Lit courses, I had begun learning that it was OK for me to stammer openly and stop pretending that this 'ugly thing' didn't exist. The Feelings and Stammering course taught me to embrace the feelings which went with that stammer. For the first time, I became aware of the multitude of negative thoughts which flitted across my mind before, during and after speaking situations. These thoughts might include: 'Why can't you ever talk properly? Nobody must hear you stammer. Stammering is ugly. Your speech is just no good. You'll never change.' I learned to bring some conscious awareness to them, which helped me begin to see where they might be coming from. I learned to challenge them, and realize they often came from my parents' beliefs which I had swallowed whole as a child.

Perhaps the most useful part of the course for me, though, was the section where we gave our feelings a voice and allowed them to 'speak' their thoughts. The idea that negative feelings might be allowed to say their piece was quite new to me. For example, I had always thought that my habitual hiding of my stammer was simply self-sabotage. I thought I was being a 'bad girl' who wouldn't do as she was told, when I couldn't disclose my stammer to strangers, as was suggested to us by a speech and language therapist in another course.

The Gestalt exercise Peter conducted with me made me explore what those hidden feelings wanted to make known. I realized they served a protective function against being further shamed and wounded. Rather than feeling like a naughty child for often continuing to hide my stammer in the world, I learned to honour that need to hide because my fears of being hurt again were very legitimate. They exposed a lifetime of experiences which I am working through in traditional psychotherapy.

The course also helped me identify why my earlier attempts at speech techniques often hadn't worked outside the clinic. The feelings were so powerful that they were blocking any attempts to work on the mechanics of speaking. Brushing them under the carpet did not make them go away, but just made them more potent.

Another thing I remember about the course was being told to really feel fear, and fully embrace it instead of ignoring it or denying it was there. Letting the fear be OK was something I had never done before. I remember several occasions becoming fearful of stammering when about to buy a train ticket at the station. I learned how to let myself feel the fear of stammering, before walking up to the counter. This gave me a strange sense of peace and calm which actually meant that, when I did stutter, all the sting was taken out of it.

The course gave me many new insights and experiences in a safe group environment. It was a springboard and an invitation for me to continue on my own journey of personal growth. I believe this is a course some may want to do more than once. The content is very rich and I certainly wasn't ready to take it all in at the start.

Evaluation of the course

All 10 participants completed the course, absences were few and they evaluated it highly. Key outcomes were:

- The course met a clear need to understand and cope better with emotions about stammering.
- People had not thought about their emotions before and tended to see them as an inconvenience, something to be mastered, or to be blotted out. So turning to face those emotions, explore and make sense of them, and experiment with new ways of coping, was new, helpful and enlightening.
- They learned a lot, so made changes intellectually. However, the process of these ideas filtering into them habitually living these ideas, and in their own way, was just begun. This was something they would need to continue without the support of the group.
- That Carolyn and I both stammered helped to create empathy, trust and safety.

There are, however, two main changes I would make. First, I would ensure that sadness was included, especially the grief felt for the loss of all those things which fluent speakers take for granted. Second, as so often happens with training and therapy, we did not follow up some months later to see whether people had maintained or, better still, developed the changes they made on the course.

What might a speech and language therapist integrate into their practice?

I want to end by offering speech and language therapists some suggestions that emerge from this chapter. I expect people who stammer might find this helpful too. My intention is to offer something that compliments and adds to what speech and language therapy can achieve.

Speech and language therapists who work with people who stammer will appreciate the importance of difficult and painful emotions in stammering: the impact they have on people's lives; how people fight their stammer for fear of experiencing those emotions; and how fear of feeling shame can prevent people from using speech and language therapy approaches, such as desensitization work.

I would therefore argue that emotional work, especially on fear, shame, anger and sadness, is essential to successful stammering therapy. I imagine it would be helpful to teach clients emotional literacy; for them to become more aware of their emotions and the possible effects they have on speech and language therapy and their wider lives; and to help them develop support systems and ways of coping.

I also want to draw attention to how much consideration Gestalt counselling has given to the process of creating lasting, meaningful change. I see this as particularly relevant to stammering therapy, as in my experience much stammering therapy tends to focus on *what* to do differently rather than *how* people change. I consider the concepts of awareness, experimentation, resolving internal conflicts, self-support and the paradoxical theory of change, were not just relevant to the course, but offer profound insight into stammering therapy more widely. I believe all of this work is easier when using basic counselling skills and having a counsellor's attitude of empathy, non-judgement and authenticity towards clients.

In particular, I suggest speech and language therapists might like to consider their clients' internal conflicts. It is important to recognize the risk of inadvertently joining forces with the client's 'top-dog' by giving them ideas they introject without consideration, or by getting them to try harder at things they do not want to do at the moment, such as voluntary stammering. To help with this I would suggest working in the following ways:

- What are a client's unchallenged beliefs around stammering that could become top-dogs? For example, 'I ought to be fluent' or 'I should use speech therapy techniques'.

- Does their top-dog punish them when its commands are not followed, leading to guilt, a sense of failure and despair?

- Allow their under-dog a voice and hear what it has to say. Normalize and honour the usefulness of this part, as well as commenting on any limitations, for example when someone has not yet developed enough inner support to risk voluntary stammering.

- With clients who seem stuck or unwilling to change, consider whether a referral to counselling might be necessary. As a counsellor, I would refer a client who stammered to speech and language therapy, if they had not already tried it.

If the therapist feels confident enough, it might help to explicitly offer clients an opportunity to explore the concept of internal conflicts.

Lastly, I imagine speech and language therapists share my experience of clients having high expectations that we can change them. These are expectations we can be seduced into wanting to meet, but that we cannot realistically deliver because only they can change. In my experience, people who stammer take many years to really let go of being fluent, if they ever really do. The temptation, I imagine, is to provide tools and techniques to promote fluency, especially in time-limited work (which I am sure can still be of much help). However, I want to encourage speech and language therapists to withstand their client's possible disappointment in them for not prioritizing fluency, and to hand the responsibility for change back to them, offering ongoing support in their struggle for self-acceptance and personal growth, and helping them to find their own way forward.

I know from my own struggle just how threatening and difficult fundamental change can be. I have had to lose cherished hopes and expectations for myself. It has taken much time, reflection, support and courage. As Fritz Perls, one of Gestalt's founders said (with uncharacteristic understatement for him):

"To die and be reborn is not easy."

(Perls in Oldham, Key & Starak, 1978, p.52)

References

Clarkson, P. (1989) *Gestalt Counselling in Action*. London: Sage.

Crocker, S. (1999) *A Well-lived Life – Essays in Gestalt Therapy*. Santa Cruz: Gestalt Press.

Goleman, D. (1996) *Emotional Intelligence – Why it can Matter more than IQ*. London: Bloomsbury.

Greenberger, D. & Padesky, C. (1995) *Mind Over Mood: A Cognitive Therapy Treatment Manual for Clients*. New York: Guilford Press.

Houston, G. (2003) *Brief Gestalt Therapy*. London: Sage.

Jeffers, S. (1989) *Feel the Fear and Do it Anyway*. London: Rider.

Joyce, P. & Sills, C. (2001) *Skills in Gestalt Counselling & Psychotherapy*. London: Sage.

Kuykendall, J. (2001) *Disorders of Fluency Special Interest Group Meeting*. London.

Korb, M., Gorrell, J., & Van De Riet, V. (1989) *Gestalt Therapy – Practice and Theory*, 2nd ed. Massachusetts: Allyn and Bacon.

MacKewn, J. (1997) *Developing Gestalt Counselling*. London: Sage.

Oldham, J., Key, T., & Starak, I. (1978) *Risking Being Alive*. Victoria: Pit Publishing.

Perls, F., Hefferline, R., & Goodman, P. (1972) *Gestalt Therapy – Excitement and Growth in the Human Personality*. London: Souvenir Press.

Williams, D. in H. Gregory (Ed.) (1979) *Controversies about Stuttering Therapy*. Baltimore: University Park Press.

12 Revealing resources

Using Neuro-Linguistic Programming with people who stammer

Debbie Mason

To begin, a story …

The Littlest God

It wasn't long after the Gods had created humankind that they began to realize their mistake. The creatures they had created were so adept, so skilful, so full of curiosity and the spirit of inquiry that it was only a matter of time before they would start to challenge the Gods themselves for supremacy.

To ensure their pre-eminence the Gods held a large conference to discuss the issue. All the Gods were very clear about one thing. The difference between them and mortals was the difference between the quality of the resources they had. While humans had their egos and were concerned with the external, material aspects of the world, the Gods had spirit, soul, and an understanding of the workings of the inner self.

The danger was that sooner or later the humans would want some of that too.

The Gods decided to hide their precious resources. The question was where?

Some suggested hiding these resources at the top of the highest mountain. But it was realized that, sooner or later, the humans would scale such a mountain.

> And the deepest crater in the deepest ocean would be discovered.
>
> And the most impenetrable jungles would give up their secrets.
>
> And the moon and planets would become tourist destinations.
>
> And even the wisest and most creative of the Gods fell silent as if every avenue had been explored and found wanting.
>
> Until the Littlest God, who had been silent until now, spoke up.
>
> "Why don't we hide these resources inside each human? They'll never think to look for them there."
>
> (Abridged from Peter McNab in Owen, 2001, p.80)

Overview

The setting of clear outcomes is central to the practice of Neuro-Linguistic Programming (NLP) so a chapter about NLP has to start with a clear statement of outcome. In the course of this chapter, I aim to answer the following questions:

- What is NLP?

- How is it useful for people who stammer (PWS)?

- What are some of the ways I have used NLP with PWS and what have their experiences been?

The chapter will initially focus on three core elements of NLP:

- **Outcome thinking**: A well-formed outcome clarifies what a client is trying to achieve.

- **Modelling**: Allows client and therapist to 'build a model' of a client's subjective experience, and thereby understand that experience. Modelling a 'problem' highlights why the client is not getting the results he wants. Modelling a 'solution' highlights what he needs to change and what resources will help him reach his desired outcome.

- **Uncovering resources**: NLP has numerous 'change patterns' and techniques to help clients access their resources.

I have then chosen five client stories which illustrate how NLP addresses the issues faced by PWS and some of the different ways it can assist them to uncover their inner resources. Two involve the use of trance to access unconscious resources, and one client describes his experience of this.

Every client story is unique and fascinating. The aim for the therapist is to respect and honour this story whilst simultaneously maintaining a focus on understanding the 'structure' of the client's experience. The 'structure' is the process beneath the level of the story; the thoughts, feelings, behaviours and internal thinking strategies that serve to 'programme' the client and create his experience. The therapist and client who understand the structures that underpin a 'problem' and 'solution' will be clear about the resources the client needs to move forward.

The reader will see that, while some elements of NLP are particular to this approach, NLP has, in fact, much in common with many of the other approaches described in this book.

What is NLP?

NLP started in the 1970s at the University of California when John Grinder, Assistant Professor of Linguistics and his student, Richard Bandler, observed the work of three renowned therapists: family therapist, Virginia Satir; founder of Gestalt therapy, Fritz Perls; and psychiatrist and hypnotherapist, Milton Erickson. All three therapists had a reputation for achieving outstanding results with their clients.

Bandler and Grinder set out to distil exactly what Satir, Perls and Erickson were doing that made them so effective and to make this information explicit. They found that all three therapists, despite superficially different approaches and personal styles, shared attitudes and common patterns in their use of language and behaviour to facilitate change.

By 'modelling' these three therapists, Bandler and Grinder created a model of successful therapy (they discovered what Satir, Perls and Erickson were doing to achieve such good results) and their exploration created a framework for understanding **how** people do what they do. This notion of modelling lies at the heart of NLP and will be explored in detail later. As NLP grew, 'change patterns' such as anchoring evolved to show people **how** to access the resources they needed to solve a problem or reach their outcome. If a client identifies that remaining calm is a desirable skill, anchoring shows him how to enter a calm state at will. The experiential nature of these patterns is a real strength of NLP.

Bandler has described NLP as an attitude (of curiosity) and a methodology (of modelling), which leave behind a trail of techniques (in Feltham and Horton, 2006, p.330). NLP is, therefore, rooted in observation rather than theory.

Bandler and Grinder (1979, p.7) state:

> "We call ourselves *modelers* ... we are not psychologists, and we're also not theologians or theoreticians. We have *no* idea about the 'real' nature of things, and we're not particularly interested in what's 'true'. The function of modelling is to arrive at descriptions which are *useful*."

Their aim was not to attribute causes to problems or develop theories, but to explore how a problem is maintained in the structure of the client's subjective experience so the client would be able to restructure this experience. Like many professionals, I have shared hypotheses about a client with a colleague – maybe speculating on what has triggered a relapse or why progress is slow. While this can be illuminating at times, it will only ever be a hypothesis. The NLP therapist trusts that the answers to such questions lie in the structure of the client's experience.

NLP is, therefore, a framework that allows you to explore your subjective experience rather than a philosophy. It can be seen as a map. A map, unlike a guide book, has no opinion and makes no judgements. It simply gives you a way of negotiating the territory (in this case subjective experience) to increase your understanding and choices.

This very practical emphasis on understanding **how** we do what we do and **how** we can change it, may be one of the reasons that NLP has been of interest to many PWS. In the stammering community, interest in NLP has been led primarily by clients rather than by research. High-profile 'success stories' such as Linda Rounds' account of her work with Bob Bodenhamer (Bodenhamer, 2004, p.165) has made NLP more accessible to PWS and led them to be curious about their potential to understand and change their own model of the world.

In the therapy world, NLP is usually described as a 'cognitive' therapy. Feltham and Horton in *The SAGE Handbook of Counselling and Psychotherapy* (2006) list it as an 'eclectic-integrative' therapy, perhaps reflecting a model that integrates many different principles and ideas.

My interest in NLP

My own interest in NLP began in 2001 when I attended a study day for speech and language therapists. The speaker, Mike Jones, had trained in NLP and used it to address his own stammering and was now able to speak fluently. I found the day interesting on many levels, not least because Mike's fluency contradicted the oft-received wisdom that adults who stammer will always stammer. At that stage of my career, I was searching for the skills that would allow me to understand and enter a client's model of the world to facilitate change. I was excited by the potential that NLP offered and could see that it would be a very useful tool in my work with PWS.

Since then NLP has taken me on a journey that has enriched my life and my work beyond anything I could have imagined. It has provided a framework for me to structure and make sense of the information a client is giving me. It has given me the skills to navigate the unique world of my client so that we both understand what is meaningful and important and can identify which interventions are likely to be most helpful. As Sheehan noted: 'Unless we understand the person, we will not understand the problem…' (1983, p.9).

Furthermore, NLP has taught me that we all possess an amazing array of resources that are frequently untapped. The use of trance in particular has revealed a powerful way of exploring and tapping into these. For me, helping a client to discover these resources is endlessly fascinating and exciting.

Outcome thinking

Outcome thinking is central to the practice of NLP. Establishing clarity about what you are aiming to achieve before acting means that your actions are likely

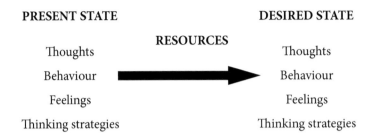

Figure 12.1 NLP as a change framework.

to be purposeful and efficient in terms of your outcome. NLP as a change framework can be summarized in Figure 12.1.

So NLP has a solution focus. Therapy is directed towards an outcome. The focus is on deciding where you want to be (desired state), noting where you are now (present state) and identifying the resources you need to reach your desired state. For a PWS, the present state may be that he blocks severely in meetings at work. The desired state may be to talk more easily in such meetings. The resources will help him reach the desired state (e.g. Does he need a new helpful belief about his ability to do this? Does he need to be able to remain calm? Does he need to use a fluency technique? Does he need to picture himself talking easily rather than picturing himself stammering?).

Maintaining a focus on the outcome does not mean there is no focus on 'the problem'. It means that when a problem is explored, it is not for its own sake but because it contains information that is pertinent to the solution. McDermott and Jago point out: 'the problem behaviour encodes a solution quite precisely' (2001, p.55). This is illustrated by Tom's story in the section on 'Modelling' below, in which an exploration of the 'problem' leads directly to the solution and the resources Tom needs.

The importance of being clear about your outcome is often illustrated by the example of buying a ticket at a train station. You have to know where you want to go. 'I don't want to be here any more, I want to be somewhere else' carries no guarantee that your destination will be desirable or preferable to your current location. 'I want to go to Edinburgh' is more helpful than 'I don't want to be in Bristol any more'.

Once you have clarity about your outcome, you will immediately begin to focus attention and energy in that direction, which is why both NLP and

Solution Focussed Brief Therapy (De Shazer, 1988) spend time helping clients to elaborate their outcome in detail and in sensory-specific terms – that is, in terms of what they are seeing, hearing, feeling etc. Wake explains this in neuroscientific terms (2008, p.143):

> "By focussing on the client's goal rather than their problem, an immediate shift in the neurology occurs such that the neuronal circuitry attached to the achievement of the goal is activated. This neuronal circuit is then flooded with neuropeptides which results in physiological changes in the mind-body system that would be necessary to achieve the goal."

An outcome can perhaps best be thought of as an intention or reason for doing something. Everything we do has an outcome, even though we do not often consciously think about it. Even when I take a shower, there is an outcome – to feel clean. For PWS, this shift in focus to considering their preferred outcome in a situation can be significant. Many have spent much time focusing on their stammering – 'the problem' – and have therefore been inadvertently giving it energy and reinforcing that neuronal circuitry. Few have explored in detail what contributes to their fluency.

Outcomes are important at every level of stammering therapy. They serve to direct attention and clients need to understand their impact. One client described how he approached meetings thinking, 'I hope I don't stammer'. This is a negative outcome – it focuses his mind on the very thing he wishes to avoid. Crucially, an outcome to be fluent can also be unhelpful, especially for clients with a covert stammer. There is little difference between saying 'I hope I don't stammer' and 'I want to be fluent' as both focus the mind on fluency. For many clients, this specific focus on fluency increases anxiety and leads to increased dysfluency.

A key part of the NLP therapist's role is to spot when a client has unhelpful outcomes and help him generate more useful ones. The following strategies illustrate just two of the ways that a therapist can help her client identify helpful outcomes:

- **Consider what promotes fluency**: For many clients, fluency is linked to certain states, e.g. 'It's easier to speak if I feel calm and relaxed'. Having an outcome that involves accessing a state such as calm can help to re-focus a client.

- **Identify a 'higher' outcome**: If a client says he wants to be fluent, asking him 'What does fluency achieve for you?' helps to put him in touch with a higher outcome, such as maintaining rapport with the listener – which can be achieved with or without fluency. This is known as 'chunking up' in NLP.

Sarah's experience is a good illustration of the importance of a helpful outcome. Following a course of therapy, Sarah was able to speak fluently in most day-to-day situations, but she still stammered in two particular situations. The first involved talking on the intercom when picking her son up from nursery and the second was having to say her name on the phone at work. When we explored these situations, it transpired that Sarah had an outcome to be fluent. She viewed both situations as a 'test'. If she were able to speak fluently it would 'prove' that she really was getting to grips with her stammer. When she set an outcome to approach the situations in a calm manner and be non-judgemental about her fluency, speaking became much easier.

Modelling

> "We need therapists who know why they were able to effect a change in a structure or who can explain why they failed."
>
> Wilhelm Reich, *Character Analysis*, 1972 (in McDermott & Jago, 2001, p.48).

Modelling has been at the heart of NLP from the beginning. The early NLP principles and techniques grew out of Bandler and Grinder's modelling of Satir, Perls and Erickson. Modelling answers the question '**how do you do that?**' (if you model someone else) or '**how do I do that?**' (if you model yourself). It allows you to understand the structure of your experience. Modelling a 'problem' or 'solution' highlights what you need to do to reach your desired state or outcome and helps you identify the resources you require.

In NLP, modelling typically involves both the observation of external behaviours and the understanding of internal thinking processes – allowing you to literally 'build a model' of how somebody does something. If you can start to understand the beliefs, feelings and behaviours of an 'expert' while s/he is performing a task, it becomes possible to experiment with those beliefs and behaviours to enhance one's own performance.

For example, when I first started studying NLP, I decided to model a friend who is a very good cook. Being a very average cook, I was keen to see what I could learn from him. I began by simply observing his external behaviours (which is what children do when they imitate adults). I noticed, for example, that he weighed and prepared each ingredient before beginning to cook (e.g. if the carrots needed grating, he did this and put them in their own bowl). He seemed very calm as he cooked – music on in the background, glass of wine at hand. I could already see differences between his behaviour and my own.

In order to build a more complete model, I decided to ask about his internal thinking processes. What did he think and feel about cooking? It transpired that cooking for him was a way to relax and he believed it gave him the opportunity to nurture himself and others. He was excited by the idea of combining ingredients in new and creative ways. This was very different from the vague sense of dread I experienced in the kitchen.

Having built my model, I now have a choice – continue to cook as I have always cooked or adopt some of the new behaviours and beliefs and see what difference they make. I will probably find a key belief or behaviour that makes a big difference (in this case, I went from seeing cooking as a chore to seeing it as an opportunity to nurture).

As well as modelling others, one can self-model, noting the differences between the occasions when one is able to be resourceful and those when one is not (e.g. the times when one remains calm versus the times when one becomes stressed).

In the case of the PWS, modelling what happens when he talks fluently highlights the salient features of fluency – the thoughts, beliefs, feelings, behaviours and thinking strategies that need to be cultivated in order to nurture fluency. Modelling what happens when he stammers highlights the thoughts, beliefs, feelings, behaviour and thinking strategies that are maintaining stammering.

The key principle behind modelling is that experience has a structure. Put simply, we take in information through our senses – Visual, Auditory, Kinaesthetic, Olfactory and Gustatory. This forms the '**Neuro**' component of NLP. Most of us have a preferred 'representational system' – some people tend to process information in a visual way, others pay attention to auditory information and some are kinaesthetic, that is, they notice how things feel. When I bought my house, it needed a lot of work. Visually it was a mess, but I liked how it felt. As someone who tends to favour the kinaesthetic representational system, this was important. If I had paid more attention to my visual impression, I probably would not have bought the house.

We then use language to interpret and define this experience, thereby giving it meaning – the '**Linguistic**' component of NLP. The study of linguistic patterns is a key component of NLP as language inevitably transforms our experience, i.e. information is deleted, generalized or distorted. The same behaviour (e.g. someone looking away while you are talking to them) can be interpreted in different ways: 'He's distracted' is a more useful interpretation than 'I'm boring him'. The ability to detect how a client's linguistic patterns may be limiting him is central to the practice of the NLP therapist, as is the ability to use language in specific and precise ways. For example, a client who says 'I stammer. I'm a bad communicator' is making two separate statements mean the same thing and this clearly needs to be challenged. These two components, the **neuro** and the **linguistic**, serve to programme us.

Modelling the structure of an experience helps us replicate it or teach it to others if it is useful (Bandler and Grinder did this with Satir, Perls and Erickson) or, if it is not useful (as is the case with stammering), destabilize and rebuild it. Like all experiences, fluency and stammering have structures that can be modelled. A process known as 'contrastive analysis' can be used to uncover the key differences. This increases understanding of the client's model of the world for both the client and the therapist. As well as understanding what is maintaining stammering, modelling allows the client to see that fluency has a structure and discover he already has a 'blueprint' for fluency.

The structure of an experience can be modelled at different levels. The following basic model uncovers:

- Thoughts (often including beliefs and meanings)

- Feelings

- Physiology

- Behaviour.

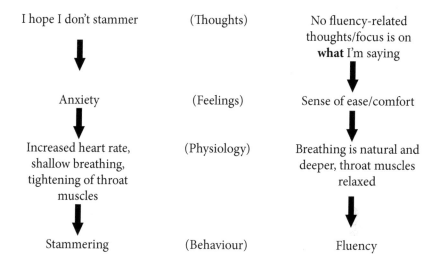

I model in this way with many clients at what Van Riper called the 'identification' stage of therapy (Van Riper, 1973). There are clear parallels with the framework used in Cognitive Behavioural Therapy (Beck, 1976).

Modelling internal thinking strategies provides more detail. This involves modelling at the level of the representational system. For example, if a client says 'I know I'm going to stammer', how does he know? Is he picturing himself stammering (Visual), is he telling himself he is going to stammer (Auditory) or does he feel he is going to stammer (Kinaesthetic)? Each representational system has sub-modalities – the smallest building blocks of our thoughts. These express subtler qualities – if you hear a negative voice in your head, what tone does it have? How loud is it? One client (described later) found reducing the volume of her negative internal dialogue dramatically changed its impact. Modelling at the level of representational systems can highlight discrepancies. One client approached speaking situations telling herself 'I can do it' whilst picturing herself stammering.

The significance of understanding internal thinking strategies can be seen in the field of education. Many teachers today are aware of children's strategies for learning and talk of 'visual learners' or 'kinaesthetic learners'. Although we use all of our senses, information is more meaningful when presented to us in a way that matches our preference. Effective teachers are those who, consciously or unconsciously, involve several representational systems in their teaching.

The importance of modelling beliefs

The meaning we take from our experiences is expressed in our beliefs. Bodenhamer describes beliefs as 'thoughts we have said yes to' (2004, p.145) A fundamental premise of all cognitive therapies is that the meaning of an experience – how it has been interpreted – is what matters. This is neatly expressed by Aldous Huxley: 'Experience is not what happens to a man; it is what a man does with what happens to him' (in Robbins, 2001, p.172).

Beliefs will support a particular behaviour or inhibit it, so modelling beliefs is vital. Exploring how a client perceives a situation will reveal beliefs; for example, asking 'Why is it hard to speak to your boss?' might reveal the belief 'I can't talk to people in authority'. Changing beliefs changes meaning and, therefore, reality.

Advantages of modelling

McDermott and Jago articulate the benefits of modelling (2001, p.56):

> "When the client begins … to unpack the structure of an unwelcome experience, they necessarily change their relationship with that experience. It is likely that in the past they have been trying to avoid, suppress or reason it away, that they may have been condemning it or themselves for experiencing it. Asked now to pay even more attention to it, but with an enquiring, scientific approach, they will automatically change their vantage point in relation to it. This is a significant intervention in itself."

Furthermore, modelling is a non-judgemental, curious and respectful process that enables the therapist to model understanding and acceptance of the client's current reality.

In the words of one client, Jack (his story follows in detail in the section on the unconscious mind and role of trance):

> "Debbie and I talked about the connectedness between emotions, thoughts and physical reactions. I was able to see the connections between a reaction, thought, behaviour

and how it manifested itself as a stammer. I worked hard on being aware of a particular stage and not fighting it or trying to change it, just being aware that it is connected and therefore if I want to stammer less I need to understand the previous stage. This helped a lot and began me on the journey to understanding my stammer – a crucial part in NLP therapy …"

As well as exploring a client's map of the world, it is important for a therapist to reflect on her *own* map of the world, especially with regard to her beliefs. A therapist who sees stammering as inevitable or permanent will work in a certain way and convey a very different message to one who believes a client has the resources they need and may be another Mike Jones (mentioned earlier, who introduced me to NLP) or John Harrison (2010) who has written about how he overcame his own stammering and authored several books designed to help others do the same. As Wake says, 'the internal world of the therapist can add or take away from the therapy relationship' (2008, p.13).

Tom's story: Highlighting the value of modelling

The following description of my first two sessions with Tom shows how modelling the structure of a problem can lead directly to identifying and accessing the resources needed to change it.

With Tom, we modelled while he was in a trance and explored an event that had been problematic. (The use of trance will be discussed in detail later.) Trance can be simply defined as a relaxed state in which the client's attention is focused on his internal experience. The steps are described in deliberate detail to show how the process unfolded within the client, with the therapist acting as facilitator. When I drew Tom's attention to the patterns at work (the structure) and highlighted his resources, he naturally accessed those resources.

Tom holds a senior corporate role that involves giving formal presentations. He described himself as a generally confident person with specific anxiety around speaking. He reported experiencing 'out of the blue blocks', especially in formal situations. He viewed his problem primarily as one of anxiety and felt the anxiety manifested itself through his speaking. His outcome was to feel comfortable in formal situations.

Session 1

We started by modelling the problem. Tom mentally walked through a recent experience of blocking in a formal presentation. He was associated into the experience – re-experiencing it as if he was there (as opposed to recalling it or watching himself). Being associated into an experience in this way helps a client to access detailed sensory information but, for obvious reasons, is only advisable for experiences that are not too traumatic.

As he re-experienced the presentation, Tom was immediately aware of his internal dialogue. He was telling himself, 'It's down to me', asking 'How will I perform?' and assuming 'They'll judge me' (threatening because a negative judgement would mean 'I'm failing'). This naturally created anxiety. Tom noticed that the anxiety made him feel 'guarded' which led to a tightness, first in his chest and then in his throat. As soon as he sensed the tightness (became aware of the kinaesthetics), his internal dialogue kicked in and he told himself 'I'm going to block'. At this point, his entire focus of attention was on speaking (very unhelpful from an outcome point of view). He blocked and then told himself 'I've let myself down', which naturally created a sense of disappointment. As he finished describing the process, Tom said two things that were loaded with emphasis:

"I **am** how I speak."

"How I speak **defines** me."

These beliefs are worth discussing because they are typical of the beliefs held by many PWS. Tom has failed to see speaking as a behaviour, something he **does** – sometimes fluently and sometimes not so fluently – and has linked it to his identity, something he **is**. As soon as we associate something with our identity, it assumes the power to say something about us as a person – to make us good/bad, a success/failure, etc.

Parents are counselled to tell children, 'That's a naughty thing you did' rather than 'You're a naughty boy'. The first statement distinguishes the person from the behaviour and carries the implication that some **things** are naughty (and some **things** are helpful). The second statement implies that the child as a person is in some way 'naughty' – a crucial distinction as it is much easier to change the things we **do** (our behaviour) and much harder to change who we think we **are** (our identity). It is very common for PWS to turn stammering into an identity issue in this way and I consider it to be one of the major goals of therapy to break this link. Removing the power of stammering to define who you are as a person is a major step.

Tom was also aware of a voice 'in the core of my head' telling him that he could not 'escape'. This voice was saying, 'Don't get above yourself' and 'I'll get you sooner or later'.

So we now have a model of the problem. We could summarize the structure of the problem as:

'I am how I speak'
(Unhelpful belief)

'It's important for me to speak well here'
(Thought)

Anxiety/guardedness ('Will I succeed or fail?')
(Feeling)   (Thought)

Tightening of chest/throat ('I'm going to block')
(Physiology)   (Thought)

Block
(Behaviour)

'I've failed'
(Thought/belief)

Session 2

In the second session, we discussed Tom's internal voice further. Tom had become aware of other things the voice was saying:

> "You're not allowed to say that word, you're not bright enough."

> "You don't have a **right** [word stressed by client] to express yourself freely ... you're not that person."

When I asked if Tom knew when these beliefs started, he began to talk about his older brother, Justin. He had always felt inferior to Justin who was a very articulate, but combative communicator. He said he sometimes wondered whether the anxiety he felt in formal meetings replicated the anxiety he had felt at home at the dinner table. It is not necessary for a client to be able to identify when a belief started but, in my experience, it can be easier for a client to change a belief if he understands it resulted from the meaning he gave to a situation and that there are other possible meanings.

To uncover what Tom had 'learned' about speaking at home, we revisited these early experiences – again in trance. Tom noticed that already at the age of five, he had looked at his older brother and decided, 'I have to be like him', but also 'I'm not as good as him, I can't do it', 'I'll never measure up'. He described the dinner table in vivid terms – as 'dangerous' and a 'lion's den'. However, Tom also had a sense that 'it shouldn't be like this'. Even at that young age, he viewed the communicative style of his brother as 'not right' and felt that communication between his family should be loving and supportive, not confrontational. This caused considerable confusion because his brother was a 'role model' within the family. Tom recalled thinking, 'I have to be that way but I can't or do I even want to?' – a 'damned if I do, damned if I don't' scenario (or 'double bind' in NLP speak).

I highlighted this confusion and pointed out that Tom's internal sense of 'This isn't right' was at odds with the external message he was receiving from his family. Naturally, Tom did what most children do; he assumed his parents and brother were 'right' and, in the process, stopped trusting himself.

Tom had been unable to develop his own style of communicating as none of his family had validated this. He had overridden his innate instincts in an attempt to be like his brother. By highlighting this, I was able to validate Tom's experience and map of the world – something that did not happen with respect to communication when he was young. The consequence for Tom of overriding his own instinct was that 'it felt false' and he was constantly worried he would 'be found out'. This naturally created anxiety about speaking. As he contemplated this, Tom said 'Justin's always been the rod – the right way to be' ... and then he paused and said, 'Maybe there is no rod'.

So I asked, 'What happens if there is no rod?'

(NB: I do not have to understand what Tom means by 'rod'. I can trust that it is meaningful for him – to explore the rod would be to go into content and I am wanting to follow the structure of the process.)

Tom's non-verbal behaviour immediately changed. His facial muscles visibly relaxed and a hint of a smile appeared. 'The pressure to conform goes with it. It's OK to be me.'

'It's OK to be me' is a hugely empowering belief, especially for someone who has spent his life believing he has to be like someone else.

We spent time allowing Tom to fully experience this new belief at a sensory level, so that it would land in his mind-body system at a somatic as well as a cognitive level. It felt 'natural', 'right', 'calm' and carried with it a sense of 'freedom' and 'release'.

Recognizing that Tom had accessed a very powerful core state, I asked:

"What happens to the negative voice in this place of calm?"

"*There is no voice.*"

"What happens to the anxiety about speaking in this place?"

"*There's no anxiety at all ... No doubt, no concern ... It feels naturally right.*"

Not only does Tom now **know** that 'it's OK to be me', he has **felt** it in his body and so experienced it at a somatic level. We have uncovered two important resources for Tom – a belief/realization that 'it's OK to be me' and a core state of deep calm which is so powerful there is no room for anxiety or negative internal dialogue.

Bodenhamer (2004) explains that negative emotions about speaking out become embodied and lead to blocking, and Tom provides a clear example of this. Updating his childhood mental map will enable him to feel that he has the 'right' to speak out. Tom described the process of modelling his experience as 'powerful' and remarked on the fact that our early childhood experiences affect us so deeply.

Tom and I met a further four times to consolidate the gains made in these initial sessions. Tom describes his experience of therapy as follows.

Firstly, I no longer regard the 'act of speaking' with as much importance as I initially did. When I started with Debbie, I genuinely felt that speaking was the most important thing I did and that it largely defined who I was. In other words, I am how I speak! I no longer place anything like this level of importance on speaking and now regard it largely as just something I do.

Second, I have a much better understanding of how I came to put so much emphasis on speech in the first place ... I've been able to better appreciate a number of family issues that caused anxiety then and which have repeatedly caused anxiety when speaking throughout my life. This understanding in itself has helped alleviate a number of the issues I've faced for a long time. As a result, I now feel I have more control over my anxiety and emotions as I tend to know what drives these emotions. This in turn has enabled me to relax more in hitherto anxious situations.

All in all, I'm no longer as bothered about how I speak and how I come across to others speech-wise, as I was before. Whilst I still block on occasions, it's really less of an issue for me and I feel it's not therefore happening as regularly.

I feel that, for Tom, being associated into the experience (that is, re-living being at the dinner table at home) contributed to the relative ease with which he accessed these resources. He had a 'felt sense' of the problem which led naturally to the solution. For me, a real strength of NLP is that it allows the client to experience such a 'felt sense'. This allows the client to access information that might not be available at the cognitive level. Gilligan (1997, p.4) explains the value of experiencing a 'felt sense':

> "The term 'felt sense' was introduced by Gendlin (1978). In his psychotherapy research at the University of Chicago, Gendlin found that the best predictor of a therapy's session success, regardless of the therapy orientation, was whether the client experienced a 'felt sense' in her body of the problem. This non-intellectual experience is not so much an emotional content as a body-mind feeling."

Wake supports this idea: 'Neurologically it is essential that a client's affective state is accessed as part of the therapeutic process, while a future-oriented state is facilitated at the same time. To provide each in isolation is unlikely to facilitate lasting change for the client' (2008, p.123).

Uncovering resources

In order for clients to reach their outcomes, they often need to uncover resources. Achieving clarity about an outcome often serves to highlight the resources that will be needed. As we have seen, modelling also highlights the resources that are required and can lead directly to the accessing of those resources, as was the case with Tom.

Bodenhamer defines a resource as 'anything that puts you in a good state, something you *apply* to a limiting situation in order to improve it. For example ... a resource could be your ability to step back or disconnect from a debilitating mass of negative beliefs' (2004, p.27).

All NLP 'change patterns' are designed to enable clients to access their resources. They allow clients to experience and learn 'from the inside out'. Sometimes a client needs help to uncover a resource he may or may not be aware of. Sometimes a client and therapist have to work out what is stopping a client using his resources. All change patterns help the client to perceive his reality in a different way and develop behavioural flexibility. Successful people are usually those who have flexibility and choice about how to reach their outcome.

There are numerous 'change patterns' and patterns can be blended to suit the needs of a client. 'In practice, effective therapists work their own variations upon the procedures they have learnt, much as great cooks have their own versions of the major recipes; but the underlying principle guides the work and leads to its successful conclusion' (McDermott & Jago, 2001, p.124).

The patterns I discuss here are those I feel to be most pertinent to work with stammering. My choices will inevitably be influenced by my clinical experience and my own belief system. The work of Bob Bodenhamer has also been hugely influential in my practice. I believe Bodenhamer's book *Mastering Blocking and Stuttering* (2004) is essential reading for anyone interested in learning more about NLP and neuro-semantics and their application to stammering. Neuro-semantics is a branch of NLP that focuses on 'higher level meanings' in the structure of subjectivity. It involves our thoughts and feelings about our thoughts and feelings, e.g. feeling anxious about being anxious or fearing the fear of stammering.

As NLP change patterns are experiential, they engage the whole mind-body system, allowing the client to access both cognitive and somatic information. Pert (1997) talks about the importance of approaches that impact the mind-body level: 'We often hear our patients say "I know I shouldn't feel this way but I *do!*". Knowing something doesn't always impact how we feel, and we may have to get past purely verbal communication to access our emotions. Some of the approaches I have found effective at getting to deeper, more fundamental levels are storytelling, hypnotherapy, neuro-linguistic programming and any of the expressive therapies that employ visualisation, music and art' (in Wake, 2008, p.8).

There are three patterns that I use with most clients: Anchoring, Mental rehearsal and Meta-stating.

Anchoring

Anchoring is a key NLP pattern that involves the client being able to access a resourceful state at will. A state can be defined as an individual's entire way of being at any given moment. This includes neurological activity, physical energy, emotions and mental activity.

Most clients initially find it easier to access a state of anxiety, for example, than a state of calm. When asked about when they last felt calm many clients will pause, think and then start talking about their last holiday. When asked about the last time they felt anxious, they will often reply 'yesterday' or 'earlier today'. Bodenhamer asserts: 'One of the key factors in learning how to run your own mind is in managing your own states. You are teaching your body to activate life enhancing states more often so that your response to any internal or external trigger will be desirable' (2004, p.12).

Mental rehearsal

Mental rehearsal involves rehearsing what a new behaviour will look and feel like. The client visualizes himself doing a desired behaviour (a dissociated position in NLP terms) and then steps into his body to experience what this feels like (associated position). I invariably use this pattern when helping a client prepare for a job interview or important presentation. It allows him to experience exactly how he would like to be.

Visualization activates the right hemisphere of the brain. Hamilton (2008, p.46) explains:

> "Visualization is not just a subjective thing, an inert
> mish-mash of mental pictures that are just there to make

you feel good, but a process that causes real chemical and structural changes in the brain. With visualization, almost immediately, mind changes matter."

Hamilton also coins the term 'feelingization' to stress the importance of feeling as well as visualizing 'strong feelings accompanying an experience will ensure that it is encoded strongly as brain cells' (2005, p.120). Research has demonstrated the effectiveness of mental rehearsal, particularly with regard to the acquisition of motor skills. Sanders et al. (2008) discuss its use in the training of surgeons.

Meta-stating

Meta-stating is a neuro-semantic pattern, which involves the application of a resource state to a problem state. In the client story above, when Tom accessed a calm state, he was no longer able to access anxiety. A powerful resource state enfeebles a problem state.

> "… every time you sift positive feelings and views into painful, limiting states of mind – you build a little bit of neural structure. Over time, the accumulating impact of this positive material will literally, synapse by synapse, change your brain."
>
> (Hanson & Mendius, 2009, p.71)

An integral part of effective therapy involves encouraging clients to be aware of the states they habitually bring to their stammering. A client who brings a state of curiosity or acceptance to stammering is ideally placed to be able to experiment and make changes.

Client stories

The following client stories show various ways I have used NLP with PWS. The first two demonstrate that change can be relatively simple and rapid. I then discuss the unconscious mind and the role of trance with two client stories illustrating why it can be helpful and sometimes necessary to work at this level. One client, Jack, provides a vivid description of his experience of this and the significant impact it has had on his fluency levels.

Stefan's story: A conversational reframe

Reframing happens instantly when you see something in a new light. Many jokes work this way. Reframing changes meaning and, as discussed earlier, when meaning changes, behavioural change tends to follow.

Stefan had attended a workshop run by Bob Bodenhamer. He learned to anchor a 'powerful' state, which he used in meetings at work. This anchor enabled him to talk fluently – something he was naturally very pleased about. When we spoke on the phone a few weeks after the workshop, Stefan reported he had not been able to use the anchor in social situations, as he did not feel congruent using 'power' in these situations. It was hard for him to identify an appropriate state to anchor for social situations. Eventually he said, 'Trouble is, I'm different.' Stefan is German and works in the UK. 'Different' was clearly seen as a problem.

When I asked, '**How** is being different a problem?', Stefan was not sure but talked about having a different outlook and sense of humour. In a slightly tongue-in-cheek fashion, I said, 'Maybe being different is a good thing' and we lightheartedly discussed what a world full of English people would look like and how boring it would be if we were all the same.

The following week Stefan reported that he had been out socially with his colleagues and allowed himself to be 'different'. This involved unleashing his sense of humour and he said he had had the most fun and fluent evening he had ever had with them. Stefan had reframed the meaning of being different; it had gone from something he saw as a problem to something that was okay, even advantageous.

> "…even a conversational reframe can have profound effects on the way a client structures a problem or difficulty, a limiting belief or past learning."

(McDermott & Jago, 2001, p.133)

Khalid's story: NLP change patterns in action

Khalid was 22 when he was referred to speech and language therapy. He had stammered since childhood, but felt his stammering was getting worse because of the pressures he was facing at university. He described his fluency as 'going to the extreme' – he would either speak fluently or stammer severely. He felt that his stammering was very affected by stress. He often avoided talking, spent a lot of time at home on his own and abandoned a presentation at university because of his lack of fluency. Sometimes he would face a long walk home from university alone rather than take the bus with friends because he was too afraid to ask for a ticket.

It was clear that there was a large cognitive component to Khalid's difficulties. His descriptions of situations in which he had stammered were littered with unhelpful thoughts and times when he had told himself he would not be able to speak. Throughout the case history, I was listening for the beliefs, feelings and behaviours that were maintaining the problem and those that highlighted resources that could be useful in therapy – in other words, I was beginning to build a model of both the 'problem' and the 'solution'.

Two pieces of information seemed particularly significant: Khalid was constantly telling himself 'you can't speak' (problem). He told me that he never stammered when he prayed (resource). As a Muslim, Khalid prays five times a day and talked about how easy it was to talk to God. Spiritual belief can be an extremely powerful resource. It took three sessions to kick-start a change.

Session 1

Our first session focused on modelling the structures of fluency and stammering to ascertain the key differences. Acceptance and judgement emerged as key themes. Like many PWS, Khalid stammered when he feared being judged and was fluent when he felt accepted. It was clear that stammering was very much part of Khalid's identity to the extent that he asked, 'How will I have a relationship and get married?' We began to discuss his negative beliefs and challenge them by contrasting them with some of the more positive ones – for example, 'I can speak fluently five times a day when praying'.

Session 2

Khalid came to the next session saying his fluency had been good in the days following the therapy session, but had then deteriorated. He identified that he felt less fearful after the session. This led to a discussion about the role of fear in driving his stammering.

We used the 'Visual Swish' – a core NLP pattern – to shift Khalid's focus away from fear and towards belief in himself. We elicited an image of his fearful self (present state) and an image of him praying with complete confidence and belief in himself (desired state). The swish involves 'swishing' from the unwanted image to the desired image so the resourceful image becomes more prominent. Bodenhamer describes it as 'rewiring the old stimulus-response linkage. The unwanted image is sent into the background and replaced with a more useful, desirable one' (2004, p.140). The swish helped Khalid to literally see 'there's a whole other side of me that I haven't paid much attention to but which could be really helpful for me ... I'd only been thinking about the fearful side of me, not the confident, positive side'.

Session 3

Khalid reported that his fluency had been 'good'. He said he was now viewing stammering as 'something that can be overcome', saying, 'It happens because I tell myself I can't do it'. Understanding this made a big difference. The swish had made him realize he wanted to cultivate 'the positive side of me'. This initiated a conversation about well-formed outcomes. In discussion, it was clear that many of Khalid's outcomes were negative and focused him on what he did not want to happen; for example, he talked about wanting to speak 'without fear and negativity'. His positive outcome was 'to feel confident and socialize more'.

To reinforce Khalid's newly-found sense of 'I can change this', we used the 'Perceptual Positions' pattern which allows a client to view a situation from varying perspectives. For example, the client may imagine that he is viewing a situation through his own eyes, then through the eyes of a chosen other, then from an observer position. Moving through the varying positions allows the client to see a situation in a new light and discover that different choices are possible. Khalid ended up in 'fifth position' sitting alongside 'God' and looking down on himself. Bodenhamer calls this a 'God's eye view' of the universe (2004, p.71). He smiled at the strange nature of this experience. From this position he could see there was no need for fear. Bodenhamer observes, 'Many who have overcome blocking have found the fifth position extremely helpful. They learn how to go there at will through consistent practice' (2004, p.75).

Session 4

Khalid was feeling very pleased. He had secured a part-time job at a well-known department store and his fluency had been 'fine' during the interview. He said he felt he had a new positive 'I can do it' approach.

I continued to see Khalid once a month for the next six months. We problem-solved certain situations and practised the Easy Onset fluency technique (Cooper, 1979: Stewart & Turnbull, 1995), which he found useful – 'it takes the pressure off'. Although he still stammered at stressful moments, Khalid continued to manage his fluency well. On discharge, we discussed what he had learnt in therapy:

- Belief in myself is key
- I can now recognize negative thinking
- I understand what's happening more now – I'm able to accept it and talk to myself positively – 'Look, Khalid …'
- It doesn't get me down like it used to
- I'm talking to more people – when I face it there's no fear; need to do it to believe it
- I'm much happier in myself – I've rearranged my room, I go for walks, feel peaceful – haven't felt this for a long time' (supporting the NLP belief that change is generative, i.e. a change in one part of the 'system' generates other changes)
- Do what makes you happy – now I understand that
- Be proactive, don't worry.

He summarized his experience as 'a big change for me, physically, socially, mentally'. He saw the therapy process as one that supported him in facing and surmounting his fear of stammering. When I last spoke to Khalid, he had been on a friend's radio show for one hour (and did not stammer) and said he felt his stammering was 'slowly going away'.

The unconscious mind and role of trance

Milton Erickson, psychiatrist and hypnotherapist, induced and utilized trance states to help his clients uncover hitherto unconscious resources. John Grinder has said that:

> "Erickson was the single most important model that he ever built, because Erickson opened the doorway not just to a different reality, but to a whole different class of realities."

> (O'Connor & Seymour, 1990, p.113)

Erickson believed the client had all the resources he needed and saw his job as helping the client to access them. He excelled at finding metaphors that encapsulated his client's experience and led to profound change. Erickson's values and skills had a profound effect on the way NLP – and indeed Solution Focused Brief Therapy (De Shazer, 1988) – developed. Wake talks of 'Erickson's incorrigible optimism in the human being as a creative, autonomous and self-balancing system that is seeking well being, even in the presentation of symptoms' (2008, p.6).

The NLP view of the unconscious mind is very different from the Freudian notion of a seething cauldron of repressed and primal urges. In NLP, 'unconscious' is used to describe anything that is not in present-moment awareness. We are aware of only a small part of our thinking process, the part that has a high enough priority to penetrate our conscious mind. NLP sees the unconscious 'as a treasure trove of experience, memory and skill' (O'Connor, 2001, p.170).

O'Hanlon and Martin (1992) who modelled Erickson's solution-oriented hypnosis, define the unconscious as:

- A repository for those things you don't keep in your conscious mind, but could recall if you wanted
- It is your deeper, wiser self
- Holding the sensory memories from life (in Wake, 2008, p.173).

Trance is the ideal state of mind to explore and recover unconscious resources. Many NLP 'change patterns' induce a light trance state naturally. Trance is a strange word that can have particular connotations for people, but the truth is we drift in and out of trance throughout the day. We are in a light trance whenever we pay more attention to our inner world than the outer one. Trance is characterized by this internal focus of attention – the further into trance you go, the deeper you go internally until, at the limit, you go to sleep. We carry out complex activities while in trance – most drivers have experienced arriving at a familiar destination as if on autopilot.

Various physiological signs indicate a trance state, such as muscle relaxation and slowed pulse and breathing. Brainwaves change from beta (active thinking) to alpha for a light trance/relaxation or theta for a deeper trance:

> "… the subjective experience of someone in trance is a rich and creative state of inner consciousness. *People in trance are more awake to themselves.*"

> (O'Connor, 2001, p.171)

A therapist induces a trance by using a soft tone of voice and matching her words to the rhythm of the client's breathing. Anyone who has ever used their voice tone to encourage a child to go to sleep has induced a trance.

The 'Milton model', modelled by Bandler and Grinder from Erickson, is a set of language patterns that induces trance. 'Artfully vague' language creates a vague surface structure and allows the client to choose his own deeper structure of meaning. A statement, such as 'there will have been times when you have experienced a deep sense of relaxation', encourages the client's unconscious mind to begin searching for experiences that match this criteria.

Why is trance useful clinically?

- Trance is a restful and relaxing state. It slows the client down and allows him to notice the details of his inner world – bodily sensations, content of thoughts, speed of thinking, nuances of emotion. It also involves heightened suggestibility (although it is not a passive state) so the therapist can use suggestion to positively frame the client's exploration. For example, "there's a part of you that knows exactly what you need right now".

- The Milton model distracts the conscious mind, which processes information in an analytical, rational way (left hemisphere) and allows the client to access the language of symbol, metaphor and intuition (right hemisphere). McDermott and Jago explain, 'the therapist has a source of information which complements what is said or done at a conscious level, and which frequently helps to open up a richer world of internal meaning that informs the work of the therapy' (2001, p.125).

- Working at the level of the unconscious makes it easier to access the positive intention behind a behaviour that is resistant to change.

NLP presupposes that all behaviour has a positive intention. Positive intention is closely allied to the concept of secondary gain. Some behaviours do not make sense at the level of the conscious mind. Few people would choose to smoke – it is expensive and will make you ill – but at an unconscious level it serves the smoker in some way, possibly perceived as comforting or relaxing. Providing comfort is therefore the positive intention of the behaviour. Sometimes the positive intention needs to be addressed before a behaviour will change, as will be seen in Fatou's story below.

Fatou's story: Addressing positive intention

The principles of the Six Step Reframe pattern are used to bring an unconscious conflict to the surface for the client to examine and resolve.

Fatou, a doctor, had a covert stammer. She was able to speak fluently much of the time, but experienced anxiety and fear in speaking situations. She described a 'self-hatred' and 'loathing' related to speaking. She said she was unwilling to accept that she had a stammer – 'I reject it and myself'.

Fatou's self-loathing was expressed mainly through her internal dialogue – a running commentary with which she metaphorically beat herself up. Fatou frequently commented on the therapist's 'calm, soothing' voice, probably because it provided a stark contrast to the punishing voice inside her head. After some initial modelling, Fatou understood the impact of her negative internal dialogue, but felt powerless to change it. She could clearly articulate outcomes that involved accepting herself and acknowledging her achievements. However, despite attempts to achieve this, the negative voice undermined all her efforts.

As the voice seemed resistant to change, we decided to explore its positive intention. The main steps in the process were:

- Anchor a resourceful state – it felt useful for Fatou to be in a calm state while we explored the voice.
- Focus on the part responsible for producing the negative voice. Fatou felt the voice started when she was 11-years-old and discovered for the first time that 'stammering can be irritating'. She had to read aloud in English Literature class and noticed, 'this gets on people's nerves'.
- Ascertain the positive intention of the voice. What is it trying to do that is important? Fatou said, 'it wants to toughen me up and to make me learn and do my best.'
- Ask if the part is willing to continue to fulfil its positive intention, which is psychologically important for the client, **without** the negativity. That is, "Will the voice continue to help you toughen up and learn **without** being so negative?"
- Fatou sensed that the part was reluctant to do this. 'I need the negative voice in order to learn.'

When Fatou said, 'I need the negative voice in order to learn', it suddenly became clear why the voice had been resistant to change. Learning is highly valued by Fatou. She had often talked about her passion for learning and there was a belief (unconscious until this point) that she needed the negative voice in order to learn. When I challenged this belief by asking, 'Can you learn without negativity?' she emphatically replied 'No'.

Fatou's only strategy for learning until this point was to be harsh with herself. This was the only method she had for reaching her outcome of learning. She needed a new strategy. I asked how she would encourage a child to learn something new and we discussed whether encouragement or punishment would be the better strategy. Fatou accepted that encouragement could be a more effective strategy, but she described overcoming the negative voice as a battle between 'good and evil' – 'overcoming it will be daunting and hard work'.

Intrapersonal battles or conflicts are as unhelpful to someone's mind-body system as interpersonal battles between different people are to a team. Approaching the voice with a battle mentality is unhelpful and usually when we fight something we encounter increased resistance. So, instead, we talked about how Fatou could reduce the power of the voice. Was it possible for her to notice the voice, but ignore it? Was it possible to reduce the volume? Fatou felt she could experiment with reducing the volume (one of the submodalities of the voice).

At the next session, Fatou said she had had a 'brilliant' week. Not only had she been able to reduce the volume of the negative voice, she had replaced it with a more positive one. Now that the link between the voice and learning has been broken, the voice was amenable to change. Previous attempts to change had been resisted because the positive intention had not been addressed. Fatou had also been able to maintain a sense of calm. This was new. Previously, she had felt calm in the therapy session, but been unable to sustain this state. Rather than focusing on fluency, Fatou had been focusing on being calm – a change of outcome. Unsurprisingly, her fluency had improved.

At the following session, Fatou described herself as 'in a very good place'. She felt she was starting to accept herself. She said there were still 'bad days', when she felt people were judging her, but she could 'turn down' her thoughts.

She had been able to access a sense of calm easily. She described the calm state as both familiar, but also new – 'I know it to be true within me but I wasn't aware of it before'. The resource was always there – now it had been foregrounded.

Fatou described this process as 'exhilarating' and talked of the 'joy in my heart' at discovering a sense of calm and being able to manage the negative voice. She talked about being able to forgive herself – 'I used to think it was all my fault'. Fatou volunteered to do a presentation at work, something she had hitherto avoided. She felt calm, was 'more eloquent than fluent', and experienced no shame, guilt or embarrassment.

Jack's experience of working with the unconscious mind

For me, Jack's story demonstrates how the innate wisdom of the unconscious mind can lead to profound change.

Jack is a teacher with his own successful business as an education consultant. When I first met Jack, his stammering was variable. There were days when he experienced tense blocking and days when stammering was more relaxed with gentle prolongations and repetitions. Although stammering was not holding Jack back professionally, it consumed a lot of mental and emotional energy and often left him feeling exhausted. It also occupied a central place in his identity. This was not entirely unhelpful as he felt that stammering had given him a certain drive and will to succeed, but it was having a detrimental effect on his quality of life.

As Jack was coping well, therapy sessions were infrequent initially – a forum to problem-solve and discuss the best way to approach situations. We spent time exploring the structures of fluency and stammering (as described by Jack in the section on modelling) so that he started to understand the factors that programmed him for either fluency or stammering. Jack observed that he had always felt he was 'managing' his stammer rather than dealing with the cause of it. He was at a time in his life when he wanted to explore beyond the level of the symptom to see if he could discover what was driving his stammering. We used trance to work at an unconscious level. The following outlines our first three sessions using this approach:

Session 1

I had a plan for the first session, but Jack's unconscious mind had another agenda. As Jack turned his attention inwards and focused on what was happening in his body, he was aware that his breathing was very shallow and there was a strong sensation around his diaphragm which he described as a 'concrete barrier' which was making breathing difficult. Jack felt that the 'barrier' had been 'inserted' (rather than being a natural part of him), but that it had been there 'forever'. As we explored the 'barrier' in sensory terms (what it looked, sounded and felt like), Jack was aware of rising heat in his body and emerging strong emotion. He simultaneously accessed a 'horrible' memory of being told to speak up by his GCSE teacher. Rather than resisting this, I encouraged Jack to focus on allowing the experience, opening his body so the experience could unfold and move through him.

Jack stayed with this process of allowing the emotion to unfold – 'visceral, hot, tingling' for most of the session. I supported the process by encouraging him to trust the wisdom of his mind-body system and to allow what was happening even though it was unfamiliar. It is important to note that Jack was, in this moment, fully experiencing what has been constantly present for him. What had been unconscious was surfacing and Jack was able to meet the experience in a new way.

At the end of the session, Jack described his breathing as 'neutral' and his head as 'empty' and said, 'I like it'. He left the session feeling 'purged' and 'relaxed'. He wrote to me later that evening to say he felt calmer than he had done in a long time.

Those with a superficial understanding of NLP often see it as a method that swaps a 'bad' experience for a 'good' one. In this case, I chose to hold the space for Jack's unconscious mind to do what it needed to do in the belief that his unconscious mind has a better understanding of his needs than I do. My confidence to do this has grown with my experience of working at the level of the unconscious mind. Using patterns, such as the Drop Down Through (in which clients drop through limiting states into powerful resource states) and Parts Integration (detailed below), has taught me that clients will lead themselves where they need to go and that it can be very powerful to allow an experience to unfold. Perls (1951) reminds us, 'It is nature that cures – *natura sant*. A wound heals or a bone knits by itself. There is nothing the physician can do but clean the wound or set the bone. It is the same with your personality' (in Wake, 2008, p.160).

Reflecting on this session, I see parallels with the process of 'focusing' described by American psychologist, Eugene Gendlin, mentioned earlier. Gendlin researched what most helps emotional healing and found that 'those of us who can allow ourselves to feel our emotions, in our bodies, in the moment, were most able to let our emotions naturally move on' (Wellings & Wilde McCormick, 2005, p.88). Wellings and Wilde McCormick further comment that John Welwood, who honed the technique of focusing, recognized its close connection to mindfulness meditation.

Session 2

Jack reported that he was learning to allow his feelings/sensations and trust that his body knew how to process them, without him needing to analyze what was happening at a cognitive level. He had noticed that at times of pressure, he had been 'able to breathe'. This was new. He had also noticed that when he stammered there was less tension.

We continued our exploration using the Parts Integration pattern. Erickson, Satir and Perls all directly refer to parts or splitting aspects of the personality. Perls (1969) explains that unacceptable aspects of the personality can be disowned by the individual: 'You do not allow yourself – or you are not allowed – to be totally yourself. We all have a number of different parts, each with expectations of fulfilment. These parts often find it difficult to get along with each other and may have inhibitory influences on one another' (in Wake, 2008, p.129). Our everyday language acknowledges awareness of these different parts. People will say 'Part of me wants X, but part of me wants Y'.

In this session we accessed both a 'problem' part and a 'resource' part. While he was in a light trance, I asked Jack to focus on the part that was making him stammer, the 'problem' part. He identified the positive intention of this part as being 'to make me slow down ... I talk too much'. This part communicated that it needed space. I then asked Jack to focus on a 'resource' part – a part that can help him. He identified a 'creative' part. As he contemplated these two parts, Jack described them as being 'like super heroes – battling for space, power and autonomy', each having their own plans and purpose. He felt his stammering arose from the conflict between the two parts and he had a sense that the creative part could easily 'take over'. The part responsible for stammering wanted space and recognition.

The goal of parts therapy is to facilitate integration between a split-off part and the rest of the unconscious self. By being aware of the conflict between these two parts, Jack was able to begin to be aware of the need to give them both space and recognition. As a teacher, he talked about this being a skill he was used to employing with children with differing needs.

Jack describes his experience of this trance process eloquently:

"... a very gradual process of talking you into listening to your body, being aware of how it feels, where any stress points are, how you are sitting, what flashes through your mind. It is a visualization technique, I suppose, a way of calming my mind, slowly filtering the hundreds upon millions of thoughts that whizz round my head all the time like a tornado. Somehow, whilst Debbie talks me down into this calm state, they dissipate and widen. They are given space to just be. They do not go or disappear, but they make room for me to step through them and look deeper – below or behind I am not sure – but past them.

"It is then when my favourite part occurs, the colours. I see my body in many different colours, feel maybe, not see ... I am aware of its hue, its texture, its shape. My stammer, currently, seems to centre itself as an orange spongy ball under my right rib cage. This is where I often feel 'tight' if I have had a non-fluent day. When I think of being fluent and the times when I am communicating freely, openly, brilliantly even, if that doesn't sound too conceited – a bright, lemon yellow wash extends from the left lung and flows through my body. It is light, warm, happy feeling – when I think of it now I am smiling. It is me at my best. And then there is this orange ball, which fights for space – my stammer."

Session 3

Jack had noticed a significant change in his fluency levels. He was still prolonging words at times, but was not blocking. He had found that moments of stammering were now accompanied by a complete absence of emotion.

The orange, spongy ball – 'my stammer' – was different too:

"It has changed. When I first started it was a hard, tight, immovable ball. It hurt. However, that tight ball has changed to a soft spongy one that has no fixed size. It changes and is much more flexible. It is recognized and allowed to be there. When I am aware of a non-fluent day, instead of getting

> angry and reacting against it, I spend a few moments just letting it be there …"

Jack reported other changes. He was experiencing a new sense of calm and had noticed himself being more assertive with people, saying "*no*" and being clear about his boundaries. He felt this new ability to communicate his needs clearly and in an unemotional way was directly linked to the Parts therapy (supporting the NLP belief that learning is generative).

This change in fluency has persisted and Jack now describes himself as 90–95% fluent, something he describes as 'fantastic' and 'life-changing' He reports feeling less exhausted and no longer needs to 're-set' himself. When he was blocking severely, he used to have to stop talking for a few hours or go for a swim in order to 're-set' himself.

He commented, 'It surprised me, the difference between what I thought consciously and subconsciously.' At an unconscious level, 'it felt very clear'. It is typical for clients to comment on a sense of clarity at the unconscious level. The part responsible for making Jack stammer communicated that it needed space. Jack has been able to give it what it needed and has seen a dramatic change in his fluency levels. In Jack's words:

> "… the thing that NLP has done for me … is given me a set of techniques to 'give my stammer space' and try to understand it, not turn away from it."

Final reflections

The importance of the therapeutic relationship

> "Therapy is not a treatment the client receives, the therapist gives or even offers but rather an ongoing collaborative dance."
>
> (McDermott & Jago, 2001, p.86)

There is a significant body of literature on the importance of the therapeutic relationship and to ignore this dimension of therapy would be to present an incomplete picture. Therapy can never be reduced to a collection of techniques; when asked to comment on their experiences of therapy, clients, unsurprisingly, talked about what Wake calls the 'relational' aspects of therapy. For example:

> "Debbie and I get on very well and I completely trust her. This is so important that I cannot stress." (Jack)

> "I can speak to you like a sibling ... You have such a calm manner." (Fatou)

O'Connor and Seymour (1990) make the point that relationship and congruence are more important than any technique you apply. Wake reminds us of the 'joy and compassion that was present in the therapy work of Erickson, Satir and Perls' (2008, p.161).

As therapists, building and maintaining rapport and being mindful and present with a client are things we probably take for granted. They are hard to measure objectively, but are undoubtedly crucial in supporting our clients to reach their outcomes. If, as Reich (quoted in the section on Modelling) suggests, we are to explain how we have effected change, we need to be cognisant of the significance of the therapeutic relationship.

A therapist's congruence (or incongruence) with an approach will inevitably communicate itself to the client in direct and indirect ways. In the case of NLP, effective therapy requires the therapist to have integrated the NLP presuppositions into her work so they are woven through everything she says and does.

Acceptance

Therapy challenges a client to change his relationship both with his stammering and with himself. Having worked with and modelled numerous clients over the years, I have observed the importance of acceptance in the therapeutic process and want to highlight this.

Sheehan noted the significance of acceptance for the PWS: 'He must develop sufficient acceptance of himself as a stutterer to stop concealing the problem from himself and others – long enough to undertake a systematic weakening of the handicapping behaviours via principles of learning' (1979, p.178).

A client's ability to accept both himself and the fact that he currently stammers seems to be central to his ability to experiment and move forward.

Clients who become stuck battling with themselves or their stammering tend to stay stuck. Establishing an increased sense of self-acceptance, therefore, has to be a key part of any therapeutic encounter with a PWS and is one of the threads that links the client stories in this chapter. Khalid articulates this when he says 'I understand what's happening more now … I'm able to accept it'.

As detailed earlier, the process of modelling alters a client's relationship to his stammering and fosters understanding and acceptance. Certain change patterns also encourage acceptance. Parts Integration, for example, helps a client to recognize that battling a part of himself is unhelpful and counterproductive. He is then able to identify an approach that will be more effective.

A client who is able to embrace his current reality and work with himself is ideally placed to change and grow. For each client, the journey to such acceptance will be an individual one, but the importance of the goal seems to be universal.

Research to support the use of NLP with PWS

Current evidence for the use of NLP with PWS takes the form of case studies, with Bob Bodenhamer being particularly prolific.

Most research into NLP to date has been carried out on selected components rather than on the entire approach. Certain elements of NLP, such as the Solution Focus and Mental Rehearsal, are well-supported by research but more is needed on the therapeutic use of NLP as a whole. Cooper and Seal (2006) point out that NLP research can be 'fraught' because:

> "Skilled NLP practitioners who have integrated NLP into their own models of the world are aware of sensory feedback within the system and vary their behaviour accordingly to achieve their outcomes. Their choice of behaviour is made in relation to the way in which the client is structuring their own experience, rather than the application of a standardized format … When NLP practitioners are working with their clients it is not their behaviour in isolation that is NLP; the NLP is in the intentional and purposeful application of the model."

(in Feltham and Horton, 2006, p.333).

Controlling such variables presents a challenge for the researcher.

Inspiritive, an Australian research and training organization, echoes the thoughts of Cooper and Seal in pointing out that researchers need to understand that NLP is 'an epistemology and a methodology, not a single theory or model'.

One study of particular interest for the stammering therapist is by Konefal and Duncan (1998), who looked at the effects of NLP training on social anxiety in adults. Much has been written about the link between social anxiety and stammering (e.g. St Clare et al., 2009: Messenger et al., 2004). Konefal and Duncan recorded a statistically significant decrease in rated anxiety and self-report avoidance behaviours post-training (using the Liebowitz Social Phobia Scale), which persisted at the six-month follow-up. The effect size for change was large, meaning changes were substantial. Previous research by these authors (1990) recorded the positive impact of NLP training on measures of 'self regard, self acceptance and the capacity for intimate contact with others'.

McDermott and Jago make the important point that NLP grew from the study of excellence in communication and therapeutic practice. "In outlining the salient features of NLP, we are also necessarily honouring good practice" (2001, p.132).

Closing remarks

It is challenging to try to capture the richness and complexity of NLP in a single chapter. I hope that I have managed to convey my view of NLP, which is one of a highly-sophisticated framework that has the power to take someone to the heart of who they are and reveal hitherto unrecognized resources.

NLP has been – and continues to be – an invaluable framework for me. It allows me to understand a client's model of the world in all its subtlety and individuality, and therefore to identify the intervention that is likely to be most meaningful for that client. Furthermore, it allows me to describe and understand these interventions and gauge why an intervention has worked or why it has failed.

Bandler (1985) claims, 'Most people don't actively and deliberately use their own brains' (in Wake, 2008, p.36). NLP shows us how to actively and deliberately use our brains to access our resources and thereby increase our choices and reach our outcomes. It shows clients **how** to reprogramme themselves to get different results so that they leave therapy with new skills and newly discovered resources.

Research in neuroscience is now showing that in learning to use our brains purposefully, we affect not just the chemistry of the brain, but also its structure:

> "The simple truth is that how we focus our attention, how we intentionally direct the flow of energy and information through our neural circuits, can directly alter the brain's activity and its structure."
>
> (Hanson & Mendius, 2009, p.v)

Maybe such research will lead more of us to share the 'incorrigible optimism' of Erickson.

For clients who stammer, my hope is that they leave therapy with not only improved fluency, but also a greatly enhanced sense of who they are as a person – a unique, creative and resourceful human being who can never be merely defined by one single aspect of their behaviour.

Acknowledgement

I am very grateful to all those clients who have and continue to teach me so much and especially grateful to those who gave permission and took the time to share their experiences in this chapter.

References

Bandler, R. & Grinder, J. (1979) *Frogs into Princes*. Moab, UT: Real People Press.

Beck, A.T. (1976) *Cognitive Therapy and the Emotional Disorders*. New York: International Universities Press.

Bodenhamer, B. (2004) *Mastering Blocking and Stuttering*. Wales: Crown House Publishing.

Cooper, E.B. (1979) Intervention procedures for the young stutterer. In: Gregory (Ed.) *Controversies about Stuttering Therapy*. Baltimore: University Park Press.

De Shazer, S. (1988) *Clues – Investigating Solutions in Brief Therapy*. New York: Norton Books.

Duncan, R., Konefal, J., & Spechler (1990) Effect of neurolinguistic programming training on self actualization as measured by the Personal Orientation Inventory. *Psychological Reports 66*, 1323–1330.

Epstein, M., Wilde McCormick, E. & Wellings N. (2005) *Nothing to Lose: Psychotherapy, Buddhism and Living Life*. London: Continuum.

Feltham, C. & Horton I. (Eds) (2006) *The SAGE Handbook of Counselling and Psychotherapy*. London: Sage Publications.

Gilligan, S. (1997) *The Courage to Love*. New York: W.W. Norton.

Hamilton, D. (2005) *It's the Thought that Counts*. London: Hay House.

Hamilton, D. (2008) *How your Mind can Heal your Body*. London, Hay House.

Hanson, R. & Mendius, R. (2009) *Buddha's Brain*. Oakland, CA: New Harbinger Publications.

Harrison, J. (2010) *Redefining Stuttering*. New York: National Stuttering Association.

Konefal, J. & Duncan, R.C. (1998) Social anxiety and training in neurolinguistic programming. *Psychological Reports 83*(3), 1115–1122.

McDermott I. (2001) *Brief NLP Therapy*. London: Sage Publications.

Messenger, M., Onslow M., Packman A., & Menzies R. (2004) Social anxiety in stuttering: Measuring negative social expectancies. *Journal of Fluency Disorders 29*, 201–212.

O' Connor, J. (2001) *NLP Workbook*. London: Harper Collins.

O'Connor, J. & Seymour, J. (1990) *Introducing NLP*. London: Thorsons.

Owen, N. (2001) *The Magic of Metaphor*. Wales: Crown House Publishing.

Robbins, R. (2001) *Awaken the Giant Within*. London: Pocket Books.

Sanders, C., Sadoski, M., Bramson, R., Wiprud, R., & Van Walsum, K. (2008) Comparing the effects of physical practice and mental imagery rehearsal on learning basic surgical skills by medical students. *American Journal of Obstetrics and Gynecology 191*(5), 1811–1814.

Sheehan, J.G. (1979) Stuttering and recovery. In: H.H. Gregory (Ed.) *Controversies about Stuttering Therapy*. Baltimore: University Park Press.

Sheehan, J.G. (1983) *Excerpts from the Writings of Joseph G. Sheehan*. Memorial Service, 26 November 1983. Distributed by the British Stammering Association, 1983.

St Clare, T., Menzies, R., Onslow, M., Packman, A., Thompson, R., & Bloch, S. (2009) Unhelpful thoughts and beliefs linked to social anxiety in stuttering: Development of a measure. *International Journal of Language and Communication Disorders 44*(3), 338–351.

Stewart T. & Turnbull J. (1995) *Working with Dysfluent Children*. Bicester: Winslow Press.

Van Riper, C. (1973) *The Treatment of Stuttering*. New Jersey: Prentice Hall.

Wake, L. (2008) *Neuro-Linguistic Psychotherapy: A Postmodern Perspective*. Hove, UK: Routledge.

Index